D1085271

Navy Football

NAVY FOOTBALL

Gridiron Legends and Fighting Heroes

Jack Clary

NAVAL INSTITUTE PRESS

Annapolis, Maryland

Library of Congress Cataloging-in-Publication Data
Clary, Jack T.
Navy football : gridiron legends and fighting heroes / Jack Clary.
p. cm.
Includes bibliographical references and index.
ISBN 1-55750-106-8 (alk. paper)
1. United States Naval Academy—Football—History. I. Title.
GV958.U512C53 1997
796.332'63'0975256—dc21 97-11916

Printed in the United States of America on acid-free paper ♾
04 03 02 01 00 99 98 97 9 8 7 6 5 4 3 2
First printing

With the exception of those listed below, all illustrations are from the Special Collections and Archives Division, Nimitz Library, U.S. Naval Academy, or the Sports Information Office, U.S. Naval Academy.
Aerial Photography, Annapolis: page 6
Buell/Whitehill Collection, Naval Historical Center, Naval War College: page 99
Tom Darden: page 217
Phil Hoffman Photography: pages vii, 185, 193, 195–98
U.S. Army: page 231
U.S. Naval Institute: pages 5, 8, 19–21, 23, 29, 41, 52 (bottom), 62, 63, 77, 79, 95 (bottom), 141, 172, 179, 201, 214

To the thousands of men who have unselfishly built the proud traditions of Navy football and, just as unselfishly, continued the proud traditions of the Naval Academy in service to their country. And to my wife, Pat, who shares not only my great affection for this sport, but also the special goose bumps that come when the band plays the National Anthem, the midshipmen march onto the field, the stirring refrain of "Anchors Aweigh" is heard, and the men of Annapolis play football for the entire Navy.

Contents

NAVY

Preface

There are college football teams, and then there are special college football teams. Navy is a special college football team with a very special tradition.

I experienced a good taste of it during World War II when my father worked at the Naval Academy, supervising the reconstruction of docks along the Severn River where the *Reina Mercedes* was berthed. I spent some vacation time with him and roamed the Yard, where I distinctly remember a clock above an old snack bar in Dahlgren Hall that told precisely how many days were left until the Army-Navy game. That certainly impressed a nine-year-old whose reading tastes had begun shifting toward the sports pages and who had already begun to develop a love for the sport of football.

That clock heightened my interest in Navy football, which was raised even more after hearing my parents talk about the games they saw in Baltimore and at Thompson Stadium in 1942, particularly the unique Army-Navy game that was played there. Being so close to Navy football that year, combined with the aura projected by the Academy, left indelible impressions on my parents. My own feelings were reinforced when they often recounted their experiences.

My interest in Navy football became even greater because the Army-Navy game was played in Philadelphia, just sixty miles from my home in southern New Jersey. That always was a special day in our home, where radio descriptions of the game provided unlimited fodder for the theater of a young mind.

In later years, when I covered the game as a sportswriter and columnist and had access to tickets, our family and many of my friends became regular attendees. The first of more than fifty books that I have written was *Army vs. Navy,* a history of that game. Working on that project exposed me further to the Academy and its gridiron heritage, and writing every year about the Army-Navy game as a major contributor to that game's program expanded my knowledge of, and appreciation for, the accomplishments and traditions that are Navy football.

Thus, it was a long-sought labor of love to have the opportunity to compile a history of the sport at the Naval Academy and to talk further and correspond with some of its greatest players. Many of their exploits on the playing field are described in this book. Just as importantly, so are some of their exploits in defense of the nation. In each instance, these men who played football for Navy upheld the highest traditions of the Naval Academy.

Acknowledgments

During forty years as a sports journalist and author, and especially while conducting research for a history of the Army-Navy football game, I acquired a vast reservoir of information about football at the Naval Academy. I talked with scores of former players and coaches, some of whose careers stretched back to the Roaring Twenties, and I was able to reconstruct many of their stories for this book. Others offered fresh recollections of their experiences and those of teammates now deceased.

Others who were invaluable with their recollections included: Tom Bates, former Naval Academy sports information director and now the compliance coordinator for its athletic teams; his successor, Scott Strasemeier, and his staff; L. Budd Thalman, another former sports information director at the Academy; Capt. William Busik, USN (Ret.), former executive director of the U.S. Naval Academy Alumni Association and himself a former Naval Academy athletic director and football star; and two other former athletic directors and great Navy players, Capt. Alan Cameron, USN (Ret.), and Capt. John "Bo" Coppedge, USN (Ret.). I am also indebted to the current athletic director, Jack Lengyel, for his splendid cooperation and encouragement.

The staff of the Nimitz Library was very helpful in steering me through its archives. In particular, former archivist Jane Price made available a treasure trove of *Lucky Bag* yearbooks dating back to 1893, as well as the files of several former superintendents. Her successor, Alice Creighton, was equally accommodating, as was picture archivist Brian Fors in searching for the early photos of football life at the Academy that are featured in the book.

The U.S. Naval Institute was a tremendous resource. My special thanks go to Paul Stillwell, who guided me through the maze of oral histories, books, and publications dealing with the history of the U.S. Navy. Paul unselfishly shared his own research as a naval historian. I also want to thank Paul Wilderson, executive editor at the Naval Institute Press, who originated the project and followed it throughout with patience and understanding.

Pat Harmon, curator and historian of the College Football Hall of Fame, provided a great deal of background information on former Navy players who now are enshrined in that august place of honor. Steve Belichick, who links some forty years of Navy football history as an assistant football coach during good and bad times, has always been an invaluable source of information. And a special thanks in this regard goes to former superintendent Rear Adm. Thomas C. Lynch, USN (Ret.), who, as a player, a midshipman, a team captain, and a naval officer, always epitomized the mission of the Naval Academy.

Navy Football

Introduction

Football at the U.S. Naval Academy is special. The Navy football team draws interest not only from every part of the country, but from every part of the world. How often have we seen pictures of naval detachments in some remote area proudly displaying a "Beat Army" banner? Or how many times have we seen photographs of ships sailing the seas with the same message painted on a stack, or on the port or starboard quarters?

At first glance, a Navy game has little that distinguishes it from a game played at any other college in the country. But Navy football is special because it is part of the fabric of tradition that has long been established within the Naval Academy—itself a very special school. Everything about the Academy is so regarded because of its stated mission:

> To develop midshipmen and to imbue them with the highest ideals of duty, honor and loyalty in order to provide graduates who are dedicated to a career of naval service and have potential for future development in mind and character to assume the highest responsibilities of command, citizenship and government.

Midshipmen must be prepared morally, mentally, and physically because, as professional officers in the naval service, they may be called upon to forfeit their lives in defense of their country. No less than any other midshipman, those who have played football for Navy have always been a part of the Academy's military mission. Many have gone on to display gallantry and attain achievements that have emblazoned their names on the honor role of American heroes, side by side with the men and women who once cheered them on the playing field.

Thus, it is expected that Navy teams will play harder, be better conditioned, and, although not always successful, will never slacken their efforts, from the opening kickoff to the final second, regardless of the score.

The spirit and rigor of the Academy has produced a pantheon of some of college football's finest players, coaches, and teams in more than a century of competition. Players like Roger Staubach and Joe Bellino, both of whom own Heisman Trophies. Teams like the "Team Named Desire," which owns one of

four Navy victories in postseason bowls. Great coaches like Paul Dashiell, the "Father of Navy Football," Doug Howard, Bob Folwell, Bill Ingram, Tom Hamilton, Swede Larson, Eddie Erdelatz, Wayne Hardin, and George Welsh. And then there are more than a dozen members of the College Football Hall of Fame, part of a veritable legion of great players: Babe Brown, Jack Dalton, Steve Barchet, Tom Hamilton, Frank Wickhorst, Buzz Borries, Slade Cutter, Bill Busik, George Brown, Dick Scott, Don Whitmire, George Welsh, Ron Beagle, the Ingrams (Jonas, "Navy Bill," and William II), the father-and-son team of Joe Gattuso Sr. and Joe Gattuso Jr., Steve Eisenhauer, Tom Lynch, Pat Donnelly, Rob Taylor, Cleveland Cooper, Chet Moeller, Eddie Meyers, Napoleon McCallum. Finally, there are the select few football players who also won the Medal of Honor during wartime: Richard Antrim, Harold Bauer, Allen Buchanen, Jonas Ingram, Frederick McNair Jr., and Carlton Hutchins.

But the tradition of football at the Naval Academy transcends coaches, players, teams, and trophies. It's "Anchors Aweigh," and Bill the Goat. It's Navy Blue and Gold, and the gold **N** that adorns blue varsity sweaters. It's the statue of the fearsome-looking warrior Tecumseh, whose countenance has been doused with thousands of gallons of paint (but who always receives a thorough cleaning after each paint job, restoring him to full, unblemished glory). And it's the Navy–Marine Corps Memorial Stadium, a shrine to the great battles fought by its graduates, and to the men who fought them.

Millions of young and old throats have sung "Anchors Aweigh" since it was composed in 1906 by Naval Academy musical director Charles A. Zimmerman and Midshipman Alfred H. Miles (Class of 1907) for Miles's June Week (now Commissioning Week) ceremonies. Following a custom in which each class composed its own march, Zimmerman wrote a tune, Miles wrote two stanzas of words, and they named it "Anchors Aweigh." Zimmerman decided to unveil the song at halftime of the 1906 Army-Navy game. Navy won the game 10–0, to break a five-game winless streak against the Cadets, and "Anchors Aweigh" began a twenty-year reign as Navy's official fight song for the annual contest. It became popular year-round after being circulated within Navy circles by the Trident Literary Society in a collection of Navy songs. When radio and motion pictures became popular in the late twenties, "Anchors Aweigh" became background music for a flood of shows with a Navy theme, giving it national exposure. It became one of the most popular college fight songs ever written. Many verses have been added to the song, but the most popular is the following:

Stand, Navy, down the field,
Sails set to the sky.
We'll never change our course, so
Army, you steer shy-y-y-y, and
Roll up the score, Navy,
Anchors Aweigh;
Sail, Navy down the field and
Sink the Army, sink the Army gray.

Bill(y) the Goat has been Navy's football mascot, first part-time, then full-time, since late in the nineteenth century. His entrance at Army-Navy games often rivals the VIP status accorded admirals and other dignitaries. Bill has been transported in limousines, luxury vans, and any number of floats. Regardless of transportation mode, each of his appearances has been met with thunderous cheers that are second in volume only to those that greet the appearance of Bill's team on the field.

During the game, Bill is tended by two midshipmen who are elected by the football squad. (They are usually players who are unable to compete because of injury.) In the 1945 Army-Navy game, one of the "goatkeepers" was Don Whitmire, who had been an All-America tackle in 1943 and 1944, but whose eligibility had expired. He was Brigade Commander at the time, was later elected to the College Football Hall of Fame, and was a much-decorated admiral. Tradition dictates that the goatkeepers keep Bill pointed toward the opposition's end zone at all times so Navy's quarterback will always know in which direction he should be advancing his team.

Credit for establishing Bill the Goat as Navy's mascot belongs to Colby M. Chester, commandant of cadets from 1891 to 1894 and the first president of the Naval Academy Auxiliary Athletic Association. He had a celebrated goat aboard the sloop *Galena* who, it seems, had made quite a mark with his "martial bearing and the grotesque character of his make-up streamers" when he rode ashore with every landing party. It wasn't too long before admirals with flag commands were acquiring goats for their flagships. They became the mascot of choice on naval vessels in part because they ate anything set in front of them, making housekeeping much easier.

By the time Chester became commandant of cadets, Navy's mascots had included two cats, a dog, and a carrier pigeon, in addition to several non-Bill goats—one, who was not named, represented the team in 1890 at the first Army-Navy game at West Point. But Chester encouraged a group of young officers stationed aboard the cruiser USS *New York* to offer their goat mascot, El Cid, to the midshipmen for the 1893 Army-Navy game at Annapolis. During halftime, El Cid was led under the goal posts in a "good luck" march. Navy scored six points in the second half for a 6–4 victory.

Early Navy football teams were represented by a goat mascot only when they played Army, and the name "Bill" was a sometimes thing. There was no game between the two schools from 1894 to 1898, and the goat did not reappear until the 1900 game in Philadelphia, when both teams had their mascots—the goat and the Army mule—present for the first time. Navy's goat again was borrowed from the USS *New York.* After winning the game, the naval cadets christened him "Bill I" and paraded him through the train that took them from Philadelphia to Baltimore after the game. In 1901, Navy had a goat named Mike from the USS *Kearsarge,* but he received a quick dishonorable discharge after Army won the game, 11–5.

Bill II became the fourth Navy goat mascot in 1904. He was succeeded the following year by a black angora animal who also was the mascot for the 6–6 tie against Army in Princeton, New Jersey, in 1905. He was succeeded by the sixth Navy goat, Bill III, who presided over 3–0 victories against Army in 1910 and 1911 that were secured by Jack Dalton's field goals. After Bill III died late in the 1911 season, his name was changed to "Three-to-Nothing Jack Dalton," and he was stuffed and mounted—and he is still displayed among Navy's athletic trophies, a lasting tribute to Dalton's right foot. There have been a succession of "Bills" ever since. The length of their military careers seems to depend as much on the team's success in the Army-Navy game as it does on their physical well-being.

Whenever he's on duty, Bill wears a blanket of blue and gold—Navy's official team colors since 1892. Before then, Navy's uniform colors were red on white canvas, or blue on white canvas, matching the designated crew color at Annapolis—red for classes in odd years, and blue for classes in even years.

No one liked alternate colors, and Lt. R. R. Ingersol was told to solicit a choice from the cadets. He reported at a meeting of the Athletic Association on February 27, 1892, that students favored the adoption of Navy Blue and Old Gold. But the word "old" was dropped, and Navy Blue and Gold became the official colors.

The varsity letter was introduced in 1890 after the first Army-Navy game. In 1911, it was decreed that a plain gold varsity letter would designate a Navy football letterman; a letter with a smaller **N** would indicate participation in an Army-Navy contest; and an **N*** meant that the wearer played in a victory over Army.

And no Army-Navy game, in any sport, is complete without redecorating the bronze statue of the famed Indian chief Tecumseh, a gift from the Class of 1891 that faces Bancroft Hall and Bancroft Court. His predecessor, a wooden figurehead of a native American warrior, was salvaged from the warship *Delaware* after it was burned in 1861 at Norfolk to prevent its capture by the Confederates. The figurehead represented Chief Tamanend, a Delaware leader who befriended the early settlers. But this peaceful man never caught the midshipmen's fancy, and they often referred to him as Powhatan, King Philip, and even Old Sebree, after a supposed resemblance to Midshipman Uriel Sebree (Class of 1867). At some point—it is not clear precisely when—the Mids did not believe that a "peaceful" warrior like Tamanend conveyed the ferocity they felt their teams should possess, so they also began referring to him as Tecumseh, a Shawnee chieftain who ravaged the American frontier during the War of 1812. When the new statue replaced the original, it was renamed Tecumseh for good. Every year before the Army-Navy game, he gets a complete paint job to make him look even more fierce. He also receives left-handed salutes and showers of pennies as victory offerings.

A Navy football victory also sets off a cacophony of bells. Ringing the Enterprise Bell—which came from the bridge of the famed World War II aircraft carrier USS *Enterprise*—has been part of Naval Academy tradition since 1950, when the superintendent, Adm. Harry W. Hill, arranged for the bell to be brought to the Academy. It sits in front of Bancroft Hall and is rung when the Academy observes morning colors and also during special ceremonies held when Navy scores a majority of victories over Army in any one of the three major sports seasons. The bell is also rung during Commissioning Week for those teams that beat Army and have not participated in a previous bell-ringing during the academic year.

The Gokokuji Bell, also set in front of Bancroft Hall, is a replica of the 1456 casting brought to this country by Commo. Matthew C. Perry following his 1854 expedition to Japan. The original bell was donated by Perry's widow to the Naval Academy, but it was returned to the people of Okinawa in 1987. Like the original bell, the replica is rung to celebrate football victories over Army—each member of the team swings the big wooden tine to designate the number of points scored by Navy.

Since its introduction in 1972, Navy has competed for the Commander in Chief's Trophy with Army—its traditional rival—and the Air Force Academy. The trophy is presented to the winner of the round-robin competition between the service academies by the alumni associations of the three schools, and is named in honor of the president of the United States.

Navy's home football games have been played in Navy–Marine Corps Memorial Stadium since it was opened on September 26, 1959. The new facility replaced the old Thompson Stadium that was the site of home football games for more than a half-century. The new stadium was paid for by bowl game receipts and private donations collected in a drive led by Rear Adm. Eugene Fluckey (Class of 1935), one of the Navy's top submarine skippers during World War II and holder of the Medal of Honor and four Navy Crosses. The dedication plaque at the stadium reads:

> This stadium is dedicated to those who have served and will serve—upholders of the traditions and renown of the Navy and Marine Corps of the United States. May it be a perpetual reminder of the Navy and Marine Corps as organizations of men trained to work hard and to play hard; in war, defenders of our freedom; in peace, molders of our youth.

On the "Blue," or west, side of the stadium, twenty-two battles are listed; on the "Gold," or east, side, twenty-one battles are honored. Inside, the Adm. Thomas Hamilton Locker Room Complex, named for the Hall of Fame player,

coach, and athletic director at the Naval Academy, is a 16,000-square-foot structure that accommodates nearly one hundred players and coaches for Navy and its opponents.

The stadium also features a Walk of Fame that lists every Naval Academy player who has garnered a principal postseason award. There are the Heisman and Maxwell Trophy winners; those enshrined in the College Football Hall of Fame; National Football Foundation Gold Medalists; NCAA Theodore Roosevelt Award recipients; first team All-Americas; and Academic All-Americas.

Still, Navy football is more than renowned players and coaches, unique traditions, stirring memories, and revered history. It is also its fans, who add so much. In hundreds of stadiums from coast-to-coast, they have cheered their team in victory and suffered with it in defeat. Regardless of where in the world they gather near a radio or a television, their emotions are no less vivid, their cheering no less rabid. But it is at Navy–Marine Corps Memorial Stadium, within sight of the Naval Academy itself, that Navy football truly comes alive. The thousands of young men and women smartly dressed in their uniforms provide a stirring backdrop for thousands of other fans. A scattering of officers in uniform spices the presence of their fellow officers and alumni. And the families of the midshipmen turn out; the parents of the players proudly wear buttons displaying their son's picture, name, and number. No less important are the "friends" of Navy football, some of whose allegiance was spawned during service in the Navy. Nearly all sport blue and gold caps, jackets, blankets, pennants, or badges as public signs of their emotion. Their enthusiasm spills out in the constant roar of cheers, in victory or defeat.

For more than a century, this panorama of Navy spirit has helped to weave that special fabric that has become the Naval Academy's football tradition. And in so doing, there was—and always will be—one theme: Anchors Aweigh!

1. The Tradition Begins 1879–1899

Football has been the centerpiece of athletics at the Naval Academy since the 1880s. The seeds for its growth were planted shortly after the Civil War, when the school was returned from its wartime location in Newport, Rhode Island, to Annapolis, where it had been founded in 1845 as the Naval School.

The Naval Academy of the late nineteenth century in no way resembled today's school. Classes were small, and naval cadets (they were not called midshipmen until 1902) spent long periods of time at sea, where emphasis was placed on learning seamanship in a canvas-sail navy. By all accounts, cadets were treated rather harshly during their training periods, partly because officers who had risen through the enlisted ranks resented the beginnings of an elite officer corps whose members would not endure the hardships they had suffered en route to their rank status.

Intercollegiate athletic competition was all but unheard of until after the Civil War—not surprisingly, since organized athletics in the country as a whole were very rare. The only record of organized sports involving the naval cadets at Annapolis prior to 1860 was a fencing match between some gun crews in 1850. Some informal fencing matches and boat races were held during the sojourn in Rhode Island.

The manner in which naval cadets were trained for their profession changed dramatically in 1865 when Rear Adm. David Porter was named superintendent. Porter, known as the "Father of the Naval Academy," was the most influential person in the school's early growth.

Porter made athletics an integral part of Academy life; he regarded them as necessary relief from the

The 1879 Navy football team, the first one organized at the Naval Academy. Led by team captain Bill Maxwell, it played under rugby rules in its only game—on December 11, 1879—and managed a scoreless tie against the Baltimore Athletic Club.

David Dixon Porter

Rear Adm. David Dixon Porter was an athletic man, broad-shouldered and barrel-chested, though he stood only five feet, seven inches. His father, Commo. David Porter, was a naval hero in the War of 1812; when he obtained command of the Mexican navy in 1826, thirteen-year-old David went to sea as a midshipman, also with the Mexican navy. Two years later his ship, *Guerrero,* was captured by the Spanish navy, and the young sailor spent a year aboard a Spanish prison ship in Havana.

Porter obtained a midshipman's commission in the U.S. Navy more than a decade before the Naval Academy was founded and distinguished himself during the Mexican War by capturing a Mexican fort. He was one of the North's foremost naval heroes in the Civil War, playing a critical role in establishing control over the Mississippi River. Among his exploits was a daring run past the Confederate batteries at Vicksburg to open communications with Gen. Ulysses S. Grant, with whom he held a lifelong friendship. Although overshadowed as a popular hero by his foster brother, Adm. David Farragut, Porter was the only naval officer to receive four different congressional votes of thanks. After Congress created the rank of admiral for Farragut, Porter was made vice admiral.

In 1862, Porter requested the post of Naval Academy superintendent, effective when the school returned to Annapolis. His interest in the job reportedly was piqued because his son had been dismissed from the Naval Academy during the Civil War, and the elder Porter wanted "to get the right sort of officers into the Navy. A new era should be instituted."

Porter worked under the unshaken conviction that anything with which he was associated had to be the very best, and that's how he trained his naval cadets during his five years as superintendent (1865–69). Porter used his considerable political clout to rebuild and expand the Academy's physical plant to accommodate an almost fourfold enrollment increase, to 566 cadets. In the process, he forged a reputation for being "ambitious, egocentric, and vengeful of any slight, real or imagined . . . a superb leader, dynamic, intelligent, and innovative," according to a history of the Academy. All of the changes he made—one of which was encouraging more athletic competition—were rooted in his memories of a cadet's grim life in the pre–Civil War Navy. Porter thought it imperative to improve the midshipmen's morale and pride. He introduced the Honor Code, scheduled more social activities, and revamped the academic curriculum. (To smother opposition to his planned reforms, Porter gave himself three votes in all dealings with the Academic Board.)

Porter took athletics seriously. When he added boxing to the physical regimen, he stunned everyone on the first day of competition by climbing into the ring and sparring a round with one of the mids. The plebe recovered from his astonishment enough to punch Porter in the nose. Later, he ordered gymnastics, boxing, and fencing competitions to be held on many Saturday evenings. He even invited President Ulysses S. Grant and his wife to one of the Saturday affairs and a subsequent dance.

students' daily regimen. He constructed the first gymnasium in 1866 on the barbette of old Fort Severn. The building had shooting galleries and a bowling alley on the ground floor and the latest gymnastics equipment on the second floor. A year later, as part of the Thanksgiving Day holiday, Porter established a series of athletic carnivals that featured track and field, baseball, gymnastics, and rowing competitions; a year after that, he hired the Academy's first physical education instructor, Matthew Strohm. Porter became so obsessed with excellence in athletics that he announced, "I don't want anyone to come down here and beat us at anything."

Football apparently escaped Porter's notice, but it would eventually benefit from the positive atmosphere he established. According to tradition, football came to the Academy in 1879, a decade after Porter's administration. A cadet reportedly returned from leave with a football and brought it to the drill field during a recreation period. A lively kicking contest ensued; before long, sides were chosen, and the rambunctious students went at each other enthusiastically. The game ended when the ball was kicked into the Severn River.

The second team in Naval Academy history, the 1882 Navy football team posted the school's first victory, an 8–0 triumph over Johns Hopkins University. The first Navy coach, Vaulx Carter, is second from left in the back row. He also played halfback. His teammates included *(front row, from left)* James Kittrell (guard), Tremlet Toney (tackle), Tim O'Leary (guard), John Alex Jackson (captain and back), Frank Hill (end), Ned Tilden (end), and William O'Malley (back); and *(back row)* George Washington Street (center), Carter, Julius Dashiell (back), Elton Dalrymple (manager), and Foxhall "Kid" Parker (tackle).

In fact, there was a semblance of football being played informally by naval cadets more than a decade before Porter's arrival as superintendent. The December 2, 1857, *Journal of the Officer of the Day* noted that, "During recreation hours, the students amused themselves with a number of footballs; almost the whole academy seemed to partake of this amusement."

Five years later, on December 23, 1862, the *Journal* recorded, "Footballs prohibited to be used in the House or in the immediate vicinity." Four days later the following appeared: "Published order prohibiting playing at football until further orders." And those orders apparently stayed in place until 1879.

They apparently were not always strictly observed, however. Cdr. H. O. Rittenhouse (Class of 1870), wrote, "About the year 1869 some progressive individual in the corps appeared on the drill field with a large round football (Rugby). The game was simply a boisterous free-for-all kick fest in which shins suffered far more than the ball. . . ."

The first attempts at organizing a football team at the Academy were twofold. According to a written account by William John Maxwell (Class of 1881), it was J. H. Robinson (Class of 1879) who deserved credit for "leading us into an interest in the type of football practice as we knew it to be under the early 'Association' or soccer rules." Captain Maxwell said that evolved into a game of "hands off," in which only the foot was used to keep the ball in play.

The game was intended to keep baseball players limbered up, Maxwell said.

Maxwell organized the first football game at the Naval Academy. It was played under rugby rules. After summer leave in 1879, he convinced two friends, Tunstall Smith and Henry Woods, who played rugby for the Baltimore Athletic Club (BAC) and who also had played at Cambridge, Eton, and Oxford in England, to agree to a game between their team and one he would form at the Naval Academy. The contest was scheduled for December 11, 1879, at the Academy.

Maxwell, who was manager, trainer, and coach of the team, knew that his opponents were bigger, stronger, and more experienced. Seeking an edge for his team, he persuaded William Bellis, the foremost naval uniform tailor in Annapolis, to make each player a sleeveless canvas jacket that could be laced in front and drawn tight to the contours of the body. Maxwell knew that canvas, when wet, was difficult to grasp, and he anticipated that a muddy field, or perhaps even body sweat, would make it difficult for the Baltimore players to grab his players.

For this bit of ingenuity, Maxwell was credited by Walter Camp, considered the "Father of American Football" and the foremost innovator of early football, with designing the first football uniform.

Maxwell drilled his players before reveille and after drills and meals; he even got them excused from supper formation. His work paid off, after a fashion, because the two teams, playing in the superintendent's cow pasture, battled to a scoreless tie. The *Baltimore American and Chronicle* declared it

> a battle from beginning to end—a regular knock-down, drag-out fight. Both sides became immensely excited and the audience was aroused to the highest pitch of enthusiasm by the spirited contest. . . . The scrimmages

The first Army-Navy Game, played in 1890. Navy defeated Army 24–0 at West Point.

were something awful to witness—living, kicking, scrambling masses of humanity surging to and fro.

If a Baltimorean got the ball and started for a run, he was unfailingly caught by one of the brawny Cadets and dashed to earth, with five or six men falling on him. The Middies were never allowed to get the ball at all.

Neither side ever threatened to score, though Navy did force the BAC team "to touch down three times for a safety" (worth no points under the rules at that time).

Cited for outstanding play that day were Maxwell, his classmate Winfield Scott Sample, and McDonough Craven (Class of 1881). Although not mentioned in press accounts, one of the Navy players was Hugh Rodman, who became America's foremost naval hero during World War I when he commanded the Atlantic Fleet and smashed Germany's U-boat threat while supervising the convoying of some four million American doughboys to France without a single casualty.

The most important result of that 1879 game was the lifting of the flagging athletic spirit at the Academy. Authorities were convinced that financial and student support would make a football program successful. But it was three years before Navy played its next organized game. It came on November 28, 1882, against the Clifton Football Club of Baltimore. Clifton was actually a team from Johns Hopkins University that played under this name because it was not sanctioned by the school. On that cold, blustery Thanksgiving Day, Navy won its first game ever, 8–0. It was the first of three straight years in which games against Johns Hopkins were the focal point of the annual holiday athletic festival started by Admiral Porter in 1867. Playing under its school name, Johns Hopkins won in 1883; in 1884, Navy won 9–6. Those were the only football games the cadets played in each of those seasons.

Midshipman Vaulx Carter was coach of the 1882 team, and thus is credited with organizing Navy's first team, as well as being its first head coach. Those accomplishments became his only claim to fame: he left the school before his scheduled 1884 graduation and disappeared from the historical record.

Playing the 1882 game was touch-and-go for a time because the contract between the schools stipulated that the game would be played only in fair weather. When day broke at Annapolis, the ground was covered by snow. Scores of naval cadets turned out and cleared the field in time for the ten o'clock kickoff. Navy's uniform that day featured maroon stocking caps and belts, white canvas pants and jackets with maroon lacings, and shoes with a strip of leather nailed to the soles to prevent slipping.

That Navy team outweighed its foes by an average of ten pounds per man. Navy's captain, John Alexander Jackson from Florida, won the coin toss and kicked off. One game account said the Clifton team dominated the scoreless first half. (At one point, the ball was accidentally kicked over the seawall and had to be retrieved by boat before the game could continue.) Navy got control early in the second half, though, and George Washington Street, a senior from Wisconsin, scored the first touchdown—and points—by a Navy player. Clifton blocked the extra point kick, but the ball landed in the hands of Cadet William

The Rutgers Connection

The first intercollegiate football game was played in 1879 between Rutgers and Princeton. One of the Rutgers players was George S. Willits (USNA Class of 1875), then prepping for admission to Annapolis. As far as is known, neither Willits nor his classmates ever tried to formally introduce the sport at the Naval Academy.

Innovations in Signal Calling

Navy's teams in the 1890s had an elementary approach to their play-calling. They used nautical commands such as "Stand by to clear anchor!" or "Down the wind!" with which all were familiar, to set their offense in motion. The calls were probably very confusing to opponents because sometimes the commands triggered specific plays, while at other times they meant nothing and were used just to confuse the opposition.

The advance to a more sophisticated system took some strange twists. For instance, numbering of the seven offensive linemen began logically enough with No. 1 as the center. But then the two guards were both No. 2, the two tackles No. 3, and the two ends No. 4. However, the distinction between right and left was made by geographical references—those on the left of the center were "western states," and those on the right were "eastern states." Positions farther from the center were states with the most letters, those closer had the fewest. Thus, the left end position was Colorado, North and South Dakota, Arizona, and New Mexico; the right end, Alabama, Connecticut, Massachusetts, and Carolina. Left tackle was designated by Idaho, Iowa, Nevada, and Oregon, while on the right, it was Delaware, Florida, and Maryland. The center was always Maine.

In the backfield, the quarterback was just that, but the right halfback was either Virginia or West Virginia, and the left halfback was California or Columbia ("District of," no doubt). The fullback was Pennsylvania or Louisiana. And the kickers? Missouri and Kentucky, of course, because they were considered "mule states!"

Games were played in forty-five-minute halves. The ball was put into play by the center who snapped it with his foot back to the quarterback, who then handed it to one of the three running backs. Substitutions were made only for injury, and teams often played two or three games a week. For many years during the first quarter-century of its football program, Navy played football on Saturday and Wednesday afternoons. The season began early in October, and the twice-a-week schedule was scattered haphazardly, even at times nudging the Army-Navy game.

Francis O'Malley, a junior from Pennsylvania. Under the rules, it was a free ball, so O'Malley ran it in for a second touchdown.

The historic significance of the game was not evident, of course. The pregame hype: a week before the game, an item in the *Army and Navy Journal* staidly noted, "It was announced that the Clifton Football Club of Baltimore, and a team of Naval Academy cadets, would engage in a game on Thanksgiving Day, if the weather permitted. A good game is expected." On game day, the duty log for the Officer of the Day at the Academy simply mentioned, "At 10, Cadets engaged in athletic sports."

During the last half of the 1880s, football at the Academy moved from its rugby and soccer roots and established its own set of rules and systems, setting the stage in 1890 to establish the crown jewel of Navy football—the Army-Navy game.

Developing talent was difficult because only first classmen were allowed to play, so there was no carryover of experience from year to year. Nor was there any coaching continuity. From 1891, when Edgar Allan Poe became the first full-time varsity coach hired from outside the Academy, until 1904, Navy employed eleven different "full-time" coaches. All were former Yale or Princeton players who were hired for the football season only. Still, they did a splendid job because Navy had a 61–25–3 record from 1891 through 1901.

Walter "Snake" Izard, a 145-pound halfback and three-year letterman in 1892–94. He scored a touchdown in Navy's 12–4 triumph over Army in 1892 and was rhapsodized in the following morning's newspaper account of the game: "Whirling like a northeast blizzard/Around the end swept little Izard." Izard was also a fine baseball player. He won the Naval Academy's baseball throwing contest twice, heaving the ball 327 and 347 feet, respectively.

With so many coaches, there were many theories about how to train a team. For example, the 1892 coach, Ben Crosby, had played at Yale. For practice sessions, he made his varsity team play two ninety-minute halves each day against a double scrub team and then swim in a cold pool before supper. Game days were a breeze after that. Navy lost its first two games—played three days apart against highly rated Penn and Princeton—but won its last five.

Preceding Crosby as coach was Edgar Allan Poe, of Baltimore, a great-nephew of Edgar Allan Poe, the famed poet and author of horror tales. There were six Poe sons and all played football at Princeton; they are the most famous coaching family in football history.

Edgar was followed at the Naval Academy in 1896 by his brother, Johnny, who, like his older brother, was fresh out of college when he signed on to coach Navy. Johnny was paid $501.25 in salary and expenses for his one season's work. By all accounts, that totaled every cent in the Athletic Association's coffers. Money was a severe problem at this time. Navy played all of its games at home, and they were free—so the Athletic Association had no ongoing means of support. That season, the Cadet Corps even chipped in to support a game against the University of Pennsylvania's Reserves, which Navy lost. The money problems weren't resolved until the team's Homecoming Day victory over the Atlantic Fleet—the famed White Squadron—with financial help from the battalion, its officers, and Robert J. Thompson, a copper magnate and member of the Class of 1867.

Knowing that his salary had drained the Athletic Association's treasury, Poe gratefully wrote, "I could not have felt unfairly treated had I received $450 for the season and no expenses."

Johnny Poe was asked to return as head coach in 1897, but he was a restless young adventurer upon whom more than a few storytellers, novelists, and

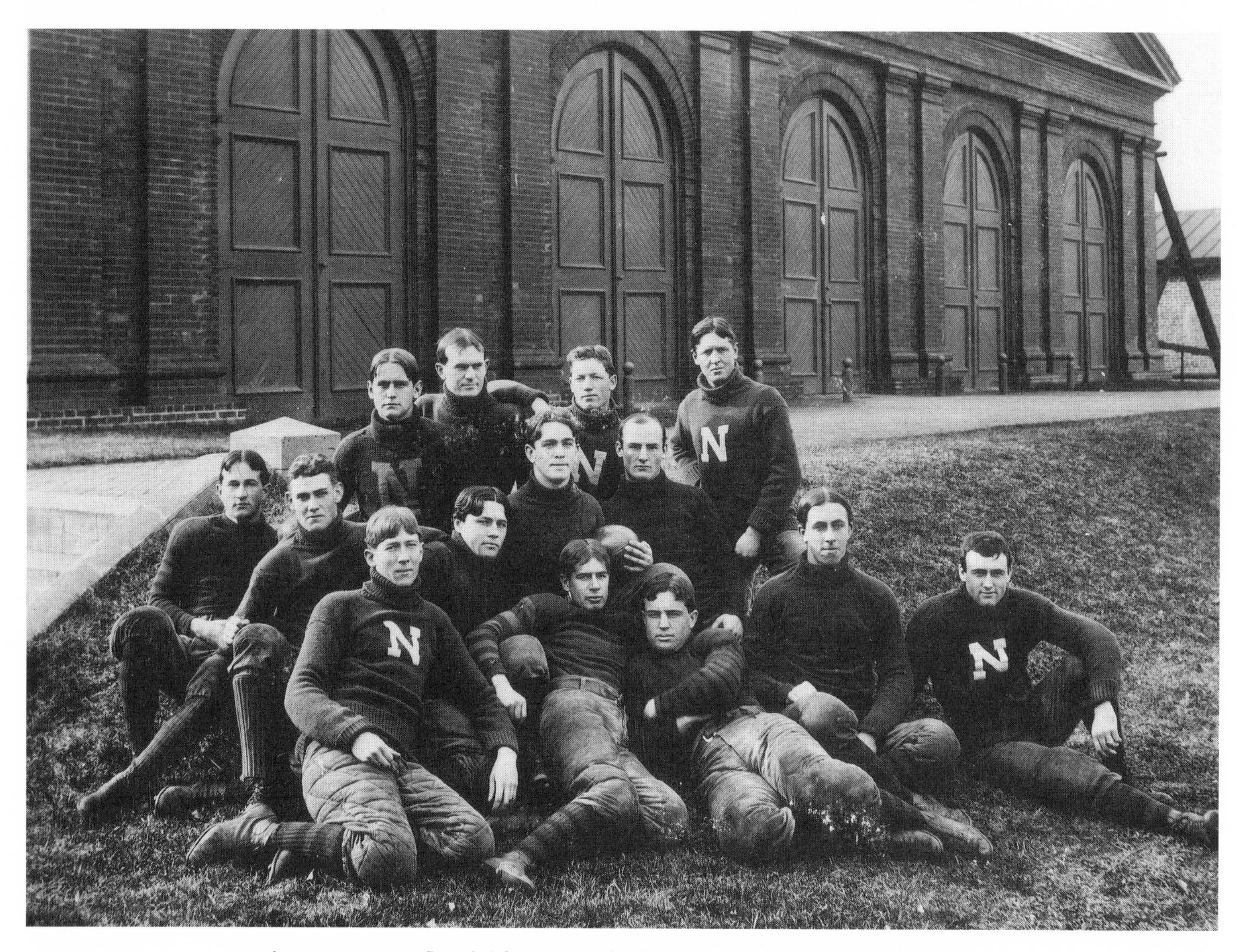

Navy's 1896 team won five of eight games with Johnny Poe as head coach. Poe's brother, Edgar Allan, had coached Navy's 1891 team. Each coached for one season only and both were descendants of famed author Edgar Allan Poe.

screenwriters based their heroes. He left Navy to take a year-round job in the Nevada mining camps as a mounted police officer. On one occasion, he single-handedly caught a gang of cattle rustlers; on another, he "thrashed" a man who had insulted the U.S. flag. Soon thereafter, he became a folk hero of sorts for helping to round up a gang of robbers in Death Valley who had looted a Wells Fargo Express office.

Poe went on to survey the boundary between the United States, British Columbia, and Alaska—and all of this before he was twenty-five years old. He fought in Cuba during the Spanish-American War and then joined the army in the Philippines. He lost his life in World War I as a member of Britain's famed Black Watch. But Poe is probably best remembered as the coach who coined the slogan, "If you won't be beat, you can't be beat."

The Poes were good coaches, despite their youth and inexperience. Edgar's 1891 team won five of seven games. Johnny's 1896 team took five of eight. The 1891 team was notable for playing—and winning—three games in one week, beating Gallaudet, Georgetown, and Dickinson. The toll for playing such a crowded schedule was heavy—the team lost its last two games, to Lafayette and Army (the latter was the first Army-Navy game played at Annapolis). This team had one of Navy's first great stars, tackle Charley Macklin, who thrived as a rusher in the "guards back" and "tackles back" formations of the day.

Also playing on that team was a young end named Homer Ferguson, who later became president of the Newport News Shipbuilding Corporation, which built hundreds of Navy and merchant marine ships during World Wars I and II. In fact, throughout the first two decades, the Navy rosters were dotted with players who later distinguished themselves during the two world wars.

In 1889, the team captain was Albertus Catlin. Determined to bring his team some national recognition, Catlin secured permission for special reveille for his teammates, turning them out for spirited practice sessions at five o'clock, an hour before everyone else arose. The work paid off—Navy won four of its six games and tied Dickinson. After it defeated Virginia 26–6, Navy claimed the championship of the South. A few days later, the team capped the season with a 24–0 victory over the Washington All-Stars.

Catlin became a Marine officer and was cited for bravery as commander of the detachment aboard the USS *Maine* when it was blown up in Havana Harbor. He also was commended for courage in the landings at Vera Cruz, Mexico, in 1914. As a brigadier general, he led the Sixth Marines in the Battle of Belleau Wood in World War I. He died from wounds after being awarded the croix de guerre.

Worth Bagley, a native of Raleigh, North Carolina, was Navy's first great football star. He was a four-year letterman and a superb quarterback from 1891 to 1894; a three-year captain of his class's football team; captain of its baseball teams for four years; and a record-setting track star. Bagley was also the first American killed in the Spanish-American War in 1898.

Navy played Army for the first time on November 29, 1890, at West Point: Navy won, 24–0. Coincidentally, that first Army-Navy game also inaugurated Army's storied football tradition. From that day on, the importance of the Army-Navy game has been an integral part of the Naval Academy's tradition.

New Tackling Techniques

During the 1880s, Navy originated some of the techniques that helped football evolve from its soccer/rugby origins. Below-the-knees tackling was one important example. Until 1888, tackling consisted mainly of grasping a ball carrier around the waist and trying to wrestle him to the ground. But in an 1887 game against the Princeton Reserves, the Navy players had great difficulty handling a 220-pound back named Hector Cowan. Finally, Cadet Montgomery Taylor (Class of 1890) dived at Cowan's ankles and flipped him in the air. Cowan landed on Taylor, and both players lay prostrate, short of breath. Finally Cadet Taylor, spicing his indignation with a few expletives, bellowed, "Get the hell off my belly." He was almost knocked breathless again when Cowan responded, in a gentle falsetto voice, "Please don't swear in my presence. I'm a divinity student."

That play is believed to be one of the first below-the-knees tackles in the game's history. The technique was legalized in 1888.

New Blocking Techniques

Worth Bagley, one of Navy's early great running backs, ran plays in 1892 with a blocker in front of him—a designation later termed "interference" after it became a popular offensive technique. The play was a product of the fertile football imagination of assistant coach Paul Dashiell, later to emerge as the "Father of Navy Football." Dashiell was one of the game's leading strategists before the turn of the century. He wanted swift, athletic ball carriers like Bagley to be the centerpiece of a more coordinated and flexible system. Previously, offense generally came down to the "V" formation—blockers packed around a ball carrier. In response, defenses developed their own tight wedges. Dashiell saw no reason to run into a mass of defenders; instead, he installed plays that allowed the swift Bagley to run to the outside, still convoyed by a phalanx of blockers.

It remains the most important game on the schedule—indeed, the prevailing philosophy has always been that every game is but a warmup until Navy plays Army.

That first Army-Navy game was such big news that the *New York Times* made it the page one lead story the following day. The two schools were pleased with the beginning of the relationship and, in 1891, played at the Naval Academy, where Army, showing much more sophistication and skill, upset their hosts 32–16. Thus was struck the one preeminent commandment that forever has ruled this series: "Always expect the unexpected!"

The schools took turns playing host. Navy won, 12–4, at West Point in 1892, and again in Annapolis, 6–4, in 1893. The emotions that spilled from this rivalry quickly helped it flourish beyond anyone's expectations. But those emotions also had repercussions. An admiral and a general, having a couple of drinks at the Army-Navy Club in New York City, reportedly became so upset while discussing Army's 1893 victory that they threatened to settle their differences with a duel. That shocked the War and Navy Departments, which stepped in and averted the confrontation. But by mutual agreement, the series was suspended, and it was not resumed until 1899.

One of Bagley's teammates during the 1892 season was a strapping tackle named Joseph Reeves, later one of the Navy's most distinguished officers during the first half of the twentieth century. Reeves was credited with inventing in 1893 the most important piece of equipment worn by a football player—the helmet.

He was the key player as a ball carrier or blocker when Navy used its tackles-back offense (the tackles dropped into the backfield and became blockers or runners). Reeves also played on his class team. Like all players at that time, he wore only a stocking cap on his head. It was an era that did not emphasize subtlety: full-speed, head-on collisions were common. The pummeling Reeves took during both his varsity and intramural play resulted in a series of head injuries. Finally, he went to a seamstress in Annapolis, and she fashioned him a beehive-shaped headgear from a piece of moleskin. Within three years, use of protective headgear became widespread on other teams, but historians have credited Reeves with devising the first.

Joe Taussig, the first in a distinguished family of Taussigs to graduate from the Naval Academy, starred as a fine quarterback during the 1897 and 1898 seasons. Taussig gained even greater fame in gymnastics, where he became known as "the man on the flying trapeze." Like Reeves, he went on to be one of the ablest staff officers in Navy history. By World War II, both men were retired admirals, but they were recalled to active duty and played vital roles in the planning of naval operations.

One of Taussig's teammates was Johnny Halligan, a fiery guard who holds the distinction of playing six varsity seasons, the most by any Navy player. He was captain of the 1897 team and graduated first in the class of 1898. Then, employing a now-defunct special designation as "Past Midshipman," which allowed graduates to return to the Academy for advanced study, Halligan played two more years. Joe Powell, captain of the 1896 team, came back and played in 1897 under that same designation.

Joseph Reeves *(middle row, center)* wears his specially made beehive helmet as a member of his Class of 1894 team. A distinguished admiral in World Wars I and II, Reeves wore this same helmet when he played with Navy's varsity team, and he is credited with using the first football helmet in intercollegiate competition.

The Helmet

Midshipman Joseph Reeves became one of the most colorful and remarkable officers in Navy history. In 1898, he was cited for gallantry aboard the battleship USS *Oregon* in the Battle of Santiago during the Spanish-American War, and he won the Navy Cross as commander of the USS *Maine* during World War I. Reeves was also striking in appearance, sporting a white mustache and goatee that earned him the affectionate nickname "Billy Goat."

His biggest contribution was as a leading proponent and pioneer in the development of naval aviation between the two world wars. He was fifty-three years old in 1925 when he qualified as a naval aviation observer, the minimum prerequisite for holding aviation commands. He developed the fleet's first air tactical doctrines and, in the early 1930s, continued to make tactical innovations in aerial warfare as Commander Carriers Battle Fleet. He commanded the U.S. Fleet from 1934 to 1936.

So great was his command ability that the aging Admiral Reeves was recalled to active duty during World War II to handle several special assignments. Reeves retired as a full admiral at the age of seventy-four in 1946.

Henry C. Mustin, who became a pioneer of naval aviation, was a quarterback on the 1894–95 teams. He was one of the first to promulgate successful aerial bombing and torpedo attack theories against naval surface forces.

Several members of the 1898 and 1899 teams, which won twelve of sixteen games over the two seasons, were destined for meritorious service during World War II. Most notable were Emory Land and Ernest J. King. Land was a four-year varsity player who started as an end but became a fine halfback during his last two seasons (1900–1901). As a vice admiral, he was appointed to the U.S. Maritime Commission in 1937; shortly after World War II began, he was appointed chairman and made responsible for the massive transport of millions of men and supplies to Europe and the Pacific.

King was Chief of Naval Operations, the Navy's top-ranking officer, during World War II. His reputation as a demanding and hard-nosed commander had its roots on the football field, where he spent four seasons playing mostly for the "Hustlers," Navy's scrub team. King so admired the qualities that the game instilled in officers that he sought former football players as his aides.

Navy's football schedule began to expand in the mid-1880s. Within a decade, teams from Penn, Princeton, Virginia, Georgetown, Rutgers, and St. John's College were annual opponents. The St. John's rivalry was particularly intense because the two schools abutted each other in Annapolis. Feelings ran so high that during a game in 1886, it took the personal, on-the-field intervention by the superintendent, Cdr. William T. Sampson, and the commandant to stop a fight between the two sides. Sampson (who had just become superintendent) was a dedicated fan; along with alumni who had been students during Admiral Porter's tenure and were now in command positions, he formed the impetus to expand the program.

Every football game was played at the Academy. Opponents came for midweek games even though both teams might have played the previous Saturday and have another game the next Saturday. At the turn of the century, a variety of schools from within a three-hundred-mile radius came to Annapolis; and until 1908, there were ten-, eleven-, and twelve-game schedules. The 1901 team played an eleven-game schedule, but six of those games were played within a two-week span. In 1903, when Navy played twelve games, seven of them were played from October 10 through October 31; Navy won three of the seven.

Schedules were far from ironclad. Nor were the rules completely settled; different games were played under different sets of rules governing the shifting of players, such as the Yale-Princeton, or Harvard-Princeton, or Harvard-Pennsylvania rules. In 1895, Virginia didn't want to play Navy under any of those formats. When Virginia also demanded that the referee and umpire alternate positions, the Mids balked. Virginia didn't show up for the game, and Navy won by forfeit, 1–0. Another rules dispute against Rutgers gave Navy a 1–0 victory two years later. In 1899, Columbia canceled a game because coach Foster Sanford said he was afraid Navy would be so tough that his team would not be physically ready to later play Carlisle on Thanksgiving Day.

That was the supreme compliment, and it was well-founded: Navy entered the twentieth century as one of the top teams in the East. All it needed was some solid direction to enable it to compete at the highest levels. That direction came from a man who was in the Yard teaching mathematics—Paul Dashiell, the "Father of Navy Football."

2. Three-to-Nothing Dalton and Babe Brown 1900–1919

Right after the turn of the century, Navy's football program began to soar. The teams had proven their ability to play and defeat the best schools in the East and South, and opponents began vying for a spot on their schedule.

Interestingly, Navy football also had begun attracting adventuresome cadets who later were pioneers of naval aviation and leaders of the Navy's carrier forces during World War II. One of those cadets was Henry Mustin, who played quarterback in 1894 and 1895 and was designated Naval Aviator No. 11. He advanced the theory that a naval air force could develop high-speed planes equipped with machine guns and bombs, and that torpedo planes would be effective weapons against battleships. Mustin also believed that fast fighter planes could protect slower bombers.

Another promising young cadet was John Rodgers, a tackle who earned three letters from 1900 to 1902 and who was designated Naval Aviator No. 2 behind Spud Ellyson. Rodgers was an utterly fearless pilot. Renowned as a long-distance seaplane flier, he attempted one of the first transoceanic flights as part of a three-plane foray from San Francisco to Hawaii. En route, the other two planes turned back. Finally, off course because of faulty navigational data, Rodgers's plane ran out of fuel and went down. In one of the most amazing survival stories in naval aviation history, Rodgers and his crewman, Lt. B. J. Connell, fashioned a sail from the fabric of one of the plane's wings and sailed the plane approximately 450 miles. The two men were within ten miles of Kauai when they were picked up by a submarine and their plane was towed into port. They set a flight record of 1,841 statute miles—a record that stood for five more years.

William "Bull" Halsey had football on his mind even when he was a young lad. The Navy's most renowned admiral during World War II won two letters as a fullback at Annapolis in 1902 and 1903.

Rodgers's 1900 team won six of nine games, including a season-ending 11–7 victory over Army. Army had won 17–5 in 1899, but in 1900 the punting of Charles Belknap—and more than just a bit of luck—helped Navy to win before 23,000 fans at Philadelphia's Franklin Field. Belknap's punts kept Army's offense backed up. The other component of the kicking game did not fare so well; Byron Long agonized as his first six field goal attempts were blocked. Army led 5–0 at halftime. In the second half, Long finally kicked a field goal, and Emory Land, who went on to help direct the nation's maritime policies during

Navy's 1901 team boasted team captain Neil Nichols *(middle row, holding the ball)*. During that season, the team played three games within a week's time and won two of them.

World War II, scored a touchdown for an 11–5 Navy lead. But the outcome was in doubt until the game's last play, when Belknap's punt was blocked in the end zone by Army's Quinn Gary. Navy's Long just beat Gary in recovering the skittering football for a safety, instead of a potential Army touchdown.

The next day, a new Navy tradition was established—the ringing of the Gokokuji Bell to represent the number of points scored in a Navy victory over Army.

There were other future aviation pioneers playing and coaching football for Navy during the first decade of the twentieth century. They included Frank Berrien, a teammate of Mustin's who lettered for three years as an end, who had a fine 21–5–3 record as head coach from 1908 to 1910, and who later was skipper of the USS *Lexington;* and one of Rodgers's teammates, future admiral William "Bull" Halsey, the nation's best-known carrier fleet commander during World War II.

Also part of that esteemed group was Ken Whiting, one of the stars of coach Paul Dashiell's first team in 1904. Whiting won four letters playing end from 1901 to 1904 and later earned the designation of Naval Aviator No. 16. He was a handsome, suave, high-flying New Englander who said he flew a plane for the "pure, wholesome hell of it." He was taught to fly by Orville Wright and later taught famed Army aviation pioneer Billy Mitchell. He commanded the first U.S. air unit to reach France during World War I and later was the first commanding officer of the USS *Langley,* the Navy's first aircraft carrier. Whiting and Mustin tested their theories of aerial warfare when Mustin commanded Pensacola Naval Station in 1915 and Whiting was in charge of its flight school. Mustin later commanded the Pacific Fleet's Air Detachment in the early twenties. Whiting later did some submarine duty. Once, while aboard a sub resting on the bottom of Manila Bay, he placed himself in a torpedo tube, ordered the other end opened, and then swam to the surface to prove that a man could survive at that depth.

Whiting and Halsey were teammates in 1903. Halsey, who was to be widely known for his peppery style as an admiral, was no less colorful as a stumpy fullback under coaches Doc Hillebrand and Burr Chamberlain during the 1902 and 1903 seasons.

A native of Elizabeth, New Jersey, Halsey came from a family of seafarers reaching back some two hundred years. His father graduated from the Naval Academy in 1862 and later taught there when Bill was young. Halsey, who had played fullback in high school, was nicknamed "Bull" when a sportswriter covering one of his Navy games misspelled "Bill." But it was an apt nickname—Halsey had fought hard to get a Naval Academy appointment.

In 1897, Halsey applied for an appointment to the Naval Academy during his senior year at Swarthmore Grammar School in Philadelphia. He was turned down. True to his gritty spirit, he appealed his rejection in a letter to President William McKinley. When he received no reply, he enrolled at the University of Virginia as a premed student. In the meantime, Halsey's mother contacted President McKinley and prevailed on him to grant her son an appointment. He made Halsey an alternate—not an admittee—in 1898, and again Halsey failed to gain entrance. The following year, he tried again, and when Congress added five more appointments, President McKinley gave one to him.

Halsey used that same determination to forge his playing career. He was not a big man—he was five eleven and weighed 155 pounds—but he was a rower and had developed a barrel chest that belied his slender legs. (A friend once described Halsey as looking like "a figurehead of Neptune.") Bull undoubtedly got some of his fire from his mother. During one of her son's games at the Naval Academy, Mrs. Halsey was seated on the sidelines when Bull was tackled. A lady in front of her jumped up and shouted, "Kill him! Kill him!" Mrs. Halsey leaped to her feet, brandishing her parasol as a weapon, and is said to have defended her son's honor until she was forcibly restrained.

Halsey was president of the Athletic Association during his junior and senior years and was awarded the Thompson Trophy Cup, given to the student who had done the most to promote athletics at the Naval Academy. He had tried out for the football team as a plebe in 1899 and didn't make it. In his second year he was a fullback on the Hustlers—the scrub team. In 1902, during Halsey's junior year, the regular fullback was injured before the season opened, and Halsey took his spot. He never relinquished it, though he often termed himself "the worst fullback who ever went to the Naval Academy." Yet, he played sixty minutes in both of his starts against Army and, in the 1903 game, had the game's longest run—thirty-nine yards.

During a meeting between Halsey and Gen. Dwight D. Eisenhower after World War II, Ike remarked, "Admiral, they tell me you claim to be the worst fullback who ever went to the Naval Academy."

"That's true," Halsey shot back. "What about it?"

"Well," Eisenhower said, extending his hand, "I want you to meet the worst halfback who ever went to the Military Academy."

Bill Halsey

In 1943, while serving as commander-in-chief of naval forces in the South Pacific, Vice Adm. William F. Halsey met Maj. Gen. Charles F. Thompson at a conference on Fiji Island. Thompson had played spectacularly at right guard for Army in 1903 against Navy when Halsey was the fullback.

"General," Halsey said, "the last time I saw you, you were rubbing my nose all over Franklin Field."

Flashing a huge grin, Thompson replied, "Admiral, how did I know you were going to be the commander-in-chief of the South Pacific?"

Paul Dashiell

Paul Dashiell was a splendid athlete. Taking advantage of the absence of eligibility rules, he played ten years of intercollegiate football at St. John's College in Annapolis, Johns Hopkins (where he was Phi Beta Kappa), and Lehigh—and he played superbly against Navy during most of those seasons. Although a small man, Dashiell was captain of both the football and baseball teams at Johns Hopkins and also was a gymnast, wrestler, and tennis player. (He was so good at tennis that in 1905 he was captain and a nonplaying member of America's Davis Cup team.)

Dashiell was a native of Annapolis who was raised at St. John's College, where his father, an Episcopalian minister, taught Latin and Greek. After his long college career, Dashiell was Naval Academy all the way. He joined the faculty in 1892 and retired as a captain forty years later, in 1932. His older brother graduated from the Academy in 1881, and his sister was married to one of his brother's classmates.

Dashiell was fascinated with the emerging sport of football. He became one of its top officials and was widely recognized by his trademark derby hat, cane, and bushy mustache. He was a member of the intercollegiate Rules Committee for twenty-seven years and was the prime mover in revising the rules in 1894 to outlaw the flying wedge, which tamed a very brutal game and enhanced its spectator appeal. A decade later he was in the forefront of making the forward pass legitimate. Above all, Dashiell never lost his consuming interest in Navy football, and he rarely missed so much as a daily practice right to the time of his death in 1934.

William Ingram II, one of Navy's great football stars in the late thirties, heard countless stories about Paul Dashiell from his father, Adm. Jonas Ingram, who had played for Dashiell and became one of his lifelong friends. It was Dashiell's influence as a Navy football coach that caused Jonas Ingram to seek the same job at Navy.

"The feeling among his players, my dad always said, was that they'd have given their right arm for him," Bill Ingram said. "That's how much they loved and respected him. He knew so much about the game, and as a teacher he knew how to make them learn and believe. He was a stickler for using the correct techniques, and everyone who played for him always felt that no opponent was better coached or more precise in their football skills."

Aptly named the Father of Navy Football, Paul Dashiell was in the forefront of developing the game as we know it today as coach, official, and innovator. He was associated with Navy football in a number of capacities for forty years, including a three-season stint as head coach in 1904–6. His teams had a record of 23–5–4.

The biggest boost to Navy's continued success occurred in 1904—the year after Halsey graduated—when Navy hired Paul Dashiell as a full-time coach. Dashiell, whose nickname "Skinny Paul" came from his association with the "Skinny Department," as the Department of Physics and Chemistry has always been called, had haunted the practice field after his daily teaching duties until he was hired as an assistant coach by Matt McClung in 1895. He then worked with Johnny Poe, Bill Armstrong, Garrett Cochran, Doc Hillebrand, and Burr Chamberlain, all former Princeton and Yale players, and all one-term coaches at the Academy. But Dashiell was at constant loggerheads with those men about how the game should be coached. When Navy had back-to-back losing seasons in 1902 and 1903, Dashiell finally convinced authorities that they could do just as well with him as coach. His subsequent efforts quite correctly earned him the sobriquet "Father of Navy Football." It was Dashiell's savvy and skill that put the Academy's program on a par with any school in the nation early in the twentieth century.

Why not? Dashiell knew more about football than any of the men for whom he had worked, and he was far more dedicated to the Naval Academy and its traditions. He imparted his love, knowledge, and enthusiasm to his players, and they responded with a dynamism rarely seen under previous regimes. In 1904, Dashiell used all of those skills to start Navy on a run of eleven consecutive winning seasons, including a record of 25–5–4 during his three as head coach. (Dashiell was later an assistant coach and adviser for eight seasons.)

Dashiell was not afraid to be innovative, even if it meant turning to West Point—Navy's foremost rival—to add a regimen that he believed would benefit his team. Dashiell immediately copied one of the conditioning programs used by his friend Herman Koehler, a very successful coach for Army from 1897 to 1900. It included boxing and wrestling. Dashiell also sharpened his players' football skills by devising a rudimentary blocking sled; he conducted spring practice until the players left on their summer cruises; and he even devised a special conditioning program for them while they were away.

His work paid immediate dividends. Navy stunned everyone by defeating mighty Princeton 10–9 in the third game of the 1904 season en route to seven wins in nine games. The following year, the Mids had their best season ever, winning nine of eleven games; they lost to Swarthmore 6–5, and tied Army 6–6, breaking a four-game losing streak against the Cadets.

President Theodore Roosevelt was in the stands for that 1905 Army-Navy game, which was played at Osborne Field in Princeton, New Jersey. The president's party included much of official Washington—in fact, so many people accompanied the

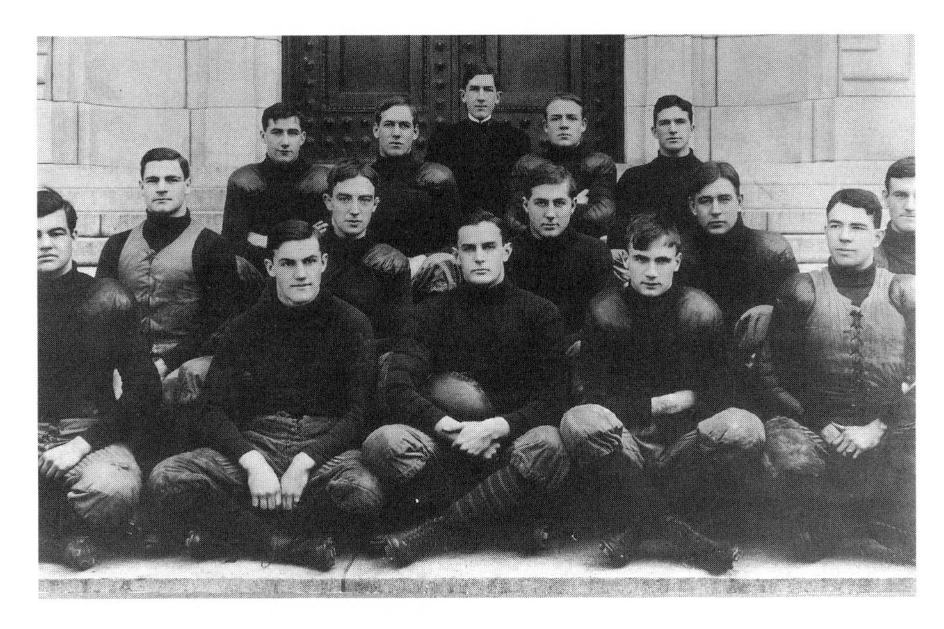

The 1906 Naval Academy team, with captain Bert Spencer *(front row, with the ball)*. The team was coached by Paul Dashiell and won eight of twelve games, including a 10–0 victory over Army. One of its stars was Bob Ghormley, who distinguished himself during some early naval engagements in World War II and as a military diplomat.

The Class of 1906

Cheering on classmate Bob Ghormley during the 1904 and 1905 seasons were three future commanders of America's carrier forces in the Pacific during World War II: Frank Jack Fletcher, Aubrey Fitch, and John S. McCain. Ghormley also distinguished himself as an admiral during the Battle of the Solomons and later as a naval envoy in London. Fletcher led American carrier forces in winning the Battle of the Coral Sea; the Navy's greatest victory of World War II at Midway; and later the successes in the Solomons.

Aubrey Fitch was a great athlete who not only played class football for four seasons, but also competed in crew, track and field, boxing, and gymnastics. He commanded the USS *Lexington*'s carrier battle group in the Battle of the Coral Sea and later became superintendent of the Naval Academy. Two other members of Ghormley's class were Rear Adm. Isaac Kidd, commander of Battleship Division I at Pearl Harbor on December 7, 1941, who perished aboard his flagship, the USS *Arizona,* and Vice Admiral McCain.

McCain commanded Task Force Thirty-eight, a fast-carrier striking unit that was part of the Third Fleet and one of the Navy's most storied fighting groups during World War II. McCain and Rear Adm. Marc Mitscher shared the force's command—when Mitscher commanded, those same ships were known as Task Force Fifty-eight.

president on his train journey that the railroad was burdened with too many special trains. At one point, the train carrying Roosevelt and many members of his cabinet was shunted aside by an overeager switcher in favor of one carrying officials from the railroad company.

None of that suppressed Roosevelt. Midway through the game, he left his box to bound up and down the sidelines, shouting encouragement to both teams. He seemed barely in control of an impulse to enter the fray. Navy, trailing 6–0 with darkness rapidly descending, was aided by the rules of the day that gave possession of the ball at the point of a penalty. Army was tagged with one that nullified a sixty-yard punt by David Howard. Instead of being backed up against its own end zone, Navy got possession deep in the Cadets' territory. The Mids' Arch Douglas scored, and Homer Norton added the two-point conversation for the 6–6 tie. (Under the rules at that time, touchdowns were worth four points and extra points were worth two.) With four minutes to play, the game was called due to darkness.

The 1905 team was loaded with future naval heroes and colorful characters. The starting right tackle, Ronan Calistus Grady, a native of East Boston, Massachusetts, was characterized by the *Lucky Bag:* "Enjoys a good rough-house—the kind where two or three people are laid out and the furniture is totally wrecked." Walter Decker, the team's quarterback, was called "the fastest quarterback in college football" by Yale coach Walter Camp after Decker came within a quarter-second of equalling the world record in the low hurdles. Halfback Stephen Doherty played four years of varsity football and in the *Lucky Bag* was called "one of Navy's greatest athletes . . . the grand old man of the football squad."

But Navy's best player was fullback Bob Ghormley, known affectionately as "Hawk-Eye," "Eagle Beak," "Stone Face," or "Hatchet Face," who led Navy in back-to-back victories over Virginia and Virginia Tech. He later was awarded the Army's Distinguished Service Medal for overseeing the transport of two million men to France without the loss of a single soldier during World War I. As a vice admiral, Ghormley received the Legion of Merit in 1943 for his work during fierce naval battles in the Solomon Islands.

Dashiell did arguably his best work as coach in 1906, piecing together a largely inexperienced team to win eight of twelve games, with two ties, and losses only to Princeton and Penn State. During the preseason, a diphtheria epidemic quarantined the Academy, but the team was moved to quarters in Annapolis and was able to practice without mishap.

Dashiell was in the forefront of restructuring how Navy football was played. He placed increased emphasis on the forward pass, and Navy used that weapon for the first time during a 28–0 victory against St. John's College in 1906, with Norton completing two passes to end Dick Bernard in the second half. The first touchdown pass by a Navy player was caught by Jonas Ingram later that season in a 10–0 victory over Army, the first win against the Cadets since 1900. Ingram caught the ball and ran twenty yards for the score.

Jonas Ingram, a hulking native of Jeffersonville, Indiana, was the star of the 1906 team—the only season in which he earned a varsity letter. (He had played class football during his early years at the Academy.) Even though his career was brief, Ingram became a legend because of his talent and competitive spirit. He was awarded the Athletic Association's Sword of Excellence, given to the most noteworthy senior athlete. Ingram was nicknamed "The Black Prince." "He can go through anything short of a stone wall, and woe betide anyone in his path," wrote the *Lucky Bag*. Ingram also was captain of Navy's track team. After his graduation from the Academy, he was Navy's head coach in 1915 and 1916 and Academy athletic director in the midtwenties. He was in that post when his brother, "Navy Bill," coached the 1926 team to the national championship.

One of the stars of Navy's 1906 team was running back Jonas Ingram, who was a preeminent figure in Navy's athletic history as well as a Medal of Honor recipient for bravery during the Battle of Vera Cruz in 1914. Ingram, who became a full admiral, was athletic director during the midtwenties when Navy claimed the national championship. He is also a member of the College Football Hall of Fame.

Dashiell's tenure lasted just three years (1904–6) because Navy decided to hire only Academy graduates as head coaches and assistants. Academy officials believed that only a graduate could fully appreciate what players underwent as midshipmen, and how that affected their lives as athletes. This rule remained in effect, with only a few exceptions, until 1948, when George Sauer became the head coach and began a succession of non-Academy graduates in the job that lasts to this day. (George Welsh (1973–81) was the exception in the post-1948 era.)

The first graduate coach was Joseph Reeves, the pioneer of the beehive football helmet in 1893, and he stayed only one season. In quick succession, came Frank Berrien (1908–10); Doug Howard (1911–14); and Ingram (1915–16). Dashiell continued as an assistant coach and adviser.

Reeves, Berrien, and Howard guided the Mids to a 55–14–8 record, including consecutive unbeaten seasons in 1910 and 1911 by Berrien and Howard. Navy strung together twenty-two consecutive games without a loss from the end of the 1909 season until early in the 1912 season. Berrien's 1910 team shut out all nine opponents, and only a scoreless tie against Rutgers in the second game spoiled a perfect season. The following year, Howard's first as head coach, the Mids allowed just eleven points and shut out seven of nine foes.

Left end Bill Dague became Navy's first All-America in 1907 when Walter Camp selected him to his prestigious team. Dague, a four-year starter, scooped

Big Jack Shafroth

One of the starting tackles on Navy's 1907 team was John "Big Jack" Shafroth. He commanded the Southeast Pacific area in 1942 and later was a distinguished admiral with the Third Fleet. He directed the task group that supported the invasion of Okinawa, where his forces were in turn supported by classmate Rear Adm. Richmond Kelly Turner. In July 1945, his Battleship Division Eight of Task Force Fifty-eight—which included the USS *South Dakota*, USS *Indiana*, and USS *Massachusetts;* the heavy cruisers *Quincy* and *Chicago;* and nine destroyers—became the first naval unit to bombard the home islands of Japan, blasting the iron works at Kamaishi. In an amazing feat of seamanship, Shafroth brought in this tremendous force undetected and then coordinated six passes across the mouth of Kamaishi harbor from a range of 29,000 yards. The two-hour bombardment shut down the plant's production of much-needed coke and pig iron for the duration of the war.

up a fumbled punt and returned it for the winning points in Navy's 6–4 victory over Penn State. His fifteen-yard run in that year's Army-Navy game set up Navy's only touchdown, scored by team captain Arch Douglas, for a 6–0 victory. Douglas, who was also president of the Class of 1908 and a four-year performer; Percy Northcroft, who was also an Academy heavyweight boxing champion; and halfback Ed Lange were named to some postseason teams.

The other end on the team was Lawrence F. Reifsnider. During World War II, Reifsnider rose from captain to vice admiral because of his genius in directing amphibious assaults. As a captain, he commanded the landing on Guadalcanal and the transport division of Operation Torch in North Africa. Back in the South Pacific, he was in charge of the III Amphibious Force at Bougainville and the Southern Attack Group at Guam. The former operation was particularly difficult because of faulty charts. At one point, when one of Reifsnider's navigation officers was asked the position of his ships, the officer replied: "About three miles inland." Despite intense enemy fire and the faulty intelligence, Reifsnider put ashore 18,000 men and some 44,000 tons of equipment from twelve ships.

Another of Reifsnider's teammates was Bill "Bully" Richardson, who inspired the chant:

First down, Navy, seven to go
The quarterback's signals are slow.
But the time-honored call
Give Billy the Ball
Makes another first down, we all know.

For many years one of the most beloved persons in Navy's football program was "Scotty" McMasters, the team's trainer. Often nattily attired in his Scotch tweeds and speaking with an accent fresh from Liverpool, McMasters worked wonders with gauze, liniment, hot baths, and his own unique philosophy of life that he freely dispensed, whether or not the young naval cadets under his care wished to hear it.

Navy's 1909 coaching staff, led by head coach Frank Berrien *(center)*. At this time, Navy utilized graduates from other schools to help its coaching staff, hence the presence of the two unidentified former Yale players at either end of the picture.

Richardson, who held all of the Academy's strength records during his playing days, was atypical of the ribald midshipmen at that time. They seemed to delight in endless roughhousing; the major casualty was usually the furniture in the dorms. Two of Richardson's closest friends were future heroes of the war in the Pacific, Adm. Frederick C. Sherman and Adm. Marc "Pete" Mitscher. Sherman was a fullback on his class team, and Mitscher won two letters in wrestling.

As a captain, Sherman commanded the aircraft carrier USS *Lexington* when it was sunk in 1942 by Japanese planes during the Battle of the Coral Sea; true to his duty, he was the last man to leave the stricken ship. Later in the war, as an admiral, Sherman and another former Navy football star, J. J. Clark, commanded task groups as part of Mitscher's Task Force Fifty-eight that sank the "unsinkable" battleship *Yamato.*

Frank Berrien took over as coach in 1908, and his team played its first four games in ten days. Navy rolled up 119 points en route to a 9–2–1 record with an interesting roster that included ends Max DeMott and Percy Northcroft, both of whom were Academy heavyweight boxing champions. Northcroft was a four-year starter whose fifty-one-yard field goal—the longest of the 1908 season in college football—beat Lehigh. Illness cost DeMott the first two months of the season, but he returned and won back his starting job in the final weeks. Also on that 1908 team was center Frank Slingluff, who joined a chain gang during his summer leave and pounded rocks to keep in shape.

Berrien's 1909 team was jinxed. When Navy played Villanova, Earl Wilson, a great athlete who had starred in Navy baseball, basketball, gymnastics, boxing,

Richard Byrd

Richard Evelyn Byrd Jr. made his fame in athletics as USNA welterweight wrestling champion for 1911–12, captain of the 1911 track team, and an expert rifleman. His *Lucky Bag* valedictory said, "Wanders around with a far away, dreamy look in his eyes and one often wonders whether he knows if he is coming or going." He later was designated Naval Aviator No. 608, and, in 1926, he and Chief Machinist's Mate Floyd Bennett were the first to overfly the North Pole, for which they were awarded the Medal of Honor. Two years later, after establishing his Little America base camp in Antarctica, Byrd was the first to overfly the South Pole.

pole vaulting, and tennis and played quarterback and safety on the football team, broke his neck. He died six months later. Shortly after Wilson was hurt, an Army tackle, Eugene Byrne, was critically injured during a game with Harvard. The day after Byrne's injury, with Wilson lying helpless in the Academy hospital, every church in Annapolis offered prayers for both players.

The next week, during a driving rainstorm, Virginia reached Navy's two-yard line before the Mids stopped them on four downs. But the referee, Gresham Poe (one of Princeton's famous six Poes) became confused and, after Navy took a timeout, penalized them a yard and gave the ball back to Virginia. On the next play, Blondie Stanton fumbled at the goal line, but the ball bounced into the end zone and was recovered by a Virginia teammate. Virginia won, 6–0.

The following week, Eugene Byrne died, and Army notified Navy that it was canceling the rest of its season. Underscoring the true spirit of Army-Navy competition, reports at the time noted that tears were shed unashamedly for Cadet Byrne during services in the Naval Academy's Chapel.

Wilson had been replaced by Gene Battle, and he was backed up by Richard Evelyn Byrd Jr., an able, tough, and gritty athlete from a distinguished Virginia family. Byrd was small, but wiry; he was captain of the gymnastics team his senior year and the Academy's welterweight wrestling champion in 1912. He was also an expert rifleman. Byrd worked hard at football but was dogged by bad luck. Injuries cost him a chance to play in 1908. He was the backup quarterback in 1909, and many people thought he would take the starter's job from Battle in 1910. But Byrd contracted typhoid on his summer cruise and missed the entire season. An ankle injury in his senior year hampered his last chance to oust Battle as starting quarterback, and Byrd again spent the season as the backup. He never earned a football letter, but he never stopped trying. His greatest fame came as a distinguished admiral and one of America's foremost polar explorers.

Jack Dalton, who was selected to Walter Camp's prestigious All-America team in 1911, booms a seventy-four-yard punt against Army at Philadelphia's Franklin Field.

Navy's undefeated 1911 team won six games and played three scoreless ties among its seven shutouts. Team captain Jack Dalton is in the second row, clutching the ball.

Howard's 1911 team included two of Navy's great stars: Jack "Three-to-Nothing" Dalton and John "Babe" Brown. Dalton, who earned his nickname because he kicked field goals in successive 3–0 victories over Army in 1910 and 1911, was a four-season varsity performer from 1908 to 1911. As a first classman, he was captain of both the football and track teams. His punting was an offensive force, moving opponents backward with each exchange to give his team better field position. He was a superb runner, scoring fourteen touchdowns in 1911. Yet some contemporaries considered him an even better defensive player. Dalton was selected to Walter Camp's All-America team in 1911. In 1970, Dalton was elected to the College Football Hall of Fame.

For most of the 1910 Army-Navy game—which capped an 8–0–1 season for Navy, Dalton was thoroughly frustrated. His first six field goal attempts went astray. Finally, with Ingram Sowell holding, Dalton hit one from twenty-five yards that produced the 3–0 victory. His nineteen-yard run had set up the winning kick.

Berrien and his staff had forged an ultraefficient team in 1910 that became the only one in Navy history ever to shut out every opponent. Dalton was the only "star," but the team was helped by four good plebes—"Babe" Brown, Charles Carey, Harold Davis, and K. P. "Gillie" Gilchrist.

Dalton's kicking and all-around great play helped Navy to its second straight unbeaten season in 1911. The defense engineered seven shutouts (three of which ended in scoreless ties). The highlight of the season was Dalton's thirty-yard field goal that capped a seventy-yard drive and gave the Mids a second straight 3–0 victory over unbeaten Army. Dalton fueled the drive with thirty-five yards on two sweeps. The goat mascot, Bill III, had died a few days before the Army game. He was stuffed and mounted in Navy's field house and

John Dalton

John Patrick Dalton, from Broken Bow, Nebraska, was a great athlete who, in addition to starring in football, set Naval Academy records in track and field. He had prepped at Christian Brothers College in St. Louis where, from 1905 to 1908, he was the star fullback on the school's national championship soccer team. Dalton always attributed his success as a punter and placekicker at Navy to his soccer background.

Dalton, who was nicknamed "Dolly," was filled with Irish charm. During his junior cruise to Queenstown, that charm made him a hero of sorts at the Academy. A young lass had received a coveted invitation to the admiral's party. Dalton convinced her that she could not enjoy it without his company. Sure enough, she got Dolly an invitation.

promptly nicknamed "Three-to-Nothing Jack Dalton" to honor Dalton and his two game-winning kicks.

Babe Brown, the first Navy player to be elected to the College Football Hall of Fame, was a teammate of Dalton's in 1910 and 1911, during the first two of his four varsity seasons. He was a great offensive guard. In the early 1900s, when linemen weighed 160 and 170 pounds, Brown was huge at 200 pounds—in his plebe season, he even played end. Brown did not wear a helmet when he played and loved the combat in the line; he waged a personal war with a zest that sometimes assumed awesome proportions.

Brown succeeded Dalton as Navy's kicker in 1912 and kicked the winning field goal in Navy's third straight victory over Army. His kicking form seemed almost effortless, yet the ball exploded off his foot and was a great weapon for a very ordinary Navy offense. Brown won a berth on Camp's 1913 All-America team; he lettered in crew and track; and in his plebe year, he set Academy records not only for the shot put, but also for the most points scored during a track season.

In the 1912 game against Army, some 30,000 fans jammed into Philadelphia's Franklin Field. Brown missed his first two field goal attempts, experiencing some of the frustration that Dalton felt in 1910. With five minutes to play in the last quarter, Brown stood at Army's thirty-yard line as if to attempt a field goal. But the ball came directly to him, and he raced downfield until the Cadets caught him at the five-yard line. Two running plays netted little, and on third down he kicked a field goal. Two minutes later, he kicked another for a 6–0 victory.

John Hall

Adm. John L. Hall was Ernest Von Heimberg's boss in the Normandy D-Day operation. He was forceful and rugged, with a dogged personality, and no one was surprised to learn that he once was a football lineman—Hall played guard on the 1910 and 1911 Academy teams. Someone once described his rugged features as "reminiscent of the less-flattering portraits of his fellow Virginian, George Washington, but he had a twinkle in his eye that Washington lacked." He was a calm, self-assured, and able leader who instilled confidence in his subordinates. Two days before D-Day, with the weather forecasts deteriorating badly, Hall calmed the apprehensions of the invasion planners by boldly proclaiming, "I do not expect to be repulsed on any beach." He secured three battleships—the USS *Arkansas,* USS *Utah* (which the Japanese thought they had sunk at Pearl Harbor), and USS *Texas*—to add more fire support at Omaha Beach. Their batteries helped to silence the German gun emplacements above the beach during the fiercely contested landing.

Like Rear Adm. Lawrence Reifsnider, Hall was a genius in landing troops and supplies under fire, regardless of topography. He was chief of staff to Rear Adm. H. Kent Hewitt in Operation Torch during the invasion of North Africa, and he landed George S. Patton's Seventh Army in Sicily. After his D-Day work, Hall commanded amphibious forces of two transport squadrons in the invasion of Okinawa with Task Force Fifty-five, the Southern Attack Force that landed XXIV Corps on Hoguski Beach.

Bates and Mitchell

Two running backs from the 1913 team, John Bates and Ralph Mitchell, became much-decorated heroes during World War II. As a captain commanding the heavy cruiser USS *Minneapolis,* Bates was cited many times for his leadership and command roles during bombardments and assaults in the Gilbert Islands, Kwajalein, Tarawa, Truk, Saipan, Tinian, Yap, Wolei, Palau, and the Philippines.

Mitchell, a Marine aviator, twice won the Distinguished Flying Cross—first as a lieutenant colonel during operations in Nicaragua and then as a major general in charge of Marine air units during the battles of New Hanover, New Ireland, Rabaul, and Bougainville.

He was commander of the northern Solomons Marine air wing, the "Airnosols Group," that perfected close-in air support for marines fighting in the jungles and plains of the islands. That support was a key component of Marine tactics during the Pacific War. Mitchell's four squadrons also helped with the Leyte invasion by providing key close-in air support that helped to break the back of the Japanese defense.

Jack Dalton kicks the winning thirty-yard field goal in Navy's 3–0 victory over unbeaten Army in 1911, climaxing a seventy-yard drive. The ball is about to pass the right upright. Dalton's running picked up half the yardage on the winning drive.

The 1913 Army-Navy game was played for the first time at the Polo Grounds in New York City, and President Woodrow Wilson and his entire cabinet were among the 42,000 spectators. The game had finally found a place in the nation's consciousness. The Mids were undefeated; their first game was a scoreless tie against Pitt, and then they reeled off seven straight victories by an average score of 42–1. (They gave up their other touchdown prior to the Army game in a 70–7 thrashing of Bucknell.) Babe Brown appeared ready to dominate Army just as he had in the previous year. Brown didn't disappoint. In the first quarter, he kicked a twenty-six-yard field goal; after Army tied the score, he kicked another one from twenty-two yards. Army went ahead 9–6, but Brown hit a third field goal from Army's twenty-eight-yard line to tie the score, 9–9. But Navy scored no more, while Army scored two more touchdowns for a 22–9 victory. Brown played every minute of that game, making him one of a handful of players to play every minute of four Army-Navy games. He finished with five career field goals against Army.

One other event during this era deserves mention: In Doug Howard's final coaching season, in 1914, Navy played its first non-Army game away from Annapolis, losing to Penn 13–6 at Franklin Field.

Jonas Ingram, with coaching help from his brother, Homer, succeeded Howard in 1915. In two seasons Ingram had a 9–8–2 record. He inherited a very young team and suffered through a 3–5–1 record in 1915, including a 14–0 loss to Army. Army All-America Elmer Q. Oliphant scored both touchdowns while President Wilson, scores of Washington and New York dignitaries, and a crowd of 45,000 watched at the Polo Grounds.

Ingram's team was 6–3–1 the following year, with major victories over Georgetown, Maryland, and Georgia offset by a heartbreaking one-point loss to heavily favored Pitt and the 15–7 loss to Army, which was again sparked by Oliphant. Bill Ingram, brother of Jonas and Homer, and Colgate transfer Wolcott Roberts formed the heart of a solid Navy offense. Ingram's rushing dominated the Georgetown and Maryland games. When Georgia came to Annapolis, the Bulldogs tried to intimidate the Mids, but a spectacular fistfight in the middle of

Babe Brown

After John "Babe" Brown kicked two late field goals in Navy's 6–0 victory over Army in 1912, T. L. Fitzsimmons of Charleston, South Carolina, penned his ode, *To All-American Babe Brown:*

Arms and the hero I sing
who first on the gridiron field
into victory came

Lads! but his placekick the thing
that made the Army men yield
and turned the rough tide of the game

With shoulders and grace of a God
mighty of stature is he
swift as Achilles and bold

Not for him the dull paths that we plod
His nature is girthless and free
as the wave-wandering tritons of old.

John "Babe" Brown *(right)* shown receiving his College Football Hall of Fame plaque in 1951. He is one of a few players ever to have played every minute of four Army-Navy games.

Babe Brown spent nearly his entire career in the submarine service, beginning with the command of two subs during World War I. In World War II, as a rear admiral, he commanded Submarine Squadron Four. But he was no desk sailor: he accompanied the USS *Narwhal* on its fifth war patrol, a forty-two-day journey that included a successful bombardment of a Japanese air base in the Kurile Islands. He was deputy commander of Submarine Force, Pacific Fleet, which accounted for fifty-five percent—more than 5.7 million tons—of the Japanese naval and maritime shipping sunk by the Allies during World War II. At the war's end, Brown commanded Task Force Ninety-two in the northern Pacific.

Brown never lost his interest in Navy football. He was athletic director in the midthirties. At this time he met a young midshipman named Slade Cutter, who became one of Brown's great submarine commanders during World War II.

"He was a marvelous judge of men," Cutter remembered. "When he talked to you, he did so as an equal. You didn't feel you were talking to God or an admiral."

Cutter also recalled in an oral history for the Naval Institute how Brown had great insights into the capabilities of his sub commanders.

"After I finished commanding my fourth patrol," Cutter related, "he told me, 'I think you need a little leave.' I hadn't been home in thirteen months and agreed it would certainly be nice.

"But he sent me home with no intention of bringing me back, but he wouldn't tell me because he knew I would fight him on it. Yet, he saved me from a fifth patrol, and I might not have come back because after you made it back from a couple you began to get careless. You didn't give a damn; you got so cocky that you lost perspective and didn't give the enemy any credit. That's when you got foolish."

Brown and Cutter share not only a page in the annals of submarine warfare but also are enshrined together in the College Football Hall of Fame.

Farragut Field between Spike McLaws (Georgia) and end Herb Jackson (Navy) only fired up the Mids and started them toward a colossal 27–3 victory.

Navy lost to Pitt (coached by Pop Warner) 20–19 only because Navy missed two extra points. One of Navy's scores was set up by a forty-eight-yard punt return by John Whelchel, who also caught a touchdown pass. Whelchel was a clever quarterback who not only returned to coach the Mids' great teams in 1942 and 1943 but later, as a rear admiral, was decorated for heroism as commanding officer of the USS *San Francisco* in 1945.

World War I cut short Ingram's tenure and, in 1917, Gilmour "Gloomy Gil" Dobie arrived on the scene. Dobie acquired his nickname because he never met a team he felt he could beat—but he hadn't lost a game in twelve seasons of coaching college football until West Virginia beat Navy 7–0 in his second game at Annapolis. He was 7–0 in two seasons at North Dakota State and 58–0–3 in nine years at the University of Washington, where his Huskies outscored their opponents 1,928 to 119, often rolling up huge scores against outmanned competitors.

Coach Gil Dobie with a Naval Academy official during the 1919 Army-Navy game in New York City.

The 1916 Team

Several of the players from the 1916 team, including non-letter-winners who were varsity performers for two or three seasons, distinguished themselves above and beyond the call of duty in World War II. For example, running back Henry Mullinix, tops in the Class of 1916, was cited for his work in antisubmarine warfare in helping guard convoys to Europe early in the war. Later, as a task force commander, Mullinix was killed in action when the carrier *Liscombe Bay* was torpedoed and sunk by the Japanese. End Ed Moran, nicknamed "Iron Mike," was cited as commander of the USS *Boise* for helping to sink four Japanese warships in the Battle of Savo Island while defending Guadalcanal in 1942, even though his own ship was damaged by enemy fire. Classmate Ben Wyatt, another end, was cited for his service commanding the USS *Chenango* in both the Atlantic and Pacific—first in the invasion of North Africa in 1942 and, a year later, in action in the central Pacific.

Gil Dobie

Prior to his tenure as football coach at the Naval Academy, Gil Dobie coached at the University of Washington. When that school's student newspaper, *Argus,* learned that Dobie was headed to Annapolis, the following biting report appeared:

"The disagreement between Dobie and President Suzzalo is caused by a misunderstanding on the part of the president. In some manner, Suzzalo has gotten the idea that the educational functions of the university are of more importance than the football team. This error of judgment, while regrettable, is excusable. For nine long years, spurred on by Dobie's zeal and profanity, Washington has waged successful football warfare. Any football fan will tell you that the university has grown and prospered solely because of the wonderful record which Dobie has achieved. Now, with a president who puts mathematics over muscle, brain over brawn, the future of the university is indeed shrouded in uncertainty."

Dobie was an enigma. He was enormously successful, but by all accounts he was disliked by friend and foe alike. The fans at Washington, instead of basking in Dobie's success, often booed and ridiculed him, and many of his players hated him for his harsh methods. For example, in 1915, after thrashing the University of California, 72–0, he made his players run twenty laps around the playing field.

Most believed that Dobie and the Naval Academy were a perfect fit because his key beliefs—discipline and conditioning—were basic tenets at Annapolis. To a point, the relationship was a good one, but Dobie's acerbic nature was no more popular with many of Navy's young players than it had been with their counterparts at Washington. Edwin Pope, in his book *Football's Greatest Coaches,* quotes Navy tackle Charley Hunt, later a rear admiral: "Dobie never bothered the low-raters, except to make us run laps after every game. But the way he goaded the first stringers was something else . . . Dobie was no leader—just a slave-driver." Ernest Von Heimberg, a great Navy end and captain of the 1917 team, reportedly had to be restrained many times from physically assaulting Dobie after being scorched by his demeaning comments.

Still, Dobie was a great coach and is a member of the College Football Hall of Fame. Like all great coaches, he was very creative—sheets of papers littered his home, where he worked like a mad scientist to devise surprises for opponents—and he overlooked no detail. Navy bounced back from the loss to West Virginia with a 62–0 victory over Maryland. A reporter noted, "A fake forward pass was one of the features of the Mids' offense, and they exploited it for gains on two or three occasions . . . the Mids' attack seemed to have more vim and dash than that which has characterized Navy teams in recent years."

Before every game, Dobie asked his squad, "What do you do before every play?" The players shouted, "Look to the sidelines." (That was to guard against sleeper plays.) Then he asked, "And what do you say before every play?" And the players answered, "It's coming at me."

After the lopsided win over Maryland, one reporter wrote, "It looks as though the Mids, in spite of having several green players, are beginning to hit their stride and show the results of the tutelage of Gilmour Dobie, whose reputation as a football mentor was much heralded in the Far West."

Later that season, after a 61–0 victory over Carlisle, one observer wrote, "Coach Dobie has simply infused all kinds of spirit into his charges. His team played with a vim and dash never before noticed in Navy elevens."

Navy lost just three of twenty games in three seasons under Dobie. As was his style, he rolled up some prodigious scores: 127–0 against Ursinus in 1918, the most points ever scored by a Navy team; 121–0 versus Colby in 1919; and 95–0 versus Western Reserve and 89–0 against Haverford in 1917.

In Dobie's first two seasons, Navy's offense was led by Bill Ingram, Wolcott Roberts, and Bill Butler; Harold Martin, who later was commander of the Seventh Fleet during the Korean War, was with them in 1917. Ingram, a lanky, tough player, was a fine runner, passer, and placekicker; he also excelled at defense and captained Dobie's team in 1918.

The star of the 1917 team was its captain, Ernest Von Heimberg, a tough end who also played baseball and basketball. He had one of the most storied

stein; backs, Ingram and Roberts.

Mr. Purman in picking von Heimburg for his All-American Team says:

"von Heimburg is very powerful and is usually able to take care of both the opposition tackle and end. He seldom permits himself to be boxed and is fast getting down the field. The Navy man is a crafty field general and his ability to diagnose plays makes him a constant menace to the opposition."

VILLA NOVA EASY FOR MIDSHIPMEN

LAST GAME BEFORE MEETING ARMY SATURDAY.

NAVY ROLLS UP 57 POINTS

NAVY HAS EASY TIME WITH N. C. A. AND M.

Registers 50 Points, the Largest Total for Midshipmen in Recent Seasons.

Annapolis, Md., Nov. 11.—With speed and dash that warmed the heart of the navy crowd, the midshipmen went at the North Carolina Aggies this afternoon, and overwhelmed them by 50 to 0.

NAVY TEAM ... G STRON... OF 1917 GRI... AGGREGA...

NAVY MASSACRES CARLISLE INDIANS

Midshipmen Play Great Football, Winning by 61 to 0.

Navy Gridders Roll Up Record Score of 95 to 0

Annapolis, Nov. 3.—For the third time this season the Navy football team broke its high score record. Western Reserve, following after Carlisle and Haverford, was sent back to Cleveland beaten by 95 to 0.

NAVY SWAMPS HAVERFORD.

Sailors Run Up 89 Points Against Weak Opposition.

Special to The New York Times.

ANNAPOLIS, Md., Oct. 27.—When they piled up eighty-nine points against Haverford College here this afternoon, the Midshipmen completed three games in which their total ran to the unusual sum of 212. In the three games, those with today's opponent, the Indian and Maryland State College, the Navy goal-line has not been seriously endangered. ... Probably because of the ...

STATE NO MATCH FOR MIDSHIPMEN

Gives Way to Navy's Great Backfield by 62 to 0.

Annapolis, Md., Oct. 13.—Gilmour Dobie's Navy football machine, with ...

MIDDIES PILE UP SCORE

State's Goal Line Is Crossed ... Times.

NAVY DISPLAYS GREAT ...

Sailors Plow Through Line, Skirt Ends And Throw Forward Passes At Will.

Annapolis, Md., Oct. 13.—The navy football players ran riot over Curly Byrd's aggregation of Maryland State College here this afternoon. They rolled up a total of 62 points, one of the ... est scores that has been registered ... navy eleven in recent years. Nin... the sailor lads invaded the ... line and Ingram was successf... of the tries for goal. State ... scoreless.

CONSTANT ... TO WE... FOR NAVY ... ERVE GOAL

MIDDIES MAKE RECORD

... Up 89 Points And Hold Haverford Scoreless.

CROSS GOAL LINE 13 TIMES

All Sorts Of Plays Used Against The Pennsylvanians—Forward Passes Are Successful.

Annapolis, Md., Oct. 27.—Working like one of the new Liberty Motors, the Navy football team completely routed Haverford College this afternoon. The ... scoring machine almost worked its way ... to the century figures. The sailors simply bowled over their opponents ... when the final whistle blew they ... piled up 89 points to nothing, a ... for a navy team. ... ford was hopelessly outclassed ...

... *Sun of November 11 said:*

VON HEIMBURG

"... existed in the minds of many as to whether the Navy has a team rated among the best, if not the peer of others in the country, is removed by the decisive victory and slashing play by which it (the defeat of Georgetown) was brought about."

The 1917 season told in headlines. The silhouette is of Ernest Von Heimberg, the team captain.

The 1918 Navy team in action. Because of World War I, the team played just five games and won four of them under head coach Gilmour Dobie. One of those victories was 127–0 over Ursinus, the most points ever scored by a Navy team.

careers in Navy history. Five months after graduating in 1918 (he was actually a member of the Class of 1919, but the Academy was on an accelerated program because of World War I), Ensign Von Heimberg served as an interpreter at the surrender of the German High Seas Fleet to the combined American and British Grand Fleet at the Firth of Forth, Scotland. Ten years later he was aboard the USS *Pope* in the Asiatic Fleet during the thorny Yangtze campaign as tiny Western naval forces warily watched the Japanese gobble up northern China. During World War II, Rear Admiral Von Heimberg commanded fleet refueling during the invasion of North Africa in 1942; the following year, he coordinated the planning and operations for the invasion of Italy. In 1944 Von Heimberg was chief of staff in charge of the detailed planning, assault, and follow-up of the XI Amphibious Force's 2,400 ships and craft that landed the First and Twenty-ninth Divisions of V Corps at Omaha Beach in Normandy on D-Day.

Game officials meet with Navy captain Eddie Ewen *(right)* and Army captain Alexander George before the 1919 Army-Navy game at the Polo Grounds.

Navy played only a five-game season in 1918 because of World War I—a good thing, because the team was decimated by the flu epidemic that swept through most of the country. At one time, Wolcott Roberts and Bill Butler were the only healthy starters; fortunately, a number of plebes, including Emery "Swede" Larson, John Orr, Clyde King, Abe Snively, Dwight Newby, Peeman Moore, and Roger Murray, showed promise.

One of the most unusual games ever played in college football was Navy's 7–6 loss to Great Lakes in that season's finale. Navy led 6–0 with five minutes to play when Lyman "Pop" Perry, later a distinguished Navy athletic director, blocked a Great Lakes punt, and Eddie

The Midshipmen get fancy during the halftime show of a 1918 season game at Thompson Stadium at the Naval Academy.

Ewen recovered the ball. The Mids drove to the Great Lakes one-yard line and appeared set to put the game away.

But Bill Ingram lost the ball trying to crash through the middle of the line. The fumble was grabbed by Harry Eileson of Great Lakes, who took off for Navy's end zone. Ewen, later a superb carrier task force commander during the Korean War, was the only Middie who saw what had happened, but he was quickly taken out by three Great Lakes blockers, including future NFL pioneer George Halas.

Eileson had a clear path—until Bill Saunders, a tackle sitting on Navy's bench, charged onto the field and tackled Eileson near midfield. A "near riot" ensued. Several Great Lakes players jumped on Saunders, freed Eileson, and allowed him to continue into the end zone. Referee Henry Heneage mistakenly —though perhaps wisely, considering the circumstances—did not blow his whistle, so the score was allowed, though even such an extraordinary transgression did not entitle the runner to a touchdown under the rules at that time.

Ironically, if one of the legal Navy players had tackled Eileson after he resumed his run, the play would have ended, Navy would have been penalized for having too many men on the field, and Great Lakes would have been almost fifty yards from the end zone. As it was, they kicked the extra point for a 7–6 victory, spoiling Navy's perfect season.

While refusing to say why he did it, Saunders recollected in Morris Bealle's *Gangway for Navy:*

> I do have a clear recollection of thinking: "This will be an awful mess if I miss this guy." The near riot following soon subsided and I played the remaining minutes of the game thinking only of getting another score for Navy which in my opinion . . . was clearly superior.

In 1919, Dobie put together his most powerful team, led by tackles Clyde King and Roger Murray and guards Fred Denfield and Ed Willkie. (Ed's brother, Wendell, ran for president in 1940.) Backs Oliver Alford, Lou Benoist, and Howie Clark, also one of the best punters in Navy history, benefited from their punishing blocking and established a dominating ground game. Navy drubbed Colby 121–0, scoring eighteen touchdowns and adding thirteen extra points. The Mids led 88–0 at the half and Dobie, who usually showed no mercy to an opponent, took it easy in the last two quarters, even ordering punts on second and third downs.

The Dobie era ended on a cold, drizzly day at the Polo Grounds in New York City, where 45,000 saw Navy break a seven-year winless drought against Army with a 6–0 victory. King kicked two field goals, and Clark's punting helped blunt Army's offense; two of his kicks soared over the head of the Cadets' safetyman and rolled dead on the five-yard line.

Four decades into its football program, Navy was more solidly established among the nation's top teams. Even greater success lay ahead in the rocking Roaring Twenties.

3. The Roaring Twenties—And How! 1920–1929

The Roaring Twenties were a raucous time in America and noteworthy for Navy football. During that dazzling decade, the Mids posted a 55–28–8 record; first tasted the glory of a postseason bowl game; claimed their only national championship; expanded their schedule to take on such national powers as Georgia Tech and Michigan and Purdue of the Big Ten; played more intersectional games in the Midwest and South; and started their immensely popular annual series against Notre Dame.

The twenties also brought to prominence some of Navy's greatest players: Steve Barchet; Tom Hamilton, who, until the days of Roger Staubach in the sixties, was the best all-around player in Navy history; linemen Tom Eddy and Frank Wickhorst; running backs Alan Shapley, Howard Caldwell, Russell "Whitey" Lloyd; and many others who responded to the splendid coaching of the decade's two dominant coaches, Bob Folwell and Bill Ingram.

Vic Noyes batters South Carolina's defense during a 1920 game at Annapolis in which the Mids rolled to a 63–0 victory. Noyes reeled off three runs of more than fifty yards in the game.

Bob Folwell

Bob Folwell was well prepared for his job as Navy's football coach. After being named an All-America at Penn, he became head coach at Lafayette in 1908 at the age of twenty-three. In three years he compiled a 22–4–1 record, including a victory over Princeton and a tie with Penn in his first year. He then coached at Washington and Jefferson College from 1912 to 1915, where he put together a 35–5–3 record. That was followed by four years at Penn, where his teams were 25–12–2. In 1917, while coaching at Penn, Folwell also was head coach of the League Island Marine team, which had a 7–3 record. Folwell was acclaimed as both an inspirational coach and as one of the game's early innovators, particularly in the development of the forward pass. He advanced the screen pass to such an art while coaching at Washington and Jefferson that it became known as the "Washington and Jefferson screen." But Folwell spent as much time coaching the line as he did overseeing the entire team. During his tenure at the Academy, Navy's teams were renowned for their great lines.

For the first time, Navy played football at home fields of schools from coast-to-coast, as well as at neutral sites in Philadelphia, Washington, and Baltimore. And, before the Roaring Twenties ended, Navy twice played before some 120,000 fans in Soldier Field in Chicago (against Army in 1926 and Notre Dame in 1928).

Bob Folwell was a splendid choice to succeed Gil Dobie in 1920. He and Bill Ingram both coached for five years—the longest tenure of any Navy coach until Eddie Erdelatz's nine-year run in the fifties. Folwell, who compiled a 24–12–3 record, came to work in September and coached the plebes until the upperclassmen returned from their summer cruises. He stayed at the Academy until the end of the football season, then returned to his home and worked at another job.

Coach Folwell inherited some fine talent, beginning with end Eddie Ewen, Navy's last two-time captain. Ewen was a five-year player, thanks to temporary eligibility rules that had been in effect during World War I. He had incurred a split kidney in the second game of his plebe year in 1916; because of a long recuperation, he had to redo his plebe year in 1917. Folwell's team also included center Emery "Swede" Larson, who would never play in, or coach, a losing game against Army.

The 1920 team got off to a rocky start. North Carolina State rolled into Annapolis the day after the Regiment returned from its annual leave—and before the Navy squad had much preparation—and beat a plebe-dominated team 14–7. But one of those plebes was Vic Noyes, who sparked Navy to a 14–7 victory the next week over Lafayette; to a 63–0 win over South Carolina, where he had three runs of fifty or more yards; and most importantly, to a 7–0 victory over Army. In the Army game, he replaced the injured Vince Conroy in the second half and drove the Mids to their only score. Noyes's touchdown was just Navy's second against Army since 1907. The game was the springboard for Noyes to become one of the team's stalwarts during the next three seasons.

With a nucleus built around Barchet, Noyes, B. G. Koehler, and Edgar Cruise, and linemen Larson, Art Carney, Clyde King, Joe Dahlgren, and Art Frawley, the Mids flirted with an opportunity to call themselves national champions in 1921 (there was no formal selection process then). Navy attracted national attention with a 13–0 victory over heavily favored Princeton. Before the game, Walter Camp, college football's acknowledged guru, wrote: "This game overshadows all others . . . for it is an early contest between strong teams and promises to furnish a direct line on important future matches, particularly how Navy is preparing toward its main goal, victory over Army." Navy was ready. The defense did not allow the Tigers a first down. Interceptions by Noyes, who had missed the first month of the season because of scholastic problems, and Pete McKee set up two field goals by King, and Carney blocked a punt and then recovered it for a touchdown.

Running back Vic Noyes, one of the stars of the 1920 team.

Navy's 1921 team won six of seven games and included such stars as Edgar Cruise *(second row, ninth from left)*, Ira McKee *(next to Cruise)*, Vince Conroy *(third row, fifth from left)*, Clyde King *(next to Conroy)*, Emery "Swede" Larson *(eighth from left)*, Art Carney *(next to Larson)*, and Bernie Koehler *(fourth from right)*.

Three weeks later, Navy played Penn State in Philadelphia. A victory would give the unbeaten Mids a strong claim to the national title. Navy took a 7–0 lead on a touchdown by Barchet. But Penn State All-Americas Glen Killinger and Harry Wilson (the latter would be a huge problem for Navy when he later played for West Point) helped the Nittany Lions to a 13–7 victory. The loss—the only one that season—cost Navy the national title. Ironically, Penn State also flubbed its championship chances when it played to a scoreless tie the following week against Pitt.

Navy closed its seven-game season with another 7–0 victory over Army. Barchet slogged through a sloppy Polo Grounds playing field and polished off a forty-five-yard drive in the second quarter with a touchdown.

So intense had this rivalry become that, at one point, John Pitzer, an Army end, entered the game as a substitute in such an excited state that he was oblivious to the fact that his leg had become entangled with an empty water bucket—and he dragged it onto the field with him. Swede Larson, Navy's captain, called time out. "Mr. Referee," he said, "I would like to call to your attention that the new Army end is using unauthorized equipment."

The 1922 Mids, solidly entrenched as one of the nation's top teams, were also one of the game's most interesting, thanks to Folwell's varied offense, and particularly his passing game. His team beat Georgia Tech 13–0 by completing ten of seventeen passes for 130 yards—amazing statistics at a time when

Eddie Ewen

Eddie Ewen was the only two-time football captain in Navy football history; he led both the 1919 and 1920 teams. As an officer, he was one of the Navy's early aviation leaders. In 1930, he was a seaplane aviator aboard the battleship USS *New Mexico;* a few years later he commanded a fighter wing aboard the USS *Lexington,* the Navy's first full-size aircraft carrier. During World War II, Ewen was much decorated. He received the Navy Cross for conducting the first night carrier operations of the Pacific War while captain of the USS *Independence* during the Battle of the Philippines. Ewen also commanded Task Force Seventy-seven during the Korean War.

Cheering by Radio

Although the Regiment of Midshipmen traveled only to the Army game, they found ways to keep abreast of what was occurring in every football game and, sometimes, even lend their vocal support. When Navy played at Penn in 1922, running stories of the game were transmitted to the Academy and then hurriedly relayed to crowds at the movie theaters in Annapolis. The following year, with Navy at Penn State, the mids used the budding technology of radio to transmit their cheers and fight songs from Annapolis over speakers that had been set up at Beaver Stadium.

passes were rarely used. Navy became a prime road attraction. The team helped to dedicate Penn's new 70,000-seat Franklin Field in Philadelphia. The Mids thoroughly dominated the first two quarters, but Penn scored twice in the second half to earn a 13–7 victory.

The following week, Navy handed Penn State its first loss in thirty-one games with a 14–0 victory at Griffith Stadium in Washington, D.C., before more than 30,000 fans—the largest crowd to watch a sporting event up to that time in the nation's capitol. Middie Carl Cullen became the game's star when the first of his two fumble recoveries set up his second-quarter touchdown; he returned the second for the other Navy score in the third quarter. The only downside to the game was noted in the *Baltimore Sun:* "the Navy goat was scared half to death by the lion [Penn State's mascot]. He refused to stand up and do any butting . . . his days are numbered. The midshipmen decided forthwith to get themselves a new goat."

Navy's great lineman and kicker Clyde King.

Billy's fate was sealed three weeks later when the Mids lost to Army 17–14 at Franklin Field in front of Vice President Calvin Coolidge and Great Britain's Lord and Lady Mountbatten. Navy led 7–3 at the half, but Army went ahead in the third quarter. With ten minutes to play, Vince Conroy's touchdown sent the Mids ahead once more 14–10. But Navy allowed Army end Pat Timberlake to get free in the end zone to catch the winning touchdown pass with less than two minutes remaining.

The bulwarks of the 1923 team were sophomores Alan Shapley and Royce Flippen. Both had gotten enough varsity experience as plebes to become competent performers. They joined a backfield that also included Barchet, Cullen, and Ira McKee, the team's best passer. Navy won five games, lost one, and

Navy's 1921 coaching staff *(from left)* included Bill Butler, Eddie Ewen, Bob Folwell (head coach), John "Billick" Whelchel, and Tommy Scaffe.

Navy vs. Army in 1921 at New York City's Polo Grounds. The running of Bernie Koehler, Vince Conroy, and Vic Noyes helped Navy to triumph, 7–0. The touchdown was the first that Navy scored against the Cadets since 1916 and only the second since 1907.

played three ties, including one (14–14) against Washington in the 1924 Rose Bowl. (That game is covered in detail in Chapter Ten.) One of the other ties was the only scoreless game in the Army-Navy series. The 1923 record was a fine one in light of the fact that Navy had difficulty replacing six starters who had graduated in 1922 because it had made two changes in its eligibility rules: Plebes no longer could play varsity football, and previous varsity experience at other colleges counted against transfers' years of eligibility at Annapolis. Those changes became thorny issues in relations with West Point; they ultimately caused the Army-Navy series to be interrupted for a couple of years at the end of the decade.

Alan Shapley, an extraordinary all-around, 180-pound athlete with great speed, replaced Barchet at fullback for the first two games of the 1923 season; he played so well that Folwell shifted him to quarterback when Barchet returned. His sixty-five yard, fourth-quarter touchdown against Colgate helped Navy win that game 9–0. Scholastic problems later forced Shapley to repeat a year, but that allowed him to play in the great 1926 backfield on Navy's national championship team.

Nothing seemed easy in 1923. Some 45,000 fans at Baltimore's Venable Stadium (later named Babe Ruth, Municipal, and, finally, Memorial Stadium) were in such a frenzy during a thrilling 3–3 tie against favored Princeton that the *Baltimore Sun* reported, "the noise cannot be described . . . [like] 10 tempests with a boiler factory and a couple dozen airship motors thrown in." Navy kicker Herb Ballinger's twenty-five-yard field goal tied the game in the final two minutes, but the Mids earlier had been turned aside three times inside Princeton's five-yard line. The week before, the Penn State series remained white hot as Harry Wilson scored three touchdowns for the Nittany Lions on runs of fifty, ninety-five, and seventy yards, dealing Navy its only loss of the season, 21–3, at State College, Pennsylvania. These games at neutral and away sites gave a clear indication that the Mids had hung out their shingle, "Have Team, Will Travel."

The following two seasons, 1924 and 1925, were training grounds for the undefeated season of 1926. In 1924 Navy replaced a dozen players from its bowl team. Up from the plebes came running backs Tom Hamilton and Howard Caldwell; linemen Frank Wickhorst, Tom Eddy, Wendell Osborn, John

Gus Lentz

Gus Lentz, a tackle and captain of the 1925 team, died when the USS *Wasp* was sunk during the Battle of the Eastern Solomons. Lentz, who weighed nearly 240 pounds, had been wounded earlier in the attack and lay in sick bay, unable to move. When the order to abandon ship was given, he knew that his size would make his evacuation a problem—he would probably jam an escape route, thereby endangering the lives of shipmates. So Lentz ordered the medical staff to leave him behind. He perished with his ship.

Cross, and Herb Hoerner; and end Hank Hardwick. Even with experienced players like Shapley and Flippen, the team was too young. Folwell compiled a disappointing 2–6 record in this, his last season, including a 12–0 loss to Army in Baltimore in which Ed Garbisch kicked four field goals.

Jack Owsley was named head coach in 1925 and stayed just one season. He was "of the Yale school," according to one observer, a quiet, calm, cool, and calculating man. He was not given to inspirational speeches, nor did he have an outgoing personality—skills and traits that many at Navy felt were necessary to succeed there.

But Owsley did develop players such as backs Ned Hannegan, Jim Schuber, and Howard Ransford; lineman Bob Pierce; and end Mike Bagdonovich. The season got off to a fine start. Navy outplayed favored Princeton in Baltimore and secured a 10–10 tie with Hamilton's late touchdown pass to Shapley. Then, unbeaten in four games, Navy inaugurated its rivalry with Michigan. In front of the largest crowd ever to see a game in Ann Arbor to that time, Navy got chewed up by future Hall of Famers Benny Friedman and Benny Oosterbaan, 54–0. (Until a game against Michigan in 1976, that was Navy's all-time worst loss.)

The Roaring Twenties were at their apex in 1925 when 70,000 spectators (another 10,000 were turned away) jammed the Polo Grounds in New York City for the Army-Navy game. The fans saw the Mids lose 10–3 after leading 3–0 on Hamilton's first-quarter field goal. Army scored its only touchdown by faking a

Georgia Tech made an ill-fated trip to the Naval Academy in 1922 and went home a 13–0 loser as Steve Barchet *(top),* running off tackle, led the Navy offense and the defense *(bottom)* slammed Tech stars Red Barron and Bill McWhorter.

field goal and throwing a pass to end Harry Baxter, who outfought three Middie defenders at the goal line to catch the ball.

Jonas Ingram, Navy's head coach from a decade earlier, took over the athletic program in 1926 and immediately hired as head coach his brother "Navy Bill" Ingram, a star on the 1916, 1917, and 1918 teams. Bill Ingram had been an assistant to coach Gil Dobie in 1918 and then coached and played for the U.S. fleet team on the West Coast that almost beat the University of California's undefeated Rose Bowl "Wonder Team" in 1921. He had resigned from the Navy in 1922.

Ingram was an imaginative coach. Like many coaches at that time, he employed the single- and double-wing formations. Ingram mixed power and finesse, with double reverses and men in motion, to take advantage of the skills of Hamilton and Shapley as receiver and passer.

Navy Bill was a clear reflection of his close friend Knute Rockne, both in style and personality. He exuded great warmth, personal magnetism, and an idealistic philosophy that decreed the good of the game should be surpassed only by love of school. Ingram was so imbued with infectious enthusiasm for

The 1925 Team

Several players from the 1925 and 1926 teams distinguished themselves during World War II. Edmund Taylor, captain of the 1925 team, was one of the Navy's top destroyer unit commanders. He commanded the destroyer USS *Duncan* in the Battle of Cape Esperance, during which he battled against two Japanese cruisers. Ultimately, the enemy's superior firepower disabled his ship, causing it to steam in circles. Still, Taylor kept his guns firing while evacuating his crew. He was the last man off the ship; he then watched helplessly as it steamed away, unmanned and out of control, before it was sunk by enemy fire.

In 1943, Taylor commanded the main body of landing craft in the Green Island Attack Group during the invasion of the Bismarck Islands. He later commanded Destroyer Division, in an area known as "The Perimeter" in the hotly contested Battle of the Bougainville; took his group into the invasions of Saipan and Tinian; and finally commanded DesDiv Eighty-nine in the Battle of the Philippines Sea as part of Task Force Fifty-eight, which covered the main American fleet battle units.

One of Taylor's former teammates, Charles Chillingworth, commanded the destroyer USS *Dewey* as part of Task Force Seventeen in the Battles of Coral Sea, Midway, and Guadalcanal. Later, in a delicious bit of irony, his flagship in DesRon Fifty, as part of Task Force Fifty-eight, was the USS *Joseph W. Reeves,* named after the great Navy player and coach.

Another teammate of Taylor's, Joe Welling, was commander of the destroyer USS *Strong* when it was crippled by a torpedo attack. While still engaging shore batteries, he had lines and cargo nets passed over to a sister ship, the USS *Chevalier,* to evacuate the 241 crew members, and then made it to safety himself. He later commanded DesRon Two, which screened the landing of the Sixth Army in the Philippines, and a task group in the Northern Attack Force as part of Task Force Fifty-three.

Steve Barchet

Steve Barchet was Annapolis born and bred, and he haunted the Naval Academy grounds as a youngster. His love of the school and the Navy was unsurpassed; fittingly, he was buried in the Academy's cemetery. He was a great all-around back who not only ran and passed well, but also place-kicked and punted. Of course, like all players in Barchet's day, he played defense in addition to offense.

Barchet, who retired as a rear admiral, commanded the LST group of the San Fabian Attack Force in Task Force Seventy-eight that landed the Army's I Corps in the Philippines. Before that duty, he was a much-decorated submariner. While commanding the USS *Argonaut* on patrol near Midway Island on December 8, 1941, Barchet made the only reported contact with the Japanese ships that had just attacked Pearl Harbor. On its return to home waters, that force began shelling Midway Island. Barchet's boat launched an attack but was quickly spotted by the Japanese screening force and wasn't able to continue. His boat's presence, however, forced the Japanese to stop their bombardment.

Alan Shapley

On December 7, 1941, Alan Shapley, a Marine officer, had been detached from duty aboard the USS *Arizona* at Pearl Harbor but was hanging around to play for his ship's softball team in the afternoon. After battle stations sounded, he joined his unit on the tripod mainmast, where it directed the firing of the five-inch broadside guns. Much of the ship was already ablaze when it was rocked by the explosion of its forward magazine. Shapley calmly led his men down the ladder to the quarterdeck. Just as they reached it, another explosion blew him into the water. He was stripped of everything but his trousers but was not seriously injured. The other men from his station dived in, too, and he led them to Ford's Island through thick oil, flaming debris, and exploding bombs. When a young corporal named Earl Nightengale faltered, Shapley towed him. Exhausted himself, Shapley nevertheless literally dragged the lad by his shirt the last yards to safety.

the game that there is little wonder that he preferred football over a naval career, but he displayed the kind of leadership and inspiration inherent in good military commanders. All of this was underscored when Ingram was inducted into the College Football Hall of Fame after a career that also included a successful coaching stint at the University of California.

Coach Ingram instituted a spring football program that included twice-weekly practices for six weeks. The coaches of some spring sports objected, but Jonas Ingram supported his brother. The extra practices paid off with an undefeated season—and the national championship—in 1926.

Navy's chief weapon that year was Tom Hamilton, who went on to prove the axiom that "the best fiction is based on fact." In Hollywood's heyday, Hamilton became the prototype for every scriptwriter whose main character was a young, handsome, and rugged naval flying officer who also had a star-studded athletic career at Annapolis.

Hamilton was all of that—and much more. He was a superb athlete: a three-year football letterman and All-America running back; captain of the basketball team that won fifteen of seventeen games in his senior year; and a catcher on the baseball team. He was also president of his class and, in his senior year, won both the Thompson Trophy Cup and the Naval Academy Athletic Association Sword as the outstanding athlete in his class.

On the football field, there was no skill outside Hamilton's province; he succeeded Barchet as the team's all-around star player. Hamilton excelled at both tailback and wingback because of his throwing and receiving skills; he mastered the art of drop-kicking extra points and field goals, leading the nation in field goals by drop kick with six in 1926; and he was a very capable defensive player.

Although Hamilton was the team's star, Ingram had great backfield depth with Shapley, Caldwell, Hannegan, Howard Ransford, and Jim Schuber. Their particular skills varied, but each was fast and an unselfish, fearsome blocker. Hannegan was a stronger inside runner than Hamilton, but not as good a passer. When Caldwell, Shapley, Ransford, or Schuber lined up behind the

Carl "Shaggy" Cullen, Steve Barchet, Vince Conroy, and Ira McKee formed the core of Navy's offense in 1923. They helped lead the Mids to the Rose Bowl that same year.

center, Hamilton and Hannegan often were wingbacks, going in motion either to become pass receivers or to carry the ball on inside reverses.

Another key to Navy's offensive success was the work of its tackles, Tom Eddy and Frank Wickhorst, the team's captain. Eddy was a slow bloomer and earned his only letter in 1926, when his game-by-game work was invaluable. His biggest individual play was blocking a field goal by Michigan's Benny Friedman that helped to key Navy's 10–0 upset of the Wolverines.

Adm. Henry B. Willson, the Naval Academy's superintendent, and his wife at the 1923 Army-Navy game at New York City's Polo Grounds, where the teams played the last scoreless tie in the series.

Wickhorst, another future member of the Hall of Fame, had attended the University of Illinois—where he had been a teammate of Red Grange as a freshman—before he received his appointment to the Naval Academy. Grange once told an interviewer, "That boy was a wonder as an Illinois freshman . . . a giant with tremendous physical power and awfully fast for his size." Wickhorst also was a magnificent leader on a team of stars. An injury in the 1926 Army-Navy game—his final game—prevented him from qualifying as an officer. After coaching at several schools, he helped Hamilton establish the V-5 Pre-Flight program in 1942. Wickhorst then served with Hamilton aboard the USS *Enterprise* during some of the most intense battles of the war in the Pacific.

Even with that talent, Navy probably wouldn't have been undefeated without end Russell "Whitey" Lloyd, who made critical plays in three come-from-behind victories. Lloyd's heroics began in the season-opening 17–13 upset of Purdue when he caught Hamilton's touchdown pass for the winning points. Against Georgetown, Lloyd's thirty-yard reception set up Hamilton's winning field goal with two minutes to play in a 10–7 win. Against Colgate, he turned in the season's most spectacular play, scooping up a fumble with five minutes to go and running ninety-five yards for a touchdown and 13–7 victory. That stunning play began when a Colgate runner was just about to leap over the goal line. Tackle Tom Wilson made a flying leap at him and knocked the ball loose, and into Lloyd's hands. Whitey took off and crossed the goal line before his closest pursuer had even reached midfield.

An unbeaten season and national championship notwithstanding, the Navy team baffled Ingram with its inconsistency. Ingram himself might have been part of the problem; throughout his career he had a reputation for "picking his spots," emphasizing some games over others. Often, this team had to challenge itself to play to its potential, because it obviously believed that it was too good to lose and it didn't respect some of its opponents. As a result, the Mids had to find some remarkable ways to win games that really should not have been so close. Ingram finally became so exasperated that he threatened to bench most of his regulars against Colgate—and he might have done it had they not asked for a chance to redeem themselves.

Yet the Mids were good enough to play—and to beat—two teams on the same day. On the season's second weekend they beat Drake 24–7, and then shut out the University of Richmond 26–0. In the latter game, every varsity player who hadn't played against Drake worked with the "B" squad against the Spiders.

When Navy played at Princeton, the Regiment gathered in Dahlgren Hall and "watched" each play as it was flashed on an electric board that was laid out in the shape of a football field. Someone announced the play-by-play action, and soon that old hall was rocking as the Mids rallied in the second half from a 14–10 deficit to a 27–14 victory on Caldwell's two touchdowns and Hamilton's field goal.

But other than the final game against Army—a heart-stopping, 21–21 come-from-behind tie (that game is covered in Chapter Nine), the season's highlight was the 10–0 upset victory over the great Michigan team that had buried Navy 54–0 the year before.

So important was the Michigan game that Jonas Ingram and Supt. Louis M. Nulton scouted a Wolverines game against Illinois while both men were en route to Chicago to make final arrangements for the Army-Navy game. They were joined by J. J. "Doc" Dougherty, Navy's regular scout, who proclaimed without reservation that Navy would win. His optimism seemed questionable.

Navy opened its 1923 season with a 39–10 victory over William and Mary on its home field, laid out against a backdrop of still-familiar Navy Academy buildings.

The Colgate Game

A controversy erupted in 1926 after Navy's victory over Colgate. The Red Raiders did not use halfback Ray Vaughn, a black player, in the game. William A. Reid, the graduate manager of athletics at Colgate University, had written to Navy athletic director Jonas Ingram to inquire about the propriety of playing a black at Annapolis; in those years, there was no interracial play below the Mason-Dixon line. There is no evidence that Ingram took a stance on the matter; evidently he allowed Colgate and the player to make the decision on their own. Vaughn did not accompany the team to Annapolis.

A couple of days after the game the *Baltimore Afro-American,* a newspaper that served Baltimore's black community, charged that the Naval Academy and, earlier, the University of Pittsburgh had refused to play Colgate if Vaughn was present.

Ingram categorically denied the charge, and Reid and Vaughn provided support. Reid sent a telegram to Ingram that read: "Ray Vaughn Negro athlete of Colgate University was not protested by either the Naval Academy or the University of Pittsburgh. The report . . . carried in various newspapers is untrue."

Vaughn also sent a wire: "Neither the Navy nor the University of Pittsburgh protested my playing against them as a member of the Colgate University football team. Knowing that the Naval Academy was an institution rather far south, I talked with athletic officials at Colgate University and came to a decision that it was best that I not accompany the team."

The *Afro-American*'s account stirred up enough controversy to reach the desk of Rear Adm. W. R. Shoemaker, who, as chief of the Bureau of Navigation, oversaw the Academy. He queried Rear Adm. Louis M. Nulton about the matter. The superintendent replied, "There was no official letter or statement or decision on the part of anyone connected with the Academy proper, officially or unofficially, either of the administration or the football squad, to the effect that the Academy would not play Colgate or any other team with colored players."

Bill Millican

Bill Millican, a running back on Navy's 1926 national championship team, commanded the submarine USS *Thresher* during World War II. Patrolling near the Marshall Islands, the sub encountered and sank a Japanese torpedo tender. The *Thresher* survived an ensuing air attack, but at least one hit caused a small leak that emitted air bubbles. The crew thought they were safe, concealed in deep waters, when in fact the Japanese could follow their every move by watching the bubbles. Suddenly, the submariners heard a banging and clanging. It was a great grapnel that a Japanese ship was towing at the end of a chain. Guided by the bubbles, the Japanese couldn't miss; abruptly, the sub's stern was lifted and the boat pitched severely. Millican ordered *Thresher* to run in fast, tight circles to get loose. The odds against escape seemed so great that Millican even destroyed secret codes. After ten frantic minutes, the boat miraculously broke free.

Navy's 1925 coaching staff *(from left)* were: Lyman "Pop" Perry, Jim Wilson, Gus Lentz (team captain), Jack Owsley (head coach), Ernest Von Heimberg, and Mac Slingluff.

Going into the game against Navy, Michigan had won seventeen straight. The Wolverines were led by Friedman and Oosterbaan—considered the greatest pass-catch combination in college football history to that time—who had been unstoppable against Navy the year before. And Shapley was injured.

But the fired-up Mids, led by Caldwell and Hamilton, outplayed the Wolverines. Caldwell was magnificent. He rolled up thirty-two yards in two runs to set up a Hamilton field goal. Then, after a Hamilton interception in the fourth quarter, Caldwell keyed another drive with twenty-eight yards rushing. The crucial play on that drive occurred on a fourth-and-two at Michigan's sixteen-yard line when Hamilton faked a field goal and passed to Maurice Goudge on the two-yard line. Caldwell scored on the next play—the first TD any team had scored against Michigan in thirteen games.

But Navy's defense in the second quarter was the key to victory. The Mids' line, outweighed by nearly ten pounds per man, battered Michigan's running game to a standstill. When Friedman turned to the air, Goudge, Hamilton, Hannegan, and Lloyd knocked down pass after pass as they came to the hands of eager Michigan receivers. After Eddy blocked a Friedman field goal attempt, Michigan could not regain its confidence. Friedman completed just seven of twenty-eight passes that day—the worst performance of his Hall of Fame career. Ingram also made a clever move when he switched Lloyd from end to defensive back and put Caldwell at end, where he helped stop Michigan's running game.

The next day, W. Wilson Wingate, the *Baltimore Sun*'s football expert, wrote, "Only a brilliant football team could have beaten Michigan yesterday and this is the type of team Navy sent on the field with the 1925 score of 54 to 0 still silhouetted against the skyline of memory."

In a move that was atypical of college football in those years, both teams had lunched at the Naval Academy before the game and then returned to the

Academy afterward for dinner together "and an opportunity to get better acquainted," according to the *Sun*.

After finishing its undefeated season with a 21–21 tie against Army, Navy claimed the national championship on the basis of its overall record and its victories over top-flight opponents. Wire service polls to select a national champion were not introduced until the early thirties. In 1926, a variety of systems in use from coast to coast claimed to designate the champ. Two of them, the Boand and the Houlgate Polls, picked Navy as the nation's best team. Others named Stanford, Alabama, and Lafayette, all unbeaten, as their national champions.

Navy made a huge move to gain more national recognition in 1927 by beginning its series against Notre Dame, which has continued unbroken to the edge of the millennium. The series was a direct result of the Ingrams' great friendship with Notre Dame coach and athletic director Knute Rockne. It also didn't hurt that Rockne had a penchant for selling himself and his school; he recognized the prestige that would result from competing against both service academies. (The Fighting Irish had started their series with Army in 1913; it lasted unbroken until 1947.)

The original agreement between Navy and Notre Dame called for the series to begin in the Midwest, possibly at Notre Dame's old Cartier Field. But that stadium had a very modest capacity, so midway through the 1926 season, the schools agreed to open instead in Baltimore the following year, where more than 50,000 fans could be accommodated. (This arrangement also allowed Navy to keep its promise to Baltimore officials to schedule at least two major opponents each year in that city.) Coming on the heels of its astonishing upset

Navy and Princeton played a 10–10 tie in 1925 at Baltimore's Venable Stadium, now site of Memorial Stadium. Alan Shapley of Navy is shown kicking the tie-making extra point in the fourth quarter.

The star of Navy's 1926 national champions was Hall of Fame running back Tom Hamilton, shown receiving an award several years before his death in honor of his long and illustrious service to Navy athletics. He was the only person ever to serve two tours as head coach at Navy.

Navy's 1926 National Champions: *(front row, from left)* Bagdonovich, Williamson, Ransford, Woerner, Born, Wickhorst (captain), Warren, Shaley, Hamilton, and Hannegan; *(second row)* Dimon (manager), Osborn, Wilson, Morse, Parish, Coffman, Burke, Hubert-Jones, Hardwicke, Aichel, Millicam, and Condra; *(third row)* Couhig, Caldwell, Taylor, Pierce, Smith, Duborg, Olsen, Lloyd, Nieman, Schuber, and Goudge; and *(back row)* Dodge, Stillman, Eddy, Hoerner, Miller, Maginnis, Truslow, Duborg, Brockman, Cross, Zondorak, and McGarry.

over Michigan in 1926, starting a series with Notre Dame was a major coup.

Rockne had his own reasons for playing Navy. He was making his school a coast-to-coast attraction, having just begun an annual series with Southern California on the West Coast. A Navy game in alternate years at Baltimore gave him a Southern counterpart to his annual visit to New York City to play Army—a game that had gained much national appeal for Notre Dame.

Notre Dame generated great excitement everywhere it played, especially among the large Irish-Catholic populations in the major cities in the East and Midwest. Thus it was on October 15, 1927, that 53,000 people jammed Baltimore's Venable Stadium on a warm, crystal-clear autumn Saturday. Special trains had brought thousands of fans from as far away as South Bend and Chicago, including more dignitaries than Baltimore had ever seen.

Even the media got caught up in the scene. The *Baltimore Sun* noted that when Notre Dame's squad came on the field for pregame warmups, "the players turned out to be the Beau Brummels of the football world. None like them have been seen on a Baltimore gridiron. The unexpected appearance of gold and silk balloon pants gave the crowd a jolt. Above the silk were Irish green sweaters."

But the writer realized that Rockne was making more than a fashion statement by dressing his team in silk: "Silk is not so heavy to carry as other material, and opposing players find it more difficult to get a hold of this material. It helps the wearer slip through tacklers."

One of the best all-around athletes in Navy history, Whitey Lloyd played offensive end and defensive back in 1926. Here he catches a pass from Hamilton during a 24–7 triumph over Drake. Later that day the Mids also played the University of Richmond in a unique college football doubleheader, and they won that game too.

On the day before the game, the Navy team played host to the Notre Dame squad at lunch at Bancroft Hall, gave them a sightseeing tour of the Naval Academy, and then allowed their opponents to use their practice facility for a "secret" workout. The next morning, Navy's team left Annapolis at 10:00 for the Baltimore Country Club, where the players limbered up for the game, one report noted, "with rounds of golf."

As was often Rockne's custom, he started his second unit, or "shock troops," to probe Navy's offensive and defensive schemes. The move backfired. Navy scored first after Notre Dame's Johnny Niemic mishandled and lost Howard Ransford's first-quarter punt at midfield. A pass interference call, and Ransford's twenty-yard run to the ten-yard line, set up Art Spring's fourth-down reverse for a touchdown. Hannegan missed the extra point.

Even after Rockne replaced the "shock troops," Navy maintained its 6–0 lead until the third quarter, when some questionable strategy caused the Mids to unravel. Whitey Lloyd's punt was downed on Notre Dame's twenty-five-yard line, but the Irish were offside. Instead of refusing the penalty and giving Notre

Jim Schuber rolls through a huge hole for Navy's first score in its thrilling 13–7 win against Colgate in 1926. Whitey Lloyd eventually scored the winning touchdown when he scooped up a fumble and ran ninety-nine yards for a touchdown.

Dame poor field position, Navy took the five yards and tried a third-and-five play. It gained nothing. Lloyd's subsequent punt was blocked by John Frederick; Chile Walsh scooped up the ball and ran for a touchdown. The extra point was missed, but the 6–6 tie was broken on Notre Dame's next possession. Christy Flanagan gained fifty-eight yards on three runs, and Charlie Riley scored a one-yard touchdown. The Irish now led 13–6. They added a fourth-quarter touchdown and shut down Navy's offense.

While the first game of the series made an explosive impact, the 1928 game was a blockbuster. An estimated 122,000 fans—the largest crowd in college football history—packed Soldier Field in Chicago and watched Navy lose, 7–0. Once again, poor punting hurt the Mids. Late in the third quarter, Lloyd's miserable seven-yard kick was downed by Notre Dame at Navy's twenty-eight-yard line. The mistake set up the Irish's only touchdown early in the fourth quarter: John Colrick scored on a play-action pass from Frank Carideo. Navy struggled mightily to come back, driving into Notre Dame territory three

---

Whitey Lloyd

There was never a more determined player in the Naval Academy's football history—nor one who played more up-and-down roles in Navy football fortunes during his three varsity seasons—than Russell "Whitey" Lloyd.

Lloyd spent at least five years (some say it was seven because he had problems as a plebe) at the Naval Academy and played three varsity seasons—1926, 1927, and 1928. He didn't graduate until 1930. He had tremendous speed, and at six feet, one inch could outleap most defensive players to catch a ball. Lloyd was such a fine athlete that coach Bill Ingram often used him to great effect as a defensive back against big, speedy receivers. His play in that position was one of the keys to Navy's 10–0 victory over Michigan in 1926. Lloyd, who became a Marine general, earned a Silver Star on Guadalcanal and also was awarded the Legion of Merit and a Bronze Star.

---

times. One drive was stopped at the Irish six-yard line. With the game on the line in the final minute, the last push was stopped at the fifteen-yard line by an interception.

The first two meetings were harbingers of things to come in the Notre Dame series. It took the Mids six years before they achieved their first victory over the Irish. In the next thirty games, Navy won just nine and tied one. Its last victory was in 1963, when Roger Staubach's team turned in a 35–14 win. Particularly since 1965, the Mids have been overmatched in nearly every game. There have been calls to break the series, but neither school has wanted to end what has become college football's longest continual intersectional rivalry. In 1996, the two teams even played a game in Ireland.

The Mids had a new cast for the 1927, 1928, and 1929 teams. New standouts included Harold and Rudy Bauer and Joe Clifton; in addition, Lloyd was moved into the backfield. Harold Bauer and Clifton were excellent inside runners—Bauer was a swift halfback, Clifton a hard-charging fullback. Coach Ingram believed that Clifton would sometimes rather run over people than try to avoid them.

Both men also excelled in their service careers. Lt. Col. Harold Bauer won the Medal of Honor posthumously for his gallantry commanding Fighter Squadron 212 at Henderson Field on Guadalcanal during three incredible weeks in the fall of 1942. No sooner had his group arrived at Henderson than it was attacked by Japanese bombers. Bauer jumped back into his plane, roared into combat, and shot down an attacker. Five days later, he attacked another raiding force, downed four planes, and damaged another; he stopped only because he ran out of ammunition. Three weeks after that, while circling to land after having led a six-hundred-mile, over-the-water ferry flight of reinforcements to Henderson, he raced to the aid of a U.S. destroyer that was being attacked by Japanese planes. Although low on fuel, he gunned down four of the attackers before crashing into the sea. Bauer's body was never found; he is still listed as an MIA.

Clifton, nicknamed "Jumpin' Joe" and "Paducah Joe"—the latter because he was from Paducah, Kentucky—was one of Navy's great success stories. He struggled academically for four years at the Academy, finally graduating fourteenth from the bottom of his class. Only the work of his classmate and personal tutor, Andrew M. Jackson, later a vice admiral, got Clifton through the Academy. The commandant gave Clifton written permission to visit Jackson at any time so Jackson could help him with his studies. Friends often heard Clifton shuffling along the hall in his bedroom slippers late at night as he went to his friend for help. Jackson, for his part, never minded the extra work, and said that helping Clifton made him work harder to keep up. On graduation day, with his diploma safely in his hand, Clifton walked up to his friend and said, "Andy, you earned two of these. Have mine as well." The special relationship between the two classmates continued in flight school, where Jackson taught Clifton the art of mastering slow rolls.

Another teammate, Mike Bagdonovich, himself a great Marine flier, said of Clifton, "He was never born to lose." The two men later worked together while training pilots at Pensacola; they also coached the football team there.

Claude Ricketts

Claude V. Ricketts, who was a little-used substitute on the 1926 and 1927 teams but won his letter in 1928, was, like his 1926 teammate Alan Shapley, a survivor of the attack on Pearl Harbor. Ricketts was serving aboard the USS *West Virginia* and was on the sick list when the Japanese attacked. The ship was soon torn apart below decks by torpedoes and set afire topside by burning debris from the *Arizona*. Nonetheless, Ricketts organized an ammunition-passing team that kept antiaircraft guns firing. In his regular billet as damage control officer, Ricketts had often concocted solutions to various disaster scenarios: now one of the world's worst—capsizing—seemed likely to come true. Ricketts had plotted how to activate flooding to counter the list and sink the ship on an even keel. And that's what he did, making the *West Virginia* much easier to raise, repair, and return to service. Ricketts later had a destroyer named in his honor. At the Naval Academy, Ricketts Hall now houses the Athletic Association offices, the football locker room, and other athletic facilities.

Joe Clifton

Joe Clifton's "football personality"—his combative nature, courage, poise under adverse conditions, and daring and competitive spirit—marked him as a flier even before he won his wings at Pensacola. On night flying training exercises he often turned off his running lights so no one could see what he was doing, and flew loops and rolls with great delight. "He treated every plane just as if it was a fighter, and made it go all out, whether or not it had the power to do all he tried," said one of his mates.

During World War II, Clifton commanded VF-12, the fighter component of the USS *Saratoga*'s Air Group Twelve. Commanding the air group was Harold Caldwell, whose spot Clifton had taken in Navy's backfield. Clifton often escorted Caldwell's bombers during operations around the Japanese fortress of Rabaul. He won two Distinguished Flying Crosses for heroism during the raids, in which he fearlessly disregarded antiaircraft fire and fighter opposition. Later, he commanded Air Group Twelve when Caldwell became the *Saratoga*'s air officer.

In 1944, the *Saratoga* was detached from Task Force Fifty-eight to help train the British carrier HMS *Illustrious* in combined operations. At one point, Clifton and another pilot were instructed to land their Hellcat fighters on the British ship. Clifton was the first to approach—but he could not locate the landing signal officer (LSO) who would direct him. (On American carriers, the LSO stood on the port side of the fantail, but on British carriers, he was stationed on the port deck edge amidships.) So, Clifton simply landed without direction and went directly to the bridge, where he presented himself to a rather startled admiral, who was quite taken aback by Clifton's daring.

Stephen Juricka, who had tutored Clifton in Spanish at the Academy, was tutored in turn by Clifton in flight school in making emergency landings. Juricka later recalled that, when the lesson was completed, Clifton would buzz his own house and do some exotic stunt flying. "That was pure Joe," Juricka said. "He was a big man, gruff, voluble, who expressed his feelings in no uncertain terms and sometimes in quite inelegant terms." Clifton proved that academic standing sometimes has little to do with officer quality. Jumpin' Joe attained the rank of rear admiral and commanded Task Force Seventy-seven during the Korean War.

Navy won six of nine games in 1927, including a 12–6 victory over Penn in which Whitey Lloyd and Rudy Bauer stunned 70,000 at Franklin Field by returning interceptions for Navy's only scores. Lloyd turned in the season's best play on an eighty-five-yard touchdown run against Michigan, though Navy lost 27–12.

The following year, Navy and Michigan returned to Baltimore and battled to a 6–6 tie. Navy led 6–0 until the fourth quarter, thanks to Johnny Gannon's touchdown that was set up by his seventy-five-yard run. Michigan tied the score early in the fourth quarter. Claude Hughes gave the Mids one last hope by blocking a Michigan punt in the final minutes. Navy drove to the Wolverines' seven-yard line, but with less than a minute to play, Lloyd's field goal attempt was low.

The Mids' captain in 1928, Eddie Burke, hadn't even considered playing football when he arrived at the Academy. But when Ingram saw him flatten a sparring partner in a plebe boxing class, Ingram ordered Burke to join the team. Burke became one of Navy's best linemen. (He later commanded Destroyer Squadron Thirty-one in the Atlantic Fleet during World War II.)

Navy turned in an 11–5–3 record in 1928 and 1929. The tie against Michigan in 1928 was the highlight.

In those years, Michigan and Notre Dame were Navy's most important opponents. The series against Army had been suspended because the schools could not agree on binding eligibility standards. Navy had long chafed at what it perceived to be a huge edge for Army. In 1927, Navy's last bit of patience expired when Harry Wilson, who played against Navy for three years at Penn State and four more at West Point, scored two touchdowns in Army's 14–9 victory.

The problem was born in 1903 when Navy protested the eligibility of certain Army stars who had played football at civilian schools before coming to West Point—notably, Charley Daly, who had been a three-time All-America at Harvard; tackle Pot Graves, who had played three varsity seasons at North Carolina; Ken Boyers; and Ed Farnsworth. Navy also claimed that Army had an edge with its higher age limit for admission—twenty-one years, compared with twenty at the Naval Academy. The Military Academy could attract more experienced players, the Navy complained.

Army maintained at that time—and held fast to its position well into the thirties—that any cadet, regardless of his prior athletic background, could engage in intercollegiate competition because it was part of West Point's curriculum. In 1904, a temporary compromise was struck: both schools signed a three-year agreement limiting participation in the Army-Navy game to those

Art Spring, his helmet askew, rolls into the end zone with Navy's first touchdown in the inaugural game against Notre Dame in 1927. Spring's score gave Navy a 6–0 halftime lead at Baltimore, but Notre Dame came back and won 19–7.

who had not played more than three years of college football, including first-team play at any of forty institutions.

That agreement was not renewed, and Army gradually returned to securing appointments for players from civilian schools. All the while, Navy felt it was unfair to send out inexperienced players to face opponents who had played up to six or seven years of college football. That Army kept winning most of those games only deepened Navy's grudge.

Brig. Gen. Douglas MacArthur, who became West Point superintendent in 1921, had been impressed with the battlefield service of athletes during World War I, and he pushed harder for the appointment of experienced college athletes. MacArthur convinced the War Department to authorize a number of "appointments at large" that were outside of the usual legislative and presidential channels and could be used to lure athletes from civilian schools. ROTC officers around the country were told to identify and encourage such athletes to transfer to West Point. The opportunity to extend their football careers was part of the bait.

Given the circumstances, Navy also allowed transfers from civilian schools to enjoy four additional years of eligibility. For example, running back Royce Flippen had played for two years at Centre College in Kentucky and played four more varsity seasons for Navy; end Hank Hardwick had three years at Virginia Tech and four more at Annapolis; and tackle Gus Lentz played two years at Rutgers and four more for Navy. But in 1923, the Naval Academy, along with most of the nation's colleges, agreed to limit eligibility to just three varsity years, regardless of where it was accumulated.

Army was not a party to this change and, once the rule took effect, Navy was at a disadvantage in its games against the Military Academy. The Cadets always seemed to have three or four superior players who had been former civilian college stars. The intensifying grumbling from Annapolis finally

Moon Chapple

Wreford "Moon" Chapple, a starter at tackle in 1927, 1928, and 1929, commanded the submarine USS *Sculpin* of the U.S. Asiatic Fleet at Manila when World War II began. Two weeks later, his boat sank a Japanese transport that was landing troops on Luzon. The *Sculpin* then made a miraculous escape through tricky shoals while under depth-charge attack. In November 1944, Chapple commanded a submarine wolfpack supporting the Seventh Fleet that was steaming west of Luzon. The wolfpack attacked and crippled the cruiser *Kumano;* the Japanese beached the ship, and she was later destroyed by planes from the USS *Ticonderoga*.

compelled West Point, in 1926, to modify its rule by barring plebes from varsity competition. That solved little, however, because transfers to West Point still had three varsity seasons of eligibility, in addition to whatever they had previously accumulated.

A few weeks before the teams played their historic 21–21 tie in 1926, a blue-ribbon officer board of former Navy football stars, plus 1926 team captain Frank Wickhorst, recommended that the Naval Academy maintain its three-year varsity rule and allow no freshman varsity competition. It also recommended that Navy not compete against any school that did not adhere to such rules. Rear Adm. Louis F. Nulton, the superintendent, agreed, and when he sent contracts to West Point for Army-Navy athletic competition from 1927 through 1930, he inserted a clause that formalized Navy's three-year rule.

Brig. Gen. Merch B. Stewart, West Point's superintendent, said that the clause that Admiral Nulton offered "would be superfluous in view of the fact that we proposed incorporating the rule in our announced athletic policy." To do so, he continued, "we were placing the Military Academy on record in a way that would make its attitude toward this point unquestioned in the future. . . . I cannot escape the conviction that the announced policies of the two Academies constitute a gentleman's agreement more binding and of greater permanence than any contract. . . ."

So Army returned the contract to Navy, minus the three-year eligibility rule but with the "gentleman's agreement" stipulation that Army would make it part of its athletic policy in the future. That really changed nothing, though, because Army continued to adhere to its old policy. Shortly before the 1927 game, there were reports that the series would be terminated. West Point athletic director Lawrence Jones called the reports "absurd," pointing out that the two schools had signed a new four-year agreement that would not expire until after the 1930 game. Shortly after Army defeated Navy 14–9 in 1927, West Point's new superintendent, Maj. Gen. Edwin Winans, approved a recommendation that Army's eligibility rule return to its 1903 status. His reasoning cited the three sticking points that had been raised in previous eligibility disputes—that varsity competition was part of West Point's curriculum and open to all students, regardless of prior experience; that the Naval Academy now set

Navy–Notre Dame at Chicago's Soldier Field in 1928. An estimated 122,000 fans jammed the big lakefront arena, the biggest crowd in college football history. Navy lost 7–0.

younger entrance age limits (sixteen to twenty years old), while West Point's age limits were seventeen to twenty-one, thus providing Navy with more men from which to choose a team; and that the eligibility rules were for the good of the service, not for the equalization of athletic teams.

Further, the Military Academy claimed that its recent ruling forbidding plebes to engage in varsity athletics was the same as Navy's three-year eligibility rule. Army said it had adopted the plebe rule as a concession to maintain athletic relations between the academies. Other schools had agreed to that rule, West Point contended, and Navy should, too. Army never budged from that position.

"Bullet Lou" Kirn, one of Navy's outstanding running backs in the 1929–31 seasons. Kirn scored both touchdowns in Navy's 13–6 victory over Dartmouth in the final game of the 1929 season. That game had replaced Army on the Mids' schedule after the two schools suspended relations for a couple of years because of a dispute over eligibility standards.

The dispute finally boiled over when the Naval Academy, the host for the 1928 game, inserted a paragraph in that game's contract declaring that players with more than three total years of varsity experience would be ineligible when the two teams played. General Winans refused to accept the clause. On January 7, 1928, both superintendents announced there would be no game that year because of unresolvable eligibility problems. Navy left open a thirty-day window in case a solution could be found, but when the deadline passed, it announced that Princeton had replaced Army on its schedule. Army replaced Navy with Stanford.

The matter reverberated through the military bureaucracy, into the halls of Congress, and even to the Oval Office. President Calvin Coolidge said it was up to the two schools to resolve the problem. When Maj. Gen. William R. Smith replaced General Winans as superintendent at West Point in March 1928, he promptly announced that Army would not change its eligibility rules. So the schools remained apart despite frequent pleadings from promoters interested in staging the game and, of course, from politicians. One congressman even introduced a bill forbidding either school from playing other schools until they restored friendly relations, but the measure never got to a vote. General Smith and Rear Adm. Samuel S. Robison, Navy's new superintendent, met in October 1929 to negotiate a settlement, but neither budged, and the breach only widened.

Navy even suggested an alternate eligibility program: play the game two years under the three-year rule, and then two years under the four-year rule. Army declined. Smith said that neither school should have eligibility rules that, he charged, were imposed because of "suspicion, mistrust and to prevent fraud."

"Army trusts Navy and feels sure that the Navy implies distrust of Army by insisting upon unnecessary eligibility rules," General Smith declared. In 1929, in place of its game against Army, Navy played Dartmouth and won 13–6; Army filled the date with another game against Stanford, and lost 34–13.

Navy and Princeton played a 13–13 tie in 1929. The Mids, shown stopping a Princeton runner, blew a 13–0 lead in the fourth quarter.

The matter disappeared from public view for the next eight months. Meanwhile, the stock market had collapsed and the Great Depression had seized the nation. Ways to alleviate some of the suffering were frantically sought. On November 7, 1930, Grover Whalen, a New York City official, headed a delegation that visited President Herbert Hoover and proposed a charity game between Army and Navy for December 13, in New York's Yankee Stadium.

A week later, with President Hoover's robust approval, the Navy Department announced that the game would be played on that date and that receipts would go to Salvation Army units in the hometowns of the players on both teams. Yankee Stadium was donated rent-free, and ticket prices ranged from five to fifty dollars.

Even with this opening, General Smith pointedly announced that the game would not be considered a resumption of the contract since it was being played for charity. He also made it clear that "West Point's team will play under its own eligibility rules." Army won 6–0 before more than 70,000 fans. A charity game also was played in 1931 at Yankee Stadium, again before a full house. In 1932, the two schools resumed normal athletic relations, with the eligibility rules still unchanged.

The issue wasn't resolved until 1938, when President Franklin D. Roosevelt, a one-time assistant secretary of the Navy, slipped a note to his military aide, Maj. Gen. Edwin M. "Pa" Watson. "From now, West Point will abide by the three-year rule," the note ordered.

But it wasn't until 1950 that the Naval Academy, through an Act of Congress specifically designed to put it on a par with West Point in attracting students and student-athletes, was allowed appointments-at-large, in addition to the regular congressional appointments.

Despite all of that turmoil, the Roaring Twenties was one great decade for Navy football.

4. Buzz, Dusty, Slade, and the Gang 1930–1938

At the same time the Great Depression gripped the country, Navy football enjoyed some prosperous years. It showcased great stars such as Gordon Chung-Hoon, Fred "Buzz" Borries, Slade Cutter, Robert "Dusty" Dornin, Bill Clark, Sneed Schmidt, and Bill Ingram II. These men helped to make a run at the 1934 national championship; played in momentous games against Notre Dame, Columbia, Pitt, and Yale; and endured continuing frustration in their contests against Army. Yet, as great as those players performed on the gridiron, their football careers were only warmups for more valorous military careers during World War II.

Dick Antrim was a fine running back for Navy's 1930 team. He is also one of six former Navy football players who have been awarded the Medal of Honor, the nation's highest military decoration.

Bill Ingram's coaching tenure ended after the 1930 Army-Navy game, which was played at Yankee Stadium in New York City. Army won 6–0. Ray Stecker ran fifty-six yards for the only touchdown with eight minutes to play. Navy had one final chance to win after Johnny Byng recovered a fumble at the Cadets' thirty-seven-yard line, but on third down his option pass missed a wide-open receiver.

The 1930 season marked the first time that Navy charged admission to its home games. Prices ranged from three dollars to fifty cents, depending upon the competition. Because of the dire times, all receipts were donated to relief agencies. That fall, Navy helped Notre Dame dedicate its new stadium, designed by Knute Rockne—and Navy lost, 26–2. Rockne was killed the following spring in a plane crash.

Despite the losses to Army and Notre Dame, Navy finished 7–4 in 1930. One of the standouts was "Bullet Lou" Kirn, a 150-pound halfback from Wisconsin who, despite his size, became the Mids' chief running threat. With his catlike quickness, Kirn got through small holes for big gains. Bullet Lou scored all three Navy touchdowns in the opening-game victory against William and Mary. On the second play of the game against Maryland, he was spun off balance at the line of scrimmage, righted himself, and, with a convoy of blockers, ran sixty-five yards for the only score in a 6–0 victory. In a game against Southern Methodist, which the Mids lost, Kirn carried the ball twenty-four times and gained 118 yards. He later put on a great second-half performance against Penn in a 26–0 victory.

Midshipmen in a pregame march-on at Yankee Stadium prior to the 1930 Army-Navy game. The series, which was terminated in 1928 over an eligibility dispute, was ordered resumed by President Herbert Hoover so that ticket proceeds could benefit relief work during the Great Depression. Army won the game 6–0.

During World War II, Kirn was one of several former Navy football stars who flew off the USS *Saratoga;* he commanded scouting group VS-3 in Task Force Sixty-one under Adm. Frank Jack Fletcher during the Battle of the Eastern Solomons. Returning from an attack on the Japanese carrier *Ryujo,* his group encountered four enemy planes. Acting more like fighter planes than lumbering scout ships, Kirn's group fought the enemy, at times just 500 feet above the sea, and shot down three and damaged the other.

Two men who were guards on the 1930 team—Charles Kirkpatrick and Gordon Underwood—also distinguished themselves in World War II. Kirkpatrick led an underwater demolition team under cover of darkness onto the island of Peleliu to photograph and scout the invasion beaches. He later performed the same risky mission on the island fortress of Yap as part of Operation Stalemate. There, he and his team battled their way through a furious firefight against the Japanese defenders before they reached the two rubber rafts that carried them back to a waiting submarine.

Underwood commanded the submarine USS *Spadefish.* On his first patrol, his boat sank nearly 29,000 tons of Japanese shipping as part of a wolf pack that sank 64,456 tons—the most sunk by any pack in a single patrol during the war. Later, working with another wolf pack commanded by Capt. Elliott Laughlin (in 1945 he was appointed athletic director at the Naval Academy), Underwood commanded the USS *Queenfish*. The subs encountered a big Japanese convoy trying to reinforce the Philippines. Underwood's submarine sank a carrier, while the wolf pack decimated the convoy. The *Queenfish* was pursued on the surface by two subchasers and, according to Underwood, "We were getting considerably more than the rated horsepower out of our ten-cylinder engines." Underwood then submerged and attacked his pursuers with four torpedoes—and heard three explosions.

The 1930 Army-Navy Game

On December 13, 1930, 70,000 people jammed Yankee Stadium to see Army play Navy. Five thousand of those spectators were lucky military personnel. Because of rumors that the stadium was sold out, many fans stayed home on game day. Finding themselves with thousands of unsold fifty-dollar tickets—the best seats in the house—the organizers gave them free of charge to soldiers and sailors.

The game, whose proceeds went to relief for victims of the Depression, had several unusual touches. Instead of the normal legion of bellowing program hawkers, squads of New York's prettiest debutantes, along with 200 Salvation Army girls, distributed programs. The ball used in the opening kickoff was auctioned off for $5,000 by Evangeline Booth, the commander of the Salvation Army, and presented to Grover Whelan, New York City's "official greeter," in appreciation for all he did to bring the game to fruition in such a short period of time.

Under the careful scrutiny of head coach Rip Miller *(on the sideline, dressed in a white jersey, with hands on his hips),* Navy's team goes through 1931 spring drills at Annapolis. Miller had succeeded Bill Ingram and his first team had a 5–5–1 record. After three years as head coach, Miller stayed at the Naval Academy as one of its great line coaches and played an influential role in recruiting athletes with his famed "Bird Dogs."

Another talented running back on the 1930 team was Dick Antrim, who became one of six football lettermen in the Academy's history to earn the Medal of Honor. In April 1942, Antrim was captured after the Japanese sank his destroyer, the USS *Pope.* While in prison, he gallantly interceded to stop the beating of a fellow officer already rendered unconscious; Antrim offered to take the blows himself. His action energized his 2,700 fellow prisoners and stunned his captors. Awed by his courage, the Japanese not only spared Antrim's life, but also dramatically improved the camp's living conditions. The POWs had been on the brink of revolting against the horrible conditions, and Antrim's action was credited with preventing an uprising that could hardly have had any outcome other than the slaughter of the prisoners. Antrim received many other decorations, including the Navy Cross, Bronze Star, and Purple Heart. He later became a rear admiral.

Ingram left the Naval Academy at the end of the 1930 season to coach at the University of California and was replaced by Edgar "Rip" Miller. Miller, a former star of Rockne's famed "Seven Mules" line at Notre Dame, had been Navy's line coach for five years. He had worked for Ingram in 1925 at the University of Indiana—on Rockne's recommendation—and came with him to Annapolis in 1926.

Miller was head coach for three years until succeeded by Tom Hamilton in 1934 when the Academy resumed its practice of hiring graduates as coaches. Miller, though, was such a fine coach that Hamilton and succeeding coaches kept Miller as line coach through 1947. He developed five Hall of Fame linemen: Frank Wickhorst, Slade Cutter, George Brown, Dick Scott, and Don Whitmire. Miller's motto was: "Hands, knees and elbows—give 'em nothing but abuse." Miller later became an assistant athletic director and was always the one continuing thread at the Athletic Association that linked a succession of coaches and athletic directors to the Academy and its traditions. His primary responsibility away from coaching was recruiting. He established his famous "Bird Dogs"—the tag given to a group of friends who apprised Miller of talented secondary school players—and was legendary for his ability to secure appointments for the athletes he wanted.

Miller was a fiery and energetic coach who was well liked by his players. Like all of Rockne's former players who later became coaches, Miller was sold on The Rock's style and "Notre Dame Box" offensive system. He installed that system at Navy when he became head coach. But it produced only mixed results over three seasons, during which the team had a 12–15–2 record. End Hugh "Fid" Murray, captain of the 1933 team, recalled that one-on-one blocking duties for the team's bread-and-butter off-tackle plays were often stymied when opposing defenses overshifted and placed a defensive tackle outside the ends, making it nearly impossible to block down on the defender and open the hole. "Our offensive successes came from reverse and inside plunges, and occasionally a pass," he said.

"Of course," he added, "we often drove Rip to distraction, none worse than the occasion when he was putting in a new play wherein both guards were supposed to pull and block. They pulled, but in opposite directions, butted heads, and sank back on their haunches like a couple of stunned bulls."

When Navy played Notre Dame in Baltimore in 1931, the Mids failed to make one first down in a 20–0 loss. In their game against Penn, however, a fake punt-pass from Kirn to running mate Harvey Tschirgi in the final moments rallied the Mids for a 6–0 victory—the biggest win of the season. Navy had a touchdown called back just before the score. The referee told Magruder Tuttle, the team captain, "I'm sorry. We had to call it."

"That's all right," Tuttle replied. "We'll get another one."

And they did.

Tuttle, who played center, had a penchant for getting into trouble. One of his indiscretions bought him and his close friend, Francis D. Foley, later a rear admiral, sixty days restricted duty and confinement in the Academy's brig aboard the *Reina Mercedes*. The infraction was an unauthorized dining hall

Kickoff for the 1931 Army-Navy game at Yankee Stadium, again played by White House order to aid relief work in the Great Depression. Navy lost for the second year in a row, 17–7, its lone touchdown coming on a pass from Lou Kirn to Harvey Tschirgi (*above*). However, both games in New York City raised hundreds of thousands of dollars for the needy.

Gordon Paiea Chung-Hoon, a native of Honolulu, was a three-year letterman as a star running back in 1931–33. His classmates always maintained that he was an even better baseball player, but that career was stymied because he spent each spring recouping his losses in the classroom. While serving aboard the USS *Arizona,* he survived the Japanese attack on December 7, 1941, and later made rear admiral.

table visit. Of course, two of the people at the table were attractive females who were wearing "white works," which resembled the Mids' white uniforms, and whose hair was tightly bobbed, making Tuttle suspect they had been overnight "guests" in Bancroft Hall. The media picked up the story, and he soon was washed by a wave of nationwide sympathy, even at the Navy Department.

Tuttle's punishment prevented him from joining preseason football training, but assistant coach John W. Byng brought him a football so he could practice his center snaps. Tuttle enlisted Foley to catch them, but they found that the capstan on the deck of the *Reina Mercedes* hindered their work. So they dismantled its head and pushed it overboard, in full view of the commanding officer. "Having fun, gentlemen?" the officer inquired—but he never took any action against them.

Two of Tuttle's teammates were running back Edmond Konrad and tackle William "Killer" Kane. Konrad, while commanding Air Group Seventeen aboard the USS *Yorktown* in 1945, led an attack on the *Yamato,* the prize battleship of the Japanese navy. His planes fired four torpedoes into the ship, causing her to list and expose her underbelly. The *Yamato* became a juicy target the next day for the *Yorktown*'s Torpedo Nine, which sank the mighty warship.

Kane was Officer of the Day at Pearl Harbor on December 7, 1941. He stayed on duty for forty-eight hours, assisting in caring for the wounded, fighting fires, and organizing the survivors. Kane won two Distinguished Flying Crosses and the Navy Cross. He was executive officer of the USS *Enterprise* in the Battle of Santa Cruz in 1942 and survived the Battle of Guadalcanal even though he had to crash-land his plane on the carrier's deck. He also commanded Air Group Ten aboard the *Enterprise* as part of Marc Mitscher's Task Force 38/58.

Killer Kane was a senior and Gordon Chung-Hoon a junior when Fred "Buzz" Borries, Slade Cutter, Robert "Dusty" Dornin, Bill Clark, and Walter Baumberger joined the varsity in 1932. This group of young men helped to form the most talented team since the 1926 champions, and several of them were ranked among the greatest players in Navy's history. Few would have predicted such stardom in 1932, when the Mids won only two games. The 1932 team captain, Jim Reedy, later became an admiral and a renowned Antarctic explorer.

Chung-Hoon, a future rear admiral, was a gritty running back who was one of the few bright spots during the dreary 1932 season. Chung-Hoon was born in Hawaii to Chinese-Hawaiian parents. He attracted much attention as a midshipman because someone had started a phony rumor that, whenever possible, Chung-Hoon walked barefoot around the Yard, supposedly because he could not adapt to regulation footwear. (In fact, he had played high school football barefoot in Honolulu.) More interesting was the fact that he had received his varsity high school letter from Knute Rockne, who was visiting Honolulu to round up two teams of barefooted players to come back to the mainland to play against U.S. college teams. Later, Chung-Hoon attended Severn School, just outside of Annapolis, where he played football wearing conventional, high-top cleats. The same footwear never seemed to deter him during three fine varsity seasons with Navy.

Along with Ulmont Whitehead, a star on the 1937, 1938, and 1939 teams,

Chung-Hoon was assigned in 1941 to the USS *Arizona,* where he replaced Buzz Borries as the ship's top football star and, eventually, coach. Both men were aboard the ship when a bomb set off a magazine on December 7, 1941. Whitehead was among the more than eleven hundred crewmen who died; Chung-Hoon survived.

But Chung-Hoon was more than his ship's star athlete; his leadership as a naval officer was legendary. His athletic feats were admired, of course, but his willingness to learn how to play the boatswain's pipe and his fair treatment of enlisted personnel also endeared him to the ship's company. As a lieutenant junior grade he observed one of the ship's officers, Lt. Clifford Janz, provoking enlisted men into doing things for which they could be disciplined. Chung-Hoon confronted Janz; their discussion became so heated that Chung-Hoon knocked the lieutenant down a ladder.

But Chung-Hoon never coddled his men; he is remembered for a direct, physical approach to maintaining order. One day, a seaman named Harold McCarty was chewing snuff while cleaning the deck. To prevent the wood from being stained, and contrary to Chung-Hoon's orders, McCarty spat the snuff into the waterway, a deck-edge gutter that was hosed down regularly. Chung-Hoon caught McCarty in the act and smacked him in the mouth. No one objected to Chung-Hoon's action; those under his command understood and accepted his approach to discipline.

He later commanded the destroyer USS *Sigsbee,* one of the ships that protected the transports of another Navy football hero, Adm. Lawrence Reifsnider, during the invasion of the Philippines. Later in the war, his ship was damaged so severely in a kamikaze attack that it was flooded to the main deck level. Chung-Hoon managed to keep it afloat so it could be towed to Guam for repair.

Navy's 1934 team became the first ever to defeat both Notre Dame and Army in the same season. Coached by Tom Hamilton, it is ranked as one of the finest in Naval Academy history. Its only loss that year to Pitt, late in the season, cost it the possibility of winning the national championship.

Slade Cutter's Musical Talent

When Slade Cutter's high school bandmaster wanted him to play the piccolo in the marching band, Cutter feared that the sight of the biggest person in the band playing the smallest instrument would make him a laughingstock. So he balked and was assigned instead the bass drum. But with the help of lessons from Arthur Kitt, first flautist with the Chicago Symphony orchestra, Cutter became such a good flautist that he won a national interscholastic flute title as a senior. He realized, however, that he didn't have the intricate sense of rhythm necessary to succeed in the world of professional symphonic music.

Chung-Hoon was the team's top rusher in 1932, but as the season progressed his stardom was eclipsed by Borries. Borries was a superb runner, passer, and kicker, and ranks with Barchet, Hamilton, 1960 Heisman Trophy winner Joe Bellino, Eddie Meyers, and Napoleon McCallum among Navy's greatest running backs.

Like Tom Hamilton, Fred Borries was a superb athlete. He earned nine varsity letters—three each in football, baseball, and basketball. (His basketball teams had a three-year record of 36–7, and he averaged 13.5 points per game when his teams were averaging forty-four; he was captain of the 1934 team.) During his three varsity football seasons, Borries scored eighteen touchdowns and kicked three extra points. "He was," Slade Cutter said, "the best running back I ever saw. He could change pace and speed; he could pass and kick; and he was probably the best pass defender we had as a safety, just about our whole pass defense by himself."

Borries was nicknamed "Buster" at the Academy. (The media gave him the "Buzz" handle because they thought its sibilant quality better suited his last name.) Though a warm, friendly person, Buzz had what Cutter called "a fighter pilot's temperament—he was aggressive and fearless, and he didn't seem to give a damn what happened to him. That's how he played football and how he flew his fighter plane."

Borries was famous for his courage. He had two carriers sunk under him during World War II—while serving as executive officer aboard the USS *Lexington* in the Battle of the Coral Sea; and while serving as air officer aboard the USS *Gambier Bay* in the Battle of the Philippines. In the latter operation, Borries managed to launch all of the ship's planes while the vessel was sinking and under heavy fire. Then, after leaving the ship, he took charge of two hundred men in life rafts for forty-eight hours until they were rescued.

Perhaps another indication of Borries's warm and caring personality was his decision to teach mathematics for five years at a preparatory school near his home in Florida after he had retired from the Navy in 1961.

Slade Cutter, who is best remembered for kicking the winning field goal against Army in an historic 3–0 victory in 1934, is one of the most remarkable athletes and officers in Navy history. Born and raised on a farm near Aurora, Illinois, the six-foot-two, 220-pound "boy" heeded his father's wishes and played the bass drum and the piccolo rather than football in high school and during one year at Elmhurst College.

But after enrolling at Severn School in 1930, Cutter met Paul Brown, a young, first-year assistant coach under Bill Hoover. It was the first coaching job for Brown, who had just graduated from Miami University in Oxford, Ohio. From those humble beginnings at Severn, he became one of the greatest coaches in football history. He led Ohio State to the 1942 national championship and founded and coached the Cleveland Browns and Cincinnati Bengals during his forty-five years in professional football. Brown was the right coach at the right time for Cutter, because his zeal for the game was boundless and infectious—particularly to someone like Cutter who was tiptoeing into the game for the first time and needed a coach he could admire intellectually and emotionally. Severn won the state title in 1930, and Cutter was named to the all-state team. He was

Buzz Borries

Running back Fred "Buzz" Borries was one of Navy's greatest players. After he died in 1969, one of his classmates wrote: "Who among us who were so fortunate to see him in action can ever forget the electrifying sight of Buster Borries under full sail? Certainly not one single opponent. In that flickering instant that it took him to get underway that deceptively awkward-appearing roll of a gait with which he walked was transformed into pure poetry in motion. . . . Bustling Buster [made] daylight with the elusiveness of a shadow, the grace of a gazelle and a power which only an opposing player whose unhappy chore it was to try to impede his progress could evaluate. . . ." The summation was perfect. Borries, who rose to the rank of captain, is a member of the College Football Hall of Fame.

one of several players on Navy's nationally ranked 1934 squad who had played under Brown during his two years at the prep school.

Cutter recalled:

> Paul Brown was just twenty-two years old, not much older than us, and he was tough. He taught us to go all out physically, and that made the transition to playing college football at the Academy much easier for all of us who had played for him at Severn. But he was always fair, always clean, he never took advantage of any of the rules. On weekends, he piled as many players as he could into an old Packard touring car and we scouted our opponents. I learned a lot of football from him, and how to motivate and work with people.

To take advantage of Cutter's speed, the plebe coaches used him as a fullback and linebacker in 1931; he also punted and place-kicked. Head injuries eventually cut down his playing time that season. When he joined the varsity in 1932, he played center behind Butch Harbold and linebacker on defense. In his junior and senior seasons, he replaced Killer Kane at tackle. Cutter gained All-America status as a senior; he later was inducted into the Hall of Fame. After seeing his son's feats at Severn, Slade's father agreed that he was well suited for football—but the only time he ever saw Slade play for Navy was in his final game, when he kicked that memorable field goal against Army.

Playing next to Cutter was end Robert "Dusty" Dornin, a big, tousled Californian whose playing had a ribald quality because he so enjoyed the physical confrontations of the game. Off the field, however, Dornin was meticulous and conscientious to the point that, while getting his uniform ready for formations, he would read a book—an indication of his determination to become the very best. "He was the same way as a sub skipper," Cutter said, "and he was one of the best."

Slade Cutter in Command

Slade Cutter not only starred in football but won a pair of letters in lacrosse and three as a boxer. Cutter had boxed at Severn School, and his pal Sam Loomis told Academy boxing coach Spike Webb that Cutter was better than anyone at the school. Early in their plebe year, Cutter and Loomis were walking together on the Academy grounds when they encountered Webb. With no warning, Webb slammed a left hook into Cutter's midsection.

"I didn't know him, I had never seen him before and I thought, 'What the hell's going on?'" Cutter later recalled.

When the 1932 U.S. Olympic boxing team was training at the Naval Academy, Webb used Cutter, then a plebe, as a sparring partner for Frank Crinkley, a former Navy heavyweight champion. Crinkley beat Cutter up so badly that he suffered a deviated septum. Three years later, Crinkley returned as a graduate student, and Cutter sought a rematch. By that time, Crinkley knew Slade's reputation—he was so tough, no one would spar with him—and he politely declined.

Cutter was unbeaten as a Navy boxer. In his senior year, he was offered $50,000 by Bill Brennan, a promoter in Philadelphia, to turn professional. Cutter's father stepped in and told him, "You owe it to the Navy to stay with them." Slade agreed, never with any regrets.

As commander of the submarine USS *Seahorse* in World War II, Cutter used his football experience to prepare his crew. "We were a team and that is how we worked," he said. "Our conditioning and drills were carried on to build teamwork, and we trained constantly en route to our patrol area. When we got there, I would tell the crew that from then on, all calls to battle stations would be the real thing, and they cheered, just as we did before we went out and played a football game at the Academy after a week's hard practice."

Cutter and Dornin achieved spectacular records as submarine executive officers early in the war. They excelled at deciphering torpedo data and had well-deserved reputations for being more successful in using the TDC control rather than the periscope in making an attack. Cutter served aboard the USS *Pompano,* where he won a pair of Silver Stars; Dornin made six patrols as executive officer of the USS *Gudgeon* and then commanded the USS *Trigger* on three more. When they commanded their own boats, they became a ferocious one-two punch in their wolf packs. Each sank a pair of enemy ships in his first attack as sub skipper and, at the end of the war, Cutter's nineteen confirmed sinkings—totaling 141,000 tons—tied him for second in the Pacific Submarine Force with Dudley Morton. He earned four Navy Crosses (Tom Hamilton recalled that he received three in one ceremony), two Silver Stars, a Bronze Star, and a Presidential Unit Citation.

During Dornin's nine patrols, his submarines sank ten enemy ships totaling more than 150,000 tons and damaged another 14,000 tons. He was awarded a pair of Navy Crosses, three Silver Stars, two Navy Commendation Medals, and two Presidential Unit Citations. On his final patrol, before becoming an aide to Fleet Adm. Ernest J. King, one of the victims of Dornin's boat was the submarine tender that was carrying the commanding officer of Japan's submarine forces.

The Navy football teams of the early thirties produced other submarine heroes, including end Hugh Rimmer and guard Dave Zabriskie, both of whom lost their lives in the war. Zabriskie commanded the USS *Herring*. Cutter saw him off on what turned out to be his final patrol; the *Herring* sank two ships before reportedly falling victim to a Japanese shore battery in the Kurile Islands. Rimmer commanded the USS *Albacore*. He won the Silver Star for successfully battling to save his ship from an onboard fire while submerged. The *Albacore* was sunk late in 1944.

One of the tackles in 1932 was Tom Chambers. In 1945, he commanded the minelayer USS *Lindsey* when it was hit by two kamikazes off Kuba Shima in the Western Islands group. The bow was blown off to the No. 1 gun, but Chambers skillfully guided the ship to safety.

Walter Baumberger and Bill Clark were perfect complements for the Chung-Hoon and Borries backfield combination in 1933; on the 1934 team, they helped pave the way for Borries's ride to All-America honors. Clark was one of the best punters in Navy history. He would tell his teammates precisely where his kicks would land so they could concentrate on covering that specific area. His booming punt that Dornin pushed out of bounds on Army's one-yard line in the 1934 Army-Navy game helped set up Cutter's winning field goal.

In the opening game of the 1933 season against Virginia, Baumberger's ninety-five-yard fourth-quarter interception return, during which he reversed his field at the fifty-yard line to avoid two tacklers, provided Navy with a 13–7 victory. Later, his twenty-four-yard pass to Borries set up Navy's only touchdown in a 7–0 victory over Notre Dame—Navy's first win ever against the Irish, and certainly that season's highlight. Perhaps the triumph was foreseen; Midshipman Sam Shaw remarked to fellow goat keeper Fred Pfotenhauer before the game, "We're bound to win. The goat smells terrible!"

Cutter and Dornin

Slade Cutter and Bob "Dusty" Dornin were close friends who had great respect for each other's feats, but who nonetheless never passed up a good-natured opportunity to make the other squirm. Those who didn't know them well mistook them for adversaries who were intensely jealous of each other's achievements, but this was never true. The misconception came about after their submarines were on the opposite sides of a target-rich Japanese convoy. After the resultant "turkey shoot," each claimed all the kills. It was just a continuation of the friendly game of one-upmanship they had engaged in since their days at the Naval Academy; the official count later sorted out the actual result of the attack.

While refitting at Pearl Harbor after a patrol, Cutter and Lou Parks of the USS *Pompano* went on a tear like those often depicted in the lighter moments of old war movies. They commandeered a Marine jeep, which had weapons stashed in the back, and raced through Honolulu firing at street lamps, water towers, and anything else in sight, all the while being chased by a Marine shore patrol. The chase ended when Cutter mistakenly turned the jeep into a brig area—where he and his passengers were immediately taken into custody.

When Dornin, who also happened to be at Pearl Harbor, heard about Cutter's incarceration, he called the duty officer and offered to bring bread and water to the jail. "If you come down here for any reason, we'll lock you up too," replied the exasperated commander, obviously fed up with the way some submariners relieved the tensions that built up during a war patrol.

On another occasion, when both of their subs were being rearmed at Pearl Harbor, Cutter decided to fete his crew with a luau. He knew a native who could procure a pig—pigs being very scarce at the time—as the centerpiece of the feast. When Dornin found out about the party, he suggested to his friend that his crew was no less worthy. Since there would be plenty to go around, both crews could celebrate together, Dornin suggested.

Cutter agreed and, twenty-four hours before the luau was to take place, the pig was appropriately buried in a bed of hot coals on a Honolulu beach. But the next night, after both crews had sloshed down enough beer to satisfy much of the entire Navy, the natural rivalry between boats began to manifest itself. About a half-hour before the feast was to begin, one of the sailors from Dornin's submarine made an inappropriate gesture to one of Cutter's officers, and one of Cutter's men forcefully stepped in. One push led to another shove, and soon, despite the efforts of the officers to keep peace, both crews were engaged in an all-out brawl, not unlike another kind of Hollywood movie scene. The shore patrol soon arrived with two wire-mesh-enclosed flatbed trucks, and each crew was loaded into a separate truck and hauled away to the brig.

"We never did get to eat that pig," Cutter said years later. "In fact, we never even saw it and I don't even know what happened to it. It probably is still buried on that beach."

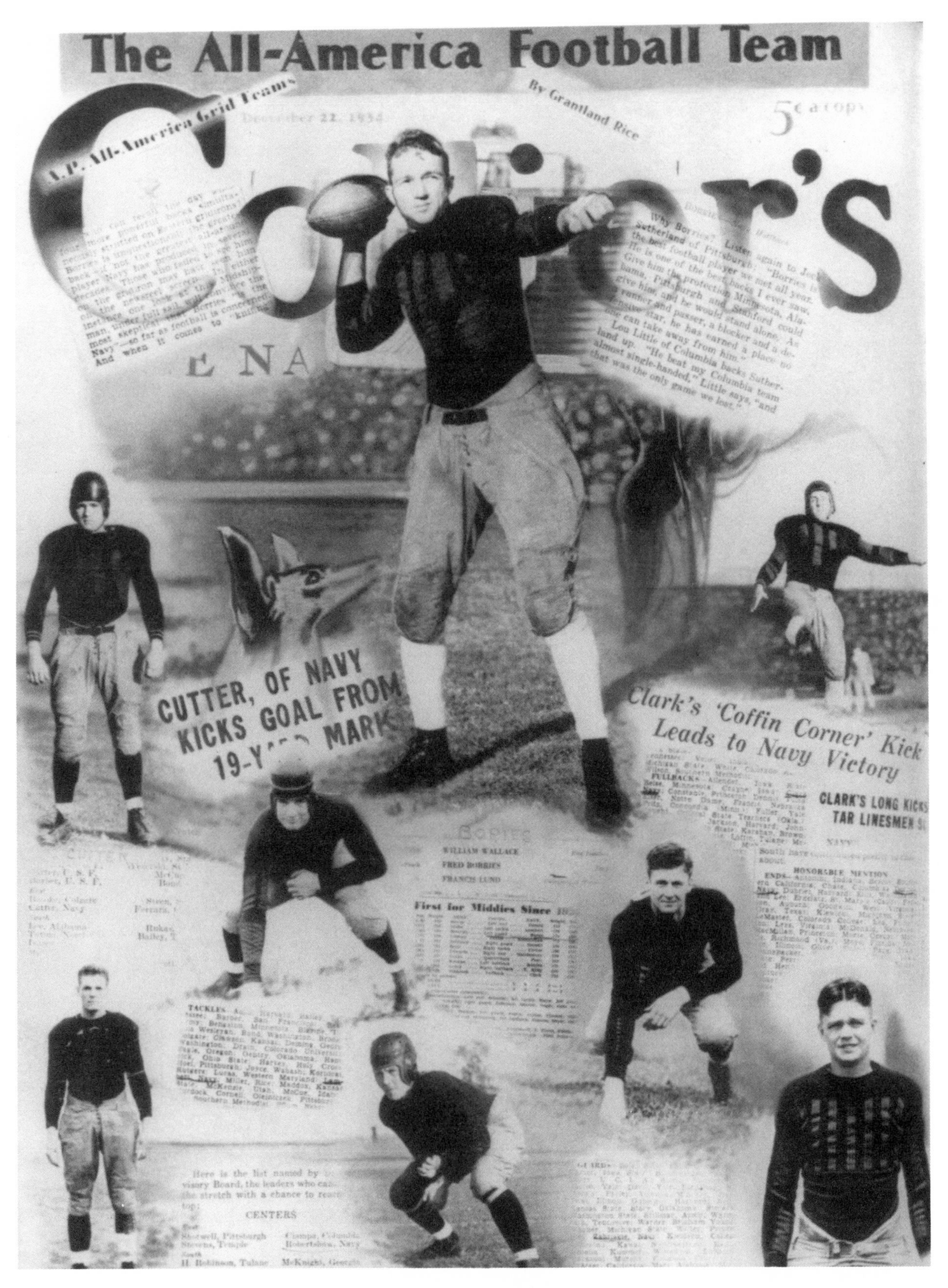

Navy's star-studded 1934 season with some of its stars *(clockwise from center)*: Buzz Borries (running back), Bill Clark (punter and back), Bob "Dusty" Dornin (back), Dick Burns (guard and captain), Lou Robertshaw (center), George Lambert (tackle), Rivers Morrell (guard), and Slade Cutter (tackle and kicker).

Dick Bull

Dick Bull, a tackle and end from 1932 through 1934, was, according to coach Tom Hamilton, "a real aviation nut."

"Once," Hamilton recalled, "when he was waiting for a punt to come down, he also noticed a plane flying overhead, so he took his eyes off the ball to watch the plane and got hit with the ball."

Bull became a fighter pilot. He was killed during the Battle of the Coral Sea.

Regardless, it was a most heroic victory for the Mids, who were no match offensively for the Irish. Their scoring drive traveled only twenty-three yards. It started inauspiciously when a five-yard penalty on first down cost them a completion to the two. But, aided by the Baumberger-to-Borries pass, the Mids fought back to the two. On third down, Clark, Baumberger, and Holman Lee cut down the Irish defense so well that Borries ran untouched into the end zone. Tackle Dick Bull kicked the extra point.

Navy's defense and punting, led by Clark and captain Hugh "Fid" Murray, also played a huge role in the win over Notre Dame. Murray had been embarrassed during an earlier 13–0 victory over Penn when he broke into the clear with a pass, yards ahead of any pursuers. He tripped and fell, ending a potential touchdown play. The *New Yorker* magazine wryly noted, "There were 65,000 people there, everybody on his feet but Murray. . . ."

Murray was a ferocious pass rusher, but in the game against Notre Dame, one of his biggest plays was calling a timeout he didn't have after Navy had stopped an eighty-four-yard Notre Dame drive less than a foot from the end zone in the final two minutes of the game. His team was exhausted and had to punt the ball safely out of danger, but it also needed a break. Murray knew that, because of the ball's placement, the penalty for calling an illegal time out would be measured in a couple of inches. The delay allowed Navy to catch its breath and Clark, who had played linebacker during the long drive, to gather his strength and boom a fifty-yard punt that he placed out of bounds for no return, helping to keep Notre Dame out of scoring position for good. Navy's victory, before 50,000 fans in Baltimore, staved off, for a few years at least, the ignominy of falling to a key rival in seven straight games. The Mids celebrated after the game by ripping up one set of goal posts and planting them in their team's shower room.

Navy–Notre Dame at Cleveland Stadium in 1934. The Mids won, 10–6, for one of only two times in which they recorded victories over the Irish in back-to-back seasons. (They had won in 1933, 7–0.)

Hamilton succeeded Miller as head coach in 1934 and inherited a mother lode of talent with Borries, Clark, Cutter, Dornin, and Bull. To that group were added youngsters Rivers Morrell, a guard; Lou Robertshaw, a center; and Sneed Schmidt, a running back. Lt. Tom Hamilton's three-year stint with Navy produced a 19–8 record.

Although he was only twenty-eight years old, Hamilton was well prepared for his coaching assignment. After graduating from the Academy in 1927, he had been an assistant for two seasons under Bill Ingram; he later coached the Pacific Fleet team. Hamilton was a very emotional coach, much like Ingram, who had patterned his style after Rockne. Hamilton diligently prepared his team early in the week and then, from Thursday until Saturday's kickoff, fanned its psychological fires.

"Tom Hamilton was the exception to the rule that career officers did not make good football coaches at the Naval Academy," said Slade Cutter, who was a senior on his 1934 team, "because he was a student of the game and a very bright and innovative guy. He scrapped Rip Miller's Notre Dame box offense, which we never should have used, and installed the single wing, whose nuances he thoroughly understood and was able to teach to us. He also was a wonderful leader and was responsible for turning around the program."

The Academy's athletic director—and Hamilton's boss—was another future war hero, Capt. John "Babe" Brown. Many players from the 1930s, including Cutter and Dornin, worked for Brown during World War II when he was deputy commander of submarine forces in the Pacific under Rear Adm. Charles A. Lockwood.

Although no one really knew what to expect from Navy in Hamilton's first year, his team roared to seven straight victories, including a 10–6 win against Notre Dame.

"Borries was the key to our success," Cutter said. "That year, he was the best back I ever saw. The team was a bunch of little guys because I was the biggest at 225 pounds, and the next biggest weighed just 185."

Hamilton brought his team along at a comfortable pace, overcoming early opponents with very conservative offensive schemes. When his team played against bigger foes, whose muscle his players couldn't match, he unveiled a dazzling display of passes and laterals whose success relied on speed, deception, and split-second timing.

The tone for the 1934 season was set in the first two games. Borries scored all the points in a 20–7 victory over William and Mary, and then Cutter's field goal salvaged a close 16–13 victory over Maryland. A week later, when Navy beat Columbia 16–13, the team attracted the attention of the preeminent sports columnist of the time, Grantland Rice, whose words about college football were taken as gospel. His unabashed praise put the Mids in the national limelight. He wrote that they incorporated "the smartest, fastest Navy attack this generation has looked upon . . . built on the modern plan—wide open and daring—executed for the greater part with amazing control in the art of handling the ball as it was flipped back and forth from Borries to Clark, or from Pratt to King." Borries gained nearly one hundred yards against Columbia. The following week, when Penn directed its defense specifically to stop Borries, Bill Clark had a field day in a 17–0 victory.

Navy hit its zenith in Cleveland two weeks later with the 10–6 victory over Notre Dame—the first of only two times Navy has defeated Notre Dame in back-to-back years. Navy scored first after Middie Dick Burns blocked Bill Shakespeare's punt, and Borries's pass to Dornin set up a Cutter field goal. In the last quarter, Clark's interception set up Borries's touchdown pass to Dornin for a 10–0 lead. The following week at home on Farragut Field, Navy, ranked second behind unbeaten Minnesota, played once-beaten Pitt, which was ranked No. 3. A shot at the national title was on the line. Pitt took the opening kickoff and marched eighty yards in sixteen plays for a 7–0 lead; the Panthers scored again on their second possession with a thundering display of coach Jock Sutherland's vaunted single-wing power. The Mids cut the lead to 14–7 on Borries's touchdown pass to Tom King, but the Panthers were clearly dominant. Hamilton removed the first team before halftime and allowed the second unit to play the rest of the game. Jim Baird, a member of that team, recalled later that Hamilton made that move because it was evident Navy couldn't beat Pitt that day and Hamilton so coveted a victory over Army in the next game that he wanted to avoid any injuries to his first unit. Pitt rolled to a 31–7 victory. But two weeks later, Navy got its win over Army, 3–0. (That Army-Navy game is covered in Chapter Nine.) Navy finished the season ranked third by the Associated Press, behind Minnesota and Pitt. That is Navy's second-highest ranking ever in a final wire service poll. (It finished second in 1963 in the AP's poll; the 1945 team also was ranked third.) Those polls have long been recognized as the "official" designator of college football champions in the absence of a playoff system.

Navy's victory over Army made the season even more special because it was the first since 1921 (they had tied in 1922 and 1926). Since the series had resumed in 1930, it had afforded Navy fans nothing but frustration. Navy lost the 1930 game 6–0. The teams repeated their charity game the following season, and Ray Stecker led Army to a 17–7 victory. Navy spoiled a magnificent defensive effort by committing seven turnovers; the Mids scored their only touchdown on Lou Kirn's forty-five-yard pass to Harvey Tschirgi. Quarterback Sam Moncure was knocked out of the game with a broken nose and concussion and spent the next day at a Navy hospital. When he returned to school, teammate Lynn Elliott told him, "I got even for you by breaking [Army tackle] Jack Price's nose."

"You got the wrong man," Moncure told him. "It was Ed Suarez, the other tackle."

The Army-Navy game was moved back to Philadelphia in 1932, and that city has been the site of the game ever since, with the exception of three years during World War II and a few forays to California and New Jersey. In 1932, before nearly 80,000 people at Franklin Field, Army coach Ralph Sasse, in a seemingly outlandish act of overconfidence, kept his team off the field until the kickoff—and then watched the Cadets win, 20–0. Years later, Peck Vidal, a player on that Army team, said that Sasse did it as a psychological ploy to upset Navy. But Sasse claimed, with some bitterness but perhaps with some merit, that Notre Dame had helped Navy

Sneed Schmidt, a 5'10", 170-pound dynamo as a running back, who in tandem with Bill Ingram II, formed a great backfield in 1935 and 1936. In 1936 Ingram kicked a field goal that gave the Mids a 3–0 victory over Notre Dame, and Schmidt scored Navy's only touchdown to beat Army, 7–0.

Fitted out in dark jerseys, Navy players score against Virginia at Annapolis in 1935. The Mids won, 26–7.

Rivers Morrell, a three-year letterman at guard and captain of Navy's 1936 team that beat both Notre Dame and Army. After leaving Annapolis he was a star on several Marine Corps teams, and during World War II and Korea, he became a much-decorated Marine Corps officer and rose to the rank of brigadier general.

coach Rip Miller prepare for the game. The Irish had beaten Army 21–0 two weeks earlier and, though Navy never seriously threatened Army, Sasse questioned how Navy seemed to know his offensive patterns so well.

Although Sasse lauded Navy's toughness, his team benefited from a half-dozen turnovers and was totally superior. Former Army coach John McEwan couldn't resist a dig at the eligibility controversy between the academies. "It was a triumph for higher education," McEwan said. "Navy will never have a team until they raise the age limit [for competition] and stop trying to play football with boys. This is a game for men."

But the gap narrowed the following year. In 1933, the Mids jumped to a 7–6 lead—the first time Navy had held a lead since the 1927 game—before a crowd of 78,000 at Franklin Field on a balmy Indian summer afternoon. Baumberger, who had replaced the injured Chung-Hoon, ran thirty-eight yards for the score in the first quarter after Army's Paul Johnson had returned a punt eighty-one yards for the first touchdown. Ironically, Navy's scouting report had noted that Johnson had fumbled several punts during the season, and coach Rip Miller told Clark, "Kick it very high, right at him." Jack Buckler's twenty-five-yard touchdown run in the second quarter gave Army a 12–7 victory.

The momentum of the 1934 victory over Army seemed to carry over into the next season as the Mids won their first three games. But then the loss of so many of 1934's stars began to show, and Navy lost the next three games. Navy snapped its losing streak with a 13–0 victory over Penn, helped by Sneed Schmidt's running and a sixty-six-yard interception return by Lou Robertshaw. The following week, in a 28–7 victory over Columbia, Schmidt had the biggest day of any Navy player that year when he gained 277 yards and scored three touchdowns, including one of ninety yards. That record lasted until 1979, when Eddie Meyers gained 278 yards against Army. But the 1935 season ended with a 28–6 defeat by Army. The Cadets led 28–0 at the half; it was the only time, Hamilton said, that one of his teams ever "froze." Hamilton never understood why his team lost four of its last six games.

Thirteen members of the 1935 team were killed in action in World War II: linemen Dick Bull (who died aboard the USS *Lexington* in the Battle of the Coral Sea), Bill Hulson, Duckett Miller, Walter Bayless, Jim Andrews, Dave Sloan, and Dave Zabriskie; and backs Bill Mason, Frank Case, Tom Edwards, Joe Evans, Charles Anderson, and Charles Reimann.

The brightest spot of the season was the emergence of sophomore Bill Ingram II, son of former star, coach, and athletic director Jonas Ingram. The fifth member of the Ingram family to star for Navy, he sparkled even more in 1936. Unfortunately, an injured hip cut him down as a senior. He was a triple-threat back who ran, passed, and kicked; his all-around athletic ability enabled him to play both center and guard on the basketball team; and he was an outfielder on the baseball team, which he captained in 1938. Ingram also became the first junior since 1923 to win Navy's Athletic Association Sword, which was given to the most outstanding athlete.

Ingram returned to the Naval Academy in 1946 and, along with ex-teammate Bush Bringle and future athletic director Asbury "Red" Coward, started the 150-pound football program. More than 450 candidates turned out for the inaugural team, which went undefeated. It even supplied a talent-starved varsity with three players for Navy's final game against Army.

Bringle, a tackle who Hamilton once said "was too tough mentally for his body and was always banging himself up," became a superb aviator. He made more than one thousand carrier landings and later commanded the USS *Kitty Hawk* from its commissioning to the Pacific theater. He subsequently became a four-star admiral and was commander of the Seventh Fleet during the Vietnam War. The other tackle on the 1936 team, Dick Ferrar, commanded a submarine that was involved in undercover operations in the Philippines; his exploits became the subject of a television drama. Team captain Rivers Morrell became a much-decorated Marine general.

Bill Ingram and Sneed Schmidt made a great tandem in coach Hamilton's final season in 1936. They helped Navy to a 6–3 season highlighted by victories over Notre Dame (3–0) and Army (7–0). Schmidt, who like Cutter had once preferred the piccolo to the football, was just five feet, nine inches and weighed 170 pounds. But he had a deceptive running gait that made him a better runner than passer as a tailback in Hamilton's offense. All agree that he would have been one of Navy's greatest stars had he not shared the limelight with Ingram.

Ingram showed his versatility when he drop-kicked a twenty-yard field goal in the third quarter to win the Notre Dame game. That victory was the third in four seasons over the Irish, and it took all of Hamilton's talents to pull it off. He

Navy stops an Army drive at its three-yard line in the first Army-Navy game played in Philadelphia's Municipal Stadium, in 1936. For all but three of the next forty-four seasons, when the game was moved during World War II, playing in the huge 103,000-capacity stadium became the national signature of this series. The last game played there was in 1979; the stadium has since been torn down.

Tiny Lynch

Frank "Tiny" Lynch's nickname was a playful misnomer. Tiny, a tackle, was six feet, two inches. He played center on the basketball team for three years and was also a record-setting shot-putter and discus-thrower. In 1937, Lynch became the first athlete in Academy history to win three "*N* Stars" in a single season when the Middies beat Army in football, basketball, and track. In 1938, he won the Thompson Trophy Cup, given to the midshipman who has done the most during the year for the promotion of athletics.

spent two evenings the week of the game showing his players films of previous games against the Irish, all the while stirring up their emotions. During halftime at the game, he revved up his team again and finished in his best Rockne-esque manner: "Remember, there are twelve of you out there—John Paul Jones is out there with you, the entire Navy is out there with you, they're watching you. Don't let them down!"

In the second half, as Notre Dame was threatening to score, Navy took a timeout and tackle Maurice Ferrera snapped, "Listen, don't let that umpire see that twelfth man or we may be in trouble."

Ingram recalled, "Notre Dame was an arrogant team when they played us, and they never believed we could beat them. They ran up and down the field between the twenty-yard lines, but we were tougher in front of our goal line."

Just as they had done in 1935, the Mids won their first three games in 1936. Then Navy lost to Yale 12–7 before 53,000 fans in Baltimore in a game marred by a controversy involving Yale end Larry Kelley, who won the Heisman Trophy that year. Navy led 7–6 in the third quarter on Ingram's ten-yard touchdown run. But Navy's Schmidt fumbled a punt at his twenty-yard line. Players from both teams scrambled after the ball. Kelley, while blocking Schmidt's attempt to fall on it, kicked it toward Navy's goal line and finally recovered it on the two-yard line. The officials ruled that Kelley's kick was inadvertent (had they ruled otherwise, Navy would have gotten possession), and Clint Frank, who would win the Heisman Trophy the following season, scored Yale's second touchdown. Frank also twice caught Ingram from behind to save touchdowns—once at Yale's twelve-yard line on a second-quarter punt return. Navy did not score after either play. Kelley, one of only two linemen to ever win the Heisman, did not catch a pass that day, but he was the game's outstanding defensive player.

The 1936 Army-Navy game moved to its most famous home—the 103,000-seat Municipal Stadium, next to Philadelphia's Navy Yard. (The stadium was later renamed Philadelphia Stadium, and then John F. Kennedy Stadium.) Over the course of the next forty-three years, until it was finally abandoned in 1980, that huge arena came to be closely linked with the game in the public's mind, particularly in the years when tens of millions watched some of that series' most memorable moments on television.

The first of those great moments occurred in that initial season. With two minutes and forty seconds to play, Schmidt broke a scoreless tie with a two-yard touchdown run that was set up by a pass interference call that nullified an Army interception. Just before that tackle-eligible Frank "Tiny" Lynch had made a spectacular one-handed catch of an Ingram pass at Army's twenty-one yard line.

In 1937, Hamilton was replaced as head coach by his old teammate Hank Hardwick. (Hamilton would return for a second coaching tenure in 1946 and 1947, when the Academy's football program was in chaos, and set the program on a course that would ultimately lead to its great successes in the fifties and early sixties.) Hardwick's stay was rocky almost from its start to its premature end just two years later. He never meshed with his players, many of whom he had coached as plebes, and he treated them as if they were veterans instead of

Vince Soballe

One of the ends on the 1937 team was Vince Soballe, who later commanded the destroyer USS *Haggard.* In an attack on a Japanese submarine, the *Haggard* forced it to surface, rammed it, and sank it. The only cost to the *Haggard* was a smashed bow. When Soballe and the *Haggard* returned to action, his ship survived a Kiksui attack at the waterline amidships; he brought it safely through that encounter.

William Thomas Ingram II, better known as "Navy Bill" Ingram II, carried on the traditions of the Ingram family at Navy by playing as a great running back in 1936 and 1937. In 1936 he teamed with Sneed Schmidt to give Navy a powerful one-two backfield punch. Ingram was a three-sport letterman, also starring in basketball and baseball. His father was Jonas Ingram, inducted into the College Football Hall of Fame after playing and coaching at Navy; his uncle was "Navy Bill" Ingram, a three-year star prior to World War I and later coach of Navy's national championship team in 1926.

young athletes trying to adapt themselves to college football. With the help of assistants Keith Molesworth and Rip Miller, Navy was unbeaten with three wins and a tie going into the 1937 game against Notre Dame. The Mids seemed to have a 7–0 victory in hand when Middie Alan McFarland, punting from his end zone, allowed a low snap to slip from his hands. He recovered the ball, but was tackled for a safety. Notre Dame then swept back down the field for the winning touchdown.

The Mids biggest win that season was a 14–7 triumph over Columbia and its All-America tailback Sid Luckman, who later was a Hall of Fame quarterback for the great Chicago Bears teams of the forties. Art Franks intercepted one of his passes and streaked sixty-five yards for the winning score. But the season ended on a sour note when Army's first-quarter touchdown stood up for a 6–0 victory as a driving rain helped to stymie Navy's good passing attack.

In 1938, Navy won its first three games and seemed to be headed for a great season. Emmett Wood provided a highlight with a ninety-four-yard kickoff return against Virginia. The Mids then hit a run of tough luck. Yale got a last-minute field goal to claim a 9–7 victory. In the next game, Princeton scored a last-minute touchdown to snatch a 13–13 tie. Wood had run sixty-four yards in two plays to give Navy an early 6–0 lead, and Cliff Lenz's five-yard TD run in the fourth quarter had put the Mids ahead 13–7. After being stung by the Yale and Princeton comebacks, Navy played a dull scoreless tie against Penn and was soundly beaten by Notre Dame, 15–0. The Mids' last bit of glory that season came in a 14–9 victory over Columbia and Luckman. The season ended in a 14–7 loss to Army. Navy rang up thirteen first downs and 125 passing yards in the first half while holding Army to just eight offensive plays and no first downs. But Army got a touchdown on Huey Long's punt return and twice stopped Navy drives inside Army's twenty-yard line. Lem Cooke finally scored to bring Navy even before halftime, but the Mids could not move the ball thereafter. In the second half, Navy had no first downs and minus eleven passing yards. Army's only offensive burst of the afternoon produced the winning score early in the third quarter.

There was little doubt that a stronger hand was needed as head coach. Standing by in the Yard to provide it was a tough, demanding Marine named Emery "Swede" Larson.

5. The Half-and-Half Forties 1939–1949

When Emery "Swede" Larson became head coach in 1939, he ushered in one of the greatest eras in Navy football history—a six-year period when Navy's football teams vied for national championships. The teams were of a caliber rarely seen before or since.

Most of those great seasons occurred during World War II, when no fewer than six future Hall of Fame players performed for the Mids under Larson and his successors, John Whelchel and Oscar Hagberg. From 1940 to 1945, Navy's record was 39–12–3. The Mids twice played Army for the national championship; won the Lambert Trophy as the East's best team in 1943; and were so richly stocked with players that there were two Navy teams during most of those seasons, either of which was capable of beating most teams in the nation. And had not it been for some questionable postwar transfer policies that stripped the teams of some great players, Navy could have continued as a national power for most of the rest of the decade.

Navy's fortunes had sagged after the midthirties regime of Tom Hamilton. When Larson took over, he needed a year to rejuvenate the Mids. By 1940, though, they had returned to the top echelon of collegiate football.

Larson was a whip-lean Marine captain, the first man from that service to coach a Naval Academy team. His booming voice could be heard at every spot on the practice field. His coaching credentials were impeccable and lengthy—he had coached Marine football teams for almost his entire career. Navy followers were especially excited to have Swede on board because he had never played in a losing game against Army, which was totally dominating Navy. The first thing Larson did after becoming head coach was to post a sign in McDonough Hall that read:

It Can, It Shall Be Done
Beat Army!

And Navy did just that: It won all three Army-Navy games during Larson's tenure, keeping his record in that competition unblemished.

Larson's discipline and hard work mirrored his belief in Marine training and helped produce a 13–3–2 record for his last two teams. During his first year

The Larson Way. When he became head coach, Swede Larson posted a sign in Navy's locker room that read: "It can, it shall be done. Beat Army." It obviously had a great impact on the field because he was 3–0 against Army while coaching Navy from 1939–41. It likewise influenced the team off the field as shown by this 1940 *Lucky Bag* photo.

The 1939 Navy coaching staff with new head coach Emery "Swede" Larson *(second from right)*. With him *(from left)* are: Rip Miller (line coach), Oscar Hagberg (ends coach), who after being one of the Navy's top submarine skippers during the early years of World War II, became head coach in 1944, and Keith Molesworth (backfield coach).

(1939), with few good players, his team had a 3–5–1 record—and the five losses were in heartbreaking succession. In a 28–0 loss to Princeton, the final game before Army, an untried back named Dick Shafer played well. "I'm the best halfback in this school," he told assistant coach Rip Miller. "But I never get a break. I think I can do a helluva job against Army. I think I really can go."

Larson agreed to give Shafer a chance and put him in the game in the third quarter with Navy leading 3–0. He carried on three of the next five plays, the last a twenty-two-yard touchdown run that ended with a headlong dive into the end zone to nail down the Mids' 10–0 victory.

In 1940 and 1941, Larson referred to his squad as his "two ocean" teams—a takeoff on the two-ocean navy strategic concept—because he had two units of almost equal strength during both of those seasons. He usually alternated them by quarters. The first unit, featuring Bill Busik and Alan Cameron, played until late in the first quarter; the second, led by Wes Gebert and Howard Clark, played into the second quarter.

Larson adeptly used his two units to create an interesting and hard-to-defend system that richly mixed power, passing, and a series of reverses and laterals. Unfortunately, Busik, Gebert, and Clark were three of more than a dozen players from those teams whose careers lasted just two seasons because the Naval Academy accelerated its academic schedule midway through 1941. The threat of World War II had rushed the nation into mobilization and, because the Navy desperately needed officers, every midshipman's education was compressed into three years.

At six one and weighing 190 pounds, Busik was nicknamed "Barnacle Bill" (this was a time when the star of every college team was given a catchy moniker). He was a fine athlete who had excelled in football and basketball at Pasadena City College (where one of his teammates was Jackie Robinson, then prepping for entry into UCLA), and who also competed in gymnastics and track and field. His football skills combined his great speed, power, and open-field running ability. He led Navy in rushing, passing, and punt returns during his two varsity seasons. Busik also was a superb punter: no Mid has topped his 40.6-yard career average, or his 43.8 season average in 1941.

Busik and Bob Zoeller were the touchdown twins of the 1939 plebe team. In 1940, teaming with Sherwood "Butch" Werner, John Harrell, and Cliff Lenz, Busik flashed a golden glimmer of his great talent in just one quarter of play in the season's opener against William and Mary—he gained sixty-five yards in ten carries, including a thirty-eight-yard run that set up Navy's first touchdown. Later, when Navy beat Princeton, 12–6, for the first time since 1931, Busik produced three big plays, including a touchdown pass to Zoeller. He engineered the two scoring drives in a 14–0 victory over Cornell.

Cameron and Busik went to prep school together in California and later were roommates at the Academy. Cameron, who played as a freshman at the University of California, shared the fullback's job at Navy early in the 1940 season with Butch Werner. Cameron added speed to the inside power running game—he had sixty-seven yards in a dozen carries in his first varsity game. He remained at fullback in 1941. But academic problems caused him to repeat a year; and when Busik, Gebert, and Clark graduated, he moved to the tailback spot and starred on the 1942 team. Cameron succeeded Busik as athletic director in 1965.

Wes Gebert and Howard Clark were almost carbon copies in their playing styles. The 145-pound Gebert, who was nicknamed "Scooter" because of his speed and elusiveness, was bigger than the five-foot, seven-inch Clark, a hard-nosed player who came to the Academy through the fleet. Gebert also was a fine passer. He threw a touchdown pass to Lars Wanggaard in his first varsity game against William and Mary, and had another against Yale.

After starting the 1940 season 5–0, Navy lost to Penn and Notre Dame and was tied by Columbia. The toughest loss was the 13–7 defeat at the hands of Notre Dame. The Mids controlled most of the game, thanks in part to Busik's great punting; once, when Navy was pinned on the one-yard line, he boomed

Navy went all-out against Notre Dame when the two teams met in Cleveland in 1939, but the Mids came up short in a 14–7 loss. Navy's only score was a fourth-quarter thirty-four-yard touchdown pass by Bob Leonard.

Swede Larson

Swede Larson's leadership as Navy coach (1939–41) was unquestioned. He was demanding of his players and an outgoing man. "A personality-plus type," one former player noted, "[who got] the most out of the players with the positive way in which he approached them. He never pretended to know all the answers, but he was a great leader who knew the game and knew how to make us a winner."

Sometimes he went to extraordinary lengths. Before an opening game against William and Mary in Annapolis, Larson sensed that his players were tense and preoccupied, suffering from the usual nerves that accompany the first game of the season and also concerned about the exams they had taken that week. Larson found the gaudiest vest extant—a dizzying scotch plaid that screamed for attention—and wore it beneath his jacket to a pregame team meeting. When he removed the jacket, his team convulsed in laughter. "Those kids laughed for ten minutes without stopping," he said later. "That little stunt relaxed tension and I knew they would be mentally into the game." They were. Navy won easily.

Joe Hunt

One of the most versatile players on the 1940 team was Joe Hunt, a halfback. In the spring of 1941, he brought Navy the NCAA tennis singles championship; two years later, he took time off from his Navy duties to capture the U.S. singles championship at Forest Hills, New York, in a grueling, four-set victory over Jack Kramer. He still is the only tennis player ever to have won the national boys, juniors, collegiate, and U.S. men's single titles.

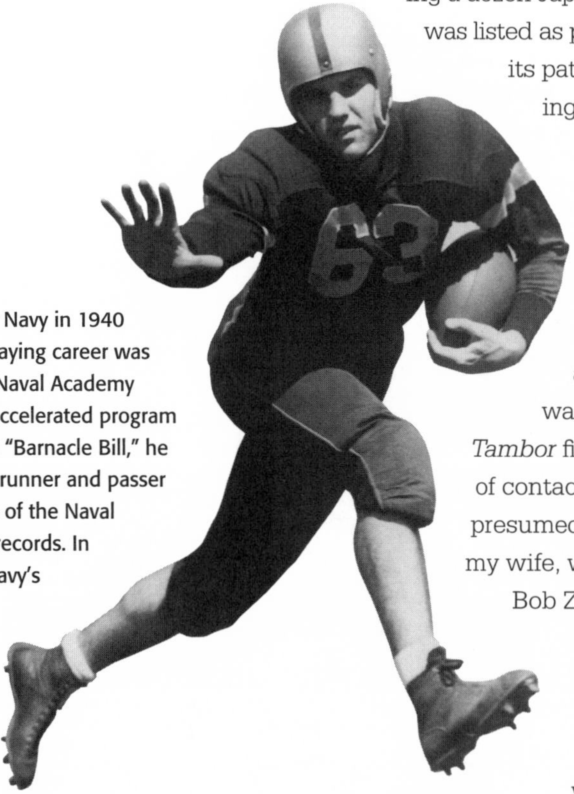

a sixty-five yarder to get them out of trouble. Navy had a decided edge in the statistics but couldn't cash in despite four scoring threats. Finally, Wes Gebert, unable to find an open receiver, dodged and twisted for a forty-three-yard touchdown run and a 7–6 lead. Navy protected its lead until there were five minutes to play. Then, the Irish's Bob Saggau, on fourth down from the six-yard line, swept right end for the winning touchdown.

The golden anniversary of the first Army-Navy game was celebrated a few weeks later, and five members of Navy's 1890 team watched the Mids beat the Cadets 14–0. The victory was fashioned on a first-quarter touchdown run by Busik and Clark's fourth-quarter touchdown pass to Everett Malcolm. Navy's defense held the Cadets to less than one hundred yards.

The 1941 team, talent-rich in every position, was ranked tenth in the nation. It didn't allow a touchdown in six games. Tackle Bill Chewning just missed making the All-America team; the other tackle, Gene Flathmann, was the team's biggest player (six feet four, 240 pounds) and also one of its fastest and most athletic. He also had experience, having played a year at Clemson. Often, while leading a runner downfield, Flathmann would yell, "Just stay behind me, I'll get 'em [tacklers]." He also was the jitterbug champion of the Academy—a good indication of his agility and nimble feet. Flathmann later played with the Washington Redskins.

Vito Vitucci, a compact five-nine, 200-pound All-East guard, was very quick. When he led Navy's backs through a hole, they put their free hands on his back while he bowled over defenders. Vitucci also did some of the placekicking.

During World War II, Vitucci served with distinction aboard two submarines—the USS *Catfish* and the USS *Tambor,* which was credited with sinking a dozen Japanese ships. He was aboard the *Tambor* when it was listed as presumed lost after it failed to report during one of its patrols. Unknown to ComSubPac, the sub, after attacking two enemy ships, had been subjected to an eleven-hour-long depth-charge attack and lost its communications antennae. It took the crew a week of repair work at sea before the boat could receive intelligence reports, but the *Tambor* still maintained radio silence. Since they still had unspent torpedoes, the crew resumed the patrol and sank another enemy skip before heading home. No one was more surprised than ComSubPac when the *Tambor* finally reported. Vitucci noted, "We had been out of contact for so long, we were declared 'overdue and presumed lost,' and you can imagine the effect that had on my wife, who was then six months pregnant."

Bob Zoeller served aboard the cruiser USS *Santa Fe,* which helped to clear Japanese forces from the Aleutians and then was part of the fast carrier task forces of the Third and Fifth Fleets.

The different designations depended on who was in command. Adm. William Halsey led the

Bill Busik starred for Navy in 1940 and 1941, but his playing career was cut short when the Naval Academy went to a wartime accelerated program in 1942. Nicknamed "Barnacle Bill," he was an outstanding runner and passer and still holds some of the Naval Academy's punting records. In the sixties he was Navy's athletic director and later was executive director of the Naval Academy Alumni Association.

Barnacle Bill in action. Busik pounds through Cornell in 1941, helped by the blocking of John Harrell, Bill Chewning, Al Cameron, and Vito Vitucci. Busik was Navy's leading rusher, passer, punt returner, and punter in both of his varsity seasons, and his career (40.6) and 1941 season (43.8) marks are still No. 1 in Navy history.

Third; Rear Adm. Raymond Spruance led the Fifth. The *Santa Fe* fought in the Battle of Okinawa and helped to rescue approximately 600 sailors from the carrier USS *Franklin* after it was nearly sunk by kamikaze attacks.

Three months after he graduated in June of 1942, Busik was aboard the newly refitted destroyer USS *Shaw,* which had lost its bow in the attack on Pearl Harbor. Its first assignment was to join a screening force in the Battle of Santa Cruz. On one side of Busik's ship, the carrier USS *Hornet* was bombed and sunk by the Japanese; on the other side, the destroyer USS *Hewitt* suffered the same fate. The *Shaw* picked up the survivors of both ships.

During the 1941 season, the only team to score more than one touchdown against Navy was Notre Dame, and the Irish won, 20–13. That was the Mids' only loss in nine games (they also played a scoreless tie against Harvard). Coach Larson called the Notre Dame game "the best played and most thrilling" of any he coached. Among the crowd in attendance in Baltimore was the actor Pat O'Brien, who had just finished filming *Knute Rockne, All-American,* in which he played the Irish coach. O'Brien sat and signed autographs in the Notre Dame rooting section, but he wore both Notre Dame and Navy buttons on his coat.

Navy beat Notre Dame in the battle of statistics and came up just six yards short of getting a tie late in the game. Howard Clark "stole the show," said Larson. His forty-yard pass to Zoeller set up his touchdown that tied the score 7–7, and Cameron returned an interception thirty-six yards for the second touchdown and a 13–13 tie in the fourth quarter. After Notre Dame scored again, Clark engineered the drive that fell short at the Irish six-yard line.

In mid-November, Navy turned down an invitation to play in the Cotton Bowl. Both Rear Adm. Russell Wilson, the superintendent, and Vice Adm.

John Whelchel

One of John "Billick" Whelchel's players on his 1926 plebe team was his brother, David. During a scrimmage, Dave went down and lay on the ground, holding his leg.

"Get up!" yelled Billick.

"Damn, Billick, I don't think I can. I think my leg is broken," his brother replied as he writhed in agony.

"Well then, just roll on off the field," Billick replied. "You're holding up the game."

Chester W. Nimitz, then chief of the Bureau of Navigation, which oversaw the Academy, noted that the accelerated program would graduate some of the team nearly two weeks before the game and "that the services of the graduates are needed at sea as early as they can be gotten there after a short leave." The rest of the team couldn't spare the class time, the admirals added.

After Navy upset Army 14–6, Larson finished his coaching tenure. With great prescience, he announced, "This will be the last game for me for quite a while. There's a bigger game coming up, and I am going to be in it."

He was correct. Eight days later, the Japanese attacked Pearl Harbor and the United States was plunged into World War II. Larson took part in the bloody battles at Tarawa and Kwajalein. He died of a heart attack in 1945 while serving as chief of the Marine Corps special services branch.

When John "Billick" Whelchel succeeded Larson in 1942, he inherited a football program that was poised for some great seasons. In 1942 and 1943, Navy not only compiled a 13–5 record, it was good enough to beat Army, which was touted as the best team in the East, in both seasons. The Mids also won the Lambert Trophy in 1943 as champions of the East.

Before becoming head coach, Whelchel, a commander, was executive officer of the Department of Ordnance and Gunnery and an assistant coach on Larson's staff. He also had a rich football background, beginning as a running back on teams coached by Jonas Ingram and Gil Dobie in 1916, 1917, and 1918. He was an assistant coach under Dobie and Bob Folwell for six seasons, and then head coach of the plebes during Bill Ingram's tenure. After that, while on active duty assignments, he coached fleet teams for eleven seasons before returning to the Naval Academy.

Whelchel was a practical man whose favorite play was an off-tackle run. One of his players, Dick Duden, called him "a tough, old Navy man, who let his team believe that 'We're the Navy, we can beat anyone, so get out of our way!'" Another characterized his style as, "Hit 'em and sock 'em," and said that his motto was, "Let's just do it!" Whelchel was a firm, demanding, insistent, and inspirational leader. He was known widely for talking down his team,

Head coach John "Billick" Whelchel *(fourth from left)* and his 1942 coaching staff. Whelchel coached Navy in 1942 and 1943, and his teams had winning seasons both years. Navy won its first Lambert Trophy as the best team in the East in 1943. Other coaches include *(from left)*: Paul Woerner, Ray Swartz, Rip Miller, Keith Molesworth, Tom Scaffe, and Pop Foster.

regardless of who it was going to play. "We could be playing the worst team in the country, and John made it sound like we would be lucky to survive the kickoff," noted Capt. Hugh Murray, who was the graduate manager of athletics at the Academy in 1942. Before the Army-Navy game that year, which President Franklin D. Roosevelt ordered played at the Naval Academy (the game is covered in Chapter Nine), Whelchel gathered his team and began citing Army's strengths in contrast to Navy's weaknesses. He finished by saying, "And God help us if it rains—we'll lose [Navy back Hal] Hamberg in the mud!"

Hal Hamberg loses the ball during Navy's 14–13 victory over Duke in 1943.

It didn't rain, Hamberg played a great game, and Navy won, upsetting Army 14–0. After the game, Coach Whelchel walked through the locker room where his players were whooping it up. He didn't say a word. "Aren't you going to talk to the guys about what a great job they did?" line coach Rip Miller asked him.

"What for?" Whelchel nonchalantly replied, without even a hint of the concerns he had expressed just a few hours earlier. "They did what they were supposed to do."

The 1942 team lost four of its first six games, primarily because the accelerated program had graduated fifteen players who still had a season's eligibility remaining. Even with fine backs such as Hillis Hume, Cameron, and Hamberg, the Mids struggled because Fred Schnurr was the only returning starting lineman. In time, though, Whelchel developed young players such as Ben Chase, Jack Martin, Al Channell, and George Brown. (Brown was later inducted into the College Football Hall of Fame.)

One of the 1942 victories was 13–6 against Yale before 30,000 in Baltimore. Cameron ran back the opening kickoff of the second half for a touchdown. Except for the Mids' 14–0 win over Army, their biggest victory was a 7–0 upset of unbeaten Penn in Philadelphia. The Regiment of Midshipmen went to the game by boat, but had not arrived at the scheduled kickoff. Nevertheless, the game began on schedule. When they finally showed up, the game was stopped, and the Mids marched on and took their seats. A few minutes after the game resumed, Hamberg passed to Ben Martin for the afternoon's only touchdown.

Hal Hamberg was a special player. Though the native of Lonoke, Arkansas, had played at the University of Arkansas before getting an appointment to the Naval Academy, his Navy football started at the battalion level. Hal was such a talent that his coach, James Bland, a mathematics professor, pressured Whelchel into giving him a tryout. Whelchel was impressed and assigned him to the "B" squad; when Hamberg proved he could pass as well as he could run, he was elevated to the varsity.

Nicknamed the "Lonoke Lancer," Hamberg, who never weighed more than 155 pounds, led Navy in passing in 1942 and 1943 and was Navy's best back in 1943 and for most of 1944. He led his teams in punt returns during three varsity seasons, and still ranks first all-time among Navy's punt returners with a 13.23 average. Above all, he was a great clutch player.

The Mids Play the Chicago Bears

John Whelchel's assistant coach, Keith Molesworth, had once played for the Chicago Bears. He arranged for a 1942 preseason controlled scrimmage in Thompson Stadium between the Mids and his former team, which was preparing for a preseason game against the Washington Redskins. The Bears were the defending NFL champions. It was a unique pairing because, except for an annual game between an all-star team of just-graduated collegians and the reigning NFL champs, the colleges and pros stayed apart at that time.

Everyone who played in the scrimmage vividly remembers the experience, played before eight thousand spectators. At one point, Bears Hall of Fame tackle Joe Stydahar overcame a double-team block by Charley Guy and Bill Barron by picking up Barron and tossing him into running back Hillis Hume to stop the play.

Don Whitmire, a two-way player at tackle in 1943 and 1944, is considered the greatest lineman in Navy football history. Inducted into the College Football Hall of Fame, he came to Annapolis after starring for two seasons at the University of Alabama. During his celebrated naval career he rose to the rank of rear admiral and, in 1975, commanded the evacuation of Saigon by elements of the Seventh Fleet.

In a 1943 game against Georgia Tech, for example, the Yellow Jackets had just tied Navy 14–14 when Hamberg returned the ensuing kickoff seventy-eight yards and then threw a touchdown pass to Dick Duden. Hamberg nailed down the victory when, on third-and-nineteen, with a tackler starting to pull him down, he threw a nineteen-yard touchdown pass to Al Channell. Two weeks later, Navy trailed Penn 7–6 at the start of the second half. Hamberg stunned a huge crowd of 71,000 at Franklin Field by returning a punt forty-eight yards for a touchdown that spurred the Mids to a 24–7 victory.

Hamberg continued his clutch play in 1944 when, late in a scoreless game against Duke, he put the Blue Devils in a hole by punting to their one-yard line. Navy got the ball back at its forty-two-yard line. Shortly afterward, facing a second-and-twenty-eight situation, Hamberg threw a perfect pass to Charley Guy for the game's only touchdown.

With World War II raging, most college athletes, like others in their age group, had two choices: Be drafted or join the various officer training programs at civilian schools all over the country. In the latter, they could play football until their officers' training was ended—usually one season, or just a part of one season. Then they went on active duty. Annapolis and West Point offered a third route: an appointment where the student-athletes could spend three years in the accelerated curriculum then in effect for all midshipmen and cadets, plus the opportunity to play football for the entire time. Then they were commissioned as officers and went on active duty. This helped Navy attract some of the greatest players in its history and, for three seasons, beginning in 1943, contend for the national championship.

In 1943, Navy got Alabama tackle Don Whitmire; running back Bobby Tom Jenkins, who had starred in the Crimson Tide's victory over Boston College in the Orange Bowl; guard John "Bo" Coppedge, who had spent two years at Virginia Military Institute; speedster Jim Pettit from Stanford; running back Bill Barron from Vanderbilt; and tackle Ed Sprinkle, who had played for one season at Hardin-Simmons and who came from the fleet.

Those players were joined in 1944 by kicker Fred Earley and guard Jim Carrington, both of whom came from Notre Dame, where they had played against the Mids. In 1945, the team was augmented by two All-America backs who had starred against Navy in 1944—Bob Kelly from Notre Dame (Kelly's appointment to the Naval Academy had already been confirmed when he played against Navy) and Tony "Skippy" Minisi of Penn. Both men stood out even on star-studded Navy teams. So did All-America running back Bob "Hunchy" Hoernschmeyer from Indiana.

Ben Martin was one of Navy's top ends for three seasons and later became a very successful head coach at Virginia and the U.S. Air Force Academy.

The 1943 team won eight of its nine games; its only loss was to eventual national champion Notre Dame. It was the most powerful team in Navy history, beating opponents by an average score of 33–9, and it was rarely pressed in any game.

The hallmark of that team—and the two that followed in 1944 and 1945—was its group of huge linemen who manhandled opponents on both sides of the ball better than any group in college football at that time. In 1943, the line included 1942 carryovers George Brown and Ben Chase at guards and newcomers Whitmire and Sprinkle at tackles. Jack Martin, who later played for the Los Angeles Rams, was at center; Leon Bramlett, Roe Johnston, Ben Martin, and captain Al Channell were the ends.

In 1944, Bramlett, Ben Martin, and John Hansen were the ends; Whitmire and Gail Gilliam the tackles; and Carrington and Chase the guards. Jack Martin returned at center. The following year, Navy switched to the "T" formation; joining Bramlett at end was former blocking back Dick Duden, a splendid pass catcher. Charles Kiser and Coppedge were the tackles, and Ed Deramee played right guard. Jim Carrington and Stansfield Turner split time at left guard. Dick Scott replaced Jack Martin and became Navy's greatest center.

Stan Turner was a dogged player on the field. In the classroom, he was a star. (He ultimately won a Rhodes Scholarship to Oxford University in England.) Turner rose through a variety of high-level positions, including the presidency of the Naval War College in 1972 and command of the Second Fleet and NATO's forces in southern Europe, before being appointed director of the Central Intelligence Agency in 1977 by his Naval Academy classmate, President Jimmy Carter.

It was common for teams using the single wing to have at least one fast, smallish guard who could pull out and lead plays. But all of Navy's guards in 1944 were big. Ben Chase, a three-year starter who also was the team's captain, had been an all-state high school fullback in California. At six feet three and 230 pounds, he didn't have the speed to compete with the other Navy backs, but he had the size, strength, and toughness to be an outstanding two-way lineman. Chase was also tough enough to win a letter in boxing. He won the Academy's heavyweight title one year, but Bramlett knocked him out in another title clash.

Jack Martin, the center, started his football career at Princeton along with his cousin, end Ben Martin. Jack was the biggest player on the Mids' line and

George Brown

Six-three, 195-pound George Brown started his Navy career as an outstanding end on the 1941 plebe team. His speed and athletic ability allowed him to fill a big hole at guard, where he was a starter in 1942 and 1943. The Associated Press placed him on its 1943 All-America team. Brown also was the NCAA's shot put champion in 1943 and received the Naval Academy Athletic Association Sword when he graduated.

During World War II, Brown served aboard the USS *Indianapolis,* and in the submarine service. In 1947, at the age of twenty-four and with one year of college eligibility remaining (he had graduated in the accelerated Class of 1945 and forfeited his final year of eligibility at the Academy), he played guard and linebacker for San Diego State. He was named honorary captain and most valuable player by his San Diego State teammates and made the Little All-America team chosen by United Press. Former Navy teammates Bo Coppedge and Don Whitmire coached a fleet team in San Diego at this time and often arranged scrimmages with Brown's Aztec team. Brown later earned a medical degree from Johns Hopkins University.

Bobby Jenkins rips off a sixteen-yard gain in the 1944 season opener against North Carolina Pre-Flight. Jenkins, who had starred at Alabama along with tackle Don Whitmire before both transferred to Navy, led the team in rushing and was named to the 1944 All-America team.

Ed Sprinkle

Lineman Ed Sprinkle, who later was a fierce player for the Chicago Bears for ten years, was awed by no one at the Naval Academy, where he played in 1943.

At dinner one evening, fellow linemen Don Whitmire and Bo Coppedge refused to pass some food to Sprinkle's end of the table. Coppedge recalls that Sprinkle stood up, looked at Whitmire—who was bull-strong at five eleven and 215 pounds and was the best tackle in college football—and growled, "Hey, fatty, I wouldn't do that."

Sprinkle got his food and a lifelong friendship with both men.

the most popular because of his leadership, sense of humor, and down-to-earth manner. Although he was not as intense a player as Whitmire (no one was), many considered Jack Martin the best offensive center in college football in 1943 and 1944. Martin later played center for the Los Angeles Rams. He also backed up the line on defense while at Navy.

Ed Sprinkle, who was six feet and weighed two hundred pounds, was a hard-nosed, raw-boned Texan whose animated playing style inspired his teammates. Bramlett, who played next to him in 1943, said Sprinkle didn't look that tough until the game started; then he was like a dervish. Nicknamed "The Snake" because he was so quick, Sprinkle seemed to take more delight in throwing himself headlong at interference wedges and battering through them to make the tackle than in slipping a block and making a clean tackle.

Sprinkle would have been an All-America player had he stayed at the Naval Academy. But he played only in 1943 because he could handle neither the academics nor the discipline. In 1944, on the recommendation of Mids assistant coach Keith Molesworth, who had once played for the Chicago Bears, Sprinkle was signed by that team. At the time, the Bears, like all NFL teams, were scrambling to cope with dwindling player resources because of the war, so they slipped the twenty-year-old Sprinkle onto their roster without ever drafting him. He had a great ten-season career with the Bears and forged a reputation for being such a terror that each opponent had an "enforcer" to deal with him.

Don Whitmire was the crown jewel of all the linemen who played for Navy between 1943 and 1945. He was a great tackle for two seasons at Alabama, in 1941 and 1942, and is a member of the Crimson Tide's all-time team. In 1941, he made the Southeastern Conference's all-sophomore team, and his performance in Alabama's 29–21 victory over Texas A&M in the Cotton Bowl earned him a spot on the all-time Cotton Bowl team. In 1942, he was an All-America, and he had two more All-America seasons at tackle for Navy in 1943 and 1944. (He benefited from wartime eligibility rules that allowed players four years of varsity competition, enabling him to play for two seasons at Annapolis, instead of just one.) Whitmire, who later made admiral and commanded the Seventh Fleet during the Vietnam War, is a member of the College Football Hall of Fame. So is his teammate George Brown, who played next to him as a guard in 1943 and 1944.

Though he played tackle, physically Whitmire was a hybrid guard/tackle. At five feet, eleven inches, he was the standard height for a guard, but his 215 pounds was considered huge for a tackle at that time.

Whitmire attended the Naval Academy almost by accident. He had joined the Marines in the winter of 1943 and was at Parris Island when Bobby Tom Jenkins, his Alabama roommate, secured an appointment to the Naval Academy from the Army Air Corps. The next summer, just before school at Annapolis was about to begin, and long after Navy had begun its preseason training, coach Whelchel summoned Jenkins and Bramlett, who had spent his freshman year at Alabama, and asked them whether they knew of any good linemen interested in coming to the Naval Academy.

"We need one badly," Whelchel told them.

"Yes, sir, my roommate at Alabama, Don Whitmire," Jenkins replied. "He's at the University of North Carolina in the V-12 program." Neither Jenkins nor Whelchel knew that Whitmire was scheduled to be North Carolina's starting left tackle that season, where he was to play alongside end Barney Poole, who later had a brilliant career at Army.

Whelchel asked Jenkins to sound Whitmire out and said that if Whitmire was interested, he could have an appointment. Jenkins called Whitmire and relayed Whelchel's message. But he knew that Whitmire hadn't been much of a student at Alabama, so he warned him, "Whit, you gotta study in this place. You're pretty much confined to the grounds and there's a lot of discipline. Do you think you could take all of that?"

Clyde "Smackover" Scott, another College Football Hall of Famer, slams for three yards against Georgia Tech. Scott, a world-class sprinter and a silver medalist in the 1948 Olympics, starred for two seasons for the Mids. He got his apt "Smackover" moniker from his hometown in Arkansas.

Don Whitmire

Tackle Don Whitmire wasn't a starter in his first game at the Naval Academy in 1943 because he arrived too late to assimilate much of the offense. Nonetheless, as he prowled the sidelines, he badgered line coach Rip Miller to put him in the game.

Tired of listening to Whitmire, Miller told him, "Go play defense." Whitmire tore up the opposition. In the second half, he went back into the game on offense. One of the few plays he knew well was a trap—"45 cross check." It came up, and Whitmire buried the defensive tackle. Back in the huddle, he told quarterback Dick Duden, "Run that play again." Duden did, again with the same results. The Mids then ran the play a third time at Whitmire's request.

Finally, Duden went to the sidelines and said to Whelchel, "Coach, get that guy out of there. He's driving me crazy. I can't run the same play all day."

Whitmire received the Knute Rockne Memorial Trophy as college football's best lineman in 1944. Yet, he said that his proudest achievement as a player was that, in the two Army-Navy games in which he played, the Cadets never scored while he was in the game. In the 1944 game, Whitmire suffered a leg injury on the kickoff. He tried to continue, but finally had to hobble off early in the second quarter. Only then did Army score. (The Cadets won the game—and the national championship that was being decided that day.)

But Whitmire, who became a rear admiral and commanded the evacuation of 82,000 personnel from Saigon in 1975, was much more than a football player. He admitted that he had "majored in football" at Alabama before entering the Academy, and he struggled at first with the tough academic regimen. But he was determined to finish and receive his commission. Although his football eligibility expired after 1944 and Brooklyn's All-America Football Conference club tried to entice him to turn pro, Whitmire stayed at the Academy to graduate with the Class of 1947. In his senior year he was brigade commander, the highest-ranking position for a midshipman.

Whitmire's crowning football achievement came in 1956, when he was inducted into the College Football Hall of Fame.

A week passed with no word from Whitmire, so Jenkins figured that he wasn't coming. Then, as he and Bramlett were walking out of Bancroft Hall, a huge, khaki-clad figure headed toward them across the parade field. "That's Whitmire," Jenkins told Bramlett.

They headed for Whelchel's office. The Navy coach said, "I hear you're a pretty good Southeast Conference tackle."

"Yes, sir, I'm pretty good," Whitmire replied.

"What do you do that makes you so good?" Whelchel asked.

With that, Whitmire got down into a three-point stance, looked up at Whelchel and said, "When the ball is snapped, I look across that line at the guy in front of me, and then I knock his goddamn head off."

Whitmire's intensity never slackened. Even in practice he played just as hard against his own teammates as he did against opponents. He was always a clean player, but he was never content to just block his man—he tried to bury him. These were the days of two-way players, and Whitmire found defense even more exhilarating than offense because he loved the less restricted play of the defensive linemen.

The backfield during 1943 had great depth with Hume, Cameron, Jenkins, Barron, Hamberg, Ben Martin, Dick Maxson, Bruce Smith, Jim Pettit, and a young blocking back named Dick Duden who had prepped at Andover Academy in Massachusetts with future President George Bush. As president, Bush often visited with his old schoolmate when he attended Naval Academy functions at Annapolis.

Bobby Tom Jenkins was a fine tailback in 1943 and 1944 because he could run and throw with equal ability. At five ten and weighing two hundred pounds, he was a more powerful runner than Hamberg and could better withstand the tailback's workload. Hamberg, though, was a better passer, so Navy's offense relied on both players. Like Hamberg, Jenkins was an intense competitor. He played best when he was used as a single-wing tailback, where his speed and power were better suited to the formation's power blocking. He and Clyde Scott became one of the nation's best backfield tandems in 1944

Navy's 1945 coaching staff *(from left)* featured: Chuck Purvis, Ray Swartz, Oscar Hagberg (head coach), Rip Miller, Keith Molesworth, and Eddie Erdelatz.

The heart of Navy's 1945 team that turned in a fine 7–1–1 record and just missed winning the national championship *(front row, from left)* were: John "Bo" Coppedge, Jim Carrington, Dick Scott, and Bob Kelly; *(middle row)* Clyde Scott, Oscar Hagberg (head coach), Dick Duden (captain), and Bob Hoernschmeyer; and *(back row)* Bill Barron, Jim Pettit, George Sundheim, Chuck Kiser, Leon Bramlett, and Ed Deramee.

Vic Finos

Vic Finos was a very reliable kicker for Navy during his two varsity seasons. He won the job during a 35–0 victory over Virginia in 1942 when he kicked all five extra points after replacing Charley Hampton, who had a charley horse. When Navy defeated Penn State 55–14 in 1944, Finos kicked six extra points; later that season, his two extra points were the difference in Navy's 14–13 victory over Duke.

His fondest football memory was of a 1943 game when he replaced Hillis Hume at fullback and scored two touchdowns. Movietone News, a distributor of newsreels that were shown in thousands of theaters around the nation, covered the game, and the narrator mentioned Finos's name when one of the touchdowns was shown. Some friends of his parents back in Everett, Massachusetts, saw the newsreel and told his parents, "Vic is in the movies."

"They raced down to the theater," Finos recalled, "thinking I had a speaking role in a film, and I think they must have blinked when the newsreel came on because the mention was so brief that they never saw it."

with their combined power and speed. When Navy shifted to the "T" formation full-time in 1945, he was not as effective taking a handoff from the quarterback. His 32.8-yard kickoff return average in 1944 is Navy's all-time season record.

Jenkins was always a big-play performer. He ran seventy-one yards for a touchdown against Penn State in a 1943 game; and in 1944 he returned the opening kickoff against Georgia Tech eighty-five yards for a touchdown (the third-longest return in Navy history).

The only times Navy was pressed in 1943—other than in losing to Notre Dame—were in back-to-back victories against Duke (14–13) and Penn State (14–6). During that Penn State contest in Annapolis, a sudden squall whipped off the Chesapeake Bay late in the game. It was so severe that the stadium clock ran backward. Barron slogged thirty-eight yards for the clinching touchdown.

Navy defeated Duke before a huge crowd in Baltimore only because a last-minute extra-point attempt by Duke sliced just inches outside the left upright. Sprinkle and Whitmire bailed out Navy time and again with their defensive play. Ben Martin flattened three Duke defenders on Hume's tying touchdown run and, with four minutes to play in the first half, Al Channell recovered a fumble and started a seventy-seven-yard drive for the winning score. It culminated in a pass from Hamberg to Roe Johnston, who then lateraled to Joe Sullivan as he streaked toward the end zone. Vic Finos kicked the winning extra point.

The 1943 national championship was on the line when Navy and Notre Dame, both undefeated, played before more than 80,000 at Cleveland's Municipal Stadium. The Fighting Irish were emotionally charged because their quarterback, Angelo Bertelli, a member of the Navy's V-12 training program, had been called to full-time Marine training and was playing his final game. His teammates responded with an impassioned performance and a 33–6 victory. Bertelli, on his way to the Heisman Trophy, threw three touchdown passes and scored another touchdown himself. That performance was just too much, even for the talented Mids, and it cost them the national championship.

Navy didn't lose another game that season and ended with a 14–0 victory over a fine Army team at West Point. (That game is covered in Chapter Nine.) Navy finished the season ranked fourth behind Notre Dame, Iowa Pre-Flight, and Michigan. One consolation for Navy was winning its first Lambert Trophy as unofficial eastern champion.

No sooner had the trophy been placed in a case than Whelchel, by then a captain, was sent to the fleet, where he soon made admiral. His successor was Oscar "Swede" Hagberg, who had been one of Rear Adm. Charles Lockwood's best submarine commanders during the early stages of the Pacific war. Most of the players were awestruck by Hagberg's war record and paid rapt attention to his combat stories. They learned more from this war hero about the perils they were preparing to face than they did about football.

Hagberg had played for Bill Ingram and Rip Miller. Like Larson and Whelchel, his coaching background was with fleet teams. Because those teams were allowed to use two officers as players, Hagberg not only coached, but often played, too.

Hagberg's biggest problem starting out as head coach at the Naval Academy was having been away from intercollegiate football for so long. The single wing of the thirties, which he knew so well, had begun in 1943 to give way to the speed and deception of the "T" formation. He considered installing the T, but Hagberg decided to stay with the single wing. It was a critical mistake, one that probably cost Navy an unbeaten season in 1944, when nearly all of its best players—including most of the line—returned.

With the addition of a young running back named Clyde Scott from Smackover, Arkansas, the Navy team was even faster than the year before. Scott had world-class speed—he later won the silver medal in the 110-meter high hurdles at the 1948 Olympic Games in London. He was built like a hurdler, too—he was a wiry five feet eleven and weighed 180 pounds. Because he played in a single-wing offense in his first season and could not pass very well, he was a fullback instead of tailback. Despite his wiry frame, he ran mostly between the tackles. He was given the nickname "Smackover" not only because of his hometown but because of what his hard, high-stepping runs could do to defenders. When Hagberg finally installed the "T" formation in 1945, Scott became a devastating offensive force and one of the finest all-round players in Navy history. He led the team in scoring for two years and in rushing, interceptions, and punt returns in 1945. He finished his college career as an All-America at Arkansas and then spent six seasons in the NFL with the Philadelphia Eagles (he was their top pick in 1948) and the Detroit Lions.

Reeves Baysinger vaulted into national prominence for his gritty performance in underdog Navy's near miss, a 21–18 loss to unbeaten Army in 1946. Then he did it again in 1948 by leading the winless Mids to an astounding 21–21 tie against another unbeaten Army team. Quiet and reserved away from the field, he was a fierce competitor during a game.

John Laboon

John Laboon was a strapping, six-two, two-hundred pounder who played end behind Bob Zoeller on the 1941 team and won All-East honors as a starter in 1942. John was called "Sleepy Laboon." The nickname was a takeoff on "Sleepy Lagoon," a popular song of the day, and also recalled the 1942 exhibition against the Chicago Bears, when Laboon had to be led, wobbly legged, off the field after he had been hit on the head while making a tackle. Laboon also was a second team All-America player on Navy's 1943 national champion lacrosse team.

During World War II, Laboon served aboard the submarine USS *Peto* and won the Silver Star for rescuing a downed Navy flier who was stranded on a reef. Laboon jumped off his boat, swam to the reef, and then towed the airman to safety aboard the submarine while Japanese planes strafed him and the *Peto*.

After the war, Laboon resigned from the Navy and later was ordained a Jesuit priest; he then returned to the Navy as a chaplain. For the next quarter-century, "Sleepy Laboon" was known as "Father Jake" to millions of Navy and Marine personnel. He served in Vietnam and earned the Legion of Merit with a combat "V." Father Laboon was the first chaplain assigned to a ballistic submarine squadron and was fleet chaplain of the U.S. Atlantic Fleet when he retired in 1980. When he served as senior Catholic chaplain at the Naval Academy he also helped coach the plebe football and lacrosse teams.

When the 1944 season began, the team had not yet acclimated itself either to Hagberg or his system, and Hagberg hadn't yet fully reacquainted himself with the collegiate game. The weaknesses showed when Navy lost 21–14 in its opening game against North Carolina Pre-Flight's Cloud Busters. Navy's problems were evident again in the season's fourth game, when Georgia Tech upset the Mids 17–15. Navy had the ball inside Tech's five-yard line in the final minutes, trailing by two points, and Hagberg ordered runs on all four downs. On fourth down, with less than a minute to play, he disdained an easy field goal attempt by Vic Finos that would have provided a victory, and Ralph Ellsworth's run was stopped just inches shy of the goal line.

Navy finally got untracked and stormed over its next four opponents, outscoring Penn, Cornell, and Purdue by a cumulative 106–0. The Mids put on an awesome display in a rollicking 32–13 victory over unbeaten Notre Dame in Baltimore. They needed only five plays in the first quarter for Scott to score two touchdowns after the defense, led by Whitmire and Jack Martin, had twice shut down the Irish inside the twenty-yard line. Navy's big linemen held the Irish to just thirty-six rushing yards, and on offense they blew apart the Irish defense, allowing Scott, Jenkins, Barron, Hamberg, and Ellsworth to roll up 338 yards on the ground.

Dick Scott, featured in the College Football Hall of Fame, was a great two-way player as a center and linebacker from 1945–47. He was an All-America in 1945 and 1947, one of only five Navy players ever accorded double All-A honors. Most consider him not only the best center in Navy history but also one of the Naval Academy's most outstanding midshipmen. In addition to winning three letters in football and serving as team captain in 1947, he was a track letter winner, Commander of the Brigade, and president of his class; he earned a Superintendent's Letter of Commendation and captured the Class of 1879 award for "outstanding leadership in the Brigade"; and he was awarded the Thompson Athletic Trophy in his senior year.

Navy warmed up for its game against Army, one that everyone agreed would decide the national championship, by walloping Purdue 32–0. Ben Martin, later a very successful coach at the Air Force Academy, scored twice on passes from Bruce Smith and Hal Hamberg, who had been injured most of the year. As the season evolved, defense had become the team's strength, as was evident in the Purdue game. In beating Penn (55–14) and Cornell (48–0), the Mids allowed each opponent just thirty-three plays. Cornell had a minus nineteen yards rushing. Navy held its nine opponents that season, including Army's national champions, to fifty-four rushing yards per game and less than two yards per carry.

It wasn't until November of the 1944 season that Army and Navy emerged as college football's two top-ranked teams. On November 4, the fourth-ranked Mids beat Notre Dame, and the following week top-ranked Army buried the Irish 59–0. Two days later, the national polls placed Army and Navy first and second. It was clear that the Army-Navy game would decide the national championship, and it suddenly became a game that everyone wanted to see.

There was one big obstacle: The game was scheduled to be played three weeks later on December 2, in tiny Thompson Stadium at the Naval Academy, which would hold only 19,000 spectators.

The Annapolis site was the result of a policy set in 1942 by President Roosevelt. He had resisted attempts to cancel the series until World War II had ended, but he ordered that the game be played in alternate years at each school's stadiums (1942 at Annapolis, 1943 at West Point, etc.), instead of at 103,000-seat Municipal Stadium in Philadelphia. These restrictions were supposed to set a good wartime example by conserving auto fuel and reducing train travel. Ticket sales, with few exceptions, were limited to those living within a ten-mile radius of the stadiums.

But with the Army-Navy game about to determine the national champion, wartime austerity had little appeal. A clamor arose within the administration, abetted by the media and the fans of both teams, to move it to a larger stadium. Minority Leader Joseph Martin took up the cause in the House of Representatives; he suggested tying the game to the bond sales for the Sixth War Loan Drive, despite the fact that the Naval Academy had already begun processing more than 19,000 ticket requests. Martin's idea met with a national surge of approval and was favorably received within the White House and Treasury Department. President Roosevelt ordered a change in locale. The matter then was handed off to Fleet Adm. Ernest J. King, chief of naval operations. King summoned one of his aides, Cdr. Robert "Dusty" Dornin, a fine end on Navy's teams in the midthirties. Dornin had just finished his combat tour as one of the Navy's top submarine commanders in the Pacific theater.

During a 1946 visit to the Naval Academy, Chief of Naval Operations, Fleet Adm. Ernest J. King, a former Navy football player himself, chats with Midshipman Stansfield Turner, who was a two-year lettermen (1944–45) at guard. Turner later achieved admiral's rank and became head of the Central Intelligence Agency.

Dornin later recalled for the U.S. Naval Institute what transpired. "Dornin," King asked him, "what do you think about the Army-Navy game? Where could it be played in a large stadium where it involved no transportation? I've got the approval of the President, who's all for playing the game away from Annapolis because he believes it's good for the morale of the country to have the No. 1 and No. 2 teams play in front of a large audience and have the midshipmen and cadets attend the game."

"I'd go to Baltimore," Dornin told him.

"Baltimore?" King replied, his eyebrows arching.

"Hell, yes," Dornin said. "The cadets could come down by steamboat and the midshipmen go from Annapolis by bus or by boat, as they usually did for a home game."

Admiral King and the White House agreed to the new venue. Roosevelt's rationale was that Navy had long played some of its home games in Baltimore; that the midshipmen would not burden the rail networks; and that because they didn't see the 1943 game at West Point "they are entitled to see this one."

In the end, both the midshipmen and the cadets traveled to the game by boat—the Mids sailed up the Chesapeake Bay as usual, and the ships carrying the cadets down the East Coast were escorted by four Navy destroyers!

Rear Adm. John Beardall, the superintendent, had just three weeks to get ready for the game at the new site, and he issued specific ground rules: Tickets for public sale were on a first-come basis, and the purchaser had to live within ten miles of Baltimore. Each must purchase a war bond valued at from $25 to $1,000 and could then buy a pair of $4.80 seats. Buying a more expensive bond meant getting a better seat location. Two exceptions were made. Navy honored its original 19,000 ticket applications for Thompson Stadium without requiring a war bond purchase or residence within ten miles of Baltimore. The Navy Athletic Association granted each U.S. Senator and Congressman temporary membership, exempting them from the war bond sale. More than two thousand tickets were sold on that basis.

All of the public's tickets were sold in one day, and it was estimated that 50,000 of the 71,000 ticket purchasers bought war bonds. Many purchasers bought bonds in $50,000–$100,000 denominations, and fifteen private boxes, each with six seats, brought a million dollars each. The total war bond take was $58,637,000.

Although the game was a financial success for the Sixth War Loan Drive, it was a disaster for Navy, which lost 23–7, partly because two of its best players—

The 1944 Army-Navy Game

Navy decided to resod the field at Baltimore's Municipal Stadium shortly before the 1944 Army-Navy game was to be played. When word reached Army coach Red Blaik at West Point, he hit the roof. "A new field at this time of the year means loose turf, and that cuts us down to a walk," he told assistant coach Jack Buckler, and immediately dispatched him to Baltimore to stop the resodding if at all possible.

Buckler later described the scene:

> The man in charge was a retired National Guard officer who was very sympathetic to Navy football. When I protested the resodding, he refused to do anything about it.
>
> "It's our home game and we will do what we wish with the field, sir!" he told me.
>
> "You may damned well do what you wish with your half of the field," I told him, "but we are also going to play in the game, so leave our half alone."

Don Whitmire and Bobby Jenkins—were lost early in the game. Whitmire, Navy's greatest lineman in those years, hurt his knee on the opening kickoff and was unable to play after the second quarter. Jenkins, the Mids' most powerful running back, suffered a concussion on the game's second play and didn't return until the fourth quarter, when the outcome had been decided.

Army fielded its strongest team ever, with two complete and talented backfields. The great combination of Doc Blanchard, who almost came to the Naval Academy in 1943, and Glenn Davis was pushed to the second unit. The game was bitterly fought. The Cadets led 9–0 in the third quarter before Smackover Scott ended a seventy-nine-yard drive with a two-yard touchdown run. But Blanchard keyed an Army drive, pounding the final nine yards through Navy's tiring defense. Davis, a Californian, got the final score on a fifty-yard touchdown run dubbed "The California Special." Army led in first downs 12–8 and, without Jenkins, the Mids were out-rushed 181–71. Whitmire's blocking was sorely missed—Army's pass rush helped force five interceptions, and Navy completed just nine of twenty-four passes for ninety-eight yards. Navy finished fourth in the national rankings behind Army, Ohio State, and Randolph Field, an Army Air Force training base in Texas.

The 1945 season began just a few weeks after World War II ended. Navy had another great team, retaining many of its stars from 1944 and attracting several new ones, including Bob Hoernschmeyer from Indiana, Tony Minisi from Penn, and Bob Kelly from Notre Dame. The talent was ideal for Hagberg's new "T"-formation offense. Navy rolled through the season unbeaten (including a 6–6 tie with Notre Dame) until a final-game loss to Army. Navy shut out its first three opponents (winning by a cumulative 96–0) and never allowed more than one touchdown until the Army game.

Skippy Minisi was a freshman star at Penn in 1944 and played just one season at Navy. When Navy played Penn in 1945, Minisi caught the winning touchdown pass from Hoernschmeyer with fifty-three seconds to play to beat his old team. In the Notre Dame game he preserved the tie with a touchdown-saving tackle at Navy's goal line. The following year, Minisi returned to Penn, where he was the key player in Penn's 32–19 victory over Navy.

Hunchy Hoernschmeyer was a triple-threat tailback at Indiana and led the nation in total offense as a freshman in 1943. Sadly, though, he was never totally comfortable playing quarterback at Navy. Injuries and problems at the position forced Hagberg to start Bruce Smith for the final three games. Hunchy left Navy in 1946 to sign with the Chicago Rockets of the All-America Football

Conference and begin a fine, ten-year professional career that included two NFL championships with the Detroit Lions.

Smith, later a distinguished admiral, was a halfback on Navy's 1943 and 1944 teams before Hagberg converted him to a "T" quarterback. He had played as a tailback in a short-punt-formation offense in high school (one of his teammates was Army quarterback Arnold Tucker). He adapted very well to the "T" formation, which allowed him to display his ability as a drop-back passer; even so, he played behind Hoernschmeyer until the season's last three games.

When Hagberg switched his offense to the "T" formation, he tried Dick Duden, a great blocking back, at fullback and then moved him to end. In his last season, Duden became one of the best ends in Navy's history, which was not surprising because he was a remarkable athlete. Duden was the first plebe ever to make the varsity football, basketball, and baseball teams, and one of only a handful of midshipmen to earn nine varsity letters.

Because Duden received his appointment to the Academy only two days before Navy opened its 1943 season, he didn't even see the opener against North Carolina Pre-Flight. He reported to the team on the following Monday and, six days later, was the starting blocking back against Cornell.

"Duden is the only man I've seen who can catch a ball thrown anywhere near him," Hagberg said at the time. Even when Duden played blocking back, both Whelchel and Hagberg utilized him in Navy's pass offense. In 1943 Duden caught the winning touchdown pass against Georgia Tech in a 28–14 victory; in 1945, when he was playing end, he intercepted a pass against Penn State and ran forty-five yards for a score. At six two and weighing 205 pounds, Duden earned the nickname "Monster" on defense because he was strong enough to handle any offensive lineman.

When the 1945 season concluded, Duden was named to every major All-America team; he won the Knute Rockne Memorial Trophy given by the Washington Touchdown Club; and at graduation, he was awarded the Naval Academy Athletic Association Sword. Duden also shared the top undergraduate rank of brigade commander. He later coached Navy's defensive line in the fifties and spent more than two decades as the Academy's most successful plebe coach.

In 1945, Navy also got Dick Scott, who was born and raised in Highland Falls, New York, just outside the main gate of the Military Academy, but could not get an appointment there. Scott left Annapolis as a Hall of Fame player after a three-season career as center and linebacker, during which he started every game at center.

Scott made countless big plays on the football field. In 1945, Navy trailed Penn 7–0 until midway through the last quarter when he blocked Bob Evan's field goal attempt. Hoernschmeyer passed for sixty-six yards with two completions to Duden; the second (a thirty-six-yarder) scored the tying touchdown. Scott led another defensive stand to maintain the tie, and then Minisi took over against his former team. With less than ninety seconds to play, Minisi gained fifteen yards on a third-

Fullback Bill Hawkins's hard-nosed style of play epitomized the best in Navy football. He led the 1947 team in rushing, but too often he preferred to run into tacklers rather than around them. Some of his coaches said he also would have made an excellent guard because of his combative football nature.

down reverse. Two plays later, Duden and Pete Williams worked a tricky pass-lateral that set up the winning twenty-two-yard pass from Hoernschmeyer to Minisi with just twenty-five seconds left.

Oddly, with two minutes to play in the game, referee Albie Booth had called the team captains together and said, "We're going to toss a coin to see who gets the game ball when this is over." Duden lost the toss.

Scott and Minisi again stepped forward the following week when Navy played a 6–6 tie against Notre Dame before a nearly-hysterical crowd of 82,000 at Cleveland's Municipal Stadium. The game was a slugfest. Navy trailed 6–0 before Scott raced sixty yards with an interception of a tipped pass.

What ensued was one of the season's most frantic finishes. With less than two minutes remaining, Notre Dame freshman quarterback George Ratterman threw a sixty-one-yard pass to Bull Leonard to Navy's seventeen-yard line. The Mids quickly called a time out they didn't own, and the subsequent penalty placed the ball on the twelve. On the next play, regular quarterback Boley Danciewicz passed to Phil Colella near the goal line. Minisi just missed knocking the ball down, but he had the presence of mind to grab Colella around the neck. Although Colella's feet were in the end zone, Minisi's lock on his upper body yanked him and the ball backward, and out of bounds, before the ball crossed the goal line.

There were still thirty seconds remaining. The Irish ran two plays: Danciewicz was stopped cold on a quarterback sneak and, on the game's final play, freshman halfback Terry Brennan ran off tackle and was thrown backward by Ed Deramee, Coppedge, and Scott.

After the players unpiled, they huddled with the officials; they appeared to be disputing whether or not there was a touchdown on the play. In fact, they were deciding who would get the game ball! Minisi walked off with it—a hero for the ages.

Though Navy barely managed to salvage a tie against Notre Dame, the last-minute heroics that prevented a loss seemed to energize the Mids. The next week against Michigan, with Adm. William F. Halsey Jr., the gritty fullback on Navy's 1902 and 1903 teams, looking on, Navy forced seven turnovers and turned most of them into touchdowns in a 33–7 victory. Bruce Smith, who had replaced Hoernschmeyer at quarterback, passed for scores to Dick Scott and Pete Williams. Minisi scored on a reverse and threw a TD-option pass to Bramlett. Navy then capped its

Dick Scott

Richard Underhill Scott had few peers on any team in the nation during the midforties. Now in the College Football Hall of Fame, Scott was undeniably the greatest center in Navy's history, and there are many who played with him who believe he also was Navy's greatest linebacker. (He worked in the era of one-platoon football in 1945, 1946, and 1947.) Some also remember him occasionally handling punting duties in 1947, when he was team captain. One of his teammates noted lightheartedly, "I don't remember who centered the ball, but it well could have been Dick himself, because he was that good."

Few midshipmen have ever matched Scott's achievements, on or off the field. Playing at six feet two and 188 pounds, he was a starter in every varsity game for three seasons and made the All-America team all three years. Scott also won letters in lacrosse and track; was awarded the Thompson Trophy at graduation for having done the most in his class to promote sports at the Naval Academy; was president of his class every year; and was brigade commander in his senior year. He spent seven years as a flier after graduation.

Scott was born and raised in Highland Falls, New York, a stone's throw from West Point. His father was manager of the Cadet book store for thirty-five years, and one of his brothers ran the Cadet restaurant for twenty-five years. "I tried so hard to go to West Point that I got my congressman all tired out and he offered me an alternate appointment to Annapolis instead," Scott said. When his appointment came through, Scott had already served nineteen months in the Army, training at Colgate and Baylor, and he considered declining the appointment and trying again for West Point—but his father dissuaded him.

"regular" season with a 36–7 victory over Wisconsin. Scott set up two scores with an interception and a punt return, while Barron and Pettit scored on runs of fifty-four and seventy yards.

The Army-Navy game returned in 1945 to Philadelphia's Municipal Stadium for the first time since 1941. All 103,000 tickets were sold almost instantly, and another million dollars worth of orders were refunded. On game day, scalpers got as much as a hundred dollars for a five-dollar ticket.

Art Markel, who played end on the 1945, 1946, and 1947 teams, established a then–Naval Academy season receiving mark of twenty-one catches (for 235 yards and a touchdown) in 1947.

Even with its decisive victories over Michigan and Wisconsin, Navy was a big underdog against Army and the national championship was again at stake. "Say a few prayers for us. We're going to need them," Navy's scouts told friends in the press box at Franklin Field after they had watched Army beat Penn, 61–0, in Army's final game before Navy.

Stopping Blanchard and Davis was imperative. Hagberg even recruited Whitmire, then a first-classman who had exhausted his eligibility, to play the role of Blanchard in scrimmage sessions.

It didn't do much good. In front of President Harry S. Truman, the first chief executive since Calvin Coolidge to attend the Classic, Navy lost, 32–13.

The outcome may have been decided when Navy lost the coin toss and Army chose to play the first quarter with a blustery wind at its back. The Mids fell on a double-edged sword: Army's defense stymied them and, when they punted, the wind prevented the kicks from traveling very far. As a result, Army continually had fine field position early in the game. The Cadets took advantage; they scored on three of their first four possessions. Blanchard had two touchdowns, and Davis added a forty-nine-yard run for a 20–0 Army lead.

Bruce Smith and Clyde Scott hooked up on a sixty-one-yard touchdown pass to close the score to 20–7 at the half. From then on, Navy's defense manhandled Army as no opponent had done that season. But Blanchard scored his third touchdown with a fifty-two-yard interception return. Navy got to 26–12 on Joe Bartos's touchdown, but Davis capped the Army victory with a thirty-two-yard touchdown run.

The contest was the first Army-Navy game to be televised. While millions heard the game on radio, a few thousand people in Philadelphia, New York City, and Schenectady, New York, watched it on a closed-circuit TV hookup.

Navy finished the 1945 season ranked third behind Army and Alabama. It was the Mids' last taste of dominance for six years. The football program nosedived in 1946 for several reasons: the influx of new players all but stopped for a year while the Academy began phasing out its accelerated, three-year classes and returned to its regular, four-year program; many of the great players from the 1944 and 1945 teams, including Barron, Bartos, Whitmire, and Coppedge, had exhausted their collegiate eligibility (even though they had not yet graduated); and several talented players, including Skippy Minisi and Clyde Scott, resigned before the 1946 season. Many contemporaries of Minisi and Scott said "good riddance" because the young men had no desire to become naval officers.

Coaching stability became another problem in 1946. Part of the culture at the Naval Academy has always been to compare itself with what is happening at West Point. During the first half of the forties, when Army had the greatest football era in its history, it had just one head coach, Earl "Red" Blaik. During that time, Navy had already had three, and it was about to hire a fourth. Discontent with Navy's graduate coaching system was starting to be heard from its fans, including many former football players. They understood that a program can only be consistently successful if there is a constant flow of good talent *and* continuity at the head coach's position. The inevitable comparisons with Army, which had won back-to-back national championships in 1944 and 1945 (and was about to share another with Notre Dame in 1946) fed the restiveness.

The difference, of course, was that in 1941, Army had abandoned its policy of using active-duty officers as head coaches and had given the job to Blaik. He was a West Point graduate and had been an assistant coach there while in the Army. But when he left the service, he became a successful head coach at Dartmouth, and when he returned to coach at his alma mater, it was as a civilian. During World War II, he was recommissioned as a colonel, but he continued to coach the football team and kept the job after returning to civilian life at the war's end.

Navy officials looked down on Army's switch to a full-time, civilian head coach, despite the grumbling from many who were familiar with the shortcomings of the Navy's system. Tom Hamilton, then a captain in the Navy and an advocate of the graduate system, was given his second tour as head coach in 1946 by the superintendent, Vice Adm. Aubrey W. Fitch, who shared the same view. "He is the only graduate who could do an outstanding coaching job at this time," Fitch said.

Ironically, Hamilton changed his mind when he became athletic director in 1948, and he hired a civilian, George Sauer, as coach. Hamilton's reversal was an important component of a comprehensive agenda to change the football

The 1948 Navy coaching staff *(from left)* were: Leon Bramlett, Vic Bradford (head coach), George Sauer, Bob Ingalls, and Roy Swartz.

program at Annapolis. It evolved from his own experiences when he ran the V-5 Pre-Flight Training Program early in World War II and when he was head coach in 1946 and 1947. He saw firsthand how college football had changed and why Navy needed a full-time head coach to provide stability and success.

But before all of that happened, he had to concentrate on coaching the football team. Originally, he agreed to coach for only the 1946 season. Then, he would become athletic director for two years before retiring from the Navy. During those last two years, he planned to implement a restructuring of the football program.

Hamilton had also handpicked his coaching successor, Cdr. Louis A. Bryan, who was a tackle on the 1929, 1930, and 1931 teams and one of the Navy's most decorated officers during World War II. Bryan became Hamilton's line coach in 1946 to acclimate himself to how college football was being played. But Bryan never succeeded Hamilton. By custom, after a Navy team finished its final practice for the Army-Navy game, the linemen tossed their line coach into the icy Severn River. When Bryan hit the water, the shock temporarily paralyzed him. Lineman Jim Carrington jumped in and saved him, but the cold plunge exacerbated an undiagnosed case of tuberculosis. Bryan spent 1947 regaining his health at the Bethesda Naval Hospital. He recovered, but his football coaching days were ended. He later retired as a rear admiral.

Hamilton stayed on as head coach for the 1947 season, the last active-duty graduate to coach a Navy football team (George Welsh, a 1956 graduate, was not in the Navy when he became head coach in 1973), and he spent 1948, his final year in the Navy, as athletic director. He had to relinquish that job because the Naval Academy continued its policy of using only active-duty officers in the post until Bo Coppedge became athletic director in 1968.

Hamilton's tenure, although not as successful as his 1934–36 tour, became the most important in Naval Academy history to that point because, in the spring of 1946, he devised a seminal plan that became a keystone in helping forge Navy's tremendous success in the fifties and early sixties.

His comprehensive plan called for numerous changes. They included asking alumni, Rip Miller's "Bird Dogs," and athletic officers in the fleet to help identify good athletes who could meet the Academy's entrance requirements; playing a national schedule of top teams; adding three hours of extra practice each week; enhancing the intramural program ("It is time the Naval Academy recognizes that competitive sports which stress human relationships are as important in the training of individuals as mathematics or other basic subjects"); and building a stadium in Annapolis to permit better scheduling and give Navy a better home-field advantage (Navy–Marine Corps Memorial Stadium is now the site for five or six games each season). At first, Hamilton also recommended that Navy retain its graduate coaching system. He believed that a civilian coach would not accept the limitations that were inherent in the rigid strictures of the Naval Academy. Furthermore, he was convinced that young naval officers, both Academy and NROTC graduates, could be given adequate preparation within the Navy to succeed as varsity coaches at the Academy. ("The Navy must recognize that duty assigned in coaching is just as much a naval assignment as training a turret crew," he said.) Hamilton later

Tom Hamilton

The two greatest contributors to Navy football are Tom Hamilton and Roger Staubach.

Both were All-America backs—Hamilton was a single-wing tailback and wingback, and Staubach was a quarterback and Heisman Trophy winner. Hamilton, though, made the bigger overall contribution to Navy's football legacy as a player, coach, administrator, and adviser.

Hamilton got his first head coaching job at Navy in 1934, when he was only twenty-eight years old. He had been an assistant for two seasons under his former coach, Bill Ingram, after graduating in 1927. When Hamilton moved west to coach the Pacific Fleet team, he again hooked up with Ingram, who was now coach at the University of California. It was, Hamilton recalled, a "valuable experience. Bill Ingram allowed me to use the University of California practice facility and work against his Cal teams."

Hamilton's true measure is reflected in his dedicated service to the expanding naval aviation program in the thirties; to athletics, particularly football at the Naval Academy; and to establishing the historic, Navy V-5 Preflight program that helped to prepare a quarter-million cadets in ground training and physical conditioning for future World War II assignments. He also supervised the selection and teaching of more than two thousand officers who would be the instructors for that program in schools and naval aviation units.

Hamilton, who retired with the rank of rear admiral, was a much-decorated war hero who served as air officer, executive officer, and captain of the famed carrier USS *Enterprise.* He was commended for his exploits in the invasions of the Gilbert and Marshall Islands; for raids on Truk and Palau; for the two mighty battles of the Philippines Sea and the invasions of the Philippines, Palau, and Hollandia; and for raids on Formosa and Iwo Jima.

He was enshrined in the College Football Hall of Fame in 1965 and later honored with the hall's Gold Medal Award for his ten years of service as coach and athletic director at the University of Pittsburgh and for his twelve years as commissioner of the Pac-Eight Conference. From the time he left the Navy until his death in 1993, Hamilton maintained his interest in Academy football and was a confidant of USNA athletic administrators.

changed his mind about civilian coaches and hired George Sauer as his successor in 1948.

Hamilton's plan could not be implemented in time for the 1946 season, and he had problems on the field. There were fewer than two dozen players of varsity caliber, and he lost some of them to chronic injuries and resignations. Navy won only one of nine games that year. Its 21–18 loss to Army, though, was a college football classic. Navy has always received as much credit as if it had won. The game made everlasting heroes of such players as Bill Hawkins, Reeves Baysinger, and Pete Williams for their gritty performances. In the final minute of the game, Navy was inside Army's five-yard line. A disputed out-of-bounds call ended the Mids' opportunity to score and handed Army's Blanchard-Davis team its only loss. (That game is covered in detail in Chapter Nine.)

Despite the great—albeit heartbreaking—finish in 1946, there still were too many holes and not enough depth to sustain Navy in 1947. The Mids defeated only Cornell and tied Duke. They lost to Army, 21–0.

The dismal records of this time mask the team-oriented, determined play of men such as Scott, Williams, Hawkins, Baysinger, Phil Ryan, Scott Emerson, Dick Shimshack, Ken Schwieck, Dave Bannerman, Bob Schwoefferman, Billy Earl, and Bill Powers. Schwoefferman was typical of this group. He was nicknamed "Bird Legs" because he weighed only 165 pounds, yet he played fullback with as much gusto as someone thirty pounds heavier.

No one displayed more determination than Emerson and Ryan. Emerson, co-captain of the 1948 team with Williams, played with great intensity and excitement and thrived in the combat of the line. So did Ryan, Navy's best pass receiver in his last two seasons and the 1949 captain. Ryan and Hawkins played on the Quantico Marines teams after graduating from the Naval Academy.

Reeves Baysinger, a hero of the 1946 Army-Navy game, never impressed anyone in practice. In a game, though, his quiet, reserved demeanor gave way to a fierce competitive spirit that more than compensated for his average passing skills and did much to hold his meager forces together.

Bill Hawkins, who had played for a year at Virginia Military Institute before coming to Annapolis, probably was the "poster boy" of these teams. He could have just as comfortably played guard as fullback, because he was a combative player who, when running with the ball, often preferred running over a tackler rather than sidestepping him.

George Sauer was a natural choice when Hamilton finally convinced his superiors to let him hire a civilian coach. The two men had worked together throughout most of World War II, first in Hamilton's V-5 Pre-Flight Training Program and then aboard the USS *Enterprise* during some of the heaviest fighting of the war. Sauer had been a great collegiate player at Nebraska and had played for three years with the Green Bay Packers. He also had impeccable coaching credentials. His teams had won two Yankee Conference titles at the University of New Hampshire before the war and two more titles in the Big Six (later the Big Eight) Conference at the University of Kansas after the war.

Sauer was well liked and respected by his players. However, his attempts to motivate them using a sharp tongue didn't work the way they did with players at New Hampshire or Kansas; the midshipmen were used to being chewed out during their daily routines at the Academy. In this respect, many later compared Sauer's approach with that of his successor, Eddie Erdelatz, who had learned as an assistant coach that tirades didn't work. Erdelatz found that it was more effective to make his players feel that they let him down when they made mistakes.

Coach Sauer introduced an innovative, wide-open, and versatile offense that featured flankers and more passing than Navy had used under Hamilton. It was run by Reeves Baysinger in 1948 and by newcomer Bob Zastrow in 1949. Throughout the 1949 season, Sauer tutored Zastrow, a pudgy-faced

Winless Navy was a three-touchdown underdog against unbeaten Army in 1948, but the relentless pounding by halfback Pete Williams and fullback Bill Hawkins helped tear apart the Cadets. Hawkins scored a pair of touchdowns and, unlike Navy's near-miss loss in 1946 when they couldn't convert any extra points, Roger Drew kicked one after each touchdown to get an astounding 21–21 tie.

Wisconsin native who didn't look like a football player. Zastrow's tenacity and spirit were often masked by his unselfishness. He so wanted his teammates to get the glory that he was, at times, reluctant to call his own signal on short-yardage plays, and had to be ordered to do so.

Despite Zastrow's appearance, no one was tougher. When he carried the ball he straight-armed tacklers to gain three or four more yards. Sometimes he was a Jekyll and Hyde quarterback—spectacularly winning games the Mids weren't supposed to win, failing to produce in games they should have won.

Sauer's 1948 team had little depth in talent, was racked with injuries throughout the season, and didn't win a game. In 1949, however, Sauer helped Navy to its best record since 1945, with upsets against Princeton, Duke, and Columbia, and a 21–21 tie against Tulane. Navy, which had copped a memorable tie against unbeaten Army in 1948, hoped for an even bigger "miracle"—a victory—against another unbeaten Army team in 1949, but the Cadets easily won 38–0. "They just beat the hell out of us and there wasn't a thing we could do about it," Sauer said afterward. Sauer compiled a two-year record of 3–13–2.

After the 1949 season, Sauer left Navy, although he had two years remaining on his contract. He became head coach at Baylor, where he had a fine career. He is best remembered at the Academy for the game that epitomized Navy football during this time—the astounding 21–21 tie against unbeaten and third-ranked Army in 1948 after the Mids had gone winless prior to that game. The key to the Mids' moral victory was having injured players, including Hawkins and Williams, healthy for the first time that season.

Army was a twenty-one-point favorite. No one seemed to heed the warning proclaimed by a Navy fan's sign: "Gallup Picks Army," the placard read, a takeoff on that year's presidential election in which the Gallup Poll had picked Thomas E. Dewey to unseat, by an overwhelming margin, Harry Truman.

Some have compared this game with the 1946 Army-Navy game, but there were some notable differences. In the 1948 contest, Navy was the pacesetter. On its second possession, the Mids moved eighty-eight yards for a touchdown, helped by Pete Williams's fifty-nine-yard sweep. Baysinger scored on a quarterback sneak, and Roger Drew kicked the extra point for a 7–0 Navy lead.

Army answered with two second-quarter touchdowns and led at halftime, 14–7. At the start of the second half, the Mids blunted an Army drive that reached their nineteen-yard line. Helped by Powers's twisting, dodging thirty-six-yard run, Navy marched eighty-one yards for the tying touchdown. Hawkins hit the line, was momentarily stopped, and then slid into the end zone for the score.

Army took the ensuing kickoff and moved to another touchdown and a 21–14 lead. A short time later, Navy began a drive at midfield with Hawkins—who didn't lose yardage on any of his runs that afternoon—pounding away with his running. Baysinger deftly mixed in his passing, and Navy was at Army's three-yard line in the final minutes.

Everyone in the crowd of 102,000 in Philadelphia's Municipal Stadium was stunned, including President Truman, who delayed his departure so he could catch the final action. (He had missed the thrilling conclusion of the 1946 game because he'd left too early.) The ending was ferocious. As he had in the third quarter, Hawkins smashed into the line, was momentarily stood up by the defense—and spun away and crashed into the end zone. Drew calmly kicked his third extra point of the day, and Navy's defense preserved the tie by stopping the Cadets at their twenty-three-yard line in the final minute. Hawkins—who else?—broke up Arnold Galiffa's fourth-down pass to end the threat.

At Annapolis, the Japanese victory bell, normally rung only after a victory over Army, tolled continuously until the football team returned home the next day for a riotous celebration by 2,000 midshipmen waiting in the rain to honor their team.

"It brought tears to my eyes," Sauer said later. "When you get kicked around all season, it's tough to keep digging. But those football players would go until they couldn't go any longer."

After the game, Army captain Bill Yoeman won a coin toss for the game ball. A week later, however, Scott Emerson and Pete Williams received a letter from Yoeman. "We won [the toss] by chance," he wrote. "You get the football."

6. Eddie Erdelatz and the Fabulous Fifties 1950–1958

A few months after Eddie Erdelatz was appointed head coach at Navy in 1950, he told the four hundred members of the incoming plebe class: "We have at least one thing in common. We're all starting out as plebes. We've got four years to do a job."

Although most of those plebes needed the four years to do their job, Erdelatz accomplished his in half the time. By his third season, in 1952, Navy had once more regained national prominence. It remained on top for the next dozen years.

The return to respectability was the culmination of Tom Hamilton's revolutionary plan to restructure Navy's football program. It was helped by an influx of good players beginning in 1948 and continuing throughout the fifties and into the sixties. (In the midsixties, seminal changes in the country itself would affect radically every facet of life at all service academies.)

During the nine years that Erdelatz was head coach, he compiled a 50–26–8 record, which ranks second in Navy history behind George Welsh's mark of 55–46–1, also compiled over nine years. Teams coached by Erdelatz had seven straight winning seasons, won two postseason bowls, were ranked five times among the nation's top twenty teams, and produced some of the Academy's greatest players.

Erdelatz was no stranger to Academy football. He had been an end coach for Oscar Hagberg and Tom Hamilton, working with such extraordinary players as Dick Duden, Leon Bramlett, and Phil Ryan. Erdelatz was the line coach of the San Francisco 49ers when athletic director Howard Caldwell offered him the head coach's job at Navy. Erdelatz was Caldwell's only choice; he agreed to the job a week after it was offered.

Football at the Naval Academy was different from the moment Erdelatz arrived. He knew his way around Academy politics from his previous stint. Publicly, at least, he appeared comfortable working under the specific conditions that were imposed. But there were huge differences in what he agreed to, and what he did.

George Sauer and Eddie Erdelatz, both civilians, ran their programs poles apart. Sauer had been too sensitive to all the suggestions offered by senior officers at the Academy and agonized too much about what he should do with them. Erdelatz heard the same suggestions, nodded his head, promptly forgot them, and did what he wanted.

His flouting of the rules became more of a problem as he became more successful. No rules or traditions were impediments to getting what Erdelatz wanted for his team. When one of his players was convicted of a Class A offense, Erdelatz went over the heads of both the commandant, Charles Buchanan, and the superintendent, Adm. C. Turner Joy, and right to the secretary of the Navy to get the player reinstated. The maneuver worked, but Buchanan never spoke to Erdelatz again. The coach battled with the three athletic directors under whom he worked from 1951 to 1958—Ian Eddy, C. Elliott Laughlin, and Slade Cutter. Erdelatz rebuffed attempts by several superintendents to strike a balance in his relationships at the Academy and the manner in which he ran his program.

Elliott Laughlin, who was athletic director from 1954 to 1957, the heyday of the Erdelatz regime, noted in an oral history he recorded for the U.S. Naval Institute, "He [Erdelatz] didn't want to conform to restrictions at the Naval Academy, which he well understood when he took the job. He wanted to keep the football team as an entity outside the Brigade."

Laughlin's relationship with Erdelatz worsened because Erdelatz didn't respect Laughlin's background as a basketball player. "Eddie, you're the coach and I'm the director of athletics," Laughlin once told him as their squabbles became more frequent. "So, let's just work together on that basis."

"And we did," Laughlin said later. But he remembered Erdelatz as "a very unreasonable person [who] had no sense of loyalty to me, the commandant, the superintendent, or the Naval Academy. . . . He wanted to have his own little kingdom and his bailiwick was the football team. He wanted separate dorms for his team and he disliked having the players live in Bancroft Hall with

The 1950 Navy coaching staff consisted of *(from left)* Ben Martin, Eddie Erdelatz (head coach), Len Eshmont, and Don Clark.

Eddie Erdelatz

Eddie Erdelatz was a self-proclaimed "football nut" from the time he was nine years old. He was a star end for St. Mary's College in California when that school was one of the nation's top independent powers during the late thirties. After graduation, he coached the line at St. Mary's and the ends at the University of San Francisco.

When World War II began, Erdelatz was commissioned in the Navy. He became a boxing coach and played football at St. Mary's Preflight School, one of Tom Hamilton's V-5 programs. A serious leg injury in 1943 ended his football playing days. He went to San Diego Navy Base as physical and military training officer before being assigned in 1945 as ends coach under Oscar Hagberg at the Naval Academy.

Erdelatz worked for two years (1946 and 1947) as a civilian coach on Hamilton's staff and was considered for the head coaching job that ultimately went to George Sauer in 1948. He was offered a spot on Sauer's staff, but the San Francisco 49ers offered him a chance to be line coach, and he took it. "I was getting in a rut coaching the ends at Navy, and there was a real challenge in coaching a pro line," he once explained.

Erdelatz was just as popular with the 49ers' players as he had been with the team at Navy. When the 49ers traveled by bus, there would inevitably be one bus carrying the team's hell-raisers and one for its quiet guys. Erdelatz always rode on the hell-raisers' bus and was in the middle of the pranks, wisecracks, and boisterous singing. This was part of a persona that earned him the reputation of being a "player's coach." But he carried that reputation too far when he tried to circumvent some of the Naval Academy's mandated routines to make life easier for his players during the season.

For all of his charm, his ability to get people on his side, including most of the media, and his skill at turning out winning football teams, Erdelatz had a darker side. He had few close friends among the college coaching fraternity (Michigan State's Duffy Daugherty, Georgia Tech's Bobby Dodd, and Oklahoma's Bud Wilkinson, from whom he had copied the split-T formation, were exceptions); he was afraid that friendship would cause him to let down his guard and reveal coaching secrets. When he decided to add the wing-T formation in 1957, he could have sought the advice of Delaware's Davey Nelson, who was a master of that offense and had a close personal relationship with Navy's great line coach, Ernie Jorge. But Erdelatz refused to take advantage of the opportunity, for fear that he'd have to give up something in return.

On the surface, Erdelatz took a relaxed approach to the job. But his wife, Agnes, once said, "Eddie thinks about football all day, every day. By the time he gets home from practice in the evening, he's had enough."

the other midshipmen. The football team was the only thing [of importance to Erdelatz]—but I must say, he was one heckuva football coach."

Erdelatz shook up things from day one. He abolished the annual spring practice game with an outside squad, which startled some Academy officials. But Erdelatz was adamant. "If you win one of those games," he said, "everybody goes around talking about an undefeated season. If you lose, all they say is, 'Well, the same old Navy team.' No matter what happens, it doesn't help morale."

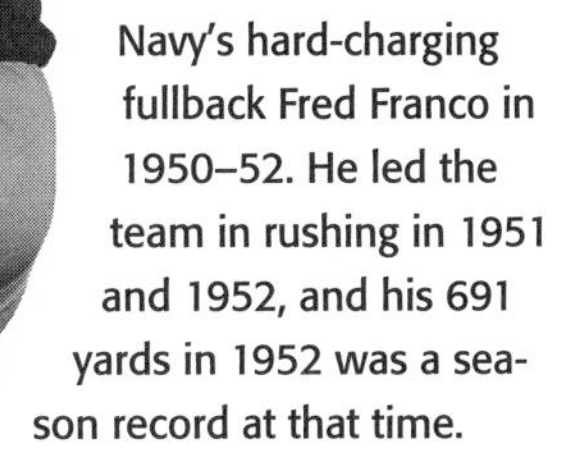

Navy's hard-charging fullback Fred Franco in 1950–52. He led the team in rushing in 1951 and 1952, and his 691 yards in 1952 was a season record at that time.

He was a very innovative coach. In his first spring practice he brought Frankie Albert, an All-America quarterback at Stanford and a star with the 49ers when Erdelatz was their line coach, to work with Navy's quarterbacks. Albert, a small man, was a ball-handling wizard who did much to help develop such fine Navy quarterbacks as Bob Zastrow and George Welsh.

Erdelatz cut the traveling squad from fifty to thirty-seven, and told those who made it that it was up to them to succeed or fail. He worked hard to build more enthusiasm and spirit among the players. Great people skills were key to his success, "and that's a coaching gift," said Red Strader, under whom Erdelatz had played at St. Mary's College in California. Erdelatz is still revered by many of the players from his Navy teams.

In 1950, Erdelatz purposely avoided automatically selecting his starters from among the lettermen and let it be known that anyone—jayvees, letter-winners and non-letter-winners alike—could become a starter. Although the two-platoon system was being used by the large civilian schools, Navy had so little depth that he insisted that every player be able to play on both units.

Erdelatz brought to Navy much of the offensive and defensive philosophy that he learned with the 49ers. His staff included two assistant coaches from the 49ers—Len Eshmont and Don Clark. Ben Martin, plebe coach under Sauer, kept the same job; Erdelatz coached the ends himself.

All of these changes gave the Mids a competitive edge over their opponents. What was missing, though, were better and more experienced players. It wasn't until 1952 that Erdelatz had the personnel and depth to match up with any opponent. From that season on, every Navy team coached by Erdelatz was ranked among the nation's top twenty.

There were several fine players on which he built his 1950 team, including fullback Fred Franco, a plebe star in 1949, and holdover backs Bill Powers and Frank Hauff. That team won just three of nine games, but two of the victories were major upsets. One was over Southern Cal; the other, over undefeated and second-ranked Army, was one of the great shockers in that series. (The Army upset is covered in Chapter Nine.)

Southern Cal, led by tailback Frank Gifford, was a twelve-point favorite over Navy when it made its first trip ever to the East Coast to play the Mids in Baltimore. Navy won 27–14 as Zastrow completely overshadowed Gifford, completing eight of twelve passes and scoring two of Navy's three touchdowns.

In its first seven games of 1951, the team tied once and lost six. Its only highlight to that point of the season came in a losing game against Maryland

Navy's brain trust in 1950 and 1951: Coach Eddie Erdelatz confers with quarterback Bob "Zug" Zastrow. Zastrow will forever be remembered for leading the Mids to a monumental 14–2 upset victory over unbeaten and second-ranked Army in 1950.

when Frank Brady, helped by a crushing block from Ira Kane, set a Navy record with his one-hundred-yard punt return for a touchdown.

The Mids got their first victory in the season's eighth game, a 21–7 win over Columbia. The contest was highlighted by a seventy-five-yard touchdown fumble return by Dean Smith, who had just been promoted from the 150-pound team. Navy then rolled over an Army team that had been decimated by a "cribbing" scandal that cost it nearly all of its veteran players. Erdelatz, who always prepared something special for the Army game, established a new pattern that year. He used the single wing and Notre Dame box instead of the "T" formation, and his team had a 14–0 lead before the Cadets even ran a play. John Raster, a plebe who had won a varsity letter at the University of Detroit before coming to Navy, had an electrifying, 101-yard interception return for Navy's third touchdown. That still stands as the longest play in Army-Navy game history. Navy poured it on for a 42–7 final score.

Erdelatz finally achieved his goal of returning Navy football to respectability in 1952. The only losses on a 6–2–1 record were against the nation's two top-ranked teams, Notre Dame and Maryland. Navy's successes were due in part to the maturing of Fred Franco, Dean Smith (the 1951 team's leading scorer), Ned Snyder, Jack Perkins, and quarterback Bob Cameron. Erdelatz then melded a group of young players for another successful season in 1953, giving Navy its first back-to-back winning seasons since 1944 and 1945. These years set the stage for the centerpiece of his tenure, the 1954 "Team Named Desire" that captivated an entire nation.

The 1952 team had a good nucleus of backs. Franco, from Newport, Rhode Island, was only five nine and 185 pounds, but he averaged more than four yards a carry during his three varsity seasons, in which he started every game. Before coming to Navy, he had won a letter at Brown University, where one of his teammates was future Penn State coach Joe Paterno.

Bob Cameron, who frequently replaced Zastrow in 1951 and won the starting job outright in 1952, was a Californian who did not fit the mold of the typical college quarterback. He was a shot-putter on the track team, a task usually performed by bigger football linemen. He also punted. Cameron's gutsiest performance was against Army in a 7–0 victory in 1952 after he had injured his shoulder so badly in a scrimmage that he could barely lift his arm to throw the ball or place it in a punting position.

Erdelatz built a solid line whose star was defensive middle guard Steve Eisenhauer. He did not letter as a sophomore in 1951, but within two seasons he was an All-American. He became the first Navy football player elected to the Hall of Fame. Eisenhauer's greatest day might have been during a 31–7 victory over Cornell in 1952: he blocked a punt, recovered two fumbles, intercepted a pass, and helped the defense hold Cornell to just two yards rushing.

One of the most interesting players in 1952 was quarterback Steve Schoderbeck, whose home address was, appropriately enough, Hero Avenue in Pittsburgh. Schoderbeck lived up to his street's name in a 31–0 victory over Yale and an upset 7–7 tie against Penn. Schoderbeck's story was a football rags-to-riches tale, and it was a product of the penchant Erdelatz had for always planning ahead to get an edge. The biggest game on Navy's 1952 schedule, beside Army, was against neighboring arch-rival Maryland in the season's fourth week. Jack Scarbath, Maryland's All-America quarterback, was a wizard at running the Terps' split-T formation, and Erdelatz knew he needed more than a week's preparation if Navy was to be successful. So, he began preparing for the game during the preseason. To ready the defense, he tried all of his quarterbacks at simulating Scarbath's moves. Schoderbeck, a junior varsity player, performed best. He became so deft that Erdelatz put part of the split-T system into his offense and let Schoderbeck run it in certain varsity game situations.

The first time was in the opening game against Yale. The Mids bumbled along to a 7–7 tie at halftime. Erdelatz knew the Eli had not practiced against any split-T plays during their preparations, so he used that offense with Schoderbeck in the second half. Navy came away with a resounding 31–7 victory. The second time Schoderbeck starred was when he helped Navy achieve a 7–7 tie against favored Penn. The Mids were awful in the first half, with turnovers stymieing every possession. In the second half, Eisenhauer helped to right the Mids' defense, and Schoderbeck relieved Cameron and performed some of his split-T magic. He not only ripped Penn's defense for ninety-nine yards rushing on his "keeper" plays, but he passed for Navy's only touchdown on a thirty-two-yard play to Fred Franco. The touchdown capped a ninety-four-yard drive.

And the Maryland game? Unfortunately, his simulations were to no avail, because Navy was crushed, 32–7. The Mids came into the game hopeful and undefeated. But the game became an all-out war, one so bitterly fought that

The Naval Academy Foundation

Eddie Erdelatz and his successor, Wayne Hardin, enjoyed a continual supply of good players, starting with an unbeaten 1951 plebe team. Much of the credit should go to aggressive recruiting. Rip Miller's twenty to thirty "Bird Dogs" were very active around the country, and Miller managed to secure "out-of-district nominations" for top prospects whose own districts had exhausted their limit.

The football program also was helped at this time by the Naval Academy Foundation, whose stated mission was "to locate, identify and determine the qualifications of young men who need an additional year of academic preparation to enter the Naval Academy." Athletic director Elliott Laughlin once admitted that the Foundation "existed solely to assist athletes to get into the Naval Academy." The Athletic Association, through the Foundation, paid the tuition bills for these prospects to attend any of sixteen preparatory schools across the country. Most of them went to Bullis Prep and Wyoming Seminary in Pennsylvania.

"Players like George Welsh, Ron Beagle, Roger Staubach, and Joe Bellino all benefited from it," Laughlin once related. "Until 1963, every decent player, except Ned Oldham, who was a walk-on, came through the Foundation's program. Navy went to three bowls in five years because of this program, which not only helped a lot in recruiting athletes but also in upgrading the caliber of the Brigade as a whole."

four Mids and three Terps were ejected for fighting and three of Navy's first four tackles wound up on the injured list. After the game, Erdelatz stood before his team and, with tears streaming down his face, said, "I'm proud of you. You never gave up. We have Penn next week . . . and we'll take it out on them."

As noted above, Navy did "take it out" on Penn, earning the surprising tie. There were no miracles the following week, however, as the Mids fell to top-ranked Notre Dame, 17–6. Navy then rebounded and upset Duke 16–6, scoring all of its points in the second half. Franco gained 115 yards and tallied two touchdowns. Next came an easy win against Columbia. Many expected the same result against Army, but Navy was fortunate to escape with a sloppy 7–0 victory. The Mids turned over the ball six times and were saved from an upset by an Eisenhauer-led defense that allowed only 106 yards and four first downs. Army did its share with seven turnovers. During a five-minute stretch in the first half, the ball changed hands six times—and there wasn't a single punt! Franco gained forty-six of his 144 yards in a sixty-five-yard drive that ended with Phil Monahan's score.

Although Navy was picked as the best team in the East in 1953, Erdelatz felt that his team still was at least one year away from deserving such a ranking. After all, Navy had finished 1952 with a so-so, 4–3–2 record. Like many schools at that time with limited player resources, Navy was affected by a new rule limiting substitutions. This forced a return to something very close to the old one-platoon football. Erdelatz had to find players capable of playing both ways and try experienced players at new positions. Thus, John Weaver, who had been a fine defensive back in 1952, became the No. 1 quarterback in 1953 so he could stay on the field and play defense; Steve Eisenhauer had to learn how to play offensive guard so that he could continue using his superb defensive skills.

The effect of the new rule was apparent in the opening game, a dismal 6–6 tie against William and Mary. The second unit, led by sophomore quarterback

Phil Monahan scored Navy's only touchdown to beat Army, 7–0, in 1952. That victory was the third straight over Army and capped Navy's first winning season since 1945.

Steve Eisenhauer

Steve Eisenhauer was probably the more popular "Ike" at the Naval Academy during the 1952 and 1953 seasons, edging out Dwight D. Eisenhower, president of the United States and commander-in-chief of all the midshipmen.

Among Naval Academy interior linemen, Eisenhauer ranks with great players such as Babe Brown, Frank Wickhorst, George Brown, Don Whitmire, and Dick Scott—Hall of Fame players, all.

Eisenhauer's trip to the Hall of Fame was a long one. In his plebe year (1950), Ike was on the sixth of six plebe teams and almost quit because he wasn't eligible for the training table. But, just before he was going to tell coach Eddie Erdelatz that he was leaving, Eisenhauer was promoted to the fifth team. He decided to stay with the program.

Ike, then an offensive guard, started the 1951 season on the jayvees and was promoted to the varsity for the last four games. He didn't earn a letter. But in 1952, Navy had such good depth at guard with Alex Aronis, Joe Pertel, and Tony Correnti that Erdelatz moved Eisenhauer to middle guard on defense. "Ike is the perfect player for the type of defense we use," Erdelatz said. The Mids used an unorthodox 5–3–3 setup, and the middle guard had to control the center of the line. Eisenhauer's keys to success were his ability to detect plays quickly and, if he was moving in the wrong direction, to reset his course without slowing down. That great quickness also helped him prevent opposing centers and guards from getting a solid block on him.

He keyed Navy's second-ranked defense, which shut out four opponents, allowed just 843 rushing yards all season, and led a tight 7–0 victory over Army when it held the Cadets to only 106 yards of total offense. Navy finished the season 6–2–1. In 1953, new rules limited substitution. Eisenhauer played both as offensive guard and defensive lineman. Despite the double duty, he was named to his second straight All-America team. Eisenhauer was inducted into the College Football Hall of Fame in 1994. He made the first Academic All-America team in 1953, and later was elected to the Academic Hall of Fame.

Eisenhauer played football for two years with the Marines before going into Navy air. He participated in the intervention in Lebanon in 1958. During the Vietnam War, he was an operations officer in 1966 and 1967, flying 120 combat missions and earning the Navy Commendation Medal with Combat "V" and the Air Medal with eight Gold Stars.

George Welsh, scored Navy's only touchdown on a sixty-three-yard run by Jack Garrow. Navy's best place-kicker, John Weaver, was not in the game, and George Textor, the second kicker, missed the extra point.

Two ends from a great 1952 plebe team—Ron Beagle, who was six feet tall and weighed 186 pounds, and John Hopkins, a sturdy, six-two, 210-pounder—made an immediate impact. Beagle not only won the Maxwell Trophy in 1954, but eventually was enshrined in the Hall of Fame. Hopkins, the 1955 team captain, first flashed into prominence during a 9–6 loss to Penn when he and Jack Reister chased Penn passer Bob Felver some thirty yards behind the line of scrimmage. Reister finally grabbed Felver's jersey. To avoid the sack, Felver flipped the ball into the air—but Hopkins grabbed it and raced forty-six yards for Navy's only touchdown. Erdelatz switched Hopkins to left tackle in 1954, and, though he missed a month during that season with a broken thumb, he rates as one of Navy's greatest linemen.

George Welsh, a five-nine, 164-pound sophomore quarterback from Coaldale, Pennsylvania, won the starting job in 1953. Except when he was injured early in 1954, Welsh held it for three seasons, during which he established himself as one of the best in Navy's history. He had attracted the attention of many schools, including Notre Dame and Penn State, but all concluded that he was too short to make it in major-college football. They didn't realize that he "played big." Erdelatz loved him. "He has the respect and confidence of the other players—and he has guts," Eddie said.

He certainly did. On the field, no one was craftier. Erdelatz called Welsh

Ron Beagle

Ron Beagle was not the prototypical end . . . but he was good enough to make the Hall of Fame after two All-America seasons at Navy. In 1954, while starring as a junior on Navy's "Team Named Desire," he also became the first Navy player to win the Maxwell Trophy, given to the outstanding college football player in the nation.

Unlike many ends, who were long and lanky, Beagle was six feet and 186 pounds. But such was his ferocity and determination that he was good enough to play offense and defense in his first varsity season (1953), when college football returned to a one-platoon system. Beagle was fortunate to play with a team that emphasized passing and had a nifty quarterback in George Welsh. Beagle was Navy's all-time leading receiver with sixty-seven catches for 859 yards and eight touchdowns when he finished his career, and he led the team in receptions in each of his varsity seasons.

Despite his relatively slight frame, Beagle was a tenacious blocker and Navy's best pass rusher. He often played an entire game without substitution.

"He was thoroughly aggressive for his size, and he had tremendous hands," said Welsh. "Off the field, he was quiet and reserved, a complete contrast to how he played."

His coach, Eddie Erdelatz, said: "Beagle is a great pass-catcher, a great blocker, a great tackler—but most of all, he's a great guy."

Beagle was also a two-time All-America lacrosse player, and lettered in that sport for three seasons. When he graduated in 1956, he received the Stuart Oxnard Miller Memorial Lacrosse Cup as the team's most valuable midfielder and the Naval Academy Athletic Association Sword.

Beagle graduated from Purcell High School in Cincinnati. Nearly a decade later, the same school produced another Navy football star who, like Beagle, became an All-America, won the Maxwell Trophy in his junior year, and was inducted into the Hall of Fame. His name was Roger Staubach.

"a right-handed Frankie Albert" because he had perfected his ball-handling under Albert's tutelage. Welsh also had no superiors at that time in running the popular split-T option offense. "He's the best split-T quarterback in the nation and he is a genius at calling plays," said Erdelatz.

Two other players also blossomed in 1953: running backs Joe Gattuso and Phil Monahan. Gattuso played linebacker in 1952 before taking over Franco's fullback chores for the following two seasons. He was built like a fireplug, with a low center of gravity. He was a sure tackler, a hard-to-bring-down runner, and, not coincidentally, a successful wrestler. After his duty as a linebacker in 1952, the one-platoon rule pushed him to starting fullback, linebacker, and punter in 1953. He led Navy's rushers in 1953 with 422 yards and a 4.2-yards-per-carry average and was No. 1 again in 1954 with 525 yards and a 7.3-yard average—the latter a record that still holds today. As a wrestler, Gattuso won four letters and twenty-one consecutive matches; he placed third in the NCAA tournament's 167-pound division on two separate occasions. He also was the Navy's runner-up candidate for the 1956 Olympic trials.

Phil Monahan played offensive and defensive halfback, and Erdelatz then deftly mixed in speedy sophomore Bob Craig, a 175-pound hurdler on the track team. Craig broke several big plays in the 1953 season as a punt returner (sixty-nine yards against Columbia) and running back (a seventy-nine-yard sweep against Princeton).

After the season-opening tie against William and Mary, in 1953 Gattuso's running—127 yards against Dartmouth and eighty-seven against Cornell—helped Navy roll to three straight wins. But the Mids went into a tailspin and lost four of their final five games. One of the season's oddities was a scoreless tie against Duke—the last by a Navy team. The Mids might have been saved from a loss by a "lost down" controversy. The officials erred by not allowing Duke to repeat a down after stepping off a motion penalty. Duke was denied a fourth-down play—which would have been a field goal attempt—at Navy's fourteen-yard line.

Although Navy was favored to defeat Army, which had rebounded from the demolition of its football program two years earlier, the Mids lost to the Cadets 20–7. Pat Uebel scored a record-tying three touchdowns for Army—the first shortly after the Cadets recovered a surprise, game-opening onside kickoff. The Mids, who lost Monahan to an injury in the first quarter and Eisenhauer in the second, tried to rally. In the fourth quarter, they allowed Army just six offensive plays, but were turned aside twice deep in Army territory. Jack Garron finally scored to avert a shutout.

Navy was ignored in the 1954 preseason ratings, which turned out to be a break because the team was able to work without the pressure of high expectations. The season became a quintessential Erdelatz production. He did his best all-around coaching job ever that season, taking a team with limited talent, a line that averaged less than two hundred pounds per man, and a backfield that averaged less than 180 pounds per man, to a 7–2 regular-season record and a Sugar Bowl victory.

The team had three outstanding assets: the coach's great knack for putting people where they would be most productive; excellent team speed; and an

The leaders of Navy's famed 1954 "Team Named Desire": Coach Eddie Erdelatz and his quarterbacks, George Welsh (11) and John Weaver (16).

indomitable spirit that produced the most famous sobriquet in Navy football history—the "Team Named Desire."

Erdelatz switched Jim Owen from tackle to right end, where he held a starting job until Earle Smith moved ahead of him at midseason. Smith had been switched from quarterback to end just before the season began. The two of them played opposite Ron Beagle, who caught nineteen passes for 243 yards and scored three touchdowns en route to the Maxwell Trophy. The Owen-Smith combination was even more productive; they accounted for twenty-three catches for 322 yards and six touchdowns. Smith scored two of the touchdowns against Army.

The line was further improved when Erdelatz moved John Hopkins from end to left tackle and made 215-pound Jim Royer, a junior-varsity guard in 1953 and the team's biggest player, the right tackle. Sophomore Wilson Whitmire was the No. 3 center when the season began, but injuries to Bob Davis and Dick Dutnell moved him to the No. 1 position at midseason. Whitmire, no relation to Navy's Hall of Fame tackle of a decade earlier, eventually became one of Navy's greatest centers.

Bob Craig was the speedster in the backfield; he averaged 6.4 yards per carry that season, second to Gattuso's 7.3. Craig and Gattuso were the nation's most formidable one-two running punch when they were in the lineup together. Craig's three interceptions that season proved his ability as a defensive back.

Dick Guest and Gattuso split the fullback chores. Guest, a junior, started the season behind Gattuso, but his defensive play, blocking ability, and punting skill pushed him into the starting position. Gattuso, though, was still Navy's leading runner and scorer, and he played linebacker and punted when he was in the game.

Quarterback George Welsh marshalled all of that talent and blended it into a perfect mix while running Navy's split-T offense with the guile of a cat burglar. Unfortunately, a leg injury cost him two games and parts of two others.

The team suffered a cruel blow when Phil Monahan, its captain, played just thirty minutes that season because of knee problems. He had had surgery on one knee during spring drills and hurt the other in preseason practice, then reinjured it prior to the Pitt game. "He gave us thirty minutes of playing time, but he gave us one-hundred years of leadership," Erdelatz said of Monahan after the season. Erdelatz compensated for Monahan's absence by moving No. 3 quarterback John Weaver to halfback, where he averaged more than four yards per carry while still performing well on defense.

Heroes came from unlikely quarters. The first was a two-year, junior-varsity quarterback named Dick Echard. He became the early catalyst for Navy's stunning success and presented the first public insight into the spirit and tenacity of this team. Echard was the No. 3 signal-caller at the start of the season, but he replaced starter John Weaver during the second game against Dartmouth and cemented a 42–7 victory with two touchdown passes during a ten-minute, three-touchdown burst in the fourth quarter.

With Welsh still injured, Echard started the following week at heavily favored Stanford. He responded by playing an almost flawless game, completing nine of seventeen passes for two touchdowns during the Mids' 25–0 victory. The game was a classic for this Navy team. The Mids were outweighed by nearly twenty pounds per man, yet their offense totally dominated Stanford's defense and produced 390 yards. Navy was tagged with 171 yards in penalties as it fought and hammered Stanford any way it could. When Hugh Webster blocked John Brodie's punt, Ron Beagle fell on it in the end zone for a touchdown; Owen caught a TD pass; and Gattuso, who never lost a yard in fourteen carries while gaining 153 yards, ran thirty-four yards for the third score.

Erdelatz, who was always a "player's coach," discovered that his team had a spirit that could not be quantified. Years later, all the players on that team agreed that the "spirit," or "desire," as it was then called, was the result of a unique chemistry among all of its members—a once-in-a-lifetime mix that allows a team to do wondrous things. Erdelatz was never introspective about what made his team tick, but he so admired its drive to succeed that he went out of his way to praise its "desire." After the Stanford game, the "Team Named Desire" tag was born when Erdelatz said, "This team has more will to win that any of the five squads I have coached at the Academy." He was seconded by his coaching foe, Chuck Taylor, who noted, "I haven't seen a bunch of boys who wanted to play football more than Navy did."

The team returned to the Naval Academy from Stanford the following night and rode their buses onto a dark and deserted Tecumseh Court. Within seconds, brilliant lights flooded the area and all 3,600 members of the Brigade—accompanied by a brass band—cheered the team. Every player was hoisted onto shoulders and carried from the buses. Cap pistols and firecrackers competed with the cheers, whistles, and

Earle Smith was the "other" end with Ron Beagle on Navy's "Team Named Desire." Smith was a crushing blocker and reliable pass catcher. He was captain of the 1956 team that had a fine 6–1–2 record.

George Welsh *(holding the ball)* was a master of sleight-of-hand as a quarterback who ran Navy's split-T formation to perfection. He gets set to bamboozle Notre Dame in a 1954 game as he heads down the line of scrimmage with guard Alex Aronis (61) sealing off an Irish defender and running back Dick Guest (30) moving outside in case Welsh decides to pitch the ball.

wooden shower clogs that were pounded together to create an almost deafening cacophony of joyous noise.

Winless Pitt—and erstwhile Navy coach Tom Hamilton—punctured the Mids' balloon the following week in one of the most emotional games of the season. Hamilton, then athletic director at Pitt, had taken over as coach after Red Dawson had to step down because of a heart problem. His team came away from the Navy game with a 21–19 victory in Pittsburgh. A fiery coach who knew exactly what to expect from a Navy team, Hamilton laid the "desire" theme on his own players. The two teams literally slugged it out in a brutal battle. The difference was missed extra points after Navy's first two scores and a Pitt blitz in which the Panthers scored twice within ninety seconds in the second quarter.

George Welsh reclaimed the starting job late in the Pitt game and led the team for the rest of the season, beginning with a stunning 52–6 win against Penn. Navy's next opponent was Notre Dame, a two-touchdown favorite. The Irish defeated Navy 6–0 on a soggy field made even worse when the ground crew, while removing the tarpaulin, allowed accumulated rainwater to empty into one end of the playing field rather than onto the sidelines. The wet turf slowed down the slick Navy rushing game, and the Irish pushed Navy all over the field in the first half, when they scored their only touchdown. But Navy dominated the second half and might have come away with a tie, or even a victory, had not Bob Craig, who played so ably at halfback, fumbled the ball as he was going into the end zone late in the third quarter.

Navy easily defeated Duke 40–7 in the first Oyster Bowl in Norfolk, Virginia. (This bowl game continued on and off for some twenty years.) After beating Columbia, Navy climaxed its season with an exciting 27–20 victory over Army, a game that is unmatched in excitement and excellence in this storied series. (The game is covered in detail in Chapter Nine.) Navy finished the season ranked fifth nationally and won the Lambert Trophy for the second time in three years.

The 1954 Army victory carried another reward—a chance to play Mississippi in the Sugar Bowl. Navy's invitation to the bowl was contingent on its defeating Army. After its victory, Secretary of the Navy Charles S. Thomas, accompanied by the superintendent, Rear Adm. Walter F. Boone, went to Navy's dressing room. When Boone asked the players if they wanted to play in the Sugar Bowl, there was a resounding "Aye!" When the dressing room doors were finally opened for the press, the reporters saw Thomas, Boone, Erdelatz, and Fleet Adm. William Halsey in the middle of a group of ecstatic Navy players, with Halsey pounding team captain Phil Monahan on the back.

Navy defeated Mississippi in the Sugar Bowl, its first postseason action since the 14–14 tie against Washington in the 1924 Rose Bowl. (The Sugar Bowl game is covered in Chapter Ten.)

In 1955, the Mids didn't have an inspiring nickname, but they did have another fine season (6–2–1), although it ended on a disappointing note. Army upset Navy 14–6 and cost the team an opportunity to play in either the Cotton Bowl or the Gator Bowl. The 1955 team was just as good as the 1954 team, but its effectiveness suffered because of injuries. Ron Beagle broke his hand before the season started and was hampered all year, although he still was named on thirteen All-America teams. George Welsh sprained his toe in the fourth game (against Pitt), which prevented him from running the option series with the same success he had achieved in 1954.

Even though he was injured, Welsh played in eight games (he missed the Penn game) and notched several season records: 1,348 yards of total offense—tops in the nation—1,319 of them from passing; and ninety-four completions, including twenty for touchdowns. On defense, he led the team with three interceptions. Welsh was awarded the Thompson Trophy that year, while Beagle, who caught thirty passes for 451 yards and four touchdowns, won the Naval Academy Athletic Association Sword.

Erdelatz came up with a pair of splendid young backs in sophomore Ned Oldham and junior Chet Burchette, both of whom teamed with Dick Guest. Oldham, a five-feet-ten, 183-pound native of Cuyahoga Falls, Ohio, was a special player during all four years of his career at Navy. He first showed his skills on the 1954 plebe team as a good, hard runner with fine outside speed. He won a starting job in spring drills and went on to lead the team's rushers with 412 yards. Oldham not only played football and lacrosse, but as a plebe he also won the brigade debating contest. He was captain of the 1957 team that won the Cotton Bowl.

Burchette was not a big player (he was five ten and weighed 163 pounds), but no one was tougher. He rose from being a third-team reserve in 1954 to a starting position in 1955. He was the team's third-best rusher, handled punt returns, and was a solid defensive player.

Navy won its first five games in 1955. After three consecutive shutouts (William and Mary, South Carolina, and Pitt) it posted a 34–14 victory at Penn State. Welsh completed fifteen of twenty passes and established a single-game passing record of 285 yards. The following week, with Welsh, Hopkins, and guard Tony Stremic on the bench with injuries, Tom Forrestal, an eighteen-year-old sophomore up from the junior varsity for just four days, directed a 33–0 victory over Penn.

The winning streak was broken by Notre Dame in a bitterly fought and emotional game that also marked the twenty-fifth anniversary of the opening of Notre Dame Stadium. When the first game was played at the stadium on October 11, 1930, Navy was the opponent personally invited by famed Notre Dame coach Knute Rockne. The Irish easily won that game 26–2. The 1955 Notre Dame team had much more difficulty taming the Mids. In the end, the Irish simply ground down Navy with a relentless running game. Oldham scored Navy's only touchdown early in the last quarter when Notre Dame led 21–0. The final score was 21–7. A week later, the slump continued. Playing without Oldham and Burchette, Navy tied Duke 7–7. Welsh passed to Beagle for the only Navy score.

Navy was favored against Army, which had turned its quarterback duties over to Don Holleder, an All-America end the previous year. Holleder had never played quarterback at any level before that season, but Army coach Red Blaik desperately needed on-the-field leadership to complement a tremendously talented team—and he prized that leadership quality so highly that he was willing to downgrade great passing and running skills. Blaik decided to switch Holleder for two reasons: One, he wanted a quarterback who could run the team for the first eight games of the season and get the most from its great talent. The Cadets won five of those games. Two, he wanted a quarterback who could match the leadership qualities of George Welsh and give his team a chance to defeat Navy. This contradicted, in part, Blaik's off-stated belief that his Army teams gave equal weight to every game on the schedule, and allowed the natural emotional surge that was endemic in the Army-Navy rivalry to carry the Cadets further against Navy. The Naval Academy, he claimed, always built its team to beat Army first and then accept whatever other success accrued during the season. Erdelatz, who did not like Blaik, ridiculed that idea; he contended he always put the best players on the field at positions where they could best perform. He was correct and, in reality, Blaik

Tackle John Hopkins (77), captain of the 1955 team, leads a phalanx of blockers that levels potential Pitt tacklers and paves the way for a big gain by running back Jack Garrow. Hopkins switched from end to tackle on Navy's offensive line during that memorable season, and he provided tremendous leadership for the fifth-ranked Mids.

Navy's defense gangs up and stops a Pitt runner as the Mids' wipe out their opponent, 21–0, during the 1955 season.

did the same thing in 1955 with his daring decision to use Holleder at quarterback. In an irony not lost on either coach, Blaik's decision to match Welsh's leadership abilities paid off with a 14–6 Army victory.

Blaik said later, "No matter what might happen before the Navy game, I reasoned that we would have no chance to win it, not with Welsh as their quarterback, unless we had a quarterback who could match him at least in dynamic leadership. This was a quality I knew Holleder to be rich in."

Holleder in fact proved to be a very good option quarterback. He possessed great athletic skills and instincts that meshed perfectly with a team that included the nation's No. 1 defense. He played an almost flawless game in helping Army to achieve this upset victory.

Blaik's offense contrasted sharply with Navy's multiple attack. Holleder missed his first two passes and never tried another. The Cadets relied instead on their defense and a solid running game. Holleder, who later was killed in Vietnam and whose name now adorns the athletic building at West Point, gave one of the most gallant and inspired performances ever by any Army-Navy participant—one that even his Navy foes richly saluted.

Navy scored on its first possession, going seventy-five yards in sixteen plays. Welsh ran for the touchdown. Oldham missed the extra point, and Navy's scoring was over for the day. Navy dominated the first half—at one point, Navy led Army in first downs 13–1. But Army scored twice in the second half, and its defense twice stopped Navy deep in its territory. The Mids blew a host of scoring opportunities throughout the game with six fumbles. Welsh had a fine game, completing eighteen of twenty-nine passes for 176 yards, including nine to Beagle for seventy-six yards.

The Welsh era ended, but the 1956 team forged a 6–1–2 record and a No. 16 ranking. The excellence continued because there was no dearth of fine players, including three young linemen, tackles Tony Anthony and Bob Reifsnider, and guard Tony Stremic, to go with Wilson Whitmire and end Earle Smith.

Coach Eddie Erdelatz and quarterback Tom Forrestal, who led the 1957 Mids to a 9–1–1 record, including a decisive 20–7 victory over Rice in the Cotton Bowl. During his two seasons as a starter, Forrestal completed 150 passes for more than 2,000 yards and 13 touchdowns. Before the 1957 season, Erdelatz said flatly that Forrestal had no peers in college football as a quarterback, and when the season ended, he underscored the remark by noting, "I've haven't seen anything yet that has made me change my mind." Forrestal was selected to many All-America teams as well as being an Academic All-America selectee that year.

Once again, Navy was a powerful offensive team. Tom Forrestal took over at quarterback and got plenty of help at running back from Oldham and Burchette, plus Harry Hurst, Dick Dagampat, Paul Gober, and Vince Monto. Navy exploded for more than five hundred yards in the opener against William and Mary and gained more than three hundred yards in four other contests . The team lost only to Tulane, tied Duke and Army, and trounced Notre Dame 33–7—the biggest Navy win ever in that series. The Mids rolled up more than 350 yards while holding the Irish to just seven first downs. Navy's scant 7–0 halftime lead ballooned in the second half. Oldham scored twice, once on a thirty-one-yard pass from Forrestal. Erdelatz was carried off the field by his team and was too emotional to speak to anyone for a long time afterward. It was the Navy's first victory over Notre Dame since 1944.

Reports were rampant that success against Army would put Navy in the Cotton Bowl. Nothing official was said by the Academy, though, so the players didn't know that they had to beat Army, not tie them, to get the bid. West Point policy forbade postseason games, so Army had no bowl ambitions of its own, but the thought of playing spoilers to Navy's hopes was obviously much on the Cadets' minds. After Dick Dagampat had gained sixteen yards to Army's eleven-yard line on Navy's only scoring drive, an Army player said to him: "You're a helluva looking mess and you're going to a bowl? But this game isn't over, and you're going to look a helluva lot worse." (Dagampat took the ball into the end zone a few plays later.)

After an Army player rode a Navy player many yards with a tremendous block, the Cadet scowled, "This ride you'll get for free, but you're going to have to pay to go to Texas."

Such trash talk marked the entire game—one in which the defenses were dominant. Navy forced five turnovers—four of them were inside the thirty-yard line—and stopped the Cadets on downs at the twenty-yard line in another series. But the Mids were done in by turnovers themselves, and Army's tough defense held Navy to just 132 yards, its worst offensive day of the year. In the first half, Navy had only one first down and crossed midfield just once; in the second half, it got into Army territory three times, and on two of those drives the Mids turned the ball over.

The game ended in a 7–7 tie. Gloom permeated Navy's locker room. Then the superintendent, Rear Adm. William R. Smedberg III, walked in and climbed atop an equipment trunk to speak to the team. "If you're not good enough to beat Army," he said, "then you're not good enough to play in the Cotton Bowl."

And with that, he stepped down and walked out, leaving behind an even more anguished atmosphere. Earle Smith, the team captain, was bitter. "This team is as good as the Sugar Bowl team and should have gone," he said.

The disappointment from the final game of the 1956 season was swept away by the achievements of the 1957 team; many believe it was better than the three that preceded it. An early clue came when Erdelatz used only seventeen of his allotted twenty days for spring practice. When the regular season ended, the Mids had won eight of ten games, and the blemishes were the results of upsets—a 13–7 loss to North Carolina and a 7–7 tie against Duke. Unlike in 1956, Navy knew before it played Army that it had to win to get the Cotton Bowl bid. The team responded with a solid victory and, one month later, capped the memorable season by beating Rice 20–7 on New Year's Day in Dallas.

When the Cotton Bowl ended, Erdelatz, not given to hyperbole when ranking his teams, flatly declared: "This was the best ball club I have ever had the privilege of coaching." His emphatic statement underscored something he had said throughout the season. "It's been fun to coach this club because I've never seen kids who wanted to play the game more."

The 1957 team easily could have been "Team Named Desire II," with two differences: It had more depth and played better defense. Oldham, the team captain, made the All-East team for the second consecutive year. In a career marked by consistent excellence, this was his finest season. He led the team in scoring with sixty-nine points; was second in rushing behind Harry Hurst with 594 yards and a 5.8 rushing average (after leading Navy the previous two seasons); and returned punts and kickoffs.

Oldham's leadership was without peer. While on defense in the season-opening 46–6 victory over Boston College, Oldham was victimized by a pass for the opposition's only touchdown. When he arrived back at the Academy and stepped off the team bus, the first person he encountered was defensive backfield coach

Running back Ned Oldham was captain of the 1957 team, lauded as much for his leadership as he was for his great play that earned him back-to-back All-East selections in 1956–57. He led Navy in rushing in both 1955 and 1956 and was second in 1957. He also returned punts and kickoffs.

The 1957 Notre Dame–Navy Game

The Brigade played a major role in Navy's 21–6 victory at South Bend in 1957. It raised $500 to lease a phone line and then connected it to loudspeakers at Notre Dame Stadium. Thus, the football team could hear the cheers from the Mids back at the Naval Academy who were watching the game on television. A replica of a football field was laid out on the basketball court with blue and gold crepe paper indicating line markers; miniature goal posts marked each end of the field. Two plebes wearing striped officials' shirts moved a blue (for Navy) or green (for Notre Dame) football down the field to track the progress of the game. Hundreds of midshipmen greeted the team when it returned to the Academy that night, and game stars Ronnie Brence and Ray Wellborn were paraded around the Yard on their fellow mids' shoulders.

Steve Belichick, who had been away scouting another team and had not made the trip to Boston.

Believing that Belichick already knew about his mistake and was going to mention it, Oldham spoke first. "Coach, that will never happen again."

And it didn't.

In fact, when Navy scored twenty-one second-half points to beat California 21–6, Oldham's interception set up Navy's third touchdown. He scored it himself, capping a 116-yard rushing day. A week later in the Oyster Bowl against Georgia, his thirty-four-yard touchdown run in the fourth quarter nailed down a 27–14 victory. After Oldham injured his knee in a 35–7 victory over Penn, he missed a smashing 21–6 victory over Notre Dame and played just one quarter of the 7–7 tie against Duke.

Tom Forrestal and Bob Reifsnider both were picked to the All-America team. Forrestal, who was also an Academic All-America, had to live up to preseason billing by Erdelatz, who said pointedly that his quarterback had no peers in the country. After Navy's Cotton Bowl victory over Rice, Erdelatz said, "I haven't seen anything yet that has made me change my mind."

The praise was deserved. Forrestal had mastered a new wing-T offensive system that complemented the split-T. The transformation was eased by the presence of plenty of weapons, with backs like Oldham, Hurst, and fullbacks Dick Dagampat and Ray Wellborn. Forrestal masterfully used the variety of reverses and passes in the wing-T, and then sprinkled in some split-T moves, particularly when Navy was in short-yardage or goal-line situations. Most importantly, Forrestal led the nation's No. 1 pass offense, accounting for 1,270 yards with his ninety-three completions, eight of which were for touchdowns.

Bob Reifsnider, at six two and 235 pounds, was Navy's biggest and fastest lineman and, in the opinion of many from that time, the best tackle of that era. He had been a fullback in high school, but Erdelatz dismissed the possibility of his playing that position at Navy. "We can't afford the luxury of a 235-pound fullback," he said. Reifsnider was an All-East tackle and honorable mention All-America player in 1956 as a sophomore, but was moved to center for the 1957 season. When Jim Martinez was lost with an early-season knee injury, Reifsnider went back to tackle. In addition to making the All-America team, he won the Maxwell Trophy as the nation's best football player. Had it not been for an Achilles tendon injury during 1958, Reifsnider probably would have been a Hall of Fame player.

The heart of Navy's success in 1957 revolved around a great, two-way line fashioned by line coach Ernie Jorge. Along with Reifsnider, the Mids started Tony Stremic and George Fritzinger at guard; Tony Anthony at the other tackle; and Milan Moncilovich at center after Reifsnider went to tackle. The ends were Wayne McKee and Pete Jokanovich, both strong defenders,who, in the victory over Army, were cited by Red Blaik for shutting down the Cadets' outside game after they found running inside to be all but impossible.

Tony Stremic, at five eleven and 205 pounds, was allowed to bypass spring drills for the 1957 season so he could secure his spot as a 191-pound wrestler (he was second in both the Eastern and National Championships that year). On the football field, his tremendous quickness, low center of gravity, and mastery of leverage techniques from wrestling allowed Stremic to uproot opposing linemen and open up holes, or control the middle of the defense. Stremic injured his leg late in the season but played the entire game against Army and then was chosen the Cotton Bowl's Most Valuable Player, though he needed a painkiller to make it through that game. Many years after graduation, he was the only non-All-America player chosen as a starter on Navy's all-time team.

Although Erdelatz was always credited for developing Navy's highly rated offense during these years, he was also a very innovative defensive coach. In 1957, he devised something the pundits dubbed the "jitterbug defense." It was keyed by the three linebackers—Dagampat or Wellborn, who both played fullback; Moncilovich; and Fritzinger. They were constantly moving in and out of gaps, hence the "jitterbug" nickname. This kind of movement disrupted the opposition's blocking schemes and jammed its running attack. Navy's defense was ranked first nationally, allowing fewer than two hundred yards per game. Opponents that season gained fewer than three yards per play. Seven of them were held to ten or fewer first downs, and Navy was so dominant that California made just three rushing first downs and seventy-one yards rushing when the Mids came from behind with twenty-one second-half points to win.

In 1957, the nation was in its early struggles to achieve racial justice, and Navy's football team became part of the battle. Its game against the University of Georgia was moved from Baltimore to Athens, Georgia, because of financial considerations, but when Georgia could not guarantee nonsegregated seating, it was moved again to the 47,000-seat Oyster Bowl in Norfolk.

The season's biggest game, outside of Army, was the 21–6 victory over unbeaten Notre Dame in South Bend. Both Oldham and Dagampat were out with injuries (though Oldham kicked the two extra points). But Ray Wellborn, who replaced Dagampat, scored three touchdowns, and Navy's offense romped with 398 yards—237 of them rushing.

Bowl fever swept the Yard for two weeks before the Army game, which pitted Army's top-ranked rushing offense against Navy's top-ranked defense. But for the first time in two decades, it rained during the game. Army's great speed, which featured Bob Anderson and Pete Dawkins, was neutralized.

Once again, Erdelatz had a surprise for Army—and for Navy. When his team returned from pregame warmups, he called them together.

"I like things fine. I like this team. I even like the rain," he said. "I like everything but your uniforms."

While his players looked quizzically at each other, he barked, "Look in your lockers."

Inside each man's steel locker was a new powder-blue jersey with gold numerals. The dressing room suddenly lit up. "The switch gave them something to chatter about and helped them stay relaxed for those last few moments before the kickoff," Erdelatz explained later. Then he added what everyone pretty well knew: "This is a pretty relaxed team anyway. When told they had to play with a leather ball instead of a rubber ball as we had planned because of the rain, one of them said, 'It's all right with us if we use a wooden ball.'"

That's how they played the game, particularly Oldham, who scored all of Navy's points that day with two touchdowns and two extra points. The first seven came on a six-yard run that ended a seventy-two-yard drive and produced a 7–0 halftime lead. In the fourth quarter, he ran forty-four yards for his second score.

Navy's defense, and the sloppy field, did a superb job containing Army. The Cadets had scored at least three touchdowns against every opponent that season and had averaged more than four hundred yards per game, including 323 rushing. Against Navy, the Cadets rushed for only eighty-eight yards and gained only forty-four more passing, while Navy intercepted seven passes. Bob Caldwell ended a second-quarter Army drive to the nine-yard line with an interception, and Tom Forrestal snatched a sure touchdown from the hands of Army end Don Usry in the end zone in the third quarter. Those were the only times Army threatened to score all day. Navy immediately accepted its long-sought Cotton Bowl bid and went on to defeat Rice. (The details of the game are covered in Chapter Ten).

Navy also looked forward to moving into its own stadium, which was then under construction. It was one of the "musts" in Tom Hamilton's plan to reshape Navy's football program. He believed the team would be more successful if it played its home games in a large, first-class stadium at the Naval Academy rather than having to travel thirty miles to Memorial Stadium in Baltimore to its "home field." Hamilton understood that any time a team boarded a bus and left its campus, it lost much of its home field advantage. At the time, Navy was playing one or two games a year at old Thompson Stadium, plus one or two in Baltimore, and another in Norfolk. Thompson Stadium was much too small for Navy's nationally ranked football program, and a desperate need for new buildings at the Naval Academy had targeted it for extinction.

Hamilton also was keenly aware of the economics of college football. He knew that a new stadium, designed to seat nearly 30,000 spectators—and

Ron Brandquist stops Michigan fullback John Herrnstein at the goal line, helping to preserve Navy's 20–14 unexpected win against the Wolverines in 1958.

with room to add even more seats should ticket demand consistently exceed its capacity—would allow Navy to schedule more home games, and thus produce more revenue.

Building plans at the Naval Academy did not allow for the construction of a stadium within the Yard. But the Naval Academy Athletic Association, through its executive director, Morris Gilmore, had acquired a large parcel of land in the Admiral Heights section of Annapolis, just a stone's throw from the Academy's grounds. That was the site chosen for what became Navy–Marine Corps Memorial Stadium.

Before it was built, though, the Academy superintendent, Admiral Smedberg, had to overcome the opposition of Thomas B. Gates, the secretary of the Navy. Gates, no doubt sensitive to some grumbling on Capitol Hill about spending money to build a new football stadium at a time when the defense establishment was cutting back, refused to sanction the project. But the Athletic Association had never sought any Navy Department appropriations, and when Gates was assured none would be solicited for the stadium's construction, he finally gave his approval.

Smedberg turned to Capt. (later Admiral) Eugene Fluckey, head of the Electrical Engineering Department at the Naval Academy, to direct the fund-raising effort. Athletic director Elliott Laughlin and Fluckey were close friends from their days as outstanding submarine commanders during World War II. Fluckey had won the Medal of Honor while commanding the USS *Barb*, which sank seventeen Japanese ships for more than 96,000 tons.

Captain Fluckey raised more than two million of the three million dollars needed, and the Athletic Association, helped by Navy's three bowl appearances after the 1954, 1957, and 1960 seasons, put up the rest. Fluckey was a natural salesman, flamboyant and persuasive. "I knew that if he took the fund-raising job, he would succeed," Laughlin said later. "He had a wealth of good, innovative ideas, including memorial chairs, and instituted competition within the various fleets, ships and even classes to see which could raise the most money."

Morris Gilmore supervised the construction of the 30,000-seat stadium. Fluckey wanted one that held 50,000 to 60,000 people to accommodate future population increases in Annapolis, but Laughlin maintained that weak Navy teams would draw no more than 18,000. If there ever was a game of such importance that all ticket requests could not be met, he said, it could be played in Baltimore's 60,000-seat Memorial Stadium. (Navy has subsequently played at times in Baltimore, as well as at Robert F. Kennedy Stadium in Washington and in large stadiums in Philadelphia and New Jersey.)

Navy played its first game at the new stadium on September 26, 1959, against William and Mary. Navy won, 29–2. More than three million fans have passed through its turnstiles. The largest turnout was 35,753 for a game against Air Force in 1993. Appropriately, the Adm. Thomas J. Hamilton Locker Room Complex was dedicated before the 1992 season—fitting tribute to the man who has done more for Navy football than anyone in Academy history.

In 1958, new starting quarterback Joe Tranchini led the Mids to a 6–3 season. Tranchini had been sought by many civilian schools, but Rip Miller's "Bird

Eugene Fluckey

Rear Adm. Eugene Fluckey, who spearheaded the stadium fund-raising campaign, was one of the submarine service's great wartime skippers and sharpshooters. He also was renowned for his colorful combat reports which, said Slade Cutter, himself a great sub commander and sharpshooter, "were written like a thriller novel." Fluckey later served as technical adviser to several submarine movies made in Hollywood.

Some of the films incorporated events from Fluckey's service. One of those occurred on his last combat patrol when eight of his crew went ashore on Hokkaido and blew up a railroad bridge. In his report, Fluckey noted that the men had watched a horse race while hiding outside a nearby track waiting to finish their mission.

Dogs," combined with some gentle persuasion from Tranchini's girlfriend back in Clairton, Pennsylvania, convinced him to accept an appointment. "Trigger Joe" missed most of his plebe season with a broken ankle; as a sophomore, he played behind Tom Forrestal and Pat Flood. Tranchini had only eighty-two minutes of playing time when he started the 1958 season, but he proved to be nearly the equal of Welsh and Forrestal.

Navy had no outstanding runner, so Erdelatz spread the workload among the quintet of Wellborn (who led the team with 271 yards), Dagampat, Joe Matalavage, Ron Brandquist, and a stumpy, thick-legged sophomore named Joe Bellino. The five combined for nearly a thousand yards in 1958, but Bellino quickly emerged as the standout. He was the team's leading scorer with five touchdowns; its leading receiver with nineteen catches; and its No. 2 rusher with 266 yards.

Navy lost to unbeaten Army, 22–6. But Navy also achieved one of its most momentous wins ever—a 20–14, come-from-behind victory over Michigan at Ann Arbor. Tranchini, who completed seven of eight passes, directed second-half scoring drives of sixty-seven and eighty-five yards to overcome Michigan's 14–6 lead. He was Welsh-like on the winning thirty-six-yard touchdown pass in the final minutes, executing a brilliant play-action fake before throwing the ball to Dick Zembrzuski, the only receiver on the play. Earlier, he had thrown a ten-yard touchdown pass to John Kanuch.

Navy's defense played a major role in the victory, turning back Michigan six times from inside the thirty-yard line—four times in the first half—without a score. One of those stops was by the Mids' second unit at the one-yard line in the second quarter. The final stop came after Navy had gone ahead, and Michigan drove to the twenty-eight-yard line. The defense drove the Wolverines back with a pair of sacks and saved the win.

Navy also posted big victories over Penn and Maryland in 1958. Erdelatz used his first team for just twenty minutes in the 50–8 blowout of Penn, allowing Jim Maxfield to do most of the quarterbacking. After losing to Notre Dame 40–20 the following week, Navy won some local bragging rights with a 40–14 beating of Maryland's Terps. Matalavage gained 102 rushing yards and scored a pair of touchdowns that broke open the game in the third quarter.

For the first time since becoming head coach, Erdelatz held Navy's practice sessions for the Army game in secret—ostensibly to devise something to combat the Cadets' new "Lonesome End" offense that featured end Bill Carpenter permanently flanked fifteen yards from his tackle. The Cadets had used this, plus the great play of Heisman Trophy winner Pete Dawkins, to fashion an unbeaten season.

Navy never figured out the Lonesome End offense, but it shocked Army at the outset by recovering Dawkins's fumble of the opening kickoff and moving to a quick 6–0 lead on Bellino's touchdown. As usual, Erdelatz had concocted a couple of offensive surprises—including occasional use of his version of the Lonesome End formation. The Mids so bamboozled Army that it seemed at first that an upset was in the making. But the Cadets stopped Bellino on a fourth-and-two at Army's fourteen-yard line, and the momentum swung. Although the Mids contained Dawkins's running, Bob Anderson scored an

In 1958 Navy had just four returning starters from its Cotton Bowl champions, and Erdelatz set up a vivid display of the setback by draping his departed players' jerseys over tackling dummies. Those departed players included Wayne McKee (end, 87), Tony Stremic (guard, 61), Tony Anthony (tackle, 76), and Pete Jokanovich (end, 86). Gone from the backfield were Harry Hurst (halfback, 34), Tom Forrestal (quarterback, 18), and Ned Oldham (halfback, 27). The four returnees who helped forge a 6–3 record were All-America and Maxwell Trophy winner Bob Reifsnider (tackle, 58), George Fritzinger (guard, 63), Milan Moncilovich (center, 51), and Ray Wellborn (running back, 33).

Army touchdown for a 7–6 halftime lead. Anderson scored again in the third quarter, and end Don Usry intercepted Tranchini's pass and returned it for another score in the fourth quarter.

Five weeks later, Earl Blaik retired as head coach at West Point. Blaik's retirement was a surprise, but that was mild compared with the announcement the following spring that Erdelatz was leaving the Naval Academy.

Despite Navy's football success, Erdelatz had begun to wear out his welcome at the Academy. The long-smoldering issue of Erdelatz's loyalty to the Naval Academy broke open after the 1957 season. Erdelatz knew that continued friction between him and the administration made his position precarious. When he learned that Paul "Bear" Bryant was leaving his job as head coach at Texas A&M for Alabama, Erdelatz quietly let it be known that he was interested in succeeding Bryant. Although still under contract at the Academy, Erdelatz even visited Texas A&M at the invitation of a prominent Aggie football booster, ostensibly to investigate the possibility of becoming head coach. In fact, Erdelatz had already convinced Bryant to push his cause with the Texas A&M administration. Bryant went so far as to assure him that he would get the job and could bring his Navy coaching staff with him. But when the alleged "agreement" became public, the Texas A&M president said he was unaware of any such arrangements. Worse still, so were Naval Academy officials, who learned what had happened from a newspaper story. Jim Myers then succeeded Bryant, and Erdelatz remained at the Naval Academy to coach the 1958 team.

It was left to Slade Cutter to wield the axe.

Cutter had succeeded Laughlin as athletic director in 1957 and was specifically charged by Rear Adm. Elton W. Grenfell, chief of the Bureau of Naval Personnel, to fire Erdelatz. Grenfell, a passionate Navy football fan, was appalled at the high-handed stunts pulled by Erdelatz. He believed that Cutter could do the job with the least repercussions among alumni because of his status as a former Navy football star and war hero. "It was one of the most miserable damn jobs I ever had in my life," Cutter said. "It was something that Laughlin should have done. The problems were there for a long time."

Cutter became concerned about the potential for a Navy version of the West Point "cribbing scandal" after he found out that Erdelatz had fixed it so that anyone who played on Saturday, regardless of how long, did not have to attend Monday classes. Further, Erdelatz had done away with Wednesday night study hall so his players could attend film sessions and had gotten them excused on Fridays to finish preparations for the next day's game. The players were missing so much class work that many of them required remedial help.

There also was tremendous animosity about the type of athlete Erdelatz was attracting to the Academy. "In 1957, my first year as athletic director, of the thirty-one players who graduated, only one went to the line," Cutter noted. "The others went to the Supply Corps or resigned. They couldn't have cared less about the Navy."

Cutter urged Superintendent Smedberg to fire Erdelatz immediately after his visit to Texas A&M became public. "We have to fire this guy," Cutter told him. "He is disloyal to you. He is disloyal to the Academy. He is turning the midshipmen against the Navy." Cutter believed that the alumni would accept the action once they learned how Erdelatz had run roughshod over the rules. But Smedberg refused. "That was really bad," Cutter said, "because Eddie became absolutely arrogant after that, and no one could control him."

Nonetheless, Cutter instituted changes regarding team privileges. Erdelatz fired back in the media, complaining about "a lack of support . . . that someone was trying to destroy my program." The last straw came just as spring practice was concluding in 1959. Erdelatz addressed a Lions Club breakfast in Annapolis and severely criticized the Academy and its new superintendent, Rear Adm. Charles L. Melson, bitterly charging that he was getting no support for his program. Sports information director John Cox was at the affair and called Cutter to warn him. Cutter also heard about the remarks from others. He confronted Erdelatz, but the coach refused to discuss the matter. Cutter then went directly to Melson and said the coach must be fired.

"He didn't even ask why," Cutter recounted. "He just said, 'It's your problem. Call a meeting of the board and see if they approve.'"

No one on the board said anything in Erdelatz's defense. Two hours later, the Erdelatz era was over. It had been a grand ride . . . but there was an even headier one upcoming. The Wayne Hardin era, featuring Joe Bellino and Roger Staubach, was about to begin.

7. The Hardin and Heisman Way: Joe Bellino and Roger Staubach 1959–1964

There were some who feared that the departure of Eddie Erdelatz signaled hard times for Navy football. But for the next six years, there were seldom major problems on the field. Erdelatz left behind a superb talent lode for his successor, Wayne Hardin. The flow of talent continued until the effects of an escalating war in Vietnam took its toll on applicants to the Naval Academy in the midsixties.

Most importantly, Erdelatz left behind Joe Bellino, who became Navy's first Heisman Trophy winner. And prepping in faraway New Mexico was Roger Staubach, Navy's second Heisman Trophy winner, considered the Academy's greatest player ever.

Bellino and Staubach helped to produce a five-year record of 38–22–2, top-ten national rankings, and appearances in the 1961 Orange Bowl and 1964 Cotton Bowl.

Wayne Hardin, thirty-two years old, was not a unanimous choice to succeed Erdelatz; several of the athletic board members thought he was too young. When they finally agreed, they wanted to give him a salary of $12,000 a year, a big cut from the $17,000 Erdelatz had received. Athletic Director Slade Cutter objected. "By God," he said, "if you are hiring a guy to replace somebody you have fired, you pay him as much as you paid the guy you have just fired." The board agreed to a slight increase.

In the end, their financial outlay was a bargain. Hardin maintained winning records, beat Army regularly, and produced two bowl teams and two great players—Bellino and Staubach. But the board paid a stiffer price in other ways, because Hardin, for all his coaching ability and suc-

To the Academy via Smackover and Stagg

Wayne Hardin was born in Smackover, Arkansas, the same town that had given Navy All-America halfback Clyde Scott during the forties. Hardin had been a superb athlete at College of Pacific (now University of Pacific), where his football coach was the immortal Amos Alonzo Stagg. He won eleven varsity letters, the most ever by a COP athlete, including four as a halfback/quarterback on the football team. Hardin had coached at COP, in high school, and at Porterville Junior College before Navy coach Erdelatz hired him as an assistant in 1955.

Hardin had great technical ability as a coach, which meshed neatly with a staff of good teachers that included Steve Belichick; J. D. Roberts, a former Oklahoma All-America guard; and Rick Forzano, later a head coach at Navy. Players on his teams have said without exception that the teaching and preparation they received during the week instilled them with the confidence that they could go out and handle any situation. Although they might not always win, they would never be surprised.

Coach Wayne Hardin *(with his hand on the football)* and his coaching staff *(from top)*: Carl Schuette, Ernie Jorge, Dave Hart, Doug Scovil, and Hugh McWilliams.

cess, caused just as many internal problems as Erdelatz. He compounded them by often becoming a public relations nightmare with his sometimes questionable coaching methods and sharp tongue.

Hardin had stints coaching the offense and the defense under Erdelatz, but no two people could have been more dissimilar. Erdelatz, with his gregarious nature, was the quintessential "players' coach," working as hard on their psyches as he did on their blocking and tackling skills. Hardin was very reserved around people. Although usually soft-spoken, he had a tendency to fire off barbed or flip comments that sullied his image. After the Middies thrashed Army 34–14 in 1962, for example, he was asked what he thought was the turning point of what was supposed to have been a very close game. "When we showed up," he responded. Such comments underscored his self-image as a rock-nosed grumbler who believed that winning was often a license for bad coaching manners—and that all sins were forgiven after each victory.

He also wove a shroud of mystery around himself. "I don't want anybody to know me or to know what I think," he once said when asked about his secretive nature. "The less they know about me, the less they know about my teams."

There were times when Hardin's coaching integrity was questioned, though often that was the result of his insatiable fascination for the gimmick plays that were liberally sprinkled throughout his playbook. Against Duke, for example, he once inserted his No. 2 quarterback as fullback, wearing a changed jersey number to disguise his real position. The player promptly fired a touchdown pass.

After Navy defeated Pitt 32–9 in the 1962 Oyster Bowl, Hardin was roundly criticized for using an illegal "sleeper play," which he always denied. After Pitt had scored on an opening drive, Navy's Jim Stewart took the ensuing kickoff while a Navy guard faked a block near the sidelines, then rolled out of bounds. Stewart jumped up from a pile of tacklers, went briefly to Navy's huddle, and then began slowly limping toward the sidelines, as if injured. Running back

Dick Ernst ran onto the field, and the Pitt players assumed he was replacing Stewart. But when the huddle broke, Ernst jumped into the guard's position. Pitt's players paid no attention to Stewart once he started limping toward the bench, and they didn't see him turn and run downfield as soon as the ball was snapped to quarterback Roger Staubach. Stewart was forty yards in the clear when he gathered in Staubach's pass and ran it in for a touchdown. Hardin said that he told the officials about the play before the game and that they had not ruled it either illegal or unethical. He insisted Stewart was indeed hurt, though not too seriously.

"That was my fault," Hardin said later, but with little contrition. "The kid limped too much on purpose. But only the press called it a sleeper. Pitt didn't." In fact, Pitt officials did consider the play unethical. The media agreed, particularly after a reporter saw Stewart limping on the wrong leg after the game. The play became a public issue that finally landed on the desk of the Academy superintendent, Rear Adm. Charles C. Kirkpatrick. When Hardin asked him to back up his action, Kirkpatrick threatened to "fire any coach who thought the superintendent was supposed to back him up in a misrepresentation of the truth."

But in 1959, Hardin's overriding concern was fielding a strong team, and no coach could have asked for a better foundation to continue a winning program than Joe Bellino. In the Sicilian language of his parents, "Bellino" means "little beauty"—and he was indeed a beauty of a football player.

Bellino was a five-foot-nine, 187-pound halfback who was compared very favorably in performance with Fred "Buzz" Borries, Navy's All-America running back from the midthirties. Physically, they were poles apart. Borries was tall and graceful and ran with a long racer's stride. Bellino exploded into action, his chunky legs churning like the drive shafts on a steam locomotive.

Bellino was built low to the ground. He had tremendous power in his legs, which measured eighteen inches in circumference at the calf and supported thick upper legs that provided so much of his power. When he was a plebe, the regulation football pants were too tight to comfortably accommodate his upper legs, so his pants had to be slit up the back of the legs to make them fit. In 1959, when Hardin ordered the players to wear stockings as protection from the cold in a game against Boston College, Bellino's wouldn't fit. The next year, Bellino had chronic problems with cramps, sometimes forcing him to come out of games. He traced the problem to pants that were again too tight; again he slit them up the back, just below the knees.

But those legs were mighty weapons for breaking tackles and bursting through tight spots in short-yardage situations. Bellino's speed was surprising, considering his build; he was never caught from behind until his final game against Army, when defensive back Paul Stanley tackled him after he had run a trap play fifty-eight yards from his own one-yard line. He could go sideways as fast, or faster, than he went forward, and he changed direction without slowing down. Some of his longest runs came after he had danced a bit, looking for an opening, before exploding into the clear.

Joe had great peripheral vision that enabled him to make cutback and stop-and-start moves to dodge tacklers. When accelerating, he was at top speed

Not Just Another Game

When Wayne Hardin joined Eddie Erdelatz's staff, he was an adherent of the time-honored coaching nostrum that every game was equal in importance, be it the first or the last game. But he quickly discovered that was not the case when the last game was Army-Navy.

Hardin witnessed his first Army-Navy game from the coaching booth in 1955. The Cadets, led by Don Holleder, pulled out a hard-fought 14–6 victory. After the game, Hardin was visibly shaken. He had never imagined that the tension and emotion of the game would touch him so deeply. He sat in the booth for twenty-five minutes afterward, numb and drained. The Army-Navy game never again would be just "another game" for Wayne Hardin. His five straight victories against Army are unmatched by any Navy coach. He got a very clear picture that football at Navy was unlike football at any other school.

Joe Bellino (27) in action against Army in 1959, taking a handoff from Joe Tranchini, who had faked giving the ball to Ron Brandquist (49). Guard Doug Falconer (67) takes aim on crashing Army end Don Usry (89). Navy end Don Hyde (81) and tackle Ron Erchul (76) have already caved in the outside of Army's defense to provide a hole for Bellino.

after his first step, and his timing for cuts and getting into and out of holes was superb. So was his balance: "He stays on his feet when he has no right to," Hardin once said.

Navy and Maryland were tied with six minutes to play in a 1959 game when Bellino caught a punt at his forty-one yard line. He was hemmed in near the sideline, and Hardin, believing he had no chance for a long punt return and wanting a clock stoppage so he could send regular quarterback Joe Tranchini back into the game without drawing a five-yard penalty—the rule at that time—screamed, "Run out of bounds!" Bellino paid no heed; he danced away from tacklers, skipped toward midfield, and ran fifty-nine yards for the winning touchdown without being touched.

"I heard coach," he said later, "but I thought I could find daylight, and we wouldn't need a quarterback if I did, except to hold for the extra point."

Bellino always used his blockers well. In a 41–6 victory over Virginia in 1960, Bellino ran off right tackle at his ten-yard line and found himself surrounded by six Virginia players. "All I could see were white shirts," he said later. "I figured I'd better get out of there." Guard John Hewitt was with him and knocked down one defender; Bellino broke free from a second, then cut sharply and shook off two more, and picked up a blocker and completed a ninety-yard touchdown play. He scored four touchdowns that day, the first time a Navy player had accomplished that feat.

Getting this great offensive player took persistence, but Navy had plenty of help from Dr. William Barone, who had delivered Bellino into the world in 1939 and who had often talked to him about attending the Naval Academy. "Maybe it was vicarious," Dr. Barone once said. "Perhaps I never got rid of the small-boy appeal Annapolis had for me. Perhaps I took advantage of my friendship with the family, but it was my ambition for Joe."

Bellino was the son of Sicilian immigrants, and he watched his brothers forego college for work after high school to help the family sustain itself. Joe's athletic skills, though, attracted some six dozen colleges, including Notre Dame, Boston College, Northwestern, Dartmouth, Penn State, Penn, Clemson, Colgate, and Indiana.

Army wanted Bellino so badly that coach Earl Blaik dispatched Doc Blanchard, then an assistant coach, to sell him on West Point. He induced Bellino to spend a weekend at the Military Academy. "West Point seemed sort of cold and gray," Bellino recalled. "Anyway, I was thinking Navy."

There was also major-league baseball. Bellino was a fine high school catcher and was offered a six-figure bonus to sign a professional contract. He turned it down. The Cincinnati Reds approached him again with a $50,000 bonus following his Youngster year at the Academy, when he batted over .400. He turned it down to play football and get his commission.

After he starred for the seventeen-man Columbian Prep team, Bellino's reputation preceded him to Annapolis. He was the outstanding player on a great plebe team in 1957. In a regulation game against a fourth-varsity unit one day, Bellino scored both TDs—one on a seventy-five-yard burst off tackle—and the plebes won 14–7. Cutter remarked, "We've only got one man in this Academy who can go all the way, and it's our luck that he's playing for the plebes."

Bellino: Tough to Catch

How elusive was Joe Bellino?

In Navy's 7–7 tie against Duke in 1960, he faked an end to the inside, then ran around him—only to meet a linebacker. So, he threw a fake at him, and ran around him—and right into a defensive back. Same story—Joe faked him inside and ran around him, too.

When Bellino finished his three varsity seasons, he had eclipsed the accomplishments of every great Navy running back. He held the Academy career rushing record with 1,664 yards, as well as career records for punt returns (833 yards and a 21.9 average), kickoff returns (577 yards and a 25.1 average), scoring (198 points), and a number of season records.

Navy Air Helped Snag Bellino

Navy finally nailed down Joe Bellino's commitment to attend the Naval Academy with the help of two formidable weapons—the aircraft carriers USS *Tarawa* and the USS *Antietam.* A year before he graduated from high school, two of Rip Miller's "Bird Dogs," Elliott Rose and future Massachusetts state Attorney General Edward McCormack, both Academy graduates, had arranged for Bellino to visit the *Tarawa* while she was berthed at the Charlestown Navy Base, near his home in the Boston suburb of Winchester. The following year, they arranged for him and end Frank Datillo, a high school teammate who also decided to attend the Academy, to visit the *Antietam.*

Tight end and kicker Greg Mather with Hardin. In 1961 Mather led the team in scoring with sixty-one points from his extra point and field goal kicking, adding a touchdown pass. He also displayed some of his defensive prowess by scoring a safety.

When Hardin was appointed head coach after spring drills had ended in 1959, the first thing he did was design his offense to get Bellino into the open as often as possible and have him run around, not over, people.

"We felt that if we gave him the ball often enough—maybe twenty times in the sixty to eighty plays we averaged in a game—and if we gave him a little blocking, he'd go a long way," Hardin said.

He did—all the way to the Hall of Fame after three great years at Navy, though knee injuries hampered him in 1958 and 1959. (The latter injury occurred in Navy's opener against Boston College.) On a fifty-yard touchdown run, during which he shed two tacklers, reversed his field twice, and even got his own blockers turned around, Bellino ran the last forty yards without escort. He pulled up lame when he crossed the goal line. "That was the greatest do-it-yourself run I ever saw," Boston College coach Mike Holovak said afterward. Holovak later signed Bellino to play with the Boston Patriots of the American Football League when his active-duty obligation was fulfilled.

When Navy opened Navy–Marine Corps Memorial Stadium with a 29–2 victory over William and Mary before 25,000 spectators, Bellino and Joe Matalavage each had long touchdown runs. The following week, though, during a 20–7 loss to Southern Methodist on a soggy field, Bellino reinjured his knee. He missed one game and played very little in two others. He finally returned to full strength against Maryland and then burst into prominence with a record-setting, 115-yard, three-touchdown game in a mighty 43–12 victory over Army.

His touchdowns against the favored Cadets were masterpieces. In the first quarter, he cut wide, faked past defender Bob Anderson, and outran Joe Caldwell for a sixteen-yard touchdown. A short time later, helped by Dick Hyde's

Navy–Marine Corps Memorial Stadium on opening day in 1959. Navy did it right, beating William and Mary 29–2. The facility now includes the Adm. Thomas J. Hamilton Locker Room Complex and a Walk of Fame that honors players who have been nationally recognized for their football and classroom achievements. The stadium cost $3 million; as of the 1996 season, more than 3.5 million fans have attended games there. Navy enjoys the home field edge because—through the 1996 season—the Mids have a 91–61–1 record. The largest crowd in the stadium's history—more than 35,000—watched a 28–24 Navy victory over Air Force in 1993.

In 1960 running back Joe Bellino was the first Navy player to win the Heisman Trophy, and he's now a member of the College Football Hall of Fame. When he finished his career, the Winchester, Massachusetts, native was Navy's all-time rusher, with 1,664 yards, and its all-time scorer, with 198 points. He also established records for kickoff and punt returns. After Bellino helped Navy upset Washington in 1960, Huskies coach Jim Owens summed up his abilities: "He made us look like we never practiced how to tackle."

A Player for the Ages

Everything Joe Bellino said or did became newsworthy during the 1960 season. Even a haircut made the news when Freddie Fernandez, one of the Naval Academy's barbers, bet Joe that Navy would not beat Air Force by thirty points.

Bellino was reluctant to bet. But the stakes were innocent enough—they agreed that the winner could cut the other's hair to whatever design the winner wished—so Bellino agreed.

Another barber in the shop, Leon Ross, asked Bellino how many touchdowns he would score. "Oh, three, I guess," Bellino replied.

"Okay, you got a bet," Ross said.

"What could I do?" Bellino said later.

He scored three touchdowns, and Navy won by thirty-two points. The following week, with flashbulbs popping, Bellino trimmed a few inches off the head of Fernandez and clipped half of Ross's mustache.

"I really didn't want to," Joe said later, "but by then I had to. Even the barbers insisted."

The next week, he received a letter from a group of Duke students offering to bet any number of shaved heads that Bellino wouldn't score three touchdowns against their school. Bellino replied that he wouldn't bet because he was going to be used as a decoy and would carry the ball just three times. "P.S.," he added, "Don't tell anyone about this."

When the 1960 season ended, Joe Bellino was honored everywhere and his grades began to suffer. The superintendent, Rear Adm. John F. Davidson, ordered a stop to the appearances.

Shortly thereafter, Richard Cardinal Cushing of Boston invited Bellino to speak at a father-son dinner, but Joe had to refuse. The cardinal asked Admiral Davidson to make an exception, but he refused. The persistent prelate then called U.S. Representative John McCormack, the speaker of the House—who also was from Boston—and sought his intercession. McCormack, ever the politician, called Davidson and, while agreeing that Bellino's grades came first, offered a compromise: If Bellino passed his midterm exams, and McCormack got Cushing to change the date of the banquet, could the ban be lifted?

Admiral Davidson agreed. Joe accordingly was at Washington's National Airport, ready to fly to Boston on the day of the event. But a mighty snowstorm closed Boston's Logan Airport. The superintendent told Bellino to return to the Academy, then called McCormack. "It seems that the cardinal's boss had other plans for Joe and decided he had to stay here," Davidson needled the speaker.

"Touché!" replied McCormack.

block, he ran forty-six yards for a second touchdown. In the third quarter, he intercepted a pass and returned it thirty-four yards, then capped a five-play drive with his third score.

Three days before the game, Hardin, ever mindful of Bellino's history of injuries and the importance of this game, lectured him. "I want sixty minutes of football from you on Saturday," he told him.

Bellino's eyes shone. "Ever since I was in high school I dreamed that some day a Navy coach would let me play sixty minutes against Army, and Coach Hardin was making that an order," he recalled. "I had dreamed that first touchdown against Army weeks before the game, that I would get the ball on a handoff, cut around Bob Anderson, and I knew I could outrun him. That's what I did, with a hip fake, but I had to outrun Joe Caldwell, the safety man, too. That wasn't in the dream, but it came out all right."

At one point, with Navy at Army's one-yard line, quarterback Joe Tranchini called a play for Bellino. Before the ball was snapped, Army jumped offsides. Navy huddled again and Tranchini called the same play. But Bellino demurred. "I've had my big day," he said. "How about giving the ball to Ronnie [Brandquist]? He hasn't scored yet." Brandquist did on the next play.

After the victory, Navy declined an invitation to return to Municipal Stadium a couple of weeks later to play in the inaugural Liberty Bowl.

Bellino was a marked man in 1960. He had a spectacular game in the opener against Boston College, accounting for all of Navy's points in a 22–7 win, and scored twice more the following week while playing just twenty minutes with President Dwight Eisenhower looking on in a 41–7 victory over Villanova. But it was Navy's defeat of defending Rose Bowl champion Washington, 15–14, in the season's third game that made him a national cover boy.

"He made us look like we never practiced how to tackle," Washington coach Jim Owens said after the game.

In Navy's first touchdown march against the third-ranked Huskies, Bellino supplied a twenty-nine-yard kickoff return, a twenty-yard option pass completion, seventeen yards on two runs, and then dove a yard for the score. Greg Mather won the game with a forty-two-yard field goal in the final seconds.

That victory elevated Navy's national stature, and the Mids then rolled off four consecutive victories. One was a 35–3 win over Air Force—the first game between the two academies. Bellino scored on Navy's first play from scrimmage, after Ron Erchul had blocked a punt, added two more touchdowns in the first half, and intercepted a pass. His quick-kicking skill—he kicked eleven times that season for a forty-seven-yard average—was also a great weapon. Early in the second half, the Mids were poised to score again when quarterback Hal Spooner, who completed fifteen of twenty passes that day, including a twenty-four-yard touchdown to Bellino, called his number.

"Hold it Hal," Bellino said, recreating the scene from the previous Army-Navy game. "I've got three. Let's let Joe [Matalavage, the team captain] get one."

Two weeks after the Air Force game, Bellino impressed 63,000 fans at Municipal Stadium in Philadelphia by scoring both Navy touchdowns in a 14–7 victory against Notre Dame. He and Matalavage alternated on five running plays in an eighty-yard drive for the first score, which came on Bellino's

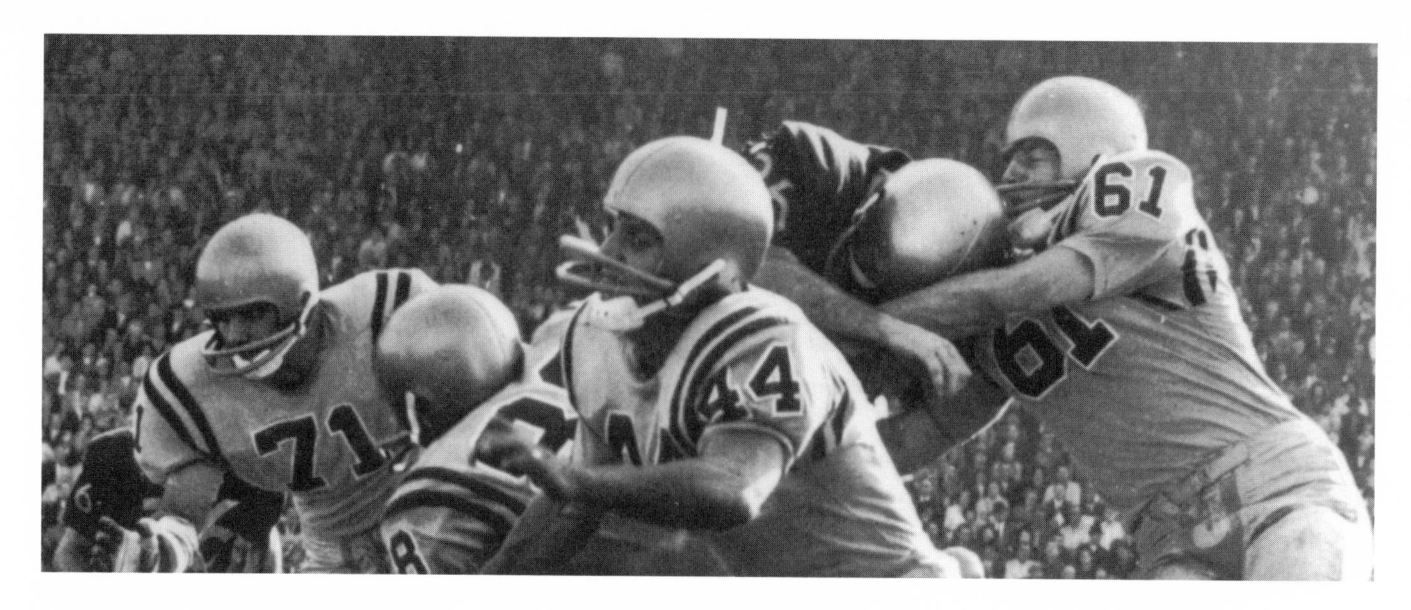

Ron Testa (71), John Zenyuh (44), and Vern Von Sydow (61) epitomized a tough Navy defense that helped upset defending Rose Bowl champion Washington 15–14 in 1960.

twelve-yard run. Al Hughes's interception set up Bellino's winning touchdown in the second half.

Duke beat Navy, 19–10, for the Mids' only regular season loss. When Navy took its 8–1 record against Army, an Orange Bowl bid hinged on the outcome, and the Heisman Trophy and Maxwell Trophy were being readied for Bellino.

Joe didn't disappoint. Vern Von Sydow's fumble recovery set up Bellino's first touchdown, a four-yard run. An Army punt put Navy at its own one-yard line in the second quarter, but Bellino extricated the Mids with one flashing play—a trap designed specifically for this game, which he broke for fifty-eight yards. That started a drive that culminated in Mather's twenty-yard field goal. Films showed that every Navy player blew his assignment, and it was only a catlike move by Bellino that allowed him to slip a pair of tacklers and escape a safety. Later, Hal Spooner threw a touchdown pass to Jim Luper, and the two-point conversion was added with a bit of trickery when Bellino lateraled to Spooner, who scored the points. That gave Navy a 17–0 halftime lead. Navy's defense did not allow Army past the fifty-yard line in the entire half.

Army closed the lead to 17–12 with six minutes to play. Then a botched handoff from Spooner to Bellino was recovered by Army at Navy's seventeen-yard line. The Cadets moved to a first down at the six. On the next play, Army quarterback Dick Eckert started to roll around right end with halfback George Kirchenbauer trailing him. Army backs were told never to use the option offense within the opponents' fifteen-yard line, but Eckert, sensing that his back would have a clear path to the end zone, tried anyhow. The ball sailed wide, and though Army recovered, its threat was blunted.

After the 17–12 victory over Army, Navy accepted an invitation to play Missouri in the Orange Bowl (that game is covered in Chapter Ten). Bellino walked into the Downtown Athletic Club in New York City a week later to become the first Navy player to accept the Heisman Trophy, and the last to wear jersey No. 27. It was no wonder that Hardin, wistful about losing such a great runner, noted in his typical sardonic style: "I'd marry the guy if I could keep him another four years."

It would have been nice to have a player with Bellino's talent around for four more years, but it quickly became obvious that Navy had another star-in-the-making. In 1961, a young plebe quarterback named Roger Thomas Staubach revealed his budding talents. In fact, Staubach was the best quarterback that Navy's varsity faced that season. During the next three years, he became the greatest quarterback in Naval Academy history. When his football career finally ended with the Dallas Cowboys in 1979, he was one of the greatest ever to play the game.

Staubach could only sit and watch on Saturday afternoons in 1961, but a group of relative "no-names" surprised many fans by winning seven of ten games. Two of the victories were over Notre Dame (13–10) and Army (the Middies' third straight win in that rivalry).

This group, led by quarterback Ron Klemick, provided an ideal intermission between two great eras in Navy football. Hardin did a masterful job of mixing and matching his resources and was aided by a tremendous team spirit that lifted performances above the talent level. He used Klemick, Bob Hecht, and Bruce Abel as quarterbacks. Klemick got four wins in the first five games before being sidelined with injuries. Later, he was flawless in beating Army.

The Mids also got a huge year from six-one, 212-pound kicker-end Greg Mather. He scored sixty-one points on twenty-two of twenty-three extra points (including twenty-one in a row); eleven field goals; and a touchdown pass among his twenty-two receptions. He also scored a safety while playing defense—two points that did not count toward his official total. His fifty-five points on kicks set an NCAA season record. Mather's twenty-one-yard field goal, set up by John Hewitt's fumble recovery, was the margin of victory over Notre Dame, complementing a fine job by Hecht, who scored Navy's only touchdown.

Joe Bellino gives the winning 1960 game ball—Navy beat Army, 17–12—a playful toss to some of his teammates.

Special in So Many Ways

What manner of man was Roger Staubach away from football?

Those who knew him as a midshipman said he was almost too good to be true. He was self-effacing about his athletic prowess and never talked about it unless the subject was broached by someone else. He attended Mass several times each week, despite his rigorous Academy schedule, and was gracious with all with whom he came in contact. Other members of the Brigade respected Staubach so much that they often stopped him in the Yard to solicit his autograph.

When Staubach was a plebe, he feared he would flunk out of the Naval Academy. He got demerits for misdeeds like everyone else and had problems solving the mysteries of mechanical drawing and metallurgy, although he finished his four years with a 2.9–3.0 average.

When Staubach graduated, the Brigade showed its thanks and admiration by giving him a gift of blue and gold rosary beads—the colors of both the Navy football team and the Virgin Mary, to whom the rosary is dedicated. It was the first and only time the Brigade so honored one of its own.

Hardin's chief worry about the game against Army, as it had been during much of the season, was Klemick's ability to spot receivers. Before the Notre Dame game, athletic director Red Coward offered a solution. The Navy always painted dummy torpedo heads bright red so they could be easily spotted and retrieved after target practice. Why not paint the helmets of Navy's ends and backs a bright color to help Klemick easily spot them? Hardin tried it in practice, but Klemick couldn't adapt to the change and the plan was dropped.

But since Army and Navy normally wore gold helmets, Klemick's problem could be expected to be twice as serious, so Hardin fell back on Coward's suggestion—and potential receivers lined up against Army wearing flaming red helmets, nicknamed "Flaming Mamies." Hardin, who loved gimmicks and catchy slogans, even had "Beat Army" sewn onto the shoulders of his team's white jerseys.

Navy did beat Army, 13–7. The hero was Greg Mather, who caught four passes; had a fifty-three-yard punt roll dead at Army's one-yard line (Hardin later called it one of the game's biggest plays); and scored seven points—the margin of victory—by kicking two field goals and an extra point. As a starting end, he wore one of the "Flaming Mamies" and caught a fifteen-yard pass on Navy's first possession to help set up his thirty-three-yard field goal. Army went ahead 7–3 in the third quarter, but reserve running back Bill Ulrich, with three blockers cleaning out Army's defense, ran thirteen yards for a Navy touchdown and a 10–7 lead. Late in the fourth quarter, Mather, who also played an outstanding game on defense, sealed the victory with his second field goal.

As Staubach sat in Municipal Stadium that day, cheering Mather and his teammates, he was poised to bring to Navy football a level of excitement never known before—or since. A six-two, 192-pound native of Cincinnati, Staubach had played quarterback only as a senior at Purcell High School, but he was a great all-around athlete, captaining both the football and basketball teams in his senior year and leading them to city championships. He later played basketball and baseball at the Naval Academy and, in 1963, won an **N** in three sports for playing in victories over Army.

Rick Forzano, then an assistant coach on Hardin's staff and later a head coach at Navy, was the prime mover in getting Staubach to commit to Navy. At the time, Navy's most serious competitors were Notre Dame, Purdue, and Ohio State. Staubach leaned toward Notre Dame at first, but he dismissed it after a weekend visit. Purdue, then about a four-hour drive from Cincinnati, was his second choice, because his parents could watch him play.

Forzano convinced Staubach that the Naval Academy offered him his best opportunity, but before making a final commitment, he advised the youngster to spend a year prepping at New Mexico Military Institute (NMMI), under the auspices of the Naval Academy Foundation. NMMI would give Staubach a good idea of what a military environment was like, and it would allow him a year to mature, become a better football player, and prepare himself scholastically.

Staubach agreed and was a junior-college All-America quarterback at NMMI. Coach Bob Shaw, a former All-Pro receiver in the National Football League, designed his offense to capitalize on Staubach's scrambling, dodging style of play. At the end of that season, after again dismissing Notre Dame,

Hardin on Staubach

Wayne Hardin had his own thoughts about Roger Staubach. Here are a few:

"He's the fastest quarterback I ever had at Navy."

"We knew he was good. He was a junior college All-America at New Mexico Military Institute and he was a good [quarterback] with the plebes."

"When it comes to reacting under pressure, I like to place Roger in the category of an (Arnold) Palmer, (Jack) Nicklaus, or (Ben) Hogan. In the pressure stretch, they are men who can deliver. Roger is the same way."

"Roger is the finest football player I've ever seen. He has a sixth sense that makes it possible for him to do the right thing at the right time."

Staubach committed himself to Navy. Forzano sent him a telegram that read, "Some day you are going to win the Heisman Trophy at Navy and have a battleship named after you."

As a plebe, Staubach worked under three former Navy stars: quarterback George Welsh, running back Joe Bellino, and plebe head coach Dick Duden. "Roger showed he had the tools," Welsh said. "It was simply a matter of time and experience. He never settled for less than 100 percent effort of himself because he was a dedicated individual. He had the scrambling, rambling style for which he's famous, but everything with him was all business. He worked on every move. He was a student of the game."

Staubach stunned everyone who watched him play as a plebe. One day at practice, while embarrassing the varsity with his running and passing, he was unnecessarily pounded every time he crossed the goal line. Capt. Charles S. Minter Jr., then the commandant (and later superintendent), watched until he could stand no more.

Minter later related the story in an oral history for the Naval Institute: "I walked right out in the middle of the field and got a hold of Hardin and said, 'Hey, Duden needs this kid for Saturday. Call off your dogs.' And he did . . . though he seemed dumbstruck that I had the audacity to tell him how to run his football practices."

Roger Staubach, the greatest player in Navy's football history. Staubach won the Heisman and Maxwell Trophies as a junior in 1963 with an astounding display of running and passing. He was nicknamed "Roger the Dodger" because of his patented scrambling tactics when he was hemmed in trying to pass. More often than not, he left opponents grasping at air as he escaped to make so many of his big plays. "He's not fast but he's quick and somehow gets where he is supposed to be," his coach, Wayne Hardin, once said. During his career, Staubach gained more than 3,500 yards with his passing and he still ranks No. 1 in Navy history with his 63.1 percent completion rate.

Much of Staubach's talent was uncoachable because it was natural. He ran with long, powerful strides, and he forever frustrated defenders with his deceptive speed. "He's not fast, but he's quick and somehow gets where he is supposed to be," Hardin once said. Staubach threw very accurately from the pocket, on the run, or even while backing up, though he was most effective in college when he was on the move. He was most dangerous when he was trapped because he used his speed and elusiveness to get free and find a receiver, or take off and run. He controlled a game by keeping defenses off balance and exercising last-second options keyed to his mobility.

Staubach combined his skills with an air of confidence that told everyone he was master of any situation and that he firmly believed he would succeed—"cool but not cocky, a quarterback with a sixth sense," Hardin said.

Despite Staubach's evident ability, Hardin made him earn the starting job. Staubach opened the 1962 season playing behind Ron Klemick and Bruce Abel. Navy split the first two games, and then lost, 21–0, to Minnesota. Late in the game against the Golden Gophers, with Navy hopelessly behind, Staubach got his first varsity action. On his first rollout pass, he was grabbed by Minnesota's two All-America linemen, Carl Eller and Bobby Bell. Bell yanked Staubach's face mask so hard that it swung him around and slammed him to the ground. Staubach wobbled to his feet, ran a few more plays, and was finished for the day.

Staubach finally got the break he sought the following week against Cornell. Klemick was injured in the first quarter and left the game. Hardin sent in

Staubach, and he led Navy to a 41–0 victory. He scored two touchdowns, completed nine of eleven passes for ninety-nine yards, and ran for eighty-nine more yards. Later that season, Commandant Minter asked Hardin, "How did it happen that Roger had such a great year as a plebe and you didn't even use him for most of the first half of this year?"

Hardin replied, "I always believe in going with experience, and he didn't have any experience. But luckily the regular quarterback got hurt, and I had to put him in."

Staubach got his first start the week after the Cornell game when Navy played Boston College; he completed fourteen of twenty passes for 165 yards and two touchdowns, as Navy won 28–6. He won his third straight game the following week in the Oyster Bowl, against Pittsburgh, where he was a principal in the infamous "sleeper play" pass to Jim Stewart. Staubach's involvement in that controversial play didn't blur a great day—eight-for-eight and 192 yards passing. Staubach had seen significant action in just three games, but already one New York City writer called him the most talented quarterback in Navy history.

The national spotlight that had begun to focus on Staubach dimmed a bit when Navy was soundly beaten by Notre Dame and Syracuse. The Mids outplayed unbeaten Southern California—the eventual national champion—but still lost, 13–6. Fullback Pat Donnelly, who had torn up the Trojan's defense, lost a fumble as he was about to cross the goal line late in the game, spoiling the potential upset. Still, Staubach put on a great show. He ran eighteen yards for a touchdown and caused USC coach John McKay to crack, "What hurt us was not the plays they had worked on, but the ones when he was trapped."

In fact, the young quarterback was not playing the improvisational style with which he was most comfortable. Hardin's very controlled, drop-back passing system was in place, and it would have been folly to install a new system in midseason. Staubach stayed with it as best he could, though he quite often scrambled to be more effective. Before the 1963 season, Hardin brilliantly devised a more mobile offense. "We've adjusted to *him*," Hardin said.

Navy had a 4–5 record going into the 1962 Army game. The Cadets were coached by Paul Dietzel for the first time. Dietzel had brought along from Louisiana State, where he had won the national championship in 1958, his designations for the three units that saw the most action: White Team, Go Team, and Chinese Bandits. The Bandits had become so popular at West Point that, when they entered a game, the Army band heralded their coming by sounding a huge Chinese gong and playing a few strains of Oriental music. The Cadets in the stands then donned coolie hats and wore them for as long as the Bandits stayed on the field.

Hardin matched Dietzel gimmick for gimmick. He had skull and crossbones decals affixed to the front of every Navy helmet. Everyone thought it was in recognition of Staubach, then nicknamed "Jolly Roger." "Not at all," Hardin said. "[The decals] represented the lore of a phantom ship that flew a skull and crossbones flag. It came from nowhere and never lost a battle."

As a talisman against the Chinese Bandits, a midshipman of Japanese descent came up with the idea of inscribing the right side of each helmet with the Chinese calligraphy for "Beat Army." Academy officials tried but failed to get the proper symbols from a Chinese restaurant owner in Annapolis. So the midshipman wrote "Beat Army" in Japanese characters. Before the game, he wrote to his mother and showed her what he had done. She wrote back immediately to say that he had made a mistake in one of the symbols. Hardin, a stickler for detail even in his gimmicks, had all the stencils changed.

On a brilliant Indian summer afternoon, Staubach put on one of the best performances in the series' history. He scored two touchdowns, passed for two more, and completed eleven of thirteen passes for 188 yards. He was Navy's leading rusher with fourteen carries—many of them his patented scrambles that bedazzled one-hundred-thousand fans in Philadelphia, including President John F. Kennedy. Thanks to television, millions more across the country had their first opportunity to see Staubach and his spectacular style of play, which so enthralled fans for the rest of his career—college and pro. It was an electrifying national debut.

With Navy ahead 2–0, Staubach ended an eighty-yard drive when, surrounded by eager Army defenders, he somehow launched a pass that end Neil Henderson snatched from two more defenders for a touchdown. Roger then climaxed a sixty-three-yard scoring drive with a twenty-one-yard touchdown run in which every member of the Army team had a chance to stop him. On Navy's first play in the second half, Staubach passed to fullback Nick Markoff for sixty-five yards and a 22–6 lead. Roger scored his second touchdown to cap an eighty-nine-yard drive early in the fourth quarter. The final score was 34–14, and the fact that Staubach had directed so many long scoring drives indicated how completely he had dominated Army's defense.

And the Chinese Bandits? When they made their first appearance and the Army rooters donned their coolie hats, the midshipmen began waving miniature American flags. This was the era of Cold War tension between China and the United States over the islands of Matsu and Quemoy off the Chinese coast. Navy's flag-waving sent those coolie hats into oblivion.

When the 1963 season began, Navy was a highly touted team, but few, save for Hardin and the players, ever expected to finish the season

Staubach: A Clutch Performer in Any Sport

Navy basketball coach Ben Carnevale, believing his team was not physically tough enough, recruited football ends Jim Campbell and Dave Sjuggerud, a pair of big, tough, hard-nosed players who simply manhandled opponents. He also invited Roger Staubach to join the team as a guard. Roger had been an all-city high school player in Cincinnati.

In February 1963, three months after he had run roughshod over Army on the football field, Staubach played against the Cadets in basketball at the Naval Academy. His assignment: man-to-man guarding of Joe Kosciusko, Army's point guard who was averaging almost twelve points a game and who had scored thirty against Penn State the previous week. Carnevale told Staubach to "meet Kosciusko at the locker room, belly button to belly button." The coach admitted the confrontation was partly a psychological ploy to remind the Army players of how Navy had trounced them three months earlier.

Staubach held Kosciusko to six points in the first half, and the Army player sat out the second half. Roger didn't score, but Navy upset Army 55–48. After the game, Maj. Gen. William C. Westmoreland, superintendent of the Military Academy, sought out Carnevale and growled, "Damn it, Carnevale, Staubach's no basketball player."

"No sir," the coach replied, "but he's a winner."

Staubach also played varsity baseball, batting .410 as a sophomore and over .300 as a junior.

In his senior year, he had a hamstring injury that was so severe he couldn't even run to first base. But when Navy played Maryland, coach Joe Duff needed someone to deliver a long hit to drive in the winning runs, so he called on Staubach.

Sure enough, Roger slashed a ball into the power alley in left center field. The runners dashed home while Staubach limped in to second base.

playing for the national championship. Staubach, of course, received a tremendous preseason buildup. Hardin flatly predicted, "Roger Staubach is destined to be the greatest quarterback who has ever played for Navy." He even was projected as a Heisman Trophy candidate at a time when juniors were expected to wait their turn. Before the season started, Navy sports information director L. Budd Thalman boldly pushed Staubach for consideration as a candidate by sending the nation's football writers, all of whom were Heisman voters at that time, a four-page pamphlet, "Meet Roger Staubach."

Four footballs represent Navy's success against Army during Wayne Hardin's era—four victories in the first four games. In 1963 the Mids' motto was "Drive for Five," and they got it, defeating Army 21–15.

There have been few seasons to compare with what Navy accomplished in 1963. It won eight of its nine regular-season games, including a pulsating 21–15 victory over Army that was not decided until the final second. It basked in the headiness of Staubach's drive to win the Heisman Trophy; and it endured the agony of President Kennedy's assassination a week before the Army game.

The Navy team and Kennedy, who was both a former naval officer and a football enthusiast, had developed a special relationship. Before the 1962 Army-Navy game, Kennedy telegrammed the team: "As President, I can't choose sides but I hope to be on the winning side of the field at the end of the game." He sat on Navy's side during the second half. Their ties grew closer in 1963 when the Mids used Quonset Naval Air Station in Rhode Island as a preseason practice site. Kennedy occasionally used the base while traveling between Washington and his compound on Cape Cod, and he sometimes visited with the team. Before long, he quietly adopted that Navy team as his own, though as commander-in-chief, he was always neutral in public.

The starting team in 1963 was a perfect blend of juniors and seniors. The juniors included Staubach; fullback Pat Donnelly, probably the best fullback in Navy history; Ed "Skip" Orr, who was switched from quarterback to flanker as a sophomore and then worked his way from the fourth team to become a starter; guard and kicker Fred Marlin; and the two tackles, Jim Freeman, a lean Texan, and Pat Philbin, a red-haired Irishman from New York.

Key seniors were Jim Campbell and Dave Sjuggerud, a pair of tough, physically skilled ends who added more muscle to the team and had enough rough edges so that few opponents took uncommon liberties with Staubach; guard Al Krekich; running back Johnny Sai, the team's fastest player; and center and team captain Tom Lynch, who later became superintendent of the Naval Academy. Lynch was an extraordinary person and an ideal team captain. He

Tom Lynch

Tom Lynch, captain of Navy's 1963 team, had a brother, Jim, who later played for Notre Dame and became a great linebacker for the Kansas City Chiefs. Navy assistant coach Rick Forzano, whose recruiting territory included Ohio, tried to recruit Jim Lynch out of Lima Catholic High School for the Academy, but could never see him to make a personal pitch. He found out later that one of the priests at the high school, anxious to ensure Jim went to Notre Dame, made sure he was never available when Rick visited.

provided great leadership and helped keep everyone level-headed when the national spotlight became hotter and hotter. He was, in the eyes of all who knew him, the model of what the Navy sought in a midshipman—then and now—and he used the same qualities that made him a splendid football captain to excel during his naval career.

Navy won its first two games against West Virginia and William and Mary by the combined score of 79–7. West Virginia served as the first test of Hardin's new offensive schemes for Staubach, and the results were perfect. The Mids won 51–7 as Staubach completed seventeen passes and amassed 185 yards of total offense. The following week, he set a single-game school record with 297 total yards against William and Mary.

Next came one of the three milestone games—against Michigan, Pitt, and Notre Dame—that made the 1963 team and Staubach special. Navy was ranked among the nation's top ten teams, and second in total and pass offense, but it had not faced a traditional power like Michigan. Though Michigan then was in the middle of the Big Ten pack, it was a big-name school, and the contest was nationally televised. The game was a crucible that measured the worth of both Navy and Staubach—who shone by gaining 307 total yards, breaking his week-old record. He had a dazzling afternoon of scrambling, dodging, and avoiding Michigan's scrappy defense, and he accounted for three of Navy's four touchdowns: A five-yard run midway through the second quarter on which he avoided a half-dozen tacklers; a fifty-four-yard pass to Johnny Sai six seconds before the first half ended; and a seven-yard pass to end Neil Henderson in the third quarter.

Staubach's style was encapsulated in a play that gained only one yard. Back to pass and finding no one open, he retreated, with Michigan defenders in hot pursuit. Back and back he went until, more than twenty yards behind the line of scrimmage and going down under an avalanche of tacklers, he finally spotted Donnelly and threw him the ball. Donnelly was tackled immediately for the one-yard gain.

"He's the greatest quarterback I've ever seen," marveled Michigan coach Bump Elliott.

The following week Navy played against Southern Methodist in Dallas. Staubach was sidelined twice with a separation of his left shoulder, but he came back and almost pulled out a victory. His last, desperate pass just flicked off Skip Orr's fingertips with seven seconds to play, and the Mustangs won 32–28. It was the only loss Navy suffered that season until Texas defeated it on the same Cotton Bowl gridiron.

The following week, wearing a protective shoulder harness, Staubach led Navy to a 21–12 victory over Virginia Military in the Oyster Bowl. Roger limited his theatrics to a short touchdown plunge: he didn't want to do anything to jeopardize his shoulder because if it popped out again, he would be through for the season.

Staubach took his second big step in nailing down the Heisman Trophy with a tremendous performance against unbeaten and third-ranked Pitt in a 24–12 victory at home while another huge television audience looked on. The previous year, Oscar Fraley, a sports columnist for United Press International,

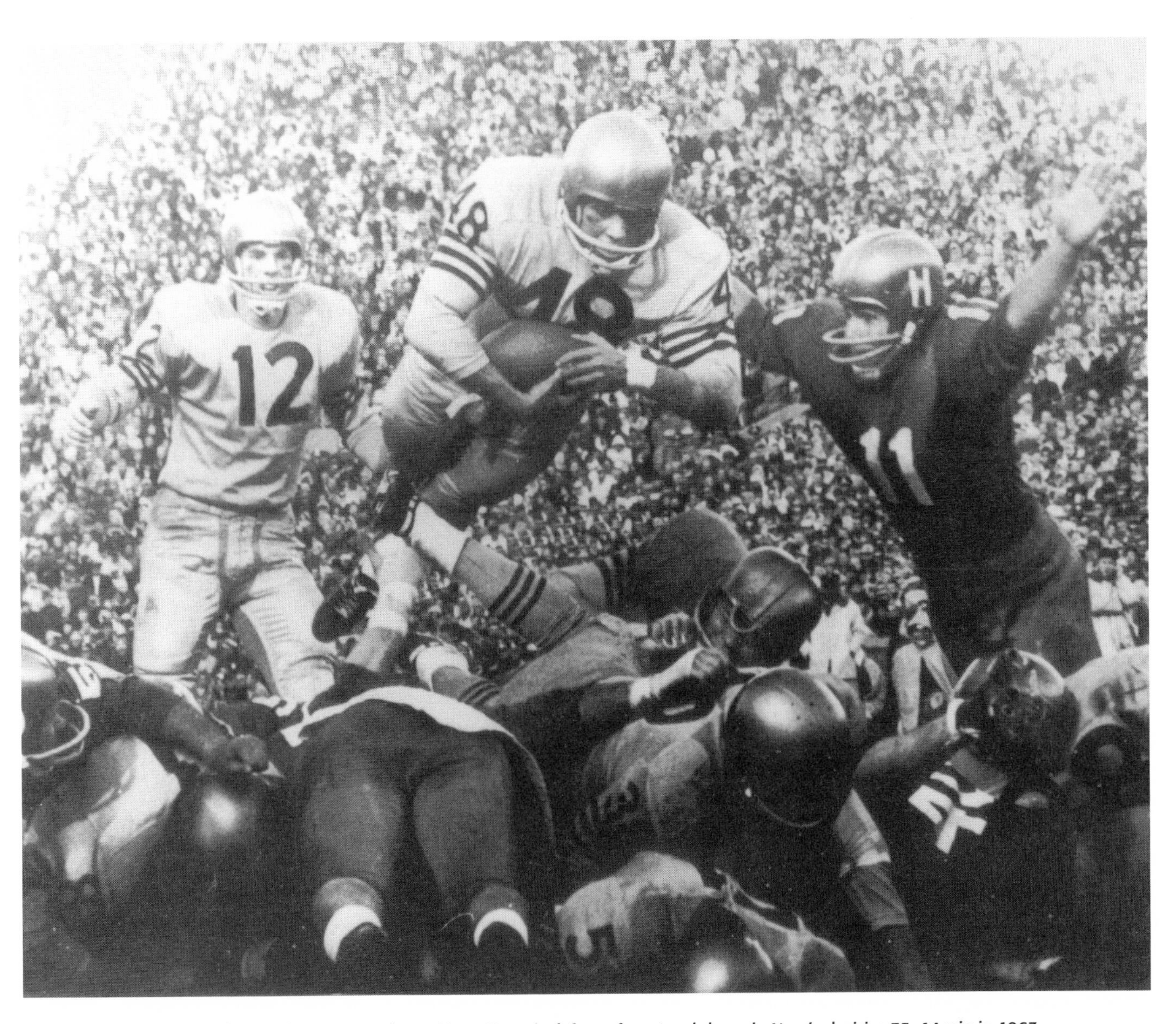

Halfback Johnny Sai goes up and over Notre Dame's defense for a touchdown in Navy's decisive 35–14 win in 1963.

Roger Staubach's 1963 Heisman Trophy says it all. He led the team to a No. 2 national ranking with a 9–1 regular-season record and also to a berth in the Cotton Bowl, where the Mids lost to national champion Texas.

had repeated a crack he had heard from Pitt's publicity director, Carroll "Beano" Cook: The famed "sleeper play" against the Panthers was the "worst sneak attack since Pearl Harbor," Cook said. At the Naval Academy, the analogy was not appreciated. Pushing tastelessness a step further, a Pittsburgh sports weekly exhumed the incident the week of the 1963 game, superimposing the headline "Pitt Remembers Pearl Harbor" over the famous picture of the burning battleship USS *Arizona*. Hardin used that to fire up his team to an emotional pitch normally seen only before Army games. Staubach completed fourteen of nineteen passes (seven to Jim Campbell) and ran for a touchdown. Meanwhile, Navy's defense forced five turnovers and allowed just seventy-six rushing yards.

The final stamp of national approval came after Navy walloped Notre Dame, 35–14. Staubach threw three touchdown passes and performed his usual breathtaking football ballet. At halftime, with the score tied 7–7, Lynch made Staubach leave the locker room and told his teammates that Roger had a good shot at winning the Heisman Trophy, but his chances would be jeopardized if Navy lost the game. The Mids scored three touchdowns in the third quarter to put the game out of reach. Pat Donnelly, who also played linebacker on defense, gained 127 rushing yards, including a forty-one-yard touchdown run. Navy polished off its final pre-Army games with a 42–7 victory over Maryland, with Staubach accounting for three scores, and a 38–25 win against Duke in which Sai ran ninety-three yards for a touchdown—the longest run from scrimmage in Navy football history.

By that time, Staubach was the toast of college football. Early in the season, the Naval Academy had decided to cut off all midweek media access to him and allow interviews only after games because there simply wasn't time in his daily schedule. Budd Thalman found that his supply of Roger's publicity pictures was disappearing and discovered that Staubach was taking them because he tried to answer the hundreds of requests on his own time and at his own expense. *Time* magazine featured him on its cover after the Michigan victory when it focused on possible Heisman Trophy winners; *Sports Illustrated* also had him on a cover; and *Life* magazine had prepared a cover with Staubach's photo to coincide with the naming of the Heisman winner just four days before the Army game.

That *Life* cover never appeared: eight days before game day, President Kennedy was assassinated. Officials seriously considered canceling the game, but members of the Kennedy family, noting how much the president had loved the contest, urged that it be played. It was postponed for a week.

Staubach had amassed 1,882 yards in eight games, including 1,474 from passing, and was named the Heisman Trophy winner a few days before Kennedy was killed. He also won the Maxwell Trophy that season, the fourth Navy player so honored. He then led Navy to a heart-stopping 21–15 victory over Army, in which Army was at the Middies' goal line when time ran out. (The details of that game are covered in Chapter Nine.)

With that win, Navy was ranked second in the nation. The Middies accepted a bid to play top-ranked Texas in the Cotton Bowl. The Longhorns had already been proclaimed national champions because, at that time, there was no final poll after the postseason games. Navy hoped to win and lay claim to the title, as it had in the 1926 season, but Texas won easily, 28–6. (The details of that game are covered in Chapter Ten.)

The Cotton Bowl loss was a bitter pill for a team that, until the Army game, had been so high. Those who were close to the team at that time cite several reasons for its less-than-stellar performance:

- The players hadn't recovered from the emotional pain of Kennedy's death
- They had not gotten over the shock of almost losing to an Army team they had so thoroughly controlled until the final ten minutes of the game
- The toll that they had paid all season as a group of overachievers whose quarterback took them on the ride of their lives finally had become too much for some of them to handle in a pressure-packed game with the national championship at stake
- Texas was a better football team, and it would have taken an almost perfect performance by Navy to win

Many expected the same kind of ride in 1964; optimists talked up the likelihood that Staubach would become the first player ever to win back-to-back Heisman Trophies. But the dream was dashed in the season's first game, a 21–8 victory over Penn State, when Staubach badly strained his ankle and Achilles tendon. The injury plagued him for the entire season. He played intermittently, showing only occasional flashes of his brilliance.

Bruce Bickel started in his place in the season's second game, against William and Mary, and Navy led 14–6 halfway through the final quarter. Not comfortable with that lead, Hardin sent in Staubach. On Staubach's first play, Kip Paskewich ran seventy-six yards for a touchdown. A couple of minutes later, Staubach threw a touchdown pass to John Mickelson. He had worked only four plays and had gotten two touchdowns in a 35–6 win. Another personal high point came against Maryland when Staubach completed twenty-five of thirty passes for 217 yards and three touchdowns. But Maryland won, 27–22.

Staubach's last glory game at Navy came against Duke in his final appearance in Navy–Marine Corps Memorial Stadium. It was vintage Staubach as he broke his own single-game yardage record with 308 yards. He almost missed the record, though. Hardin wanted Staubach to enjoy one final salute from the Annapolis fans, so he took him out of the game in the fourth quarter. The thousands of spectators rose and gave him a thunderous ovation. Hardin didn't

Paterno on Staubach

When Roger Staubach quarterbacked Navy against Texas in the 1964 Cotton Bowl game, Joe Paterno was looking on. Paterno was then an assistant coach at Penn State and was scouting the Mids because they were his team's first opponent the following season. After the game, he had this appraisal:

"He's the greatest third-down-and-long-yardage quarterback the college game has ever seen. He's the greatest I ever watched. His poise under pressure is amazing. He refuses to become rattled."

Paterno compared Staubach to Y. A. Tittle, the star quarterback of the New York Giants and a future Hall of Fame player (like Staubach). "When things are not going right, Tittle will carefully study the situation and then pick out a play or two and go to work. The next thing you know, the Giants have a couple of touchdowns, just when you have written them off the books. Staubach is the same way. What makes him go? I wish I knew. I'd pass it on to our quarterbacks."

Fullback Pat Donnelly hammers the California defense during a 1964 game. Donnelly led Navy in rushing during the great 1963 season with an average of six yards per carry, rolling up 613 yards. He was also a fine linebacker on defense. In 1964, injuries to Staubach and Donnelly cut down Navy's effectiveness.

realize it, but Staubach needed ten more yards to break the record. Thalman had kept track, though. Before the cheers had subsided, he told Navy's coaches in the spotting booth, and they informed Hardin. So Staubach came right back into the game. He set the record, and then for a second time, Staubach trotted off the field, while the Navy–Marine Corps Memorial Stadium rocked again with cheers.

Staubach's injury seemed to set off an epidemic—Navy suffered some forty injuries that season, including a leg injury to Orr and a midseason knee injury that felled Donnelly until the Army game. Missing both Staubach's dazzle and Donnelly's power running, Navy finished 1964 with a dismal 3–6–1 record.

The previous year, the Mids coined a motto for the Army game: "Drive for Five," which meant five straight victories over Army. When that happened, Navy was just one victory short of evening the series record. So, the motto for 1964 was, "Even the Score in '64."

It didn't happen. Army won 11–8. Pregame barbs and gimmickry abounded. The most blatant gimmick was Hardin's changing captain Fred Marlin's jersey number from "64" to "65." When asked why, Hardin tartly replied, "This is the sixty-fifth game."

Roger Staubach and his future wife, Marrianne, on graduation day in 1965. Staubach served his time as a naval officer and then had a brilliant career as quarterback of the great Dallas Cowboys teams of the seventies. He twice led Dallas to Super Bowl victories and is enshrined in both the College and Pro Football Halls of Fame.

Hardin had remade his backfield by using Calvin Huey, the first African-American football player in Navy history, at halfback and Danny Wong, a five-foot-six sophomore of Chinese-American extraction, to replace Donnelly at fullback. Donnelly was healthy enough to start at fullback against Army, but he and a semihealthy Orr were needed to bulwark a badly mauled defense.

Staubach was caught for a safety on Navy's first series, and an Army touchdown a short time later gave the Cadets an 8–0 lead. Hardin then moved Donnelly back to fullback, and Staubach drove his team for a touchdown—scored by Tom Leiser—with just a few seconds remaining in the first half. Staubach passed for the two-point conversion to tie the score 8–8. He did it in his best "Staubachian" manner: He was chased by several Army linemen—at one point, he switched the ball from his right to his left hand to fend off a tackler, then switched it back to the right. Driven back to the fifteen-yard line, with two Army players grabbing him and three others closing in, he fired the pass to Phil Norton.

That was Staubach's last grand gesture. Army's defense never let him get on track in the second half. When the game ended, he left the field, head bowed. Arguably the greatest player in Navy history walked almost unnoticed past thousands who poured from the stands to embrace the winning Cadets.

One week later, Hardin was finished as Navy's head coach. Throughout his tenure, he was resented by those outside the football program, including Naval Academy brass and the Brigade, all of whom felt he treated them with disdain. Trouble had brewed since early in his tenure because, like Erdelatz, Hardin tried to remove the team from life within the Brigade during the football season.

During the 1961 season, for example, Hardin had scheduled Friday night film sessions so that the first classmen on the team didn't have to attend a series of lectures that had been personally arranged by the superintendent, Rear Adm. John F. Davidson. The series included talks by the U.S. ambassador

Navy athletic director Capt. Bill Busik and assistant athletic director Edgar "Rip" Miller, who presided over Navy's great success during the Staubach era.

to the Soviet Union, the chairman of the joint chiefs of staff, and the chief of naval operations. Admiral Davidson, an avid football fan whose nickname was "Big Daddy" (his wife was called "Big Mama") and who regularly attended practice, went on road trips, and was a fiery orator at pep rallies, switched the series to Tuesday nights to accommodate the players. Hardin then switched his film sessions to the same night.

Furious, Davidson called Hardin. "Hey, I'm still running the Naval Academy," he said, "and I've gone to a lot of trouble to do this. You can have your movies any night of the week except Tuesday. That's my night."

After Hardin appropriated the lacrosse team's lockers in McDonough Hall the following spring for his team, Admiral Davidson called him into his office.

"If you keep on trying very hard, you're going to be just as impossible as Eddie Erdelatz," he told him. "If you get that impossible, then things have to happen."

"Things" finally did happen. Capt. Bill Busik became athletic director in 1962 and proved to be a hands-on supervisor. He quickly became disenchanted not only with the way that Hardin conducted his program but with his abrasive treatment of everyone at the Academy. Busik did away with the special privileges Hardin had secured for his team and made it clear that the players would adhere to the same Academy routine as other midshipmen. In 1963, Busik took everything but Hardin's coaching duties away from him. That may have contributed to Navy's grand success: Hardin had nothing to do but concentrate on football. Afterward, Busik was so pleased with the team's No. 2 national ranking that he restored all of the duties he had earlier taken away.

Hardin was telling friends that he wanted to escape the emotional strain of coaching and get into the administrative arena. Some people thought he meant that he wanted to replace Rip Miller as assistant athletic director. Hardin always denied that was so; he maintained that he only wanted something that would provide him some security. But Miller, who had clashed with Erdelatz when he thought Eddie had ambitions for his job and who had been instrumental in his ouster, had no intention of leaving. Before the 1964 season, he squelched any of Hardin's ambitions by telling the superintendent, Admiral Minter, that Wayne had not acclimated himself too well to the "people" part of some administrative duties he had been given. Minter had crossed swords with Hardin before, so Miller's views reinforced his own perceptions of the situation. Any hopes that Hardin might have harbored about moving into an administrative post at Navy were weakened.

The situation remained rocky throughout the depressing 1964 season. Hardin and Busik clashed after Navy lost to California because Hardin had used a badly hobbled Staubach in a losing effort when he had promised that Roger would not play until he was healed.

Just before a pep rally for that season's Army-Navy game, Hardin went to Busik's quarters and said, "I've found a great way we can beat Army. Let me tell the team this is my last game as head coach."

"Is it?" a surprised Busik asked.

"It could be," Hardin said.

Busik refused to allow the ruse—assuming it was a ruse—but that was the last straw. The following week, he convened a meeting of the athletic board and asked for Hardin's dismissal. There was no objection.

Thus, within the space of one week, Navy bade farewell to one of its most successful head coaches and to Roger Staubach, its most legendary star.

8. Changing Times and Rough Sailing 1965–

Since 1964, when the Roger Staubach era ended, Navy football has never reached the heights attained during the previous fifteen years when Navy was nationally ranked, played in postseason bowls, produced Heisman Trophy winners, and enthralled fans around the country.

Bill Elias, head coach at Navy from 1965–68, during which his teams won fifteen games. He had a break-even 4–4–2 season in 1965 and a winning season in 1967 with a 5–4–1 record. Elias was the first coach to feel the pinch from the effects of the Vietnam War; the Naval Academy's change of attitude toward recruiting athletes; and societal changes that affected all of the military academies and radically affected the number and quality of their student-athletes.

The aftershocks of the geopolitical shifts caused by World War II were rumbling across the country—major wars have seismic effects on society that last long beyond an armistice—and their combination, plus other social changes, had a devastating effect on the Naval Academy, and thus on Navy football. Hostility toward anything military became so pervasive in some quarters that, many times, Navy coaches were turned away at the front door by a prospect's parents; on occasion, stones were hurled at Naval Academy Athletic Association vehicles during visits to schools. This attitude, and the fear of going to fight a war with an ill-defined mission, affected applications to the Academy and cut down the number of good athletes seeking admission. From 1965 to 1972, Navy had just one winning season—a 5–4–1 record in 1967.

There were other factors that contributed to the decline in the sixties:

- Careerists at the Academy, including some in the athletic association, were disturbed that so many athletes who had helped bring the football program such success left the Navy as soon as they could. They began placing more emphasis on recruiting those who wanted to stay.
- College athletics changed, and admission standards fell. Schools welcomed high school athletes whose academic qualifications would have been unacceptable in the past. But at the Naval Academy, the admission standards became tougher, and good players became fewer, even as the competitive levels of football opponents rose.
- The Naval Academy Foundation's athletic scholarship program was altered in various schools around the country, hampering the ability to prep good athletes like those who made up the great teams of the fifties and early sixties. Rip Miller's "Bird Dog" program also declined as some of his group passed from the scene and new recruiting rules lessened the impact of those who remained.

- Professional football's popularity soared, spurred in the sixties by a talent war between the National and American Football Leagues that rewarded the best players with huge amounts of money. The Academy's postgraduation service obligations were a serious drawback to high school stars hoping to cash in on these opportunities by going straight to the pros after college.

All of these factors contributed to ten subpar seasons. The good times didn't reappear until after George Welsh became head coach in 1973; he compiled a 55–46–1 record that included five winning seasons. His teams also won one of three bowl appearances and, most importantly, had a 7–1–1 record against Army.

But in the late seventies and early eighties, when it appeared that Navy football had returned to the success it had enjoyed two decades earlier, the academic profiles at the Naval Academy were toughened. The reasons cited included the need to attract superior students who could understand and manage the complex systems that were becoming part of naval warfare. In so doing, the Academy dropped some "friendly" majors that had once opened the door to many athletically gifted young men who were little better than average scholars. Those student-athletes were by no means "dummies" or "football majors." During the turmoil of five wars in the twentieth century, they had proven the thoroughness of their preparation by the Naval Academy by making sound and heroic decisions that often reflected the experiences of intense athletic competition.

Head coach Rick Forzano and quarterback Allan Glenny discuss strategy during the 1972 Army-Navy game. Forzano bore the brunt of the seismic changes that affected Navy football in the early seventies. While his teams won just ten games in four seasons, his resilience and respect for the Naval Academy and its traditions were the correct platform that ultimately helped to reinvigorate the program.

The new academic standards, though, further hampered Navy's ability to attract and keep good players because a prospective student-athlete either had to be able to cope with the new, tougher courses, or go to another school. Too often, they chose the latter, and Navy's football talent pool began to diminish.

There were other internal problems as well, particularly the frequent reassignment of commandants. When the commandant was changed, rules governing the midshipman population, including the athletes, usually changed as well. This particularly bothered George Welsh, who tried, within the rules of the Academy, to provide some relief for his players as they juggled their intense scholastic requirements with their twenty to twenty-five hours a week of game preparation. This factor, plus the increasing difficulty of attracting enough good players to compete with a tough schedule of opponents (problems his successors would face, as well), finally was too much for Welsh, and he left the Academy after the 1981 season to become head coach at the University of Virginia.

Following Welsh's departure, there was a lack of consistently successful head coaches. Taking into account the quality of their available talent and the strength of the opposing teams, it is unfair to judge them solely on the basis of win-loss records. The lack of top-flight players became an increasingly serious problem, particularly when injuries struck down key starters and there were no talented replacements waiting on the sidelines.

Even after the conclusion of the Vietnam War, the outlooks of young Americans continued to change, as did the face of intercollegiate athletics. The prospect of a military commitment for several years and a tightly regimented college life versus the prospect of a less structured college and the possibility, regardless of how remote, of playing professional sports, prevented Navy from gaining access to the talent pool necessary to sustain a top-flight program.

The bottom line has been the biggest victory drought in Naval Academy history. From the time that George Welsh left after the 1981 season through the midnineties, there have been just two winning seasons, in 1986 and 1996. Worse still, success against Army has diminished.

Still, during the three decades following the Staubach era, some fine, outstanding Navy players captured national attention: Napoleon McCallum, Eddie Meyers, Phil McConkey, Chet Moeller, Rob Taylor, Terry Murray, Joe Gattuso, Jr., Cleveland Cooper, John Cartwright, Mike McNallen, Jim Kubiak, Bob Kuberski, Bob Leszczynski, Bob Tata, Steve Fehr, Sean Andrews, and Chris McCoy. And there were some great games and fine teams.

Welsh's two predecessors, Bill Elias and Rick Forzano, bore the brunt of Navy's descent in the late sixties, though both did everything possible to produce good football teams while working within the spirit of the Naval Academy. There was one constant: No Navy team ever quit, or appeared to give less than its best effort, regardless of the circumstances or the opposition. Never was this better illustrated than in 1969 when the Mids were getting blown out by eventual national champion Texas. Late in the game, the Longhorns were ahead 56–13 and had a first down inside Navy's five-yard line. Allowing one more touchdown wouldn't have made any difference, but Navy held fast.

By the time Wayne Hardin left after the 1964 season, selling Navy football had already become more difficult, and athletic director Bill Busik knew that it was more important than ever to get a coach who was a top-notch recruiter. None was better than Elias, a charming man who had done an extraordinary job at Virginia for four years. He was the ACC Coach of the Year in his first season, when Virginia won more games than it had in the previous eight. Getting the job at Navy was the fulfillment of a lifelong ambition that began when, as a sixteen-year-old kid, Elias watched Notre Dame defeat Navy 14–7 at Cleveland Stadium.

The four-season tenure of Elias brought mixed reaction. Some at the Naval Academy thought that he did as good a job as possible, considering the decline of talent; others believed that he did not work hard enough and that the results should have been better. Yet, he was fully supported by the man who hired him, Supt. Draper Kauffman, and by Busik and his successor, Capt. Alan Cameron. When Elias was hired, Rear Admiral Kauffman made it clear that the football team could not be segregated from the Brigade in any of its daily routines, and he assured Elias that the only official evaluation of his work as coach would come from the superintendent's office. Elias got a unanimous "thumbs up" after a 4–4–2 record in 1965, which included a 7–7 tie against Army and two losses by only a touchdown, and after a 4–6 record in 1966, which included a 20–7 loss to Army. Elias stayed for four seasons, but there always were rumblings of discontent from those who were nostalgic for a rapidly disappearing era and unable to comprehend the constraints of the present.

There was a handful of outstanding players during the Elias years, beginning with Staubach's successor at quarterback, John Cartwright, a quiet redhead who had quarterbacked the plebes to a 5–2 record in 1964. He was the

During his three seasons as quarterback, John Cartwright broke all of Roger Staubach's passing records. He finished his career in 1967 as Navy's all-time career and single-season passing leader.

fourth quarterback on the depth chart in spring drills but made a remarkable move to become a starter in 1965, supplanting veteran Bruce Bickel, who had started three games in 1964 when Staubach was injured. Bickel went on to play a key role in 1965 as a backup.

Cartwright became Navy's all-time passing-yardage leader with 3,626 yards, bettering Staubach's record. He also set a season passing record in 1967 with 1,537 yards and a season touchdown record with nine. (Those marks have since been eclipsed.) Though he had better statistics than Staubach, Cartwright's achievements were largely unappreciated because he was always being compared with Roger—a once-in-a-lifetime player. Cartwright differed from Staubach in personality and playing style, and he played with less talented teams. Staubach had an edge because of his ability to scramble and improvise big plays, but Cartwright was every bit as good a passer as Staubach and provided some outstanding performances.

Cartwright's best season was 1967. It included a wild-and-woolly 35–35 tie against Vanderbilt, in which he broke Staubach's single-game total offense record with a total of 358 yards—123 yards on seventeen rushes, and 235 yards on sixteen of twenty-nine passing. The crowning achievement that day also was "Staubachian"—a fourteen-yard scoring pass to Rob Taylor with forty-four seconds to play that got the tie.

Two weeks later, Cartwright put on a magnificent display by directing Navy to a 19–14 victory over Army. He engineered a seventy-two-yard scoring drive that ended with a thirty-six-yard pass to Taylor; a nine-play, forty-five-yard drive that was capped by Dan Pike's touchdown; and a ninety-three-yard drive that included forty-four yards in passing and closed with Jeri Balsy's thirteen-yard touchdown run.

Cartwright's best running back was Terry Murray, who became a career Marine Corps officer. Murray's 174 pounds were tightly wound over his six-foot frame, and he was one of the toughest players in Navy history. Murray led the team in rushing and scoring in 1965 and 1966 and in punt and kickoff returns in 1966 and 1967.

He first starred in the third game of the 1965 season, scoring three touchdowns against William and Mary in a 42–14 victory. He had three one-hundred-yard rushing games while setting a team record with 171 carries in 1966. Elias switched Murray to flanker in 1967, and he and end Rob Taylor combined to catch eighty-four passes for more than a thousand yards. Murray ran twenty-five yards for the winning touchdown in a 26–21 victory over Michigan and caught a fifty-two-yard touchdown pass from Cartwright as Navy upset Syracuse 27–14.

Taylor, a six-two, 189-pound Californian, was the best pass receiver in Navy history. "Rob Taylor could catch a football in a revolving door," one his coaches once quipped. His 1,736 yards is the school's career record, achieved on 129 catches that included thirteen touchdowns. His 818 yards in 1967 still ranks No. 1, and his sixty-one catches and six touchdowns that year is a shared record.

Taylor left behind a litany of big-game performances. In 1966, when he caught fifty-five passes for 727 yards and four touchdowns, he set a Navy

End Rob Taylor (82) and quarterback John Cartwright were the best pass-catch combination in Navy history. Taylor was without peer as a receiver and still is considered the finest ever to play at the Naval Academy. His career figures of 129 receptions for 1,736 yards and 13 touchdowns from 1965–67 all rank No. 1.

single-game record with 130 yards on six catches in a 24–7 win over Pitt. He caught another six—two for touchdowns—when Navy beat Vanderbilt 30–14, and he got Navy's only touchdown and tied a Navy record with nine catches in a 20–7 loss to Army.

He started his 1967 season with a record-setting ten-catch, 140-yard day, including two touchdown receptions, in a 23–22 upset of Penn State. The second touchdown came with fifty-seven seconds to play; he repeated the script later in the season when he caught Cartwright's fourteen-yard touchdown pass with just forty-four seconds to get the tie against Vanderbilt.

Elias's first team produced a huge 10–0 victory at Oklahoma by holding the mighty Sooners to just eighty-three yards of total offense. Cartwright tossed a thirty-three-yard touchdown pass to fullback Al Roodhouse. Phil Bassi kicked the extra point and later added a thirty-six-yard field goal in the final moments of the second quarter. Against Maryland, in a 19–7 victory at Navy–Marine Corps Memorial Stadium, the defense allowed the Terps just forty-nine total yards while Cartwright and Taylor hooked up for a pair of touchdown passes as part of a rollicking 432 yards of offense.

Navy in 1965 also had players like Calvin Huey and Danny Wong. Huey, who finished second in receiving, was the first black man to play at Georgia Tech's Grant Field, where the Midshipmen lost 37–16. Wong, who had played on Staubach's 1964 team, was the No. 2 fullback behind Al Roodhouse in 1965 and Carl Tamulevich in 1966 and was a tough inside running back.

The 1965 season ended with a 7–7 tie against Army. The Mids trailed 7–0 with less than two minutes left in the first half, but Cartwright cranked up a thirty-six-yard drive that ended with his eight-yard touchdown pass to Murray.

Phil Bassi kicked the extra point, and that ended the day's scoring.

Navy could easily have been 6–4 rather than 4–6 in 1966, and the 1967 season brought a return to a winning record (5–4–1). The season was a sparkling tribute to hard work and dedication. The first half of the season saw the upset victories over traditional powerhouses Penn State, Michigan, and Syracuse. Navy came up with another hero in kicker John Church, who calmly kicked a thirty-two-yard field goal with less than four minutes to play for a 22–21 win over Pitt. The 19–14 victory over Army in the final game for Cartwright, Murray, and Taylor capped the only winning year during Elias's tenure.

Rick Forzano replaced Bill Elias in 1969 and suffered through the trough in Navy's football fortunes, compiling a 10–33 record in four seasons. Forzano came from the Cincinnati Bengals' new franchise, where he had worked for coaching great Paul Brown, who was his mentor. Brown had specifically recruited Forzano from the University of Connecticut, where he was head coach, and got him a job in 1967 at St. Louis, with the assurance he would join the Bengals staff when the club started operations in 1968. He spent the 1968 NFL season with Cincinnati before he was approached by Navy to replace Elias. Brown warned him that he was heading into a no-win situation and strongly advised Forzano to stay with the Bengals if he still aspired to become

Carl Tamulevich (33) was a hard-charging fullback for Navy and later a longtime athletic administrator at the Naval Academy.

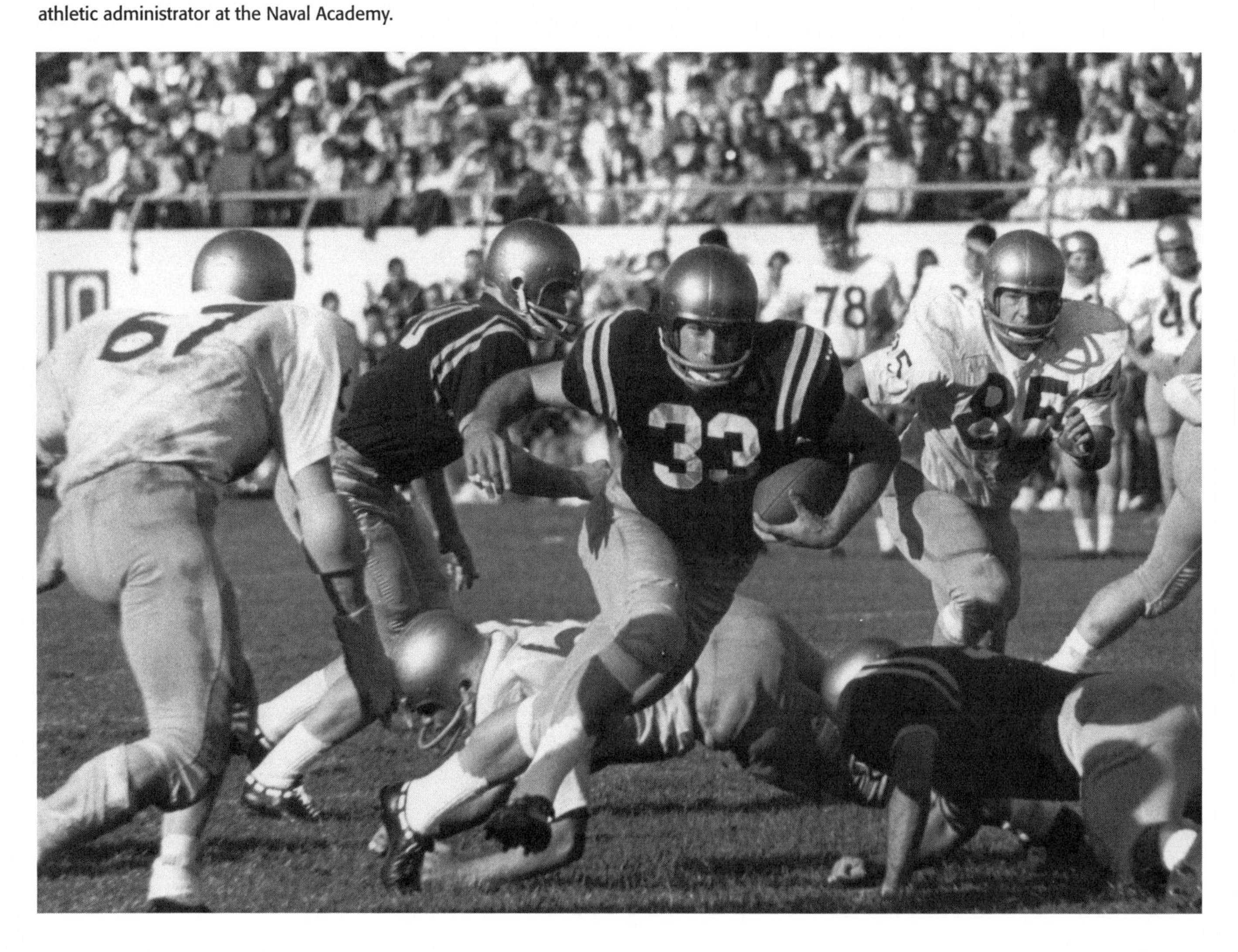

an NFL head coach. But Forzano's five-year stint as an assistant coach at Navy a decade earlier had been so special to him that he ignored Brown's counsel. Forzano was fired after the 1972 season, but the story had a bittersweet ending. Brown helped him get a job as an assistant coach with the Detroit Lions. When head coach Don McCafferty died suddenly in 1974, Forzano succeeded him and fulfilled his dream of being an NFL head coach.

Fullback Dan Pike carries against Army in 1969. Pike was atypical of most of Navy's football players at this time—limited physical skills but all-out players who never gave up.

Forzano was the right coach at the wrong time for Navy. His superb coaching skills, which included a brilliant mind and a great knack for recruiting—he was responsible for Roger Staubach, Tom Lynch, and Pat Donnelly, bulwarks of the 1963 team, coming to Navy—were diluted by the paucity of good players.

"He was so caught up in his love for the mystique of the Naval Academy that he believed he could replicate his prior experiences," noted L. Budd Thalman, the sports information director at the time. "He reveled in coaching the Army-Navy game, in being around dedicated young men, and he was someone who really believed in the 'God and Country' concept. He still has tremendous rapport with everyone at Navy whom he coached."

Forzano inherited a fine quarterback in Mike McNallen, a six-one, 195-pound native of Chicora, Pennsylvania. In 1968, he was the first sophomore quarterback since Bob Zastrow to start the season's opener, and he finished his career in 1970 as Navy's all-time passing leader, a ranking he held for the next sixteen years. McNallen was one of those "rare exceptions" who come to the Naval Academy when they very easily could go to a civilian college and be national stars with NFL potential. McNallen rose above a lack of supporting talent and produced very consistent seasons, including two years in which he gained 1,342 yards—sandwiched around one with 1,312 yards—for a career total of 3,996 yards and thirteen touchdowns.

He had offensive help from running back Dan Pike, who gained 141 yards and scored seventeen- and eighteen-yard touchdowns during Navy's 35–14 win over Georgia Tech in 1968. "Dan was a great player, though he really didn't have the size to be a featured running back," Forzano said of the five-nine, 182-pound halfback from DeQueen, Arkansas. "But no one ever told him that, and it wouldn't have made any difference. He had better-than-average speed, but no one had a bigger heart."

Forzano's first year (1969) was the nadir of Navy's troubled times. The Mids won just one game—10–0 against Virginia in the sixth game of the season.

Cleveland Cooper

Cleveland Cooper, a native of Rochester, New York, was one of ten children. He delighted in playing the saxophone. He delighted even more in slashing through opposing defenses with a blinding quickness.

"He was cat-quick," coach Rick Forzano recalled. "I never coached a running back who could change direction as quickly as he could, and with his low center of gravity, he did it without losing any speed or momentum. Very few sophomore backs ever had as great a season as he did in 1972." (Cooper gained more than 1,000 yards that season and had a 5.4-yards-per-carry average.)

When George Welsh inherited Cooper in 1973, he was equally awestruck. "He had great natural ability to start with, but it wasn't just that natural talent that made him outstanding. It was his extremely good football sense and his great concentration," Welsh said.

It certainly wasn't his size, because Cooper was just five nine and played between 175–180 pounds. "I thought my size would hold me back when I came to the Naval Academy," Cooper said. "When I tried to add ten or fifteen pounds, I felt sluggish, so I cut back and played very comfortably at about 175 to 180 pounds."

Jack Detweiler kicked a thirty-eight-yard field goal, and McNallen threw a sixty-two yard touchdown pass to Karl Schwelm. The Mids' defense stopped seven Virginia fourth-down plays—two at the goal line in the fourth quarter. Navy then lost its last four games, including a 27–0 pasting from Army during which the Cadets' Lynn Moore set a series rushing record with forty carries for 206 yards.

Navy recovered very slowly over the next few seasons. It won two games in 1970 (2–9), three in 1971 (3–8), and four in 1972 (4–7). George Welsh succeeded Forzano in 1973, but Navy's record stuck at 4–7 during his first two seasons.

The highlights were few, but there were some fine individual performances. Mark Schickner, a cornerback who had not even played football as a sophomore, set a school and series record with four interceptions in Navy's 11–7 win over Army in 1970, his junior year. In 1972, Glen Nardi made the All-East team as a defensive tackle. His approach was unconventional. He was six-five and 225 pounds when most nose tackles were no taller than six-two, and he charged almost straight up, although the accepted technique was a low, hard charge to disrupt blocking schemes and burrow into the backfield. The key to Nardi's success was his mastery of the leverage techniques that he used as a wrestler, plus great consistency and tenacity.

Navy had nine sophomores in its 1970 starting lineup. McNallen threw three touchdown passes and scored a fourth in a 48–22 opening game victory over Colgate, but Navy then proceeded to lose every game until the gritty 11–7 victory over Army. The Mids overcame Army's 7–0 lead when Bob Elflein, helped by good blocks from Karl Schwelm and Andy Pease, ran forty-nine yards for a touchdown. Roger Lanning added a thirty-three-yard field goal. Schickner got his record four interceptions—his last one nailed down the victory—and much acclaim. He attributed his feat to "reading the eyes" of Army quarterback Dick Atha. He had simply followed the scouting report that noted that Atha watched his primary receiver until he delivered the ball. A few days after the game, Schickner got a letter from West Point warning him to forgo visiting that academy with his classmates during exchange weekend.

In 1971, Navy won its opening game against Virginia, 10–6, then lost five in a row. The most frustrating loss in that string was a 36–35 squeaker against Pitt. Navy led 35–10 at halftime, but the Panthers stormed back and scored the winning touchdown with twenty-seven seconds to play. Against Duke, Navy turned the tables: after trailing 14–0, the Mids came back and won 15–14 on Fred Stuvek's touchdown pass to Andy Pease with twenty-nine seconds left.

In that game, Chuck Voith had one of the greatest games ever by a Navy defensive player; he recovered three fumbles, forced two more, made fifteen solo tackles, and assisted on nine others.

The Mids spotted Army a 16–0 lead and then, helped by George Berry's rushing—he gained 127 yards in nineteen carries—fought back to grab a 21–16 lead in the third quarter. Stuvek ran for two touchdowns and hit Steve Ogden with a twelve-yard pass for the other. Army regained the lead, 24–21, but Navy drove to Army's eight-yard line. On fourth down with just seconds to play, Forzano, true to the spirit of this game, disdained an easy, tie-making field goal. But Stuvek's pass slipped off Pease's fingers. Army conceded which team was better when, rather than punting the ball from its end zone and risking a blocked kick, the Cadets deliberately took a safety on the game's final play.

Cleveland Cooper wasn't even a starter when the 1972 season began, but he became the first Navy runner to gain more than a thousand yards in one season. He finished with 1,046, breaking Joe Bellino's school record and establishing himself as one of Navy's greatest runners ever. Cooper made his mark in the season's third game, against Boston College, when he ran seventy-one yards for a touchdown that nailed down a 27–20 victory. In a 21–17 victory over Air Force, Cooper got his first start and gained 144 yards. Dan Howard's six-yard touchdown run got the winning points with thirty-nine seconds to play. Cooper went on to rush for one hundred more yards in six consecutive games. When the Mids defeated Pitt 28–13, he rolled up 158 yards and set up three touchdowns by Howard. An eleven-yard run against Georgia Tech broke Bellino's 1960 season record.

Cooper set a Navy career mark in 1973. His 898 yards—then the second-best season total ever—brought his total to 1,944 yards after only two seasons. The record was broken during a 22–17 loss to Pitt in which he gained 123

Glen Nardi *(dark jerseyed No. 76)* reaches for a Syracuse running back. Nardi, a defensive tackle, was one of the East's outstanding players during his three seasons at Navy (1970–72). Defensive end Wes Bergazzi (75) moves in to help.

Quarterback Fred Stuvek runs the option as Navy defeats Pitt 28–13 in 1972. Tackle Steve Oswald (56) throws a block, as does back John Ashmore.

yards. Fullback Bob Jackson had 101 yards, making it the first time in ten years that two Navy runners had gone over one hundred yards in the same game. In 1974, Cooper added 638 yards to finish his career with 2,582 yards, a record that later was broken by both Eddie Meyers and Napoleon McCallum.

Cooper's 1972 record-setting season ended in disappointment when Army beat Navy 23–15 in a game that had two distinct parts, a Navy first half and an Army second half. Cooper scored on a one-yard run and Howard caught an eleven-yard touchdown pass from Al Glenny to give Navy a 12–0 halftime lead. But the Cadets took the lead in the third quarter when Army's Scott Beaty recovered Roger Lanning's blocked field goal and ran eighty-four yards for a touchdown.

The following year, George Welsh became the first Naval Academy graduate to be its head coach since Tom Hamilton. Nine seasons later, he had won more games than any coach in Navy's history. Welsh's football pedigree, as much as his familiarity with the Naval Academy, landed him the job. He coached quarterbacks for Wayne Hardin in 1960 and 1961. After he finished his active-duty career in 1963, Welsh spent ten years as an assistant coach at Penn State, where he worked for Rip Engle and Joe Paterno. At both the Academy and Penn State, he impressed everyone with his quiet ability to make improvements.

Welsh knew it would take time to build the resources to have a successful program. In the meantime he never deviated from his belief in attracting "good people" who were also capable athletes, and who understood their roles and the limitations under which they worked. Welsh was a stickler for fundamentals and thorough preparation: one of his prime commandments was to do only that which made sense. His offenses and defenses were always tailored to fit his personnel, and always well-conceived.

Though he worked in the post–Vietnam War era, when the Academy found recruiting a little easier, Welsh never attracted the number of quality athletes who comprised the outstanding teams of the fifties and early sixties. But even when his teams produced back-to-back 4–7 records in his first two seasons, he maintained the course he had set, and, in 1975, it paid off in a 7–4 record—Navy's first winning season since 1968.

Not only did Welsh earn the devotion of Navy alumni with his 7–1–1 record against Army, he also brought Navy all five of its Commander in Chief's Trophies by defeating Air Force and Army in the same season. The first was in 1973, during Welsh's first season as head coach, when the Mids defeated Air Force 42–6 and Army 51–0, the latter the biggest margin of victory by either team in series history. The Mids rolled up 460 yards against Army, including 366 from rushing. Ed Gilmore ran for 123, and Cooper added 102 and three touchdowns. Navy led just 6–0 after the first quarter, but scored thirty-one points in the second quarter, including two touchdowns by Cooper and one by Larry Van Loan on a thirty-nine-yard touchdown pass from Al Glenny.

Navy had several very fine defensive players during this time. Chet Moeller, a six-foot, 190-pound defensive back, was a unanimous All-America selection in 1975. He played the "rover" in the Mids' defensive secondary—that is, he was moved around to fulfill specific assignments on nearly every play.

"Moeller was one of the best defensive backs ever to play at the Naval Academy," Welsh said. "He played the run so well that we always felt teams ran away from him, and that was the ultimate compliment. It certainly helped us to set up a run defense knowing an opponent would pretty much stay away from one area. But Chet made it easy on himself in that he had a fantastic memory for detail. He not only knew his responsibility in every coverage but those of everyone else in the secondary, as well. He also had deceptive speed—he wasn't as fast as he appeared, but he reacted so quickly to a play that he got to his area before the offense could react."

When Navy upset Penn State 7–6 early in the 1974 season, Moeller had thirteen tackles, three of them behind the line of scrimmage, and recovered one of the five fumbles that Navy forced that day. Ed Jeter knocked down a pass on a two-point conversion attempt in the final minutes to preserve the win. Lineman Jeff Sapp, a third-team All-America selection in 1976 at middle guard, and defensive backs Gene Ford, Mike Galpin, and John Sturges were also superb players in the same era.

The Sturges-Galpin duo played together for three years. While Ford led the team with six interceptions in 1975, Galpin, a versatile player, shifted to wide receiver. He caught seventeen passes, second on the team, for 299 yards and three touchdowns. In 1976, Galpin was back on defense. He led the team with seven interceptions, including three in Navy's 27–10 victory over Syracuse. Sturges had a team-record eight interceptions in 1977, and finished as Navy's all-time leader with thirteen. He was named a third-team All-America.

The Army-Navy game celebrated its Diamond Jubilee in 1974, and among the 103,000 spectators was President Gerald Ford, the first chief executive to attend the game since

Cleveland Cooper was one of the best running backs in Navy history. When he finished his three-year career in 1974, he was then Navy's all-time rusher, with 2,582 yards. His 1,046 yards as a sophomore in 1972 made him the first Navy runner to gain 1,000 yards in a season. Here he picks up a good gain during Navy's 21–17 triumph over Air Force in 1972.

George Welsh

The Naval Academy superintendent in 1973, Rear Adm. William Mack, recalled, in his oral history for the Naval Institute, his interview with George Welsh before he was hired.

According to Admiral Mack, Welsh told him: "You pay me whatever you think I'm worth and I won't ask for a contract. At the end of the year, we'll know whether I want to stay and whether you want me to stay."

"Do you think you can produce winning teams at the Naval Academy?" Mack asked, then added, "I don't think you can because the requirements for academics to get in here and stay are too stringent."

"I think I can do it," Welsh insisted.

"How?" Mack asked.

"I'll do it on a quality rather than a quantity basis," he replied.

"Well," Mack replied, "recruiting has been done on a mass basis where we get as many nominees as possible, we try and get all the athletes possible, and hopefully some good ones will be in the group."

"That won't work," Welsh replied. "You must go after the really blue-chip athlete who is academically sound, and concentrate on getting a few good ones of that type in here.

"I want young men who are 'good people'—a good man, a smart one who is athletically able. He knows he's not a pro prospect, but I believe we can get some who are just below that level, who are smart. If he's a lineman, then we build him up to 250 pounds and allow his other virtues to take over."

"Where will these kinds of athletes come from?" Mack asked.

"I'll concentrate on New Jersey, Pennsylvania, Florida, New York, and California because I believe we can find people in those areas who like the Navy and would come and stay at the Academy," Welsh said.

In 1973 George Welsh *(left)* took over as head coach, the first Naval Academy graduate to hold the job since Tom Hamilton left in 1947. Walsh—the nifty quarterback of the Sugar Bowl champion "Team Named Desire" of 1954—became Navy's winningest coach, with fifty-five victories in his nine seasons at the helm (1973–81). His teams also ranked nationally and played in three postseason games. Best of all, he was 7–1–1 against Army. Standing next to him during the 1973 Penn State game is quarterback Al Glenny (14).

Mack agreed, and he never questioned his coach's work, even though Welsh did not have winning seasons during Mack's tour as superintendent.

"He never once asked for anything for his football team, no special privileges," Mack said. "He just told them they had to be midshipmen first and football players second. The morale of the football team was outstanding, but he had a hard time changing the attitude of the Brigade that football players got special privileges when they didn't."

John Kennedy in 1962. Welsh installed a "Power-I" offense for the game, and the Mids churned out 290 rushing yards in a 19–0 victory. Cooper, playing his last game, had 105 yards—making him the first player to rush for more than 100 yards in each of three Army-Navy games. Bob Jackson scored twice, while the defense intercepted three passes, recovered two fumbles, and scored two points when Tim Harden tackled Army passer Scott Gillogly in the end zone for a safety.

Welsh truly proved his worth as a coach in 1975. Navy's quarterback, Phil Poirier, was inexperienced. Rather than force him to carry too much of the offensive load, Welsh established a solid running game. Jackson and Gerry Goodwin each gained more than 800 yards that season. In an opening 42–14 win over Virginia, Goodwin equaled Bellino's record of four touchdowns in one game as he rolled up 166 yards. With the powerful running game, Poirier threw just 104 passes all season. Navy won four of its first five games and captured the Commander in Chief's Trophy. In one of the most exciting games, the Mids overcame a 16–3 deficit to defeat Miami 17–16. Jackson's option pass to Joe Gattuso, Jr., got a touchdown in the third quarter, and Ford returned an interception twenty-four yards for the decisive points in the fourth quarter.

Navy's defense was ranked third nationally. It didn't allow Syracuse beyond its own thirty-seven-yard line in the second half and used interceptions by Ford and Moeller to set up two scores in a 10–6 victory. In a 17–0 win over Pitt, Moeller made a touchdown-saving tackle on future Heisman Trophy winner Tony Dorsett and then recovered his fumble a few minutes later to key Navy's first scoring drive. He also intercepted an option pass and returned it fifty-four yards to set up Larry Muczynski's forty-yard field goal. Muczynski scored a

President Gerald Ford visits the Navy football team in Annapolis. Ford also attended the 1974 Army-Navy game, when Navy won, 19–0. Starting early in the century, the Army-Navy game once was a "must do" on the calendars of many presidents. In 1905 President Theodore Roosevelt spent the second half on the sidelines, encouraging both teams.

Chet Moeller was one of the finest, most versatile defensive players in Navy history. He was a defensive back but played the "rover" position in the Mids' secondary, moving to different areas on every play. He was a unanimous selection to the 1975 All-America team.

record sixty-three points that season with his kicking. (The mark was later broken by his two successors, Bob Tata and Steve Fehr.) He later distinguished himself by shooting down a Libyan jet during an air battle over the Mediterranean Sea.

Navy revved up its ground game one last time in 1975 to beat Army 30–6. Navy's defense held Army to 192 yards. Bob Jackson gained 133 yards and became Navy's No. 2 all-time rusher with 1,667 yards, three more than Bellino.

Welsh always had a marvelous knack for moving players from positions that had too much talent to ones that didn't have enough, and getting the most from the moves. In 1976, Bob Leszczynski started the season as one of four sophomores behind starting quarterback John Kurowski. Kurowski struggled, while Leszczynski performed well in relief appearances against Boston College and William and Mary. So Welsh made Leszczynski the starter, shifted wingback Joe Gattuso, Jr., to tailback, and put Kurowski at wingback. This offensive combination operated with deadly efficiency for the rest of the year.

In Leszczynski's second start, against Notre Dame, he set a school record by passing for 294 yards, completing twenty-one of forty-five attempts. His touchdown tosses to Dave King and Larry Klawinski put Navy ahead 14–3 in the second quarter, but heavily favored Notre Dame scored three straight touchdowns and won. Leszczynski then led Navy to wins in the season's last three games, including a 38–10 trouncing of Army. He completed ten of fourteen attempts for 145 yards and threw touchdown passes to Phil McConkey and Dave King as Navy beat the Cadets for the fourth consecutive time. When Leszczynski finished his career, he was rated Navy's most efficient passer behind Staubach and second in yards behind McNallen with 3,945.

"Bob came a long way very fast," said Welsh. "He showed great judgment for a sophomore when we had to put him in. But he also had a great understanding of the passing game and pass coverages; and he was such a good athlete that we used him to run an option offense."

Joe Gattuso was a physical and stylistic replica of his father, who was a teammate of Welsh's on the 1954 "Team Named Desire" and led Navy in rushing in 1953 and 1954. Like his father, Gattuso Jr. had only moderate speed, but he had the same great instincts to pick his way through a defense and was just as tough and fierce a competitor.

Gattuso was the starting wingback for the final six games of the 1975 season but didn't cause much of a ripple. But after Welsh moved him to tailback in 1976, he gained 159 yards and scored two touchdowns against Syracuse; ran for eighty-one yards, including twenty-five for a touchdown, and caught a seventy-five-yard touchdown pass in a 34–28 win over Georgia Tech; and scored three times and ran for 128 yards in the win over Army.

"Like his father, he was never flashy," Welsh said of Gattuso. "But also like his dad, he was a winner and did everything so well. There weren't a lot of players who could have moved from wingback to tailback and then learned the job on the fly as well as he did. The positions are so different that he really had to learn how to run with the ball all over again, yet it seemed he'd been at that spot from day one."

Gattuso was certainly master of the position in 1977, when Navy won five of

Running back Gerry Goodwin (43) racks up significant yardage against Air Force in 1975. The Mids won the game, 30–6, and captured the Commander in Chief's Trophy, given each year to the team that wins the interlocking competition between the three schools.

eleven games. He set an all-time Navy season rushing record with 1,292 yards; caught twenty-two passes; returned kickoffs; and was the team's No. 2 scorer with thirty-six points. Gattuso rolled up several one-hundred-yard games that year, and was the key player in Navy's 10–7 win over Air Force, climaxed by Bob Tata's winning twenty-five-yard field goal. In a 42–17 victory over William and Mary, he put on one of the greatest individual performances in Navy history: 250 rushing yards and two touchdowns; a twenty-yard touchdown pass to McConkey; three pass receptions for twenty-five yards; and two kickoff returns for thirty-four yards—for a total offense of 329 yards!

Gattuso became the second Navy player to break the one-thousand-yard rushing barrier for a season when he gained 132 yards against Syracuse, even though Navy lost 45–34. The following week, with President Jimmy Carter, a Naval Academy alumnus, at Navy–Marine Corps Memorial Stadium, Gattuso broke five Navy records, including Cooper's season rushing mark, in a 20–16 win against Georgia Tech. The defense saved the game in the final minute after Georgia Tech got inside Navy's twenty-yard line. Charlie Thornton got a sack, and then Glenn Flanagan came up with an interception.

Two weeks later, Army jumped to a 10–0 lead in a game played in a zero-degree wind chill. Leszczynski threw an eighteen-yard touchdown pass to Kurowski, but Army scored again for a 17–7 halftime lead. Gattuso's third-quarter touchdown made it 17–14. With just a minute to play, Navy faced a fourth down at Army's eight-yard line, in easy range for a game-tying field goal by Tata. But Welsh knew that Army-Navy games were played to win or lose—not tie—and he called for Gattuso to throw an option pass. The ball skittered off Phil McConkey's fingers in the end zone, and Navy lost. Gattuso finished his career that day with 1,890 yards, second-best behind Cooper at that time.

George Welsh brought Navy football back to national prominence with winning records in his last four seasons, during which the team was 31–15–1, including 3–0–1 against Army. The Mids capped three of those seasons with appearances in postseason bowl games and defeated Brigham Young 23–16 in the first Holiday Bowl. (The details of all three games are in Chapter Ten.)

During that time, two of Navy's three famed "M Boys"—wide receiver Phil McConkey and running back Eddie Meyers—were key players and leaders in the team's success. The third "M Boy," Napoleon McCallum, played with Meyers in 1981 and then broke all of his records during the 1982 through 1985 seasons.

McConkey, a five-ten, 180-pound son of a Buffalo, New York, policeman, who later was the inspirational soul of the New York Giants' 1986 NFL champions, wasn't recruited by any Division I school except Navy. His drive and determination helped him become one of the Academy's all-time leading receivers and return specialists. The same traits helped him make it in the NFL after five years on active duty as a helicopter pilot.

Phil McConkey was co-captain of the 1978 team that won its first seven games, Navy's best start since 1960. In the first quarter of the season's 32–0 opening win against Virginia that year, he caught five balls for 141 yards (he had 149 for the game) en route to leading Navy in receiving for the second straight season. McConkey was third in the nation in 1977 in punt returns with a 13.5 average (he led Navy in punt returns in 1976, 1977, and 1978, and he led the Mids in kickoff returns in 1978). He finished his career tied with Rob Taylor for the most touchdown catches (thirteen) and holds the school record with eighty punt returns. "He was always the guy who made big plays for us," Welsh said with characteristic understatement.

Eddie Meyers was a five-nine, 203-pound running back from Pemberton, New Jersey, whose father was a retired twenty-year Army man. Eddie's older brother, Charlie, was a starting Navy defensive back in 1977, 1978, and 1979. Eddie Meyers finished as Navy's all-time rushing leader with 2,935 yards and was co-captain of Welsh's final team in 1981. He established a single-season record that year of 1,318 yards. (McCallum would soon eclipse both his single-season and career marks.)

Later, Meyers used his annual leave while a Marine Corps officer to play with the Atlanta Falcons during the NFL preseason for six straight years. "I don't see how he did it," said Falcons running backs coach Steve Crosby. "It took such self-discipline, such determination."

That was Meyers. A sparkling personality that won him many friends among midshipmen and faculty alike masked his bulldog tenacity as a player. At the beginning of 1979, his sophomore season, he was the third-string fullback and the No. 4 tailback. Navy won its first six games; finally, a freshman quarterback at Pitt named Dan Marino completed twenty-two passes for 227 yards and shot the Mids down 24–7. Meanwhile, Navy's tailbacks were tumbling: Steve Callahan, Duane Flowers, and Mike Sherlock all were injured midway through the season. Meyers was placed full-time at tailback. Finally, given a start in the tenth game of the year, he gained 183 yards on twenty-seven carries in a

Running back Joe Gattuso, Jr., dives over Army's defense for one of the record-tying three touchdowns that he scored in Navy's 38–10 stomping in 1976. Gattuso's dad was one of the backfield stars of the 1954 "Team Named Desire" that included young Gattuso's coach, George Welsh.

Wide receiver Phil McConkey was an inspirational force for his Navy teams from 1976 to 1978. He was a steady wide receiver and the most valuable player of Navy's 1978 Holiday Bowl win after making the game-deciding catch. He was an equally fearless kickoff and punt return specialist and ranks third in total kick returns, with more than 1,000 combined yards and an 11.2-yard average. When his active-duty naval career ended, his fiery play became a mainstay for the New York Giants. McConkey played on their 1986 NFL championship team. Standing next to him is Leon "Red" Romo, one of Navy's legendary athletic trainers for whom the Romo Physical Training Center is named.

Phil McConkey

Phil McConkey suffered perhaps the cruelest fate that could befall a commissioned naval officer from Annapolis: He had chronic seasickness.

"Whoever heard of a naval officer suffering from chronic seasickness?" said McConkey, who was a helicopter pilot. "But that was me. I was on a four-month cruise of the Mediterranean. The ship would start rocking, and I'd jump in a helicopter and fly around—just to get off the ship."

He was reassigned to a desk job, but the lack of action frustrated McConkey so much that his parents suggested he consider trying out for pro football.

"Are you crazy?" he said. "Roger Staubach did it, but . . . ?"

Nonetheless, he worked out for five months. The biggest plus was his consistent time of 4.5 seconds in the forty-yard dash—the measuring stick used to grade the potential of NFL players. Navy assistant coach Steve Belichick, whose son, Bill, was defensive coach with the New York Giants, strongly recommended McConkey, and he used his regular leave time to attend the Giants' training camp. Head coach Bill Parcells was impressed enough to sign him as a free agent.

"But some admirals saw me playing a preseason game on TV, and went nuts," McConkey recalled. "I thought I'd be sent to Cuba. Instead, they denied me an early discharge and shipped me off to Pensacola [Naval Air Station]."

He continued to work out with ex-Navy teammate Kit McCulley and with New Orleans Saints' quarterback Richard Todd, who was a neighbor. When McConkey finally was discharged in 1984, he rejoined the Giants and made the team, where he played as a pass receiver and return specialist until 1989.

The millions of Giants' fans loved him as much for his enthusiastic towel-waving and spirit as for his timely feats on the football field. He capped his career in Super Bowl XXI against the Denver Broncos by scoring a touchdown in typical McConkey fashion: A pass popped out of the hands of tight end Mark Bavaro and directly into his hands as he tumbled into the end zone.

24–14 loss to Georgia Tech. Meyers had a record-setting, 278-yard, three-touchdown day against Army during a 31–7 win that tied the series for the first time since 1923.

Late in the game, Meyers was sitting on the bench and basking in his good day's work—270 yards on 38 carries—when Welsh was informed that Meyers was on the brink of setting two records. He was just eight yards shy of breaking Navy's single-game rushing mark of 277 yards, set by Sneed Schmidt against Columbia in 1935; and was within three carries of eclipsing the record of forty rushes in an Army-Navy game set by Army's Lynn Moore in 1969.

"Do you want to try breaking them?" Welsh asked him.

"Sure, let's go for it, why not?" Meyers replied.

Welsh sent him back into the game, and he gained four yards on his first two carries. On his third play, Meyers took a pitchout and headed around left end. Seeing an Army player coming up to stop him, he just lowered his shoulder, knocked over the defender, and picked up four yards. And two records. All told, he set five records that day. Including three Army-Navy game marks. For the season, Meyers and Sherlock combined for more than 1,200 yards rushing.

In 1980, Meyers's national reputation grew when he gained 114 yards during a nationally televised 24–10 Navy victory over eighteenth-ranked Washington. Against Army that same year, he added 144 yards as Navy won 33–6.

But Meyers is forever remembered for his best performance in 1981 against Syracuse. Little-used Jeff Korn played quarterback because of injuries to Marco Pagnanelli and Tom Tarquinio. To offset the inexperience at quarterback, Meyers carried the ball on play after play. He produced a record 298 yards and four touchdowns, one on a seventy-eight-yard run, in a 35–23 win.

Something new was added to Navy football in the seventies when female cheerleaders first appeared, reflecting the Naval Academy's coeducational status.

Navy players celebrate their 6–3 upset of Syracuse in 1980 at the Carrier Dome. Steve Fehr kicked two field goals for all of Navy's points, and his field goal early in the fourth quarter broke a 3–3 tie and gave Navy the upset victory.

In his final three games in 1981—which also were Welsh's last three as head coach—Meyers helped Navy beat Georgia Tech 20–14 with 196 yards; gained 119 in a 3–3 tie against Army (he had a record 547 yards against Army in three games); and was chosen Most Valuable Player in the Liberty Bowl after gaining 117 yards, the most any runner got against Ohio State that season. Despite his effort, Navy lost to the heavily favored Buckeyes, 31–28.

Quarterback Bob Leszczynski rolled up nearly 4,000 yards passing from 1976 to 1978. He led Navy to a thrilling 23–16 victory over Brigham Young in the 1978 Holiday Bowl.

While talented players such as Meyers helped Navy achieve national ranking in the polls, the real secret to the Mids' success was Welsh's great coaching ability. He again displayed his knack for shuffling players to positions where they were most productive. No move was bigger, in 1980, than making a quarterback of Fred Reitzel, who had led the team with five interceptions as a defensive back in 1978. Navy won eight games, including a 24–10 upset of Washington's Rose Bowl–bound team. Against Army, Reitzel accounted for three touchdowns, and the defense forced three turnovers in the 33–6 victory.

Meyers's 957 yards relieved some of the pressure on Reitzel, as did Steve Fehr's kicking. Fehr kicked seventeen field goals, including the winner early in the last quarter in Navy's 6–3 upset of Syracuse; four in a 19–8 victory over Georgia Tech; and four in the victory over Army.

Welsh also rebuilt his defense in 1980, with middle guard Tim Jordan, linebacker Mike Kronzer, and defensive backs Elliott Reagans and Jeff Shoemake the cornerstones. They seldom made mistakes, except for a 33–0 loss to Notre Dame and a last-minute touchdown pass that allowed Air Force to win 21–20. The Mids again were nationally ranked.

For the first time, the Army game was played at

Quarterback Fred Reitzel *(arms upraised and clutching the game ball)* exults after leading Navy over Washington's Rose Bowl–bound Huskies, 24–10, in 1980. Reitzel had been Navy's top defensive back the previous season, but he responded to his new position by leading the Mids to an 8–4 season in 1980. Mike Dolan (center, 75) and Bob Teufel (guard, 57) join the celebration.

Steve Fehr kicks a field goal for Navy's only points in a 3–3 tie against Army in 1981 at Philadelphia's Veterans Stadium. Fehr, whose 189 points are the most ever by a Navy kicker, is No. 3 in career scoring, and for three consecutive seasons (1979–81) he led Navy in scoring. His forty-two field goals are the most in Navy history. He followed Bob Tata, another great kicker who had amassed 161 points.

Philadelphia's Veterans Stadium, across from fabled JFK Stadium where so many of the game's greatest moments had taken place for more than forty years. Navy's 33–6 win gave the Mids the lead in the series for the first time since 1921. Navy's defense allowed the Cadets just 144 yards—the same number that Meyers gained with his thirty rushes. Navy controlled the ball for more than forty-two minutes. Reitzel completed twelve of eighteen passes for 138 yards, scored twice, and threw a nine-yard touchdown pass to Dave Dent, who caught six passes for sixty-six yards. Fehr had fifteen points—the most ever scored by a kicker in the series—including a record-setting fifty-yard field goal. Three weeks later, Navy ended the season with a 35–0 loss to the University of Houston in the Garden State Bowl. (That game is covered in Chapter Ten.)

Welsh carved out his fourth straight winning season in 1981 with a 7–4–1 record. It began with Navy's 500th victory, 17–7 over the Citadel, but the team slumped to 2–2. Then, despite injuries to seven starters, Navy won five of its next six games. A 30–13 victory over Air Force not only helped to secure the fourth straight Commander in Chief's Trophy, but also gave Welsh more victories than any Navy coach. The season ended with a disappointing 3–3 tie against Army and the narrow loss to Ohio State in the Liberty Bowl.

Meyers finished fifth in the nation that season with a 131.8-yards-per-game average and had seven games of 100 yards or more en route to his single-season record; he also set five other Academy rushing marks. Steve Fehr set ten Academy field-goal kicking records, including a school record seventy-six points. Navy's defense, led by linebacker Andy Ponseigo, Jordan, and Shoemake, again was ranked. What delighted Welsh most of all, though, was the number of non-letter-winning seniors who stepped up and supplied the needed depth to survive the schedule and produce the winning record.

That kind of help was critical for Navy football to prosper because former prep stars did not line the bench like they did at many of the high-profile civilian college football programs. Welsh scraped and scratched to accumulate the talent that had returned Navy's football program to such competitive heights, and he had succeeded in large part because of his extraordinary ability to get the most from his talent and get players to perform successfully in areas where he needed help. The work exacted a heavy personal toll on Welsh, just as it had on everyone who had coached a Navy football team. Only Eddie Erdelatz had stayed as long as Welsh but, unlike his old coach, Welsh still operated at the end of his tenure within the boundaries imposed at his hiring.

By 1981, the challenge to produce successful teams became even more formidable because, as noted earlier, the Academy tightened its admission policies and toughened its curricula. Welsh often found more of his energies directed toward trying to cope with those hurdles than toward coaching football. The breaking point probably came before Navy lost to the University of Houston in the 1980 Garden State Bowl. While Houston's team was practicing for the game, Navy's players had to stay in their hotel and take final examinations. Welsh knew that his counterparts at civilian schools had no such problems, and the dismal loss to Houston underscored how difficult it had become to consistently produce successful teams at Navy.

Welsh had long been pursued by civilian schools where he could coach without the impositions placed upon him at the Naval Academy, and with far more rewards. So he left Navy after the 1981 season and became head coach at Virginia, where he continued his winning tradition and raised the Cavaliers to high national standing. Gary Tranquill, who had coached quarterbacks and receivers for four years under Welsh at Navy and then been an assistant at Ohio State and West Virginia, succeeded Welsh in 1982 as the Academy's thirty-first head coach.

Gary Tranquill, one of college football's most imaginative offensive strategists, succeeded George Welsh as head coach in 1982. He immediately produced a 6–5 season, Navy's last winning season until 1996.

Running back Mike Sherlock, helped by a block from tackle Frank McCallister, wedges out some yardage. Sherlock finished his career with 1,600 rushing yards, placing him among the top ten rushers in Navy history.

McCallum Owned the Record Book

When Napoleon McCallum graduated, he was in Navy's record book as:

- Career rusher with 4,179 yards record. He averaged 4.6 yards on each of his 908 carries.
- Single-season rushing record with 1,587 yards for a 4.8 average and ten touchdowns in 1983. (Also No. 2 season leader with 1,327 yards and fourteen touchdowns in 1985, and his totals for his other two seasons rank among the eleven best in Navy history.)
- Most games with one hundred or more yards rushing (nineteen).
- Career all-purpose leader with 7,172 yards, also an NCAA record.
- Season all-purpose yardage leader with 2,385 in 1983.
- Career kick returner (kickoffs and punts) with 133 returns for 2,197 yards, both records, and a 16.5 average.
- Season punt return leader with 372 yards in 1982.
- Career punt return leader with 858 yards.
- Career kickoff return leader with 1,339 yards.
- Career scoring with two hundred points, mostly with his record thirty-three touchdowns. (No. 2 single-season scorer with eighty points in 1985.)
- McCallum has nearly a dozen other records sprinkled through various offensive categories.

Running back Napoleon McCallum touched off salvos whenever he touched the ball during his five seasons. He is Navy's all-time leading rusher, with 4,179 yards. His 908 rushing attempts and 31 rushing touchdowns are also school records. McCallum and Eddie Meyers gave Navy a solid one-two running punch in 1981.

Just as Welsh got a huge boost in his first seasons by inheriting Cleveland Cooper, Tranquill inherited Napoleon McCallum, a native of Milford, Ohio, who became Navy's most heralded player since Roger Staubach. McCallum became college football's all-time leader in all-purpose running (rushing, receiving, and punt and kickoff returns combined) with 7,172 yards. His jersey number, 30, was retired, joining those of Bellino and Staubach.

McCallum, who spelled Meyers at tailback during Welsh's final season, was six-two and 208 pounds. He had superb athletic skills, including the speed to run away from people in the open field and the power to break all but the most determined tackles. Like all great running backs, he always got better and better in a game the more he was involved.

He was an All-America in 1983 after gaining 100 or more yards from rushing in a record-setting eight games, and he gained more than 200 yards against Princeton and Air Force. His total of 332 all-purpose yards against Princeton that season is an all-time Navy record.

McCallum started the 1984 season as a sure-fire All-America player and possible Heisman Trophy winner, but he broke his ankle with only eighty-four seconds to play in the second game, against Virginia, and missed the rest of the season. For the first time in the modern era, the Naval Academy waived a rule that had limited varsity competition to only those years before graduation, and McCallum was granted an extra year of eligibility as a postgraduate while studying for a second major.

"I had wanted to make the 1984 season the best year for Navy and myself," McCallum said in explaining his decision to go for the fifth year. "I had high hopes of great things being accomplished, and when I was injured, my dreams

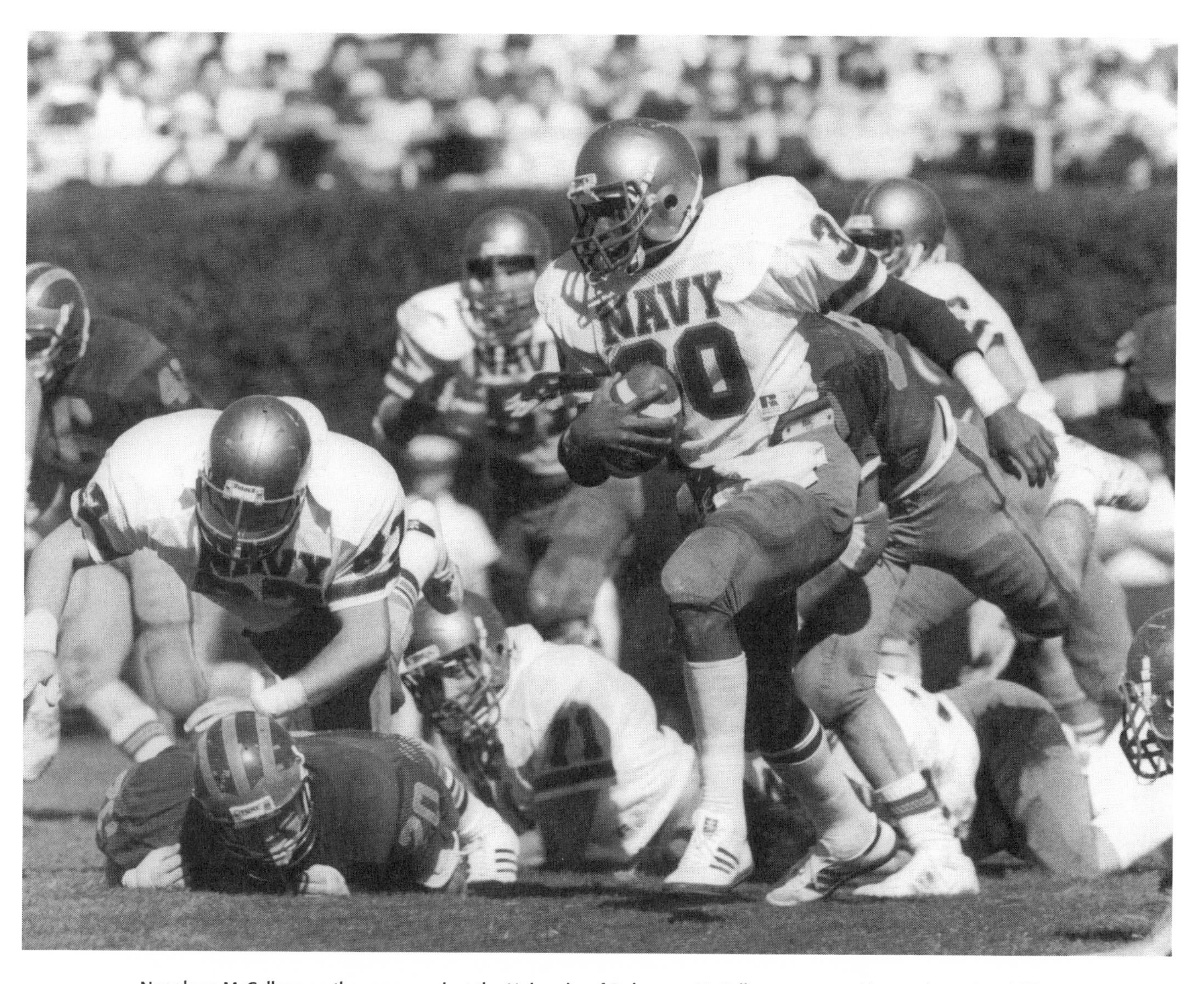

Napoleon McCallum on the move against the University of Delaware. McCallum was a workhorse player: in addition to being Navy's all-time rusher, he is the top career kick returner, with 2,197 yards from 133 punts and kickoffs. He also ranks fifth in pass receptions, with ninety-six for 796 yards.

Only seconds before the end of the second game of 1984, Napoleon McCallum—a Heisman Trophy candidate that year—broke his ankle and had to be helped off the field. He missed the rest of his senior season, but in a rare move, the Naval Academy allowed him to play a fifth year of varsity football in 1985, with NCAA approval, and pursue graduate work.

had left me. I love to play football and I had the option of playing the final game that year against Army and calling it a career. But playing only the last game of the season at great risk of reinjury was not a good alternative to take the place of the dreams I had."

So he came back in 1985 and had a great season. He led Navy with 1,327 rushing yards, second only to his 1983 school record, and was first in pass receiving, punt and kickoff returns, and scoring. He was named to the All-America team again, but fell short in the Heisman race because Navy won only four games and his achievements were diminished—at least in the eyes of the Heisman Trophy voters. To the Brigade, he was the best: McCallum's classmates carried him off the field at Veterans Stadium on their shoulders after his final game, a 17–7 victory over Army during which he gained 217 rushing yards on forty-one carries.

There have been some very fine players at the Academy since 1985: quarterbacks Bill Byrne, Alton Grizzard, and Jim Kubiak; running back Chuck Smith; all-purpose back Jason Van Matre; defensive players Jim Dwyer, Dave Pimpo, Bob Weissenfels, Andy Kirkland; and those who followed McConkey's path to the NFL, such as defensive tackle Bob Kuberski, tight end Kevin Hickman, and tackle Max Lane. But there has not been another of McCallum's caliber.

In 1982, Marco Pagnanelli complemented McCallum's running and set a school record by completing fifteen of seventeen passes for 171 yards in a

McCallum's Part-Time Pro Career

Napoleon McCallum won the Naval Academy Athletic Association Sword after the 1985 season and was named Most Valuable Player in the Senior Bowl and Blue-Gray Game en route to being the fourth-round draft pick of the Los Angeles Raiders. With the Raiders, he was the first service academy player to serve on active duty and play pro football at the same time. He was assigned to the USS *Peleliu* at Long Beach, California, but he attended Raiders practices during his off hours and played on Sundays.

"I have no idea where he got his perseverance," former Raiders all-pro defensive end Howie Long said. "In your career, you run across very few guys like him. He was a Navy highlight film come to life. They should have put him on every recruiting poster."

McCallum had a fine pro career, considering the constraints. He finished second among the team's rushers in his rookie season. He was then transferred to the USS *California* at the Alameda Naval Air Station outside Oakland. Ironically, the Raiders had played in Oakland until only three years before he joined them, but he was too far from their new home to play and keep up his Navy commitments. The transfer was done at the direction of Secretary of the Navy James Webb, himself a Naval Academy graduate who had never favored McCallum being granted an extra year's eligibility at Annapolis. Webb saw a way to work his will.

McCallum missed two years of football, during which time he was traded to the San Diego Chargers while he and his ship joined the Seventh Fleet. Still, when he returned to pro football, he had been traded back to the Raiders. After he left the Navy, McCallum continued to play in the NFL through the 1994 season, when a knee injury forced him to retire.

Eric Wallace (86) celebrates his ninety-five-yard touchdown kickoff return in the 1983 Army-Navy game in the Rose Bowl at Pasadena, California. With him is Todd Hastings. Navy ran a reverse on the opening kickoff and Wallace took a handoff from Napoleon McCallum that completely fooled the Army coverage unit. It was the first opening kickoff score in the series history and opened the floodgates for Navy to win, 43–12.

victory against Duke. But his career was ended three games later when he broke a leg during the Mids' 28–3 victory over the Citadel. Tranquill's very effective pass offense now was completely subordinated to the running game, led by McCallum and tailback Rick Clouse. They responded with three victories to close the season, including the win over Army, which was made even more significant because sophomore quarterback Rick Williamson started his first game. The Navy defense held the Cadets to just one rushing yard in the second half and only fifty-eight for the game—the least any Navy team had allowed since 1952.

Navy slipped to a 3–8 record in 1983. The season was notable only for the Army-Navy game, played before more than 81,000 at the Rose Bowl in Pasadena, California. It was the first time the game was played west of the Mississippi River and the first time since 1944 that it was played anywhere but Philadelphia. The event produced one of the biggest peacetime weekend military airlifts ever as 9,000 students from both schools were flown to the game.

For the first time, a West Coast audience had a chance to experience the unique spirit and feeling that is showcased by the midshipmen and cadets, beginning with their march-ons and continuing throughout the game with a zany array of hijinks. Californians are usually blasé about such things, but the throng at the Rose Bowl was impressed by all they witnessed. When the game was over, there was more talk about the spirit of the two student bodies than about Navy's devastating display of football in its 42–13 victory.

Navy zoomed to a 21–0 lead in the first four minutes, sparked by the first opening kickoff touchdown in the series' history when McCallum handed the ball on a reverse to defensive back Eric Wallace, and he raced ninety-five yards for the score. It was the longest kickoff return ever in the series. McCallum had 182 rushing yards, almost a hundred more than Army gained, giving him his eighth straight one-hundred-plus-yard game of that season.

After McCallum was lost to injury in the second game of the 1984 season, Rick Clouse and Mike Smith carried the rushing load. Bill Byrne, a sophomore, took over at quarterback and piled up more than 1,400 yards passing and eleven touchdown throws. He became one of the finest passers in Navy history, finishing his career with 381 completions for 4,582 yards, a record broken by Jim Kubiak a decade later. But his accomplishments never got the recognition they deserved because his teams never had winning records, and he played in McCallum's considerable shadow. He also was dogged by bad luck—a broken foot ended his sophomore season prematurely, and a torn spleen cost him the last two games of the 1985 season after he had already set a season record with 1,692 passing yards.

After Byrne broke his foot, his successor, Bob Misch, helped pull off one of Navy's biggest upsets of this era with a 38–21 win over second-ranked South Carolina. It was only the third time that a Navy team had defeated an opponent so highly ranked. Navy scored thirty-one straight points. Clouse had a fifty-three-yard touchdown run, and Misch tossed two touchdown passes, while Navy's defense, led by co-captain Eric Rutherford (eleven tackles, four sacks, and a blocked field goal) held South Carolina to just 102 rushing yards. Misch had another good game against Army, passing for a series record 280 yards. But Navy's rushing defense collapsed, allowing the Cadets 432 on the ground. Army won, 28–11.

Though McCallum and Byrne were a great combination in 1985, Navy lost seven games—five by a total of fifteen points, and two of its first three in the final minute. The Mids finally performed some late-game magic themselves against

There is no denying the feelings of these midshipmen as they march into the Rose Bowl for the 1983 Army-Navy game, the first one ever played west of Chicago.

Elliott Uzelac, once an assistant coach at the Naval Academy, returned as head coach in 1987 for a three-year stint.

Army, as Misch directed Navy to ten fourth-quarter points and a 17–7 win. The defense contained Army's second-ranked rushing offense.

The Tranquill era ended in 1986 after Navy won three of its first four games, then lost every game thereafter, including a 27–7 shelling by Army.

Alton Grizzard was a prolific yardage producer at quarterback for the Mids, churning out a combined total of 5,666 yards during his career from rushing and passing.

Tranquill was replaced by Elliott Uzelac, who had been an assistant coach under Forzano in 1970 and 1971. Uzelac's first move was switching his offense to the wishbone formation, which had been a staple in college football during most of the sixties and early seventies but was out of favor by the eighties. Army had switched to the wishbone a few years earlier and had been more successful against the types of physically powerful and talented opponents that were beating Navy. Uzelac hoped that the switch would help the Mids mirror Army's success. Ideally, the biggest advantage was that an opponent had to change much of what it did defensively for this single game. A little confusion and tentativeness were likely to result, and Navy hoped to gain some advantage. Although his teams produced several rushing records during his three seasons as head coach, the system yielded only eight victories—and just one, in 1989, against Army. (That game is covered in Chapter Nine.) Navy's offense was usually respectable, but its defense was porous.

Uzelac found a marvelously gifted and upbeat athlete to run his offense. Alton Grizzard, a six-foot, 195-pound son of a retired Navy chief warrant officer, had played quarterback only in his senior year in high school, but he became a starter in the fifth game of his plebe season in 1987. Four years later, Grizzard finished as Navy's all-time total offense leader with 5,666 yards, averaging five yards every time he ran or threw the ball. He was Navy's fourth all-time rusher with 2,174 yards and its seventh all-time passer with 247 completions for 3,492 yards and twenty touchdowns.

Defensive lineman Bob Kuberski bears down to smother Delaware's quarterback. Kuberski was one of the Mids' best players on defense in the early 1990s. He won the George Fritzinger Memorial Award, which is given to a senior interior lineman who excels as a student-athlete and contributes to the team's overall leadership and spirit. Later, he was a member of the 1996 NFL champion Green Bay Packers.

In Grizzard's final season, new coach George Chaump switched gears and ran a multiple, pro-style offense. Grizzard adapted easily and helped to produce five wins, the most since 1982. But, in the 100th year of Army-Navy competition, Navy blew its chance to have a winning season, losing 30–20. Army had a 17–0 lead before Navy scored on Grizzard's six-yard touchdown pass—a record twelfth of the year. Brad Stramanak later scored another touchdown on a forty-five-yard run.

It was downhill after that for Chaump's regime. He finished with a 14–41 record, including consecutive 1–10 seasons in 1991 and 1992. In 1991, Navy scored first in nine of its ten losses, yet was on the brink of having its first all-losing season going into the Army game. Army scored first—and Navy roared back for a rollicking 24–3 victory. Jason Van Matre, who played both quarterback and halfback, and Kubiak, then a freshman, combined to produce 309 yards. Van Matre had perhaps the greatest all-purpose performance in Army-Navy game history: He scored a touchdown after shifting to quarterback from halfback to run a five-play option offense; threw a twelve-yard touchdown pass to Kevin Hickman; rushed for eighty-nine yards; and caught five passes for thirty-eight-yards—accounting for 139 yards and two touchdowns.

The following year was a disaster from the start. Navy didn't score a point during the first fifteen quarters of the season; Kubiak was lost for the year after dislocating his shoulder in the third quarter of the season's opener against Virginia; and the Mids defeated only Tulane, 20–17, on Tim Rogers's third-quarter field goal. The worst blow was losing to Army after leading 24–14 going into the final quarter. Army scored on a sixty-eight-yard pass play and passed for a two-point conversion to trail by two points with more than seven minutes to play.

Then, in the final minute, Army's Patmon Malcolm kicked a forty-four-yard field goal, the longest of his career. But as the joyous Cadets ran whooping to their bench, certain that the game was won, they saw a yellow penalty flag laying on the field. Stunned, they froze in place. A moment later, a roar erupted from the Navy fans. The ball had been hiked just a fraction of a second after the thirty-five-second play clock expired, and the Cadets were tagged with a five-yard delay penalty. That not only negated the winning field goal, but it pushed the ball beyond Malcolm's usual kicking range.

What followed was sublime football theater. A great hush fell over Veterans Stadium as the young man lined up to try a second kick. His first had traveled well over the needed forty-four yards, but kicking is an art, not a science. Could he do it again? Malcolm had only a few moments to regain the icy composure that a kicker needs in such pressure-filled situations, forget the disappointment of the negated kick, and block out the pressure of being center stage with the outcome of an Army-Navy game at stake.

Malcolm didn't flinch. His second kick sailed between the uprights, and Army won, 25–24.

Matters improved only slightly in 1993. The biggest of four victories was a 28–24 upset of Air Force, breaking an eleven-year winless streak against the Falcons. Navy twice came back from ten-point deficits. Brad Stramanak scored

Dan Prather (50) and Dave Osaba (39) celebrate Navy's 24–3 victory over Army in 1991, as much in jubilation as in relief because the win prevented Navy from suffering its first winless season since the 1883 team lost the only game it played.

three one-yard touchdowns, two of them in the fourth quarter as Navy made up a 24–14 deficit. Once again, though, the Mids were dogged by hard luck against Army. They lost 16–14 in the rain at Giants Stadium. A dramatic fourth-quarter rally went for naught when plebe Ryan Bucchianeri missed an eighteen-yard field goal in the final six seconds.

About the only bright spot in the early nineties was Kubiak's passing. He finished as Navy's all-time leading career passer with 558 completions for 6,008 yards, both records. He capped his career with a great performance against Army in 1994, setting Army-Navy game records with his 361 passing yards and twenty-four completions. Kubiak's fifty-six-yard pass to Hickman gave Navy a 20–19 fourth-quarter lead. But the Mids lost 22–20 when Navy was victimized by a field goal for the third straight year—a record-setting, fifty-two-yard kick by Kurt Heiss midway through the last quarter.

Another new era began in 1995 when Charlie Weatherbie became head coach. In only his second year the Mids posted an 8–3 record—their first winning season since 1982—and earned a berth in the Aloha Bowl, Navy's first postseason contest since 1981.

Charlie Weatherbie brought new hope and anticipation to Navy football when he became head coach in 1995. A former quarterback at Oklahoma State, Weatherbie had been head coach for three seasons at Utah State before coming to Navy, and he also had been an assistant coach for six seasons at the U.S. Air Force Academy.

Weatherbie came to the Naval Academy after six years as an assistant coach at the Air Force Academy and three as head coach at Utah State, where his 1993 team won the Big West Conference and the Las Vegas Bowl. He produced immediate enthusiasm at Navy and startled many with his hands-on approach to the game. To give his assistants firsthand knowledge of the pressures the players endured away from football, he had them attend classes with the midshipmen. He was so positive in his approach at every level of Academy life that he even received a standing ovation from the Mids when he walked through the dining hall. It was not unusual for him to read a passage from the Bible to his players when he wanted to drive home a point.

His style of football followed the same directed approach. He brought to Navy a little-used wishbone offense that he had learned at Air Force and that Army had also adopted. The service academies enjoyed a significant measure of success with this system because it compensated for the talent advantages (particularly on defense) enjoyed by most of their Division I-A opponents. When these schools played against Navy or the other academies, they were forced to devise a special defensive scheme for the game in order to contain an offense they rarely faced. That makeshift scheme inevitably failed at some point during the game because players were too focused on trying to recognize what was happening across the line of scrimmage instead of automatically reacting to it.

Weatherbie came up with a solid one-two punch at quarterback in Chris McCoy and Ben Fay and moved Navy from the bottom of the rankings in rush-

Fullback Tim Cannada against Villanova in 1995. It was his first start, and he responded with 108 yards and a touchdown. Tackles David Petko (73) and Bryce Minamyer (72) clear the way.

ing and scoring offense to near the top. McCoy, a defensive back as a plebe, had been an option quarterback in high school, and during spring drills he requested a tryout as a quarterback in Weatherbie's new option-oriented offense. Fay, a junior who was a better passer than a runner, was hurt, so McCoy won the starting job for the first two-thirds of the 1995 season. He produced more than 1,300 yards of offense, including more than 800 yards on the ground. In 1996 he gained 1,228 rushing yards, becoming the first Navy quarterback to run for more than 1,000 yards in a season. He became No. 4 among Navy's all-time rushers.

In 1995 Weatherbie also propelled Navy's defense into the top twenty nationally thanks to such outstanding players as Andy Person, Fernando Harris, Joe Speed, Andy Thompson, and Sean Andrews. All of this helped the team compile a 5–6 record. The Mids served notice of their improvement with a 33–2 victory over Southern Methodist to start the season, McCoy providing a record-setting 398 yards of total offense. They also defeated unbeaten Delaware in decisive fashion, 31–7. Wide receiver Matt Scornavacchi caught a

Quarterback Chris McCoy led Navy to its first winning season in 1996 since the 1982 team posted a 6–5 mark. He quickly demonstrated his ability when, in his first start in 1995—against Southern Methodist—he set a Navy single-game yardage mark of 398 yards, with 273 rushing and 125 from passing. In 1995 McCoy set a season record for rushing by a quarterback with 805 yards; in 1996 he was in charge of Navy's option offense and produced more than 2,000 yards from running and passing, as well as a rare win at Air Force.

school-record eighty-seven-yard touchdown pass in a 35–7 win over Tulane.

Hopes burned bright for the biggest upset of them all when Navy led Notre Dame for the first forty minutes of their 1995 contest in South Bend, but the Mids eventually lost, 35–17. And they saw their chance at a winning season slip away when Army drove ninety-nine yards in the final minutes to eke out a 14–13 victory.

In 1996 Navy beat Rutgers of the Big East Conference 10–6 in the opener, and Tom Vanderhorst's thirty-eight-yard field goal on the game's final play topped Southern Methodist by a score of 19–17. The Mids blew a ten-point third-quarter lead over heavily favored Boston College and lost 43–38 as McCoy missed two open receivers for touchdowns and another potential score was lost on a muffed interception. Navy then ran off three straight wins, including a 20–17 victory at Air Force—the Mids' first triumph at Colorado Springs since 1978, and only their second win over the Falcons in the last fifteen tries. Once again, Vanderhorst provided the margin of victory with a twenty-five-yard field goal in the game's final seconds.

The winning streak came to an end at Croke Park in Dublin, Ireland, where Navy moved its home game against Notre Dame. It was the first time that the Mids had ever played outside the United States; the 1996 season was also the first time that Navy games were played at sites more than 9,000 miles apart (Dublin to Honolulu). More than 30,000 sometimes bewildered natives, who were supposed to give Notre Dame a huge emotional advantage, and several thousand visiting Americans started to think about an upset in this "homecoming" for the Fighting Irish when Navy trailed by just 14–7 late in the second quarter. But Notre Dame took a 21–7 lead just fourteen seconds before the end of the first half and increased it to 35–14 in the third quarter on its way to a 54–27 rout. But Navy assured itself of a winning campaign with a 30–14 victory over Delaware and flirted with a national top twenty-five ranking as it rolled to an 8–3 regular-season record.

But its continuing inability to defeat Army cast a shadow on these accomplishments. A pair of galling defeats in 1995 and 1996 extended the losing streak against the Cadets to five games—games that were decided by a total of only ten points. In 1995 Weatherbie experienced for the first time the unique pressures of an Army-Navy game, discovering the hard way that the outcome—not the margin of victory—is all that matters. Ahead 13–7, he chose not to kick a field goal from the one-yard line midway through the fourth quarter. McCoy's fourth-down pass landed behind Corey Schemm and set the stage for one of the greatest drives in Army-Navy history. The Cadets marched more than ninety-nine yards in nineteen plays, including a crushing twenty-eight-yard completion from Ron McAda to John Graves on fourth-and-twenty-four that put the ball on Navy's one-yard line. John Conroy scored the winning touchdown with sixty-three seconds to play, giving Army the 14–13 victory.

After the game, with tears rolling down his face, Weatherbie took responsibility for the loss and promised his team that it would never happen again. One year later the circumstances were different—but the result was the same. Navy surrendered a 21–3 lead and misfired on eight tries from inside Army's ten-yard line in the final four minutes.

In a constant downpour and with President Bill Clinton in the stands (he was the first president since Gerald Ford in 1974 to attend the game), Navy exploded for three second-quarter touchdowns within a span of 4:19 to take a 21–3 lead. Pat McGrew ran seven yards for the first score; helped by a turnover, the Mids then scored on a fifteen-yard pass to LeBron Butts and a two-yard keeper by McCoy.

But Army, the nation's top-ranked rushing team, shredded Navy's defense for 340 yards and outscored the Mids 25–3 over the next two and a half quarters. Its defense held Navy to 153 yards on the ground. Still, Navy had its chances to win. There was irony in the fact that the halftime festivities in Philadelphia honored those who played in the 1946 Army-Navy contest. In that game's final seconds, underdog Navy had the ball inside the Cadets' five-yard line and had four chances to pull off the greatest upset in college football history. Army held on for the victory in 1946—and did it again in 1996, causing Jim Carrington, one of Navy's players from that earlier era, to wonder aloud whether he and his mates were "a jinx."

A forty-three-yard pass from McCoy to Astor Heaven gave Navy a first down at the Cadets' four-yard line with four minutes to play. Fullback Omar Nelson gained two yards, but a penalty moved the ball back to the seven-yard line. A pass to LeBron Butts fell incomplete, and a line plunge picked up only two yards. When Butts dropped McCoy's fourth-down throw in the end zone, it appeared that Navy was dead.

But the Mids' defense held, and Navy took over at its own forty-three-

With Ross Scott (80) leading the way, fullback Tim Cannada bursts through Notre Dame's defense. This 1996 game, played at Croke Park in Dublin, Ireland, was the first played by Navy outside the United States.

Trainer Leon "Red" Romo gets a well-deserved ride atop the shoulders of Navy's players after his final game as trainer, the 1996 Aloha Bowl. Renowned for his positive attitude and keen sense of humor, Romo provided physical and psychological assistance to thousands of Navy athletes over his forty-one-year tenure.

yard line with fifty-six seconds to play. Onto the field came the little-used Fay; he immediately completed two passes for thirty-seven yards. A ten-yard penalty put Navy at the Cadets' ten-yard line with forty seconds to play. From there, Weatherbie called on Fay to lob four consecutive passes into the end zone. All four missed their receivers. The last one was intercepted when Navy receiver Corey Schemm fell over an Army defender at the goal line.

Nonetheless, 116 years after Capt. Bill Maxwell's first Navy team played a scoreless tie against the Baltimore Athletic Club, Navy's approach to the sport remains the same as the mission of the Naval Academy: to prepare future officers to win every battle. And the battles often begin on the playing field.

9. Army vs. Navy

Navy's football program was maturing in 1890 when it was announced that, at long last, a game had been arranged with West Point. The two academies were several hundred miles apart geographically, but they were very much aware of each other as rivals—and they were frustrated by the lack of some kind of competition with which to claim "bragging rights."

The first attempt to arrange inter-academy athletic competition reportedly occurred in 1868 when the Naval Academy Practice Squadron, consisting of the *Savannah, Macedonian,* and *Dale,* anchored in the Hudson River off West Point. According to accounts from that time, some of the naval cadets aboard the ships challenged the Army cadets to a baseball game or a boat race. Though the alma mater of Abner Doubleday—the man credited in baseball legend with inventing the sport—West Point had no organized baseball program, nor organized sports of any kind. So, Navy's challenge was rejected. But the Army cadets, noting there were some good marble players among their ranks, challenged Navy to a game of agates. The Navy lads demurred, pointing out that it was difficult to develop marbles skills on the pitching decks of naval vessels.

Navy's football team that defeated Army 24–0 in the first Army-Navy game. It was played at West Point on Saturday, November 29, 1890. Team captain Charles Emrich *(second row, third from left)* scored the first touchdown in the series history.

In the late 1880s, Army started an intercollegiate baseball program, but Navy was not on its schedule, so the natural rivalry between the two schools found no outlet until 1890. That summer, Dennis Michie intervened. Michie, a West Point cadet, was born at the Military Academy, the son of Col. Peter Smith Michie, the most influential member of the powerful academic board that established all of the activities for the Corps of Cadets. Young Michie was tired of listening to friends at the Naval Academy talk about their football team, which was playing a six-game schedule. Football was played only on an informal basis at West Point, mostly by young men who, like Michie, had played the sport at prep schools. Michie worked on his father to make football an official Military Academy activity. At the same time, he got his friends at Annapolis to challenge West Point to a football game, which he hoped would prick the pride of the brass and convince them to allow the match.

Colonel Michie at first refused to consider the proposal, echoing the general feeling at the Military Academy that football would disrupt academic and military routines. His opinion was bulwarked by the low repute in which the game was held because of the sport's brutal nature at that time.

According to an account from those times, Michie and his football-playing friends simply pushed ahead and hoped that approval would come. They were "still smarting from their unfulfillment of an athletic challenge from Annapolis [in 1889], [and] countered with a proposal for a meeting in football in view of the fact that a more liberal policy toward athletics had set aside most of the restrictions. This challenge hung fire until the following year, but finally led to the first Army-Navy game of 1890."

The okay came in early October of 1890, leaving Michie just eight weeks to recruit a team, coach it, and make all the arrangements for a November 29 game. Remarkably, he did it. From that first game grew college football's most enduring classic.

November 29, 1890—West Point

Navy 24, Army 0

The first time is supposed to be the most memorable.

And so it was with the Army-Navy game which, on this date, marked the beginning of the foremost rivalry in American football. For Army, the game marked the birth of its own football program, which has built a great tradition over more than a century.

Navy had won four of six games in 1890 before embarking for West Point, the first time any Navy team had played away from Annapolis. Army had only three men—Michie, Leonard Prince, and Butler Ames—who had played football on an organized basis before getting to West Point. When the game was agreed to, an order was issued at West Point decreeing that anyone who weighed more than 180 pounds must report to the football team. Michie coached the team, though he was helped during the final week by William Hyndman, who had played at Yale. Reggie Belknap, a Navy player who was injured, and Hyndman were the game's officials.

Navy's team traveled by train from Annapolis and arrived at West Point at 1:45 on Saturday morning. There is no record of how the midshipmen spent the hours before dawn, except that some of them watched the posting of the guard at 7:15. Later, they were greeted by a special reception committee and taken to one of the barracks around 10:00. They paid a courtesy call upon Col. John W. Wilson, the superintendent, and Lt. Col. Hamilton Hawkins, the commandant. At one o'clock, they dined with the Corps of Cadets in Grant Hall.

The opening kickoff of the first Army-Navy game on the Plain at West Point. Navy *(at left)* received the kickoff and scored midway through the first forty-five-minute half.

A large number of naval officers from ships anchored in New York harbor came to see the game and were entertained at West Point's Officers' Club. Afterward, they joined a crowd estimated at more than six hundred who had gathered on the Plain, the huge parade ground that sits atop the ramparts overlooking the majestic Hudson River Valley. Many Navy rooters sported red and white—then the team colors—while Army's fans wore black, gray, and orange. The colors represented the colors of the cadet uniform: orange stood for the brass buttons, gray for the cloth, and black symbolized the braid. Years later, the official West Point colors became black, gold, and gray, symbolizing the components of gunpowder—charcoal (black), saltpeter (gold), and sulfur (gray).

On the east side of the Plain were cadets from both academies, visiting naval officers, and other Navy fans; on the west side were Army officers, other cadets, and ladies. Seats were provided for the latter just beyond the ropes that ringed the playing area, and sentinels marched within the line during the entire game. Colonel Hawkins sat and cheered for his team with an enthusiasm that surprised many who were accustomed to his stuffy military bearing. Just before the game began, he yelled to his team, "I shall slug the first man who leaves the field in an upright position." Many around him, unfamiliar with military jargon, were stunned, believing he would physically manhandle a player. Actually, "slug" was slang for issuing demerits, and the comment was made more to inspire than to threaten.

The Army band played "Red, White, and Blue" at 2:00, and a few moments later, both teams received a rousing ovation when they appeared on the field. They were a marked contrast in uniform colors. Navy, first to appear, was dressed in red and white stocking caps, red stockings, and white canvas jackets and breeches. The team immediately impressed—and perhaps awed—their hosts, as one account noted: "The condition of the costume showed that the match about to be played was by no means a maiden effort. The grace and dexterity with which the ball was handled in some preliminary by-play occurring before the actual game were only too fully appreciated by the anxious eyes of many of West Point's friends."

Army appeared quickly thereafter dressed in black woolen caps edged in orange; black woolen stockings; and contrasting white-laced canvas jackets and breeches. Immediately upon their appearance, the band played "Annie Laurie." ("On Brave Old Army Team" would not become the team's official fight song for another twenty-one years.)

Some of the Navy team had conscripted a goat from the front yard of a noncommissioned officer stationed at West Point and brought it along as a traditional good luck symbol. After Navy's 24–0 victory, the goat was returned to its owner, who no doubt kept secret forever that his pet had been a talisman in Navy's first victory over Army.

The lineups for that first game were:

NAVY—Ends: George Laws and John Buret; Tackles: Heber Ward and Charles Macklin; Guards: Rufus Lane and Martin Trench; Center: Noble Irwin; Quarterback: Moulton Johnson; Halfbacks: Charles Emrich (team captain) and Renwick Hartung; Fullback: Adelbert Althouse, who also played end at times.

ARMY—Ends: James Moore and Leonard Prince; Tackles: Joseph Crabbs and Francis Shoeffel; Guards: John Heavey and Truman Murphy; Center: Sterling Adams; Quarterback: Kirby Walker; Halfbacks: Dennis Michie (team captain) and Ed Timberlake; Fullback: Butler Ames.

Navy won the coin toss and, after choosing to defend the south goal with a slight wind at its back, took Army's kickoff at precisely 2:30 P.M. Navy charged forward in a "V" formation on the first play, and Emrich gained twenty yards. When they lined up again, quarterback Moulton Johnson, the only plebe on Navy's team, called out the signal "Reef the topsail!" Emrich charged forward again for another sizable gain. Whenever Johnson barked "Tack ship!" Emrich ran around right end. When he called out "Stand by to clear anchor!" Emrich

In the 1890 Army-Navy game, Red Emrich scored four of Navy's five touchdowns, a series record that still stands. He also ran for two extra points, giving him a total of twenty—touchdowns were worth four points and extra points were worth two back then. That point total also remains an Army-Navy game record.

headed off tackle. Emrich's center plunges were keyed by the command "Splice the mainbrace!"

All of this was new to Army, which in reply concocted a series of meaningless signals such as "Front into line, gallop left, march!" "In battery, right heave!" "As skirmishers, march!" Quarterback Kirby Walker later revealed that he got the ball moving merely by pressing his thumbs against the leg of center Sterling Adams because Army simply had not had enough time to master the voice commands.

The game was fairly even until Navy's experience and coaching, helped by Emrich's tricky change-of-pace running, tipped the balance. Midway through the first half (the game was played in forty-five-minute halves, which referee Hyndman timed by the clock atop West Point's chapel tower), Emrich ran three yards for the first touchdown ever scored in the series. It was one of four that he scored that day, a record that stood into the series' second century, as did his total of twenty points (touchdowns were worth four points, extra points two). Shortly thereafter, Johnson barked "Anchors in sight!" and skirted Army's left end for a score. Emrich again added the extra point for a 12–0 halftime lead.

Emrich scored twice more in the second half. One report noted that "Emrich seemed to delight in rubbing his bristling crop of red hair into the faces of his tacklers." Michie was clearly the best Army player, both in calling plays and running with the ball. On defense, he made most of the tackles.

Navy was far better at the game's intricacies. In the second half, Emrich ran with a fake punt for a touchdown. Army's cheering section demanded that the officials nullify the play, claiming that Emrich, preparing to be an officer and a gentleman, had tricked the Army players; such deceit should not be tolerated! Michie only laughed and gave Emrich a good-natured slap on the back.

On another play, Army's Truman Murphy hit Emrich, turned him completely around, and released him—and he scored his third touchdown. When asked later why he let the Navy back get away, Murphy said rather disconsolately, "When I stopped him I heard a lot of yelling from the sidelines. I thought I had done something wrong, so I let him go."

The game was roughly played. In the first half, Army's Kirby Walker lost three teeth making a tackle, and it is said that a forever anonymous Army cheerleader stepped in at his position for one play while blood was cleared from his mouth. Late in the second half, Walker was knocked out making another tackle and was carried from the field, never to return. So hasty were Army's preparations that it forgot about substitutes and played with only ten men after Walker's injury.

Frank Lyon was the only "official" substitute that Navy used in the game. He replaced Althouse after he was twice knocked senseless. Emrich also was knocked out twice, but he was revived and continued to play each time. One Navy player had his pants torn off and had to borrow a pair from his friend, Reggie Belknap, one of the officials.

As the last vestiges of daylight began to disappear, Hyndman ended the game at 4:30, with Navy the victor.

New York's newspapers gave the game front page treatment in their Sunday editions. It was the top story in the *New York Times,* which heralded it thus:

The Six-Year Rift

After Army defeated Navy 6–4 in 1893, the teams didn't play each other again until 1899 because the infant series had already sparked such partisanship that, after a heated argument one afternoon in the Army-Navy Club in New York City, an admiral and a general threatened to settle their differences with a duel. The duel was averted, but when Washington heard of the incident, the 1894 game was canceled.

Such impassioned discussions continued and were creating bad feelings between graduates of the two schools.

The series was suspended because "the Army-Navy game constituted a distracting influence out of character with the orderly routine of the two schools."

THE NAVY WHIPS THE ARMY
ANNAPOLIS' FOOTBALL MEN CONQUER WEST POINT'S BEST
THE YOUNG ADMIRALS SWEEP ALL BEFORE THEM,
SMITING THE ENEMY HIP AND THIGH AND FORCING COMPLETE CAPITULATION

An anonymous *Times* reporter called the game "the greatest victory the Navy has achieved since Decatur and John Paul Jones." He added, "The result was watched with national interest . . . it was generally regarded as the beginning of a new era in the athletic training of two institutions. . . ." With prescience, he added, "With coaching, the Cadets in gray will give the Cadets in blue their feel of football. . . ."

Army got even the following year at Annapolis, beating Navy 32–16. With Michie as Army's head coach in 1892, Navy returned to West Point and won 12–4, as Walter "Snake" Izard and Moulton Johnson scored the touchdowns and Worth Bagley added the extra points.

Michie, rightly acclaimed the Father of Army football, and Bagley, a four-year letterman, were forever linked. Michie was killed on July 1, 1898, while preparing to lead a charge of the Sixth and Sixteenth Regiments up San Juan Hill in Cuba during the Spanish-American War. Bagley was the only U.S. naval officer killed in that war when a shell from a Spanish gun hidden in the jungle near Cardenas Harbor struck the USS *Winslow*.

November 27, 1926—Chicago

Navy 21, Army 21

The Roaring Twenties were in high gear in the fall of 1926, and the Army-Navy game was the crown jewel of college football's unprecedented popularity.

No game ever topped the 1926 Army-Navy contest—a 21–21 standoff dubbed "The Classic Tie." It was played before more than 115,000 spectators at Chicago's Soldier Field. The mammoth stadium had been dedicated the previous day after having been built in recognition of the American servicemen who fought in World War I.

This was the first time the game was played away from the East Coast; it was arranged by Chicago Congressman Daniel Britten, chairman of the House Committee on Yards and Docks and the influential Naval Affairs Committee. Britten was very pro-Navy.

Both academies had misgivings about the site. The Naval Academy superintendent, Rear Adm. Louis B. Nulton, who would have been host to the 1926 game, and his counterpart at West Point, Maj. Gen. Fred W. Sladen, feared that the game sites would be manipulated by politics. But despite their concerns that they were establishing a precedent that would haunt their successors, they consented.

Agreement was reached in mid-January to play the game on the Saturday following Thanksgiving Day, so the teams would have to miss only Friday's classes. The City of Chicago agreed to pay all expenses for each school. There were more than a half-million requests for the 115,000 available seats, and there were no free tickets. The academies were each allotted 29,000 tickets, and they had 9,000 more requests than they could handle.

The 1926 Army-Navy Game

Getting almost all the student bodies from both schools to the 1926 game in Chicago produced a logistical marvel. Two railroad lines, the Pennsylvania and the Baltimore and Ohio, were the prime carriers for Navy, while the Pennsy and the New York Central Railroad moved the West Point contingent. The total cost for each midshipman and cadet was $51.41, which included round-trip sleeper car travel, five meals aboard the trains, and a hotel room and four meals in Chicago. The game sponsors in Chicago picked up the tab.

The exodus from Annapolis began after Thanksgiving Day dinner. Everyone was transported to Camp Meade Junction between Washington and Baltimore, and then transferred to four special trains from each railroad. Each train consisted of two dining cars, a baggage car, and nine sleepers. There was a total of seventy-two sleepers for 1,850 Academy personnel. Rear Adm. Louis B. Nulton, the superintendent, also got extra cars in case of breakdowns and arranged a cut-rate rail package for Athletic Association members.

Each train left an hour apart, the Pennsy going to Union Station in Chicago, the B&O to LaSalle Street Station. After the game, the trains from both lines were parked on sidings adjacent to the stadium; the midshipmen marched directly from their seats onto the trains and then waited for the staggered departures for the twenty-one-hour trip that brought everyone home to Annapolis Sunday night.

The Pennsylvania Railroad's special trains were due to arrive in Chicago thirty to sixty minutes earlier than the B&O's because of differences in the routes. The B&O trains arrived a half hour to two hours late in Chicago. But all returned home ahead of schedule.

When the Regiment arrived in Chicago, 900 taxi cabs took the men to Navy's headquarters at the Palmer House. Four to six mids stayed in a room (all the furnishings had been moved out and replaced by cots), and the three meals each midshipman ate at the hotel cost $1.50 per meal. A week after the game, it was discovered that there were an additional $134.50 in valet and miscellaneous charges, and the middies responsible paid the tab.

It was an outing not to be equaled until 1983, when the two teams played at the Rose Bowl and the students were airlifted across the country.

Navy's Ned Hannegan *(second player from left)* skirts the left end in the 1926 Army-Navy game. The Mids jumped to a 14–0 lead, then had to battle back from a 21–14 deficit in the fourth quarter to get a 21–21 tie.

Scalpers had a field day and made more than a half-million dollars—almost as much as the South Park Board, which oversaw the game, and twice as much as the academies—by selling an estimated 10,000 tickets. Ten dollar seats went for $30 each; $15 seats cost $60 to $75 each; and box seats brought $100 each.

Each naval cadet received one ticket to attend a musical comedy and two tickets for a vaudeville show. They also received an open invitation to attend a regimental ball Friday night at Chicago's Parker House hotel, to which 1,600 of the city's "prettiest girls" were invited. Most of the midshipmen and young ladies attended.

The game was worthy of all of its trappings. Navy grabbed a 14–0 lead in the first quarter and looked as relaxed and confident as anyone could recall during that season. Part of the reason for its confidence was Coach Bill Ingram's approach to the game. Before the pregame warmup, he told his players, "I want you to stop at the end of the runway and look as long as you want at the largest crowd ever to witness a football game, 115,000 people, and then to forget them."

Army coach Lawrence "Biff" Jones used Knute Rockne's "shock troops" theory, in which he started the second team to discover the key elements of Navy's game plan, and then tried to soften up the opposition a bit before using the best players to apply an early knockout blow. Rockne was at the game, forgoing his own team's game against Carnegie Tech. (The Irish lost that game, costing them a perfect season and the national championship.)

"At the start of the game, I don't think we even realized that Army had its second team in the game," Tom Hamilton said later. "We were such an offensive-minded team that all we thought about was attacking the other defense."

Navy scored on its first two possessions. A thirty-eight-yard pass from Jim Schuber to Hank Hardwick set up Howard Caldwell's touchdown; then a pair of fake punt-pass plays from Hamilton to Schuber, and key runs by Caldwell, set up Schuber's two-yard touchdown run.

Midway through Navy's second scoring drive, Jones sent out his first teamers, and they soon turned the game around. The Cadets were led by two great running backs, "Light Horse" Harry Wilson, who had been a Navy nemesis when he played at Penn State for three seasons, and Christian Keener Cagle, such a great star at Southwest Louisiana College that larger schools refused to schedule his team. Before the first half ended, they helped Army to a 14–14 tie, scoring on

Tickets to Soldier Field

The best ticket deals for the 1926 Army-Navy game in Chicago went to three Notre Dame students. Earlier in the fall, the three had been returning home from the Army–Notre Dame game in New York City when they happened upon Brig. Gen. M. B. Stewart, commandant of West Point, out of gas on a road in upstate New York. The students provided four gallons of gas. When they refused to accept any money, the general handed them tickets to the Army-Navy game.

The University of Chicago football team also made out well. It had played so badly that season—at least by coach Amos Alonzo Stagg's standards—that Stagg threatened to withhold the coveted Army-Navy football tickets. But the day before the game, he called in twenty-five prospective letter-winners and handed each a ticket to the game.

Some people made the scene even without tickets. A parachutist leaped from an airplane near the end of the first quarter and narrowly missed plummeting into the huge crowd. The roof of the multistory YMCA building, though located a mile from Soldier Field, also was jammed with spectators who brought binoculars or particularly sharp eyes.

Wilson's sixteen-yard run and a recovered punt fumble by Skip Harbold.

Cagle sent Army to a 21–14 lead on the first series of the third quarter with a thirty-four-yard touchdown run. Hamilton later called the Wilson-Cagle tandem "the best that Army had until Blanchard and Davis."

The game was fiercely fought. For the only time in the series history, two brothers—Army end Chuck Born and Navy guard Art Born—played against each other. Early in the second half they got into a heated argument. Fearing Born might draw a penalty and be thrown out of the game, Hamilton rushed up and snapped, "Knock it off!"

"Stay out of this," his teammate snapped back. "This is a family fight."

Navy got the ball at its forty-three-yard line with four minutes to play in the third quarter, and team captain Frank Wickhorst, a Hall of Fame tackle, gathered his team about him. "This time we're going to cross that goal line," he told them, pounding the frozen ground with his fist.

Navy executed an eleven-play drive that ended with Alan Shapley's touchdown with four minutes gone in the fourth quarter. Hamilton or Shapley touched the ball on all but two plays. On fourth and three at the eight-yard line, Howard Ransford, who had replaced the injured Caldwell in the second quarter, took the ball and slipped it to Shapley on a double reverse. Ransford executed such a beautiful fake that the defense stayed after him long enough to allow Shapley to run untouched around right end for the touchdown.

Wickhorst, a superlative leader, then chased Hamilton out of the huddle and told him to concentrate on the extra point kick. Hamilton stood behind his team's huddle and cleaned the mud from his shoes. "I never worried about it," he said later. "Each night I practiced dropping the ball and kicking it through a small window in the closet in my room so it had become a very routine action for me. Everything was automatic, and I have no recollection of the crowd noise, the Army players or anything other than getting the ball from center, dropping it as I always had and kicking it." And kick it he did—right through the goal posts for a 21–21 tie.

There still were nearly nine minutes to play. Army reached Navy's sixteen-yard line, but with less than six minutes to play, Wilson missed a thirty-two-yard field goal. The Cadets got to Navy's forty-nine on their next possession, but on fourth down, Tom Eddy slammed Cagle to the ground for no gain. That was Army's last gasp.

Two great teams and their great players had lived up to their notices. Navy outgained Army 367–250, with the Mids' edge coming on 110 passing yards. Wilson was brilliant with 124 yards in seventeen carries, and Cagle had eighty in thirteen tries. Schuber and Shapley each gained seventy-two yards. Caldwell had sixty-three on sixteen carries before he was injured; Ransford, with fifty-three yards, was an able replacement.

Many believe the game was the greatest in the series' history. Navy claimed the national championship, and an inscribed football rests in its trophy case testifying to that feat. The definitive word on the game was flashed later that night by the Officer of the Watch at the Naval Academy to the football team in Chicago:

"The Navy is still undefeated."

Hage Rawlings (1926)

Navy coach Bill Ingram had a key psychological weapon at his disposal for the 1926 Army-Navy game in Chicago—the dying wish of a former Navy halfback named Hage Rawlings that the Mids beat Army. Rawlings died a few weeks before the game, but his wish for a victory became an important part of Navy's game plan.

Rawlings had been a member of the 1923 team and had suffered grave injuries while on active duty in 1925. He told his mother, Elizabeth Rawlings, that he would live for a Navy victory over Army in 1925. Before that game, the Navy players sent him a letter dedicating their efforts to him, and the Navy Department set up a radio alongside his bed for greetings from the field.

Navy lost 10–3, but Hage, according to his mother, was unfazed. "They will do it next year, and I'll fight to live to see it," he told her.

Rawlings actually got stronger as he avidly followed Navy's progress in its unbeaten 1926 season. When experts picked Michigan to beat Navy, Hage said, "They can't do it, this is a Navy year."

Hage evidently hit an emotional high during Navy's victory over the Wolverines; afterward, his health failed. Before he died, he asked his mother to take a personal message to the team, and Ingram allowed her to tell her story to the players just before the Army game.

The Depression

Army and Navy stopped playing each other after the 1927 game because of differences over their eligibility rules. But in early November 1930, with the nation hurting from the Great Depression, President Herbert Hoover ordered the two schools to resume their series with a special charity game at Yankee Stadium. The game's slogan was, "They play for the unemployed." The profits helped the Salvation Army fund its charity work in the hometowns of players on both teams.

The atmosphere in New York City and at both academies resembled times past despite the gloom of the Depression. But the Middies lost 6–0 when, with about eight minutes to play, Army's Ray Stecker raced fifty-six yards for the game's only touchdown. Navy had one final chance to score after Johnny Byng recovered a fumble at the Cadets' thirty-seven-yard line. On third down, though, his option pass fell short of a wide-open receiver.

The charity games were held for four years and raised more than one million dollars for Depression relief.

December 1, 1934—Franklin Field, Philadelphia

Navy 3, Army 0

Tom Hamilton, one of the stars of the 1926 game, had returned to Navy as head coach in 1934. He gathered a talented, though undersized, group of mostly senior players, including All-Americas Fred "Buzz" Borries, Slade Cutter, and Bill Clark, and won seven of eight games. Navy hadn't beaten Army since 1921 but was favored over the Cadets, who had a 7–2 record.

Some 80,000 fans jammed Franklin Field and sat through a driving rainstorm that turned the gridiron into a giant bog. Instead of dominating the game with its speed and power, as expected, Navy won principally because of the kicking skills of Cutter and Clark. Those skills became decisive early in the first quarter.

A Clark punt was knocked out of bounds at Army's one-yard line by end Bob "Dusty" Dornin who, like Cutter, became one of the Navy's great World War II submarine commanders. Army's Jack Buckler punted on first down, refusing to take a chance with the bad conditions at the edge of his end zone. But Cutter, playing right tackle, put on a mighty rush and got a hand on the ball, causing it to wobble only to the Cadets' thirty-seven-yard line. Borries returned it for four yards.

Borries carried the ball on five straight plays to Army's seven-yard line. On third down, Norm Edwards tossed him for a five-yard loss, making it fourth and nine at the twelve-yard line. Quarterback Dick Pratt called the fourth-down play: "Cutter back to place kick."

Cutter was stunned and later recalled, "I thought he was out of his mind in the damn mud, and I said, 'Time out!'"

But Pratt stayed with his decision.

Cutter had made all three of his placement tries that season, including game-winners against Maryland and Notre Dame. But in pregame practice that day, he was awful.

"I didn't make one damn kick, not even the extra points," Cutter said. "I had longer mud cleats on my right shoe, which was my kicking foot, so when we went in after warming up, I told our equipment manager, Red Rasmussen, to put the regular ones on my right shoe. Those mud cleats were catching the dirt when I kicked so I wasn't striking the ball correctly.

"Bill Clark, my holder, and I hadn't worked together in pregame practice because he was working on his punting, and a placekicker's success is 75 percent the work of the holder," Cutter noted. "Bill was very good at putting the ball where he said it would go, and he built a little mound from the mud and patted it down to remove the water and make it as firm as possible so the ball wouldn't move."

On the sidelines, Hamilton and his staff watched as Cutter removed his helmet and laid it on the muddy ground. They were certain that Pratt had called for the special fake kick play they had installed for the game.

"Rip Miller [Navy's line coach] told me later that when the coaches saw that I was really going to kick the ball, they said, 'The goddamned fool. He's going to kick it,'" Cutter recalled, "and after it went through, they shouted, 'Great!'"

The ball went between the uprights some thirty yards away; Cutter vividly recalled it sailing deep into the stands at the closed end of Franklin Field. "There really wasn't any pressure on me when I kicked the field goal because I thought we were going to run up a score on them," Cutter said. "I knew I had a field goal from the moment I stepped up to boot it. That damn thing would have gone from forty yards out."

Slade Cutter's father was in the stands, watching his son play football for the first time. Neither knew it at the time, but his dad had only four months to live. Cutter always treasured the fact that his father saw him play at the crowning moment of his career, after having been so against his playing when Slade was in high school.

Navy protected its 3–0 lead for the rest of the game, although doing so wasn't easy sometimes. Army pounced on a fumble at Navy's thirty-four-yard line in the second quarter and moved to the twenty-five-yard line before Navy held. Clark broke up another threat early in the fourth quarter when he intercepted a pass at the Mids' fourteen-yard line. Navy couldn't move the ball, and in the huddle Pratt called for a punt.

"Cover this thing good because it's going over that guy's head," Clark said, nodding in the direction of Army's safetyman. He then produced the second biggest play of the game—a mighty seventy-six-yard punt that rolled dead at Army's twelve-yard line.

Clark credited his kicking success to a summer cruise stop in Italy where the midshipmen, including Borries and Cutter, were guests at a reception and audience with Pope Pius XI. When the Pope was imparting the Papal Blessing, Clark stuck out his foot and Cutter extended his right leg a bit, as if to "catch" the blessing. Cutter had just begun learning his kicking art that spring and figured "I needed all the help I could get." But Clark was certain he now had divine assistance; he told his teammates that the blessing touched his kicking toe and that all of his future kicks would be good ones.

Slade Cutter kicks the most famous field goal in Navy history—a thirty-yard kick in the first quarter that propelled Navy to a 3–0 triumph over Army in the 1934 game. The victory broke a ten-game losing streak against the Cadets.

The superintendents from West Point and Annapolis—Maj. Gen. Francis Wilby *(left)* and Rear Adm. John R. Beardall—greet each other before the start of the 1942 Army-Navy game at the Naval Academy. Because of World War II travel restrictions, the game was played in Annapolis and only those living within ten miles of the Academy could purchase tickets.

Clark recalled his prediction after the game and raced up to Rip Miller, shouting, "Rip, it worked!"

"What worked, the field goal?" the puzzled Miller asked him. "Of course it worked."

"No, no," Clark said. "The toe! The toe! The Pope's blessing worked on my toe!"

Borries played the entire game and carried the ball on thirty-six of Navy's forty-seven running plays. He got all three of Navy's first downs (Army had only two) in the terrible field conditions. On defense, he stopped Army's Maurice Simmons after the latter had intercepted a pass at Navy's thirty-five-yard line. He saved another score in the fourth quarter after Army tackle "Moose" Miller recovered a blocked punt and started toward Navy's goal line. Borries missed his first chance to tackle Miller, but he recovered and, with his speed, caught Miller from behind.

November 28, 1942—Annapolis
Navy 14, Army 0
November 27, 1943—West Point
Navy 13, Army 0

Though the Army-Navy game had been booked for Philadelphia's 103,000-seat Municipal Stadium in 1942 and 1943, for the first time in a half-century it was played at each of the academies because of World War II travel restrictions.

With the war in full swing, some in Washington wanted the series dropped. But one of President Franklin D. Roosevelt's closest advisers, Maj. Gen. Edwin "Pa" Watson, a close friend of Army football, convinced him that playing the games was good for the nation's morale and its armed forces.

The very scaled-back games symbolized the sacrifices being made on the home front, where everyone was urged to abstain from all but the most essential travel to aid in conserving rationed gasoline and tires and to relieve the scarcity of space for nonmilitary railroad travel. Normally, thousands of cadets and midshipmen, their friends, families, and fans traveled to the game by auto and rail.

Ticket sales totaling $100,000 already had been made when the 1942 game site was changed to Annapolis in early October. That money was returned, though some was donated to the schools for their War Relief Funds. New rules limited the sale of tickets to people living within ten miles of Maryland's State House in Annapolis. In 1943, the ten-mile limit was measured from Army's Michie Stadium. The ticket sellers at both academies drew a radius on their maps that stretched the limit to the very last foot. There were no gate sales at either Navy's Thompson Stadium or at Army's Michie Stadium, each of which seated slightly more than 20,000.

In 1942, each midshipman was allowed one "guest" ticket, presumably for his "drag" (date); in 1943, the cadets were each given one ticket. In both years, officers were allowed to purchase two tickets for guests scheduled to arrive that weekend, and it was generally understood that any officers exercising the privilege would honor the spirit of the rules and invite guests who lived within the proscribed ten-mile radius of the stadium. With such intensive policing of ticket applications, barely 12,000 people, including the midshipmen, showed up for the 1942 game in Annapolis; only 16,000 came to West Point in 1943.

Tickets in 1942 were limited to four groups: the 3,200 midshipmen; personnel attached to the Severn River Naval Command; Navy Academy Athletic Association members; and nonmembers who lived within the ten-mile limit. That last category excluded the thousands of graduates from both academies who lived in Washington, D.C., plus the legion of politicians who annually attended the game.

Navy's athletic director, Capt. Lyman "Pop" Perry, set up an entire bureaucracy apart from his office to handle ticket sales. It was headed by Cdr. Morris Gilmore, treasurer of the Naval Academy Athletic Association, who did his job so meticulously that he was dubbed "Chief Ticket Detective."

Ticket applicants had to sign a form declaring that they did not live outside the ten-mile limit, and their addresses were then verified by Gilmore and his staff through postal authorities, phone and municipal directories, and, in some cases, by personal phone calls. If there was a question of validity, the money was refunded.

1942 Ticket Rules

Even Navy's football coach was not immune to the special ticket rules imposed on the 1942 Army-Navy game at Annapolis. A few days before the game, Morris Gilmore, who oversaw the ticket distribution, noted that he was still holding the tickets that coach John Whelchel had ordered. "He sent the application all right—but he forgot to sign it, and he's not getting the ducats until he comes over here and signs for them. Rules are rules."

Navy defense *(wearing dark jerseys)* stops an Army runner in the 1942 game at Annapolis. Half of the midshipmen were forced to "cheer" for the Cadets, though all of them seemed to root for Navy when it scored its two touchdowns and defeated Army, 14–0.

Jimmy, the rented mule, at the 1942 Army-Navy game at the Naval Academy. Wartime travel restrictions not only forbade the transportation of the Corps of Cadets to the game but also Army's regular mule mascots. So a farmer outside Annapolis agreed to "rent" his mule to the Cadets for the game.

No tickets were sent to business addresses. Local merchants who wanted to buy tickets for employees were required to have the employees submit applications for each ticket. "They did it too, and we checked up on them," Gilmore said. "We didn't have much evidence of cheating, and when someone tried, they didn't fool us."

One application carried an unfamiliar RFD address, but Gilmore's investigation proved that the applicant was living on a boat within the limit; only his mail was being delivered to the suspicious address. He got his tickets. On the day of the 1942 game, Maryland's Office of Price Administration, in charge of all rationing activities, checked license plates and parking permits on cars in the parking lot to be certain that all originated from inside the ten-mile zone. Violators were issued traffic citations.

The war forced other radical adjustments to the historic contest. Since the Corps of Cadets was forbidden to travel, half of the mids were designated to cheer for Army; West Point even sent packets of cheers and songs for them to learn. Two Army cheerleaders, reinforced by some of Navy's cheerleaders, led the borrowed cheering section, which included West Point superintendent Maj. Gen. Francis B. Widby. Of course, there was only the remotest semblance of objectivity. Forty years later, Capt. Daniel Webster Herlong, one of the Navy cheerleaders detailed to the duty, recalled huge ovations from this group when Navy scored its touchdowns. "Everyone told us later we acted like we meant it when we led Army's cheers, and I guess we did. I certainly felt good about the job we did, but I felt better about Navy winning. And I still do," Herlong said.

Army's coach, Earl "Red" Blaik, recalled that when his team came out for pregame warmups "there wasn't anyone in the stands. No one! It was eerie. The juice that was always there before this game couldn't get turned on . . . we were just flat as hell without our own Corps behind us."

Army's mascot couldn't travel, either, so the midshipmen rented a stand-in, a seven-year old mule from the nearby farm of Clarence Bausum. They named him Jimmy. The handlers for Army's two mules, Mr. Jackson and Pancho, sent the mids instructions for proper mule care, including specifications for a GI mule haircut, which were dutifully followed. But when Army's mule riders tried to ride Jimmy, he tossed them to the ground several times.

For the first time, the game had a radio sponsor—Esso Marketers, which contributed $50,000 each to the Navy Relief Society and the Army Emergency Relief Fund. More than 160 stations on two radio networks carried the game from Maine to Florida, and it was flashed by short-wave to the armed forces worldwide.

Navy shut down Army stars Hank Mazur and Doug Kenna, and Navy's Gordon Studer's thirty-four-yard punt return set up a one-yard touchdown plunge by Joe Sullivan. The Mids nailed down their fourth straight win in the series, 14–0, with Hal Hamberg's twenty-one-yard touchdown pass to end Ben Martin after an interception by Hillis Hume. Navy's defense twice stopped Army inside the ten-yard line in the fourth quarter.

A disappointed Blaik wryly noted afterward, "A team plays a game like that once in a season, and Navy saved that once for us today."

The next day, the *New York Times'* Kingsley Childs wrote, "It was the strangest Army-Navy football clash of modern times."

But it was just as strange in 1943, when the entire scenario was replayed at West Point. It was the first Army-Navy game played there since 1892. West Point athletic director Lawrence "Biff" Jones, strapped for revenue after losing the receipts from the 1942 game, wanted the game moved to Yankee Stadium, but the War Department refused. Earlier that season, Army had played Notre Dame before 70,000 fans there, including the Corps of Cadets, without a murmur about rationing and rail transportation. Congressman Samuel Weiss from Philadelphia noted that, in Great Britain, thousands of U.S. servicemen would watch a soccer match between England and Scotland "within a half-hour of

In 1943 the Army-Navy game was played at West Point under the same travel restrictions that were enforced in 1942 at Annapolis. Half of the Corps of Cadets donned white cap covers and were ordered to cheer for the Mids. They did a pretty good job, though the roar was less than deafening when Navy scored both of its touchdowns in a 13–0 win.

Members of Navy's 1939 team take turns ringing the Gokokuji Bell following their 10–0 win against Army. The bell was brought to this country by Como. Matthew C. Perry following his expedition to Japan in 1854 and later donated by his widow to the Naval Academy. The bell was returned to the people of Okinawa by the Navy in 1987, but an exact replica stands at the Naval Academy and is rung to celebrate football victories over Army.

the real danger of the Luftwaffe. If they can enjoy a soccer football game, for goodness sake, what has happened to the good, old U.S.A.?" he asked.

All pleas were rejected. It was announced on October 6, 1943, with the football season well underway, that the game would be played in Michie Stadium under the 1942 rules.

The First Regiment of the Corps of Cadets lost a coin toss with the Second Regiment and had to cheer for Navy. Members of the First wore white caps to symbolize their allegiance and, according to Glenn Stewart, one of the Navy cheerleaders who helped to conduct the cheering, "did it in good spirit, almost as if they didn't know the difference nor did they really care who they cheered for, though there was a considerable difference in volume from the cadets who cheered for Army."

Navy's team included two future Hall of Famers—lineman Don Whitmire, who had starred for Alabama, and guard George Brown. Nonetheless, Army was favored; the Cadets had a platoon of great backs such as Glenn Dobbs, Max Minor, Bobby Chabot, Johnny Sauer, and a young plebe named Glenn Davis. But the Cadets lost their fifth straight to Navy, 14–0. The contest was so bitter that Whitmire noted afterward, "Hell, I thought Tennessee and Alabama was a rough game. This was something else again."

The game was scoreless into the third quarter. Navy finally mounted a forty-four-yard drive, which Bobby Jenkins completed with a fourth-down, two-yard touchdown run with Army tackle Joe Stanowicz hanging on his back. Hume's running led the Mids to their second touchdown a short time later, scored on Jim Pettit's one-yard run.

November 30, 1946—Municipal Stadium, Philadelphia

Navy 18, Army 21

In 1946, Navy won its opening game against Villanova 7–0, and lost every other game for the remainder of the season.

Army, with Doc Blanchard and Glenn Davis playing in their final season, won every game except for the famed scoreless tie against Notre Dame, marring Blanchard and Davis's perfect record during three years of collegiate competition.

At Municipal Stadium, Navy almost did the impossible. The team came within three yards and three points of achieving the greatest upset of all time before losing to Army 21–18 in one of the most astounding finishes in the series history. By overcoming its huge underdog status and coming so close to beating the mighty Blanchard-Davis team, a scrappy group of Mids earned no small measure of satisfaction and a place of honor in the annals of the great rivalry.

Blanchard and Davis's Army teams had beaten Navy in 1944 and 1945, with the national championship on the line, and this game was the finale of their great careers. Everyone expected it would be the duo's one last hurrah against a poor Navy team.

Tom Hamilton, back for a second stint as head coach, fielded a squad that had fewer than two dozen players of varsity caliber. The team had been stripped by graduation, resignations, loss of eligibility, and physical disability; Hamilton had to force-feed jayvee players and plebes.

But Army had problems, too. Blanchard, the 1945 Heisman Trophy winner, played far below the level of his previous two seasons because of a knee injury, and quarterback Arnold Tucker had injured his shoulder so badly that he could not throw a pass. Instead, Tucker tossed the ball back to Davis, who threw halfback-option passes with great success. But with Davis so critical to the offense, he could not play defense, so Army was without its best defensive back.

Navy went on the attack a week before the game. Don Whitmire, the two-time Navy All-America tackle who had exhausted his football eligibility, and a group of Middie "commandos" were captured at West Point while they were trying to steal Army's mules and paint "Beat Army" in red and blue on the Academy's venerated statues. While they were expunging their handiwork, West Point's superintendent, Maj. Gen. Maxwell Taylor, issued a communiqué that read in part: "if the remainder of the Navy works as hard next Saturday as these prisoners are working this Sunday, then the Army high command views the coming battle with considerable concern."

Prophetic.

Just before the game, the Navy team got a telegram from a destroyer in the Pacific. It read simply: "Please!"

Phil Ryan, a plebe end and later captain of the 1949 team, remembered Army players playing volleyball over the goal post crossbar with a football, laughing and overconfident, before pregame practice. "We got the message," he said.

Bill Hawkins, the gritty Navy fullback who had played so well throughout the season despite a knee injury that required daily treatment, looked across the field at Blanchard and Davis before the game and felt compelled to ask them for their autographs.

Navy won the toss and, led by quarterback Reeves Baysinger, dominated most of the first quarter. But it was Army that scored first, on Davis's fourteen-yard run late in the quarter. Jack Ray kicked the first of three extra points—the ultimate difference in the game.

Navy came right back and drove eighty-one yards for a touchdown. The Mids alternated between the "T" and single-wing formations, and "Pistol Pete" Williams and Myron Gerber tore up Army's defense. Baysinger added two big passes to team captain Leon Bramlett and Art Markel and then ran two yards for Navy's first score. Bob Van Summern's extra point was blocked.

Army responded. Blanchard, looking like the Doc of old, ran fifty-two yards for a touchdown. Then, after Bill Yoeman intercepted a pass, Davis, on the option play, passed to Blanchard for a twenty-six-yard touchdown and a 21–6 halftime lead.

While Hamilton gathered his team for the halftime break, the Academy superintendent, Vice Adm. W. Aubrey Fitch, walked into the locker room, and everyone became quiet. It was unheard of for the superintendent to talk to the team during the game.

"Coach Hamilton," Fitch said, "I want to tell you and the team that the secretary of the Navy and I wish to congratulate you on a great first half of football."

Bramlett stood up and said, "Admiral, you haven't seen anything yet!"

Inspired, Navy came out and stopped Army's initial drive at the thirty-two-yard line, then rolled sixty-eight yards for a touchdown. Hawkins ran it in from two yards out. But Hawkins, pressed into emergency duty as the kicker, missed the extra point. Navy now trailed 21–12.

The momentum turned Navy's way for good late in the third quarter. Army faced a fourth and one at its thirty-five-yard line. Hamilton later recalled: "We knew Army always felt that Blanchard could make one yard every time he carried the ball, so we put in an extra lineman to tie up their blockers and free Dick Scott, our great linebacker, to make the tackle. Sure enough, Doc tried, but Leon Bramlett and Dick met him head-on and stopped him cold."

Army coach Red Blaik admitted later "that was the turning point, because on that one play, Navy snatched the game's emotion and held it to the very end."

From Army's thirty-five-yard line, Baysinger needed just four plays to get Navy's third touchdown. It came on a pass to Bramlett. Hawkins again missed the extra point. Navy now trailed 21–18 with thirteen minutes to play.

Williams's interception halted Army on the next series, and the teams exchanged punts until there were about four minutes to play. Just as Navy got the ball at its thirty-three-yard line, President Harry Truman and his party left the stadium. The police ringing the field, relieved of a huge security responsibility, turned to watch the game. They paid little attention to the thousands of fans who, frenzied by Navy's resurgence, streamed onto the sidelines at the closed end of the stadium.

Lynn Chewning, who played behind Hawkins, came in and pounded away at Army's defense. Williams added a seventeen-yard option pass to Ryan and then worked with Al McCully to get to Army's twenty-three-yard line with just over two minutes to play. Three running plays gained little, but on fourth down Chewning burst through Army's defense on a counter play and ran to the three-yard line.

There were ninety-two seconds to play, and Navy had no timeouts. The clock became Navy's biggest nemesis and the focal point of a controversial ending. Years later, Hamilton recounted those last minutes:

> We could have thrown a pass out of bounds to stop the clock, but I had a fixation that ninety-two seconds were enough in which to run four plays. But the conditions had changed dramatically. Thousands had jammed the sidelines and spilled onto the field so that I could not see the sideline markers. They were making so much noise that the players could barely hear the play being called in the huddle.
>
> Baysinger called a trap play on first down, not a good call at the goal line, and they stopped us. On second down, Barney Poole, their great end, made a fine play to stop Chewning for no gain.
>
> We had no time outs left, so I took a penalty to stop the clock by sending in a substitute. That put the ball back to the seven-yard line with about thirty seconds to play. I often thought that it probably was dumb as hell, but it was my responsibility and I paid for it.
>
> We could have tried a field goal from that point and gotten a well-deserved tie, and I asked Rip Miller, our line coach, what he thought.
>
> "Hell," Rip growled, "you wouldn't go for a tie."
>
> "You're damn right," I replied. "It's all or nothing in this game."

No space is too small to express a Mid's feelings about Army. Even the cymbalist in Navy's Drum & Bugle Corps gets his message across.

Then came the play that has left unanswered the question: Did he or didn't he go out of bounds and stop the clock? "He" was Pistol Pete Williams. Baysinger called a buck lateral. He faked to Hawkins running inside, then pitched the ball to Williams, who was going around right end on the short side of the field and toward the thousands who had spilled onto the sidelines. Poole stayed with him and cut off his path to the end zone. As he tackled Williams, both of them disappeared into the crowd near the three-yard line. The officials ruled that Williams had been tackled in bounds; Hamilton later said that the game films were inconclusive, "though when I looked at them I kept thinking, 'We're going to win!' but we never did. While there was more glory from losing, it was all very unsatisfactory."

There were still twelve seconds on the clock when the play ended. Hamilton immediately sent Billy Earl in as an illegal substitution to stop the clock with another penalty. Earl ran right up to referee Bill Halloran to be recognized, but Halloran looked at him, then looked at the clock, and then looked away, refusing to acknowledge him. The final seconds ran off the clock without Navy running another play.

Later, Hamilton asked Baysinger what he would have called had he gotten a fourth down. He replied, "A little flare pass to Hawkins which I know would have scored."

"That's what we wanted, too," Hamilton recalled. "It would have been a touchdown and we would have won the upset of the century.

"When I got to the locker room, there was nothing but heartbreak," Hamilton said. "I had such a great feeling for those wonderful guys that day and it was so sad that they came so close and couldn't win. None of us ever had gone through such disappointment, and it was a tragedy that I felt forever."

While the players were downhearted, fans who remembered how long the odds against Navy were and appreciated an intense contest were in a celebratory mood. When Hamilton returned to the hotel, he was warmly greeted in a small hospitality suite by Naval Academy officials, all of whom were excitedly reliving the team's great performance. Acting as bartender was Adm. William F. "Bull" Halsey, the Navy's greatest Pacific War hero. A former Navy fullback and athletic director, he was so thrilled that he had postponed a trip to Delaware to prepare for eye surgery so he could be a part of the postgame excitement and have the opportunity to speak to the team later that evening.

"It was," Hamilton later recalled, "an absolutely unforgettable day."

December 2, 1950—Municipal Stadium, Philadelphia

Navy 14, Army 2

Jim Baldinger battles an Army defender to catch a thirty-yard touchdown pass from Zastrow for one of Navy's two touchdowns in its 14–2 upset victory over Army in 1950.

It was almost 1946 all over again. An unbeaten Army team, which had given up just twenty-six points all season and had shut out four opponents, played a three-touchdown underdog Navy team that had won just two games and tied another during the 1950 season.

Eddie Erdelatz, Navy's new head coach, had been through three Army-Navy games as an assistant coach during his previous shift at Annapolis. He knew precisely the mental and emotional demands for this rivalry. He instilled in his team a cocky attitude: the players believed that they could not be

Army captain Dan Foldberg and Navy captain Tom Bakke chat with President Harry S. Truman before the 1950 Army-Navy game. Truman was reelected in an upset victory over Thomas E. Dewey in 1948 and was present a few weeks later when a winless Navy team miraculously tied unbeaten Army, 21–21. Again, in 1950, Truman presided over a huge 14–2 win by the Mids against another unbeaten Cadets team.

beaten, regardless of their poor record. During a pregame press session, some media people harped on the fact that Army was so upset that it was ranked second in the country behind Oklahoma that it would try to run up the score against Navy to gain a No. 1 ranking. Reporters repeatedly asked Erdelatz how his team could respond.

The coach finally exploded. "Listen," he said, "we're burned up, too. We're ranked sixty-fifth, and we should be sixty-fourth."

Army's attitude set the tone during pregame warmups. The players ran onto the field with knees kicking high, a tactic that Blaik believed was intimidating. "They ran all the way around the field, right around us as we were warming up," said Jim Baldinger, a Navy end. "They were saying a few things about how bad they were going to beat us. We looked at each other and said, 'We can do it.'"

The heroes were Bob Zastrow, Navy's redoubtable quarterback, and the Mids' defense. Army smothered punter Bob Cameron on Navy's nine-yard line in the first two minutes, but the Mids drove Army back seven yards in four plays. Navy employed an array of different defensive sets that completely frustrated the Cadets. At halftime, Army had just three rushing yards and one first down.

In the second quarter, Army fullback Al Pollard lost a pitchout, and right end Bob McDonald recovered for Navy. A penalty set Navy back to Army's thirty-two-yard line, but four plays later, Zastrow broke two tackles and ran for a touchdown. Roger Drew, who had helped Navy get its surprising 21–21 tie in the 1948 game, kicked the first of his two extra points.

With only two minutes to play in the first half, Zastrow marched Navy sixty-three yards in just five plays for the Mids' other touchdown. Army was bunched to stop running back Dave Bannerman, who led all rushers with

The Mids wheel in one of the countless floats—this one is a replica of the Navy goat—that make up the hijinks and color surrounding the game. This pageantry has always been as much a part of the Army-Navy game as the football on the field, and it is just as competitive within the student bodies of both academies.

Army-Navy Hijinks

An integral part of the Army-Navy game—indeed, often more interesting than the game itself—is a constant kaleidoscope of pranks and hijinks performed by the Mids and Cadets, aimed at that precious bit of one-upmanship that often is as important to its perpetrators as winning or losing.

There have been full-page ads in the *New York Times* decreeing the Middies' excellence and guaranteeing dire consequences that would befall their rivals; there have been tons of leaflets dropped on both Academies from airplanes; a succession of Navy goats have accumulated thousands of miles being spirited to and from West Point; and even the Army mules, once thought to be totally secure, have been kidnapped.

No effort is too much, no risk too dangerous. Back in the fifties, a Navy destroyer was anchored in the Hudson River adjacent to West Point shortly before an Army-Navy game. Naturally, the ship was a juicy target for adventuresome Cadets. Some rowed out at night, evaded the ship's watch, and painted "Beat Navy" on the ship's starboard side. The next day, despite the certainty that the crew would be furious at having been duped and would also be extra vigilant, the Cadets ventured to photograph the results of their feat. They were quickly captured and made to scrape off the paint and clean the starboard side of the ship.

Prior to one Army-Navy game, a shocked West Point exchange officer watched in horror as some Middies drove his car onto Bancroft Court and then destroyed it with repeated sledgehammer blows. But no sooner had the destruction been completed than one of the Middies presented him with a check for $4,500—representing a dollar donated from every midshipman—to replace the car.

The Mids celebrate their upset of Army in 1950. Part of the credit went to its defense, which reduced the Cadets' powerful running game—they had averaged more than two hundred per game—to a mere seventy-seven yards. The defense also allowed only sixty passing yards. During the second half Navy stopped Army six times inside the twenty-yard line, and four of those stops, including two turnovers, came in the fourth quarter.

sixty-seven yards, but on first down, Zastrow faked a toss to him and slid off right guard for eleven yards. Zastrow missed a pass, but Navy then fooled the defense with a reverse run by Bill Powers for twenty-two yards to the Army thirty-yard line. Another pass fell incomplete, but on his next try, with forty-five seconds before halftime, Zastrow scrambled until Baldinger got free in the end zone to catch his touchdown pass.

Army's only points came in the second half. Zastrow foolishly backpedaled twenty yards into the end zone trying to pass, only to be caught for a safety.

Navy's defense stopped Army six times inside the Mids' twenty-yard line in the second half—four in the last quarter—and recovered fumbles at Navy's nine- and six-yard lines in the last quarter. The left side of Navy's defense, supposedly its weak point, was never better. Fritz Davis and McDonald led the gang-tackling that held Army to just seventy-seven rushing yards after the Cadets had averaged more than two hundred per game. Navy's defense harried Army quarterback Bob Blaik, one of the nation's leading passers, so mercilessly that he completed just five of twenty-two passes and was intercepted twice. The second interception was by John Gurski on the game's final play when Army had the ball at Navy's three-yard line.

After the game, Erdelatz, with tears streaming down his face, was carried off the field by his players. He kept shouting about "the greatest team effort I've ever seen."

And it was, a classic among those special Army-Navy contests where the Mids have done the impossible.

Navy running back Bob Craig breaks into Army's secondary for a big gain in the 1954 Army-Navy game. The Mids and Cadets, both powerful teams, staged one of the best offensive shows in the series history before Navy and its "Team Named Desire" came from behind to win, 27–20, thus sewing up a bid to play in the Sugar Bowl.

When the team arrived home the next day, more than ten thousand people turned out as Erdelatz rode triumphantly atop a fire engine to a huge celebration in front of Bancroft Hall. There, he attacked the Japanese victory bell with such gusto that he broke the string on the gong.

Overhead, near the terrace of Bancroft Hall, a banner fluttered from a window:

Somewhere birds are singing
Somewhere children shout
But there's no joy at West Point
Mighty Army has struck out.

November 27, 1954—Municipal Stadium, Philadelphia

Navy 27, Army 20

The anticipation for the 1954 game had not been seen since 1945—the last time both teams were nationally ranked when playing each other. Scalpers got as much as $125 for a pair of $5 tickets. Navy, with its storied "Team Named Desire," had a 6–2 record, and had lost only to Notre Dame and Pitt by a total of eight points. Army, picked to retain the Lambert Trophy as the East's best team, had won seven of eight games.

Both were among the nation's best teams, and the game reflected their excellence. The teams surged up and down the field in one of the greatest shows of offense in series history. Navy's offense, run by the crafty George Welsh and featuring Joe Gattuso, John Weaver, Bob Craig, and All-America end Ron Beagle, was equal to the Cadets' unit of Pete Vann, Pat Uebel, Tom Bell, and its All-America end, Don Holleder.

On the game's first play, Navy recovered a fumble at the Cadets' twenty-seven-yard line. Welsh, a master of the split-T offense, started with a keeper and squirmed seventeen yards to the ten-yard line. On fourth down from the six, Welsh sucked in Army's pass rush and flipped a screen pass to Craig, who, helped by blocks from Wilson Whitmire and Jim Royer, crashed between two defenders for a touchdown. John Weaver kicked the first of three extra points for a 7–0 Navy lead.

Army roared back with a sixteen-play scoring drive. Ralph Chesnauskas missed the extra point, so Army still trailed 7–6, but it had shown that it could move the ball against Navy's great defense, which was ranked No. 2 in the nation.

The Mids then moved to midfield and faced a fourth-down punting situation when the teams changed goals to start the second quarter. Army coach Blaik always inserted his second unit to start the second quarter, so Welsh, figuring that Army's subs would be very anxious to fall back and cover the kick, called for a sweep. Weaver zoomed around end for twenty-three-yards. A couple of plays later, Welsh passed to Earle Smith for a touchdown and Navy was ahead, 14–6.

A little later in the quarter came a rapid-fire series of events that left everyone breathless.

Navy's punter, Dick Guest, muffed the center's snap. When he recovered the ball, he saw it was impossible to get his kick away and began to run. Guest lost the ball again, and Holleder recovered at Navy's three-yard line. Uebel scored on the first play, and Navy's lead was just one point—but only for sixty-two seconds. On Navy's first play after receiving the kickoff, Uebel intercepted Welsh's pass and ran to the Mids' forty-two-yard line. Vann hit Bob Kyasky on the next play with a touchdown pass, and Army led 20–14.

Then came the game's critical play. Vann, without any order from Blaik, told

Navy linebacker Pat Donnelly lines up Army quarterback Rollie Stichweh for a tackle early in the 1963 Army-Navy game. Donnelly, who also played fullback, scored three touchdowns to help Navy beat the Cadets, 21–15. Stichweh bedeviled the Mids most of the day and drove his team to Navy's three-yard line before time ran out so that the Mids escaped victorious in one of the series' most exciting games.

Running back Johnny Sai zooms through Army's defense to help set up one of Navy's three touchdowns in their victorious 21–15 game against Army in 1963.

Chesnauskas to try an onsides kick—but failed to inform the other members of the kickoff team. They did not use their special coverage (many ran past the short kick), and Navy recovered at its forty-seven-yard line. Weaver broke a twenty-six-yard run and made a twenty-seven-yard reception, and Welsh scored for a 21–20 lead.

Navy widened the margin in the third quarter with a ten-play, fifty-nine-yard march that ended with Welsh's second touchdown pass to Smith. The extra point was missed, and Navy led 27–20. Army still had a chance, and the Cadets gave it one mighty try in the fourth quarter, driving to Navy's eight-yard line. But on fourth down, Gattuso roared in on a blitz and hit Vann's arm as he was throwing. The ball wobbled harmlessly to the ground.

The game had been worthy of all of its hype. A bid to play in the Sugar Bowl awaited the winners. Erdelatz, as was his custom after Navy's victories that season, said that "desire" had won for his team. So did guts—Beagle, guard Glen Benzi, Weaver, and Craig played the entire game.

December 7, 1963—Municipal Stadium, Philadelphia

Navy 21, Army 15

The nation was still in a state of shock two weeks after the assassination of President Kennedy, but more than 100,000 fans jammed Municipal Stadium (later to be renamed John F. Kennedy Stadium) for the 1963 Army-Navy game. The game had been scheduled for Saturday, November 30, and some wanted it canceled because of the assassination. After consulting with the Kennedy family, and bearing in mind the president's enthusiasm for the series, both sides agreed merely to postpone the contest for a week.

"It was a terrible blow," recalled team captain Tom Lynch. "All of us had looked forward to seeing him at the game, and I particularly looked forward to the coin toss ceremony at midfield because he was a part of it."

Until that terrible moment in Dallas on November 22, Navy's season had been a dream, sparked, of course, by the dazzling play of junior quarterback Roger Staubach. Four days after Kennedy's death, he won the Heisman Trophy; he later got the Maxwell Trophy.

Navy was ranked No. 2 nationally and had won eight of nine games, losing only to SMU when Staubach was injured. A victory over Army meant a Cotton Bowl bid and a chance to play Texas and make a claim for the national championship, which had already been awarded to the Longhorns. (At that time, postseason results were not factored into the final poll results, and Texas had finished the regular season as the top-ranked team.)

After Kennedy's death, Navy's team flattened out. The emotion that had done as much to carry the team as Staubach's great play seemed to disappear. It was the rampant emotions of the crowd that would cause problems this day, though.

Staubach's opposite number at quarterback, Rollie Stichweh, drove Army to a 7–0 lead in its first possession, setting the tone for the day. Navy was stopped at Army's one-yard line early in the second quarter, with a holding penalty nullifying a Staubach touchdown pass. But on Navy's next possession, Pat Donnelly's four-yard trap play capped a six-play scoring drive, and the teams were tied 7–7 at the half.

Each year, scores of homemade banners, similar to the one hung by the Mids at Veterans Stadium, are produced by each academy for the game.

Navy exploded for two scores in the third quarter. Staubach gained twenty-eight yards with completions to Neil Henderson and Skip Orr; Donnelly's pet trap play got nineteen yards; and it was Donnelly again for the one-yard score. Fred Marlin's extra point gave Navy a 14–7 lead. Navy's defense, led by Al Krekich, stopped Army at the Mids' five-yard line, and the offense stormed back with a ninety-three yard, five-play blitz that ended with Donnelly's record-tying third touchdown. Navy led 21–7 with eleven minutes to play.

Many felt that the Mids had locked up the win and the bowl bid. But not Stichweh and his teammates. They quickly scored a second touchdown, and Stichweh ran for the two-point PAT to cut Navy's lead to 21–15 with six minutes to play. They would be six of the most dramatic minutes in Army-Navy history.

Army tried an onsides kick that went precisely ten yards, and Stichweh—the "other RS"—fell on it at the fifty-yard line. Continuing to keep Navy's defense off balance, he drove his team to the twenty-three. On fourth and one, and with the Mids expecting a run, he tossed a perfect play-action pass to Don Parcells at Navy's seven-yard line.

There were ninety-eight seconds to play, and Army had no timeouts—a reprise of the 1946 game when the clock helped sustain an unbeaten record for Army's Blanchard and Davis. As happened then, thousands of fans streamed onto the field. It was now clear that Navy's defense had to win the game.

The noise was deafening. Several times, Stichweh stepped back from center because his team could not hear him call signals. Each time, referee Barney Finn stopped the clock until the noise subsided. On the first play, Ray Paske got two yards to Navy's five-yard line. Navy's players dawdled as they unpiled and Army couldn't stop the clock, so there was less than a minute to play when Ken Waldrop gained a single yard at the middle of Navy's defense on second down.

Lined up to run a third-down play without huddling, his teammates could not hear Stichweh. He backed away, and Finn stopped the clock. Stichweh then huddled his team, costing it a dozen seconds, before running a third-down play on which Waldrop was smothered by Lynch, Krekich, and Marlin at the two-yard line.

It all came down to one last play. There were twenty-two seconds left as Army quickly lined up and Navy's defense set itself. Again, the crowd noise was too much for Stichweh, and he got a clock stoppage from Finn. Again, he took his team back into a huddle. Finn restarted the clock while Army's players huddled, seemingly unaware that the last few seconds were ticking away. Stichweh later maintained that he was aware of the time and just wanted his players to have all the time possible to catch their breath, before running one last play.

The Army players seemed oblivious to the urgency as they broke from their huddle and lined up. Again, the noise made it impossible for the players to hear the signals, so Stichweh turned to Finn for another stoppage. But Finn ignored him, and the clock ticked off the final seconds.

"Finn was getting pretty frustrated with our requests and when we got to the line of scrimmage there were eight seconds to play, enough time to run a play," Stichweh later said. "But the noise started and I turned to him again to ask for quiet. He looked at me and wouldn't do anything."

Tom Lynch recalled, "I was at linebacker, about three yards in our end zone, when the clock showed eleven seconds to play and Army broke the huddle. They still hadn't noticed the clock moving, but I started to count the seconds and when the clock reached three and Stichweh was looking around to get quiet, I began to move. As soon as it hit zero, I had that ball in my hands and I was gone."

At the same time, line judge Ray Barbuti, who kept the time on the field, began running down the line of scrimmage, waving his hands and shouting, "It's over! It's over! It's over!" It was.

Lynch had the final word. "If they had run the play, there was no way they would have made it. We all knew it."

Frank Schenk *(right)* exalts with his holder Alton Grizzard after kicking the winning thirty-two-yard field goal in the final eleven seconds of the 1989 Army-Navy game. It gave Navy a 19–17 victory. Schenk became the first Navy kicker since Slade Cutter in 1934 to win an Army-Navy game with a field goal.

December 9, 1989—East Rutherford, New Jersey

Navy 19, Army 17

There were a couple of splendid Army-Navy games after 1963, and in each Navy upheld the principle that victory—not a tie—is the only acceptable outcome in these games. In each instance, the Mids passed up a field goal that would have given them a well-earned tie. Instead, they walked off a rain-swept field in 1971 with a 24–23 loss, and six years later, they just missed on a fourth-down pass play in the final seconds that cost them a 17–14 loss.

Last-minute heroics are another hallmark of this series, and Navy performed some in grand style in 1989. It seemed only fitting that Roger Staubach, who set so many total-yardage records when he was Navy's quarterback, was at Giants Stadium to see Alton Grizzard put on a dazzling performance that ranks with the best of any Navy quarterback in history. He accounted for 222 of Navy's 336 yards, and his work in the winning drive was breathtaking.

Before the game, coach Elliott Uzelac had Staubach and several other former Navy stars give the team a pep talk. Already eager to break a three-game losing streak against the Cadets, the Mids were ready emotionally when they took the field.

The game's pace was all-out. Grizzard and Army quarterback Bryan McWilliams staged a duel of a kind rarely witnessed in Army-Navy competition. In the end, Grizzard won out, and kicker Frank Schenk won immortality.

Grizzard wasted no time. On his sixth play of the game, he threw a fifty-four-yard touchdown pass to B. J. Mason, who caught the ball in the middle of the field, sped to his right, and reached the end zone. Grizzard muffed the snap on Schenk's extra point kick, and Navy led 6–0.

A missed extra-point kick often takes away some of the momentum that is gained from a touchdown, but on its first two plays following the Mids' touchdown, Army handed the edge right back to Navy. Steve Tazza threw Mike Mayweather for a four-yard loss on first down. Army then tried to fool the Mids with a pass to Sean Jordan in the left flat—a play it had never shown before from the wishbone formation. But Navy's Bob Weissenfels intercepted. Seven plays later, Schenk kicked a thirty-eight-yard field goal, and Navy led 9–0 with just half the first quarter played.

The 1989 Army-Navy Game

Alton Grizzard, the hero of Navy's great victory over Army in 1989, was an outstanding midshipman, on and off the field. He was not only a great quarterback but also an outstanding leader in the Brigade.

It was a shock when he died three years later, the innocent victim of a shooting incident. The 1993 Navy team dedicated its game against Army to his memory, and every player wore a patch bearing Grizzard's No. 12.

One of those players was kicker Ryan Bucchianeri, a plebe, who was sent into the game in the final seconds to attempt an eighteen-yard field goal that would give Navy a 17–16 victory. As he trotted onto the field, he tapped the patch with Grizzard's number and silently dedicated the kick to him, even though they had never met.

Alas, his kick missed, and Navy lost 16–14. The young kicker, though, became a hero nonetheless for the manner in which he conducted himself in the aftermath of this disappointment.

But there was more. Early the next morning, three of Bucchianeri's friends were killed when the car in which they were riding skidded on a rain-slicked highway near the Naval Academy and crashed into a downed tree. He didn't find out about that tragedy until after he had returned to school with his teammates, and then had to shoulder an even greater burden.

But he did, in a manner far beyond his years.

Navy quarterback Alton Grizzard stiff-arms Army linebacker Triton Gurganus as he rolls for some of his 222 yards (of Navy's 336-yard total) in leading the Mids to a 19–17 come-from-behind victory in 1989. Grizzard, who lived up to his reputation as an crafty operator of Navy's option offense, stunned the Cadets when he threw a fifty-four-yard touchdown pass to B. J. Mason on the game's sixth play.

To that point, Army had possessed the ball for thirty-six seconds. For the rest of the first half, Navy had it less than five minutes as it fought relentlessly to try and hold McWilliams and Mayweather, who would break the Army career rushing record this day, in check. Army's Calvin Cass scored on two of the Cadets' next three possessions—one an exhausting fifteen-play, sixty-eight-yard drive that consumed eight-and-a-half minutes, the other a twelve-play, sixty-two-yard drive that took nearly six minutes—to put his team ahead, 14–9.

Since 1972 the Commander in Chief's Trophy goes each year to the overall winner of the interlocking competition between Navy, Army, and the Air Force. Navy won its first trophy in 1973.

Navy's defense improved in the second half. Early in the third quarter, Bill Yancey caught Cass for a loss that forced Army to punt for the first time, and the kick went only twenty-six yards. Grizzard was magnificent as he directed a fourteen-play, fifty-four-yard drive, even overcoming a fifteen-yard clipping penalty. The march consumed more than six minutes and ended with Rod Purifoy's three-yard touchdown run and a 16–14 Navy lead. Grizzard, a junior, either passed or ran the ball himself on ten of the fourteen plays, accounting for fifty-four yards. At one point, he faced a third and twenty-one, but he hit Jerry Dawson with a nineteen-yard pass, and then got the first down on a ten-yard keeper.

Back came Army with a sixty-seven-yard drive that ended with Keith Havenstrite's twenty-one-yard field goal and a 17–16 Army lead. Navy's defense cut down an Army drive early in the fourth quarter, and the Mids got a break with less than six minutes to play when Army was penalized before it could run a fourth-and-one play and was forced to punt.

Navy took possession with 5:02 to play, and Grizzard conducted a drive for the ages, controlling the ball until there were just eleven seconds remaining. He ran the ball five times for thirty-five yards, including three straight keeper plays—for seven yards on third and nine to Army's thirty-five; for a first down by fighting through a horde of tacklers; and then for ten more yards on the next play.

With only thirty-six seconds remaining, Purifoy's eight-yard run put the ball on Army's fifteen. Grizzard missed on a pass to Dawson in the left flat, and coach Uzelac decided that was enough. He sent Schenk onto the field to try a thirty-two-yard field goal with eleven seconds left.

Schenk, who had missed a field goal earlier that season that could have given Navy a victory against Delaware, said later that he felt before the game the final outcome would depend on his kicking.

"When Havenstrite kicked that one to put them ahead 17–16, I knew it was coming down to the end," Schenk said. "I just tried to put the crowd, the fact it was the Army-Navy game, and how much time was left, out of my mind. I knew it was going to be good when it left my foot because I hit it pretty well."

And it was—all thirty-two yards of it!

The 1991 Mulenapping

Navy's 24–3 upset of Army in the 1991 game averted a winless season. It also shared the spotlight with Navy's greatest off-field caper ever—Operation Missing Mascot, the kidnapping two days before the game of Army's four mascot mules, Spartacus, Trooper, Ranger, and Traveler.

The prank was all the more remarkable because West Point's veterinary area, which housed the mules, was considered impregnable to any would-be mulenappers. That is why there had been few attempts to snatch the animals during the series' century-long history. (In contrast, Navy's goat, housed on a farm outside Annapolis, was a comparatively easy target for pranksters. Before that, its home was a cage under old Thompson Stadium.)

The mulenapping had all the elements a screenwriter could ask for: revenge; undercover reconnaissance; a sudden aborted attempt when plans went awry; infiltration in disguises; the capturing of a building located in the middle of enemy territory; a lightning subjugation of the enemy; flawless getaways with the victims; thrilling car chases—and a helicopter chase—and a last-minute rescue to save the mission.

It happened on December 5, 1991. The invasion team consisted of seventeen midshipmen, two military advisers, and an Annapolis area farmer named Wier "Tennessee" Denton. D-Day in Europe or Operation Desert Storm were never as meticulously planned—nor as completely successful.

The revenge factor lay with Denton, a sixty-seven-year-old mule farmer who had been a "victim" of a goat-napping by Army in the late forties while he was working at the Navy Dairy Farm near Annapolis. He and a half-dozen Marine guards were watching over Bill the Goat when some crafty cadets opened a gate and let dairy cows out into the road. While Tennessee and the Marines rounded up the cows, the Army commandos snatched Bill. More than thirty years later, Denton was happy to serve as Operation Missing Mascot's outside consultant on mule-handling, instructing the kidnappers to make certain no harm came to the mascots and to ensure they would leave docilely with their captors.

The mulenappers were divided into four teams. There were an intelligence and electronics team that stood ready to handle phones and alarms; man-handlers—big guys picked for their size and readiness to place an enemy in submission according to the mission brief; and a door man who controlled entry to West Point's Veterinary Clinic, in the heart of the post. The planners didn't miss a point. The cars they used to infiltrate West Point bore "I Love My Cadet" and "Beat Navy" stickers. Some team members were dressed in fatigues with Army insignia, and others were disguised as MPs. The uniforms had been purchased by an adviser two weeks earlier from an Army post exchange.

The mule-handlers had to leap a steel and concrete fence and enter the pen housing the four mules, and in less than three minutes, catch and bridle the animals. The operations plan instructed that they should "look natural and do not draw attention." Tennessee Denton and an adviser, dressed as an MP, were the transportation team; they casually arrived in a pickup truck towing a four-horse trailer.

The operation inside West Point lasted just thirty-three minutes. Thirteen members of the team entered the Veterinary Clinic, claiming that they had come to pick up mule feed laced with molasses for the Army-Navy game. Locks were cut (and later replaced by the team); the Army sergeant who admitted them was quickly tied up and others in the office made prisoners; phone lines were disconnected and alarms silenced; and a "Sorry, We're Closed" sign was hung on the door. The team collected and bagged souvenirs such as West Point saddles and the Black Knight helmet.

Meanwhile, the mule-handlers made friends with the mules, giving them the candy feed at the front barn door. When the van arrived, it took less than a minute to load the compliant victims—they leaped on in hot pursuit of a bucket of the sweet feed that was strewn on the trailer's floor.

Two cadets approached the barn door while the mules were being loaded.

"Where are they going?" one asked.

"A rabies virus vial has broken, and the mules are being evacuated," one of the disguised MPs answered.

"Oh, I hope they're alright for the game," a cadet replied.

No sooner had the van with the mules departed than one of the human prisoners broke a window, rolled into the open, and sounded an alarm. That quickly set off a wild car chase involving a rear guard of three Navy men who had stayed behind to ensure the van had a clear escape route from the clinic, and a car belonging to a soldier at West Point. The rear guard jumped into their car and sped away as soon as they heard the alarm. But their escape was blocked by the soldier's car. The interlopers headed in the opposite direction, speeding up a hill to another exit just five hundred yards away. The soldier took a shortcut toward the exit and got to the exit ahead of the Navy team. The Navy adviser who was driving crunched the gas pedal, leaned on the horn, swerved around the soldier's vehicle, and made his escape. The Army man wisely dove for cover.

Security at the Military Academy scrambled three UH–1 Huey Cobra helicopters and notified federal forces. The roads south of West Point were all covered by state and federal authorities. But the mulenappers drove north to Albany, New York, then southwest to Scranton, Pennsylvania, and thence to Denton's farm outside Annapolis.

There was more. The mules were scheduled to be the guests of honor at a huge pep rally and bonfire at the Academy, scheduled for 7:30 that evening. When the convoy carrying them drove through Gate 8 at the Naval Academy, federal authorities were waiting. They forced everyone from their vehicles, spread-eagled them on a nearby baseball backstop, and charged them with the federal crime of grand theft, mule.

But Bill Wiseman, one of the team, had seen the feds when he drove through the gate a few minutes earlier and had notified Lt. Angela Smith, the command duty officer, who was technically in charge of the naval station. She sped to the gate and ordered the agents to release the midshipmen and escort them—and the mules—to the pep rally. If she hadn't come along, the 'nappers would have been forced to return the mules to West Point.

The prized trophies stood placidly at the rally as the crowd went into a frenzy. The mules had their pictures taken more often than a rock star. The following day, the mulenappers rode the animals in T-Court and then, by agreement, returned them to Army—though the mids had fervently hoped that the exchange would take place at Veterans Stadium in Philadelphia.

While this caper was under way at the Veterinary Clinic, six West Point personnel downstairs in the building never guessed that the MP who was bantering with them was a member of the assault team. He told them the men upstairs were MPs, "and they're doing a security check because we think Navy is gonna try to take the mules."

"They'll never do it," one of the Army men said.

10. The Bowls

Navy's legacy in postseason games is modest by most standards—eight games, in which the Mids won three, lost four, and tied the first one they played, against the University of Washington in the 1924 Rose Bowl.

It wasn't until thirty-one years later, on January 1, 1955, that Navy, with its "Team Named Desire," played in another bowl game, upsetting Mississippi 21–0 in the Sugar Bowl. Three years later, the 1957 team went to the Cotton Bowl and beat a good Rice University team 20–7.

Navy also had its two Heisman Trophy winners—Joe Bellino and Roger Staubach—as centerpieces in bowl games. Bellino's 1960 team lost to Missouri in the Orange Bowl 21–14, and Staubach played in the biggest postseason game in Navy football history in the 1964 Cotton Bowl, when the second-ranked Mids lost to national champion Texas, 28–6.

Since then, Navy has played in four bowls—a 23–16 victory over Brigham Young in the 1978 Holiday Bowl; a 35–0 loss to Houston in the 1980 Garden State Bowl; a 31–28 loss against Ohio State in the 1981 Liberty Bowl; and a 42–38 victory over California in the 1996 Aloha Bowl.

Until Navy went to the 1955 Sugar Bowl, there was a "no-bowl" policy at the Naval Academy. The season-ending Army-Navy game was, in effect, Navy's bowl game; by Academy standards, anything else was anticlimactic. Further, Academy officials believed that players had already lost too much academic time and that more football only exacerbated the loss. When that policy changed—and it did so to provide additional revenue for the Naval Academy Athletic Association and its much-needed expansion projects, and to provide increased exposure to attract more students and student-athletes—Navy at first accepted a bowl bid only if it beat Army. Now, the entire menu of bowl games is drawn up even before the traditional first Saturday in December date for the Army-Navy game. So winning or losing against Army probably will not be a factor.

January 1, 1924—Rose Bowl

Navy 14, Washington 14

The Rose Bowl was the only postseason game played in 1924. Navy knew it was going to the game a week before it had played the first game of the 1923 season. But it didn't know that its opponent would be the University of Washington because, for the first time, the Pacific Coast Conference (PCC) named its representative when the season ended.

Rear Adm. Henry B. Wilson, the Naval Academy's superintendent, was asked early in September to consider sending his team—sight unseen, its final record still to be decided. Wilson declined at first, but he took up the matter with the Navy Department and Academy officials. Three factors persuaded Wilson to change his mind. The game would give the Naval Academy national exposure; it would be an opportunity to build better relations between citizenry and the tens of thousands of naval personnel stationed on the West Coast; and it would give those Navy people, particularly Naval Academy graduates, a chance to see their football team.

When Leslie B. Henry, chairman of the Tournament of Roses, told Wilson that Navy's opponent would be the PCC champion and that it could approve the game officials, he agreed to play. On September 26, three days before its opening game against William and Mary, Navy accepted the bid. Henry wrote to Wilson shortly thereafter, "Your announcement . . . to play here broke as a veritable bombshell in Pacific Coast collegiate circles."

During the 1923 season, Navy won five games, lost only to Penn State (the 1923 Rose Bowl champion), and played two ties, including the last scoreless deadlock with Army. Washington had lost only to unbeaten California, 9–0, and got the invitation only because Cal declined to play.

Navy declined an offer from a group in Texas to play a Christmas Day game in Dallas against either Texas, Texas A&M, or SMU, and receive $2,500 in

Ira McKee runs off tackle during the 1924 Rose Bowl game against the University of Washington.

expenses. Instead, the team spent three weeks in Annapolis practicing for the Rose Bowl. On Christmas Day, a party of twenty-six players, head coach Bob Folwell and two assistants, and three Academy officials departed shortly after noon for a cross-country train trip. They arrived in Chicago the next morning, worked out for two hours at the University of Chicago, dined at the University Club, spent the rest of the afternoon sightseeing, and departed by train that evening for the West Coast. After stopping on December 29 for a daylong tour of the Grand Canyon, they arrived in Pasadena, California, on the afternoon of December 30 and checked into the Huntington Hotel. The team was so chipper that it donned full gear and worked out. On December 31 the Mids had a two-hour drill at two-year-old Rose Bowl Stadium, which seated 52,000 at that time.

But not everything came up roses.

Rear Adm. S. S. Robison, commander of the Pacific Battle Fleet, enthusiastically backed the plan, at first. He had pamphlets containing Navy cheers and songs distributed to all personnel and ordered that they be practiced at least twice a week under the direction of "capable cheerleaders, preferably an ensign recently graduated." Fleet cheerleaders were also to be designated and were to conduct combined cheering practices during December.

The biggest administrative problem was tickets. Admiral Wilson was told that the payout for the game would be at least $45,000, all from ticket sales. So certain were the Navy and the Tournament of Roses Committee that Navy could sell 20,000 tickets to its personnel that Academy officials evidently took their $45,000 cut in additional tickets and then sold them to make even more money.

Robison originally was told that the fleet could have 5,000 tickets at $3.00 each, and that 2,000 of those would be between the fifteen-yard lines. On December 5, he was notified that seats between the fifteen-yard lines would cost $5.50 each. He protested to Wilson that the new price was "very excessive. It will preclude [the] presence of enlisted rooting party, [and] also prevent a large attendance by [the] Navy contingent [on the] Pacific Coast."

The matter festered. With thousands of tickets still to be sold, Robison suddenly ordered his fleet to sea on December 31. Thousands of the tickets went unused. On the day of the game, officials in cars with sound systems circled the stadium and tried to sell the unused tickets. Attendance was estimated at 40,000 instead of the anticipated 52,000.

Back in Annapolis, officers, faculty, and midshipmen jammed the auditorium in Mahan Hall to follow the game's progress, via telegraph, on a large blackboard that was rigged on the stage. Two midshipmen read the play-by-play, and two others charted the team's fortunes on the blackboard, using orange chalk for Navy and white for Washington. On every play the hall rocked with cheers— just as, a continent away, the Rose Bowl echoed with shouts from the throng watching the brutally tough game.

Navy, under Folwell, who was paid an extra $500 to coach the game, used its wide-open style of football to control most of the game. Navy quarterback Ira McKee completed his first fourteen passes, eleven in the first half, and the running of Steve Barchet and Alan Shapley ably supported him. Navy outgained Washington 363 yards to 202.

The Mids were stopped at Washington's three-yard line early in the first quarter, but McKee and Charley Cullen combined on a twenty-two-yard touchdown pass on the first play of the second quarter. McKee kicked the extra point. But the Huskies came back to tie the game on George Wilson's twenty-three-yard run.

Later in the quarter, McKee and Cullen linked up again for twenty-six yards to Washington's eight-yard line. Shapley then pitched a touchdown pass to McKee. McKee also kicked the PAT, and Navy led 14–7 at the half.

Navy kept control of the game until midway through the final quarter. Then, with the ball at his twenty-seven-yard line, Steve Barchet started to the left and the center snap went to his right. Washington recovered at the Mids' twelve-yard line, and four plays later the Huskies tied the game. The Huskies threatened to win, but they missed a thirty-two-yard field goal in the final minute.

One newspaper columnist wrote the next day, "Washington had no right to tie this game. Navy outplayed the Huskies by a rather wide margin."

The Navy team made no stops en route home, returning January 6. On February 2, the entire Brigade watched movies of the game.

In 1945, the Rose Bowl Committee wanted to choose two teams from among Alabama, Army, and Navy to make up the January 1, 1946, pairing, but both service academies turned down the bid.

January 1, 1955—Sugar Bowl

Navy 21, Mississippi 0

Navy's decision to accept the 1955 Sugar Bowl bid for its "Team Named Desire" to play Mississippi was a turnaround from the two previous seasons, when it had declined invitations to the Orange Bowl.

However, with Navy's team capturing so much national attention in 1954, all bowl invitations were considered under the category of "special exceptions." Navy needed bowl revenue to supplement the fund-raising drive to build a new stadium and bowl exposure to prop up declining applications.

Navy was 7–2 and sought by every bowl except the Rose Bowl, which had its own arrangement with the Big Ten and Pacific Coast Conferences. The Mids wanted to play against the highest-ranked team possible, so the Sugar Bowl sponsors named fifth-ranked Mississippi as an opponent when it made its presentation to Capt. C. Elliott Laughlin, Navy's athletic director, in mid-November. Payment was to be "at least" $160,000—enough to convince the Athletic Association's Executive Committee to ditch the long-standing "no-bowl" policy. The change became official after Navy's 27–20 victory over Army.

Several starting players were injured. Tackle Jim Royer was replaced by Pat McCool; Bob Craig, the Mids' fastest runner, was stricken by tonsillitis and replaced by Jack Garrow (who himself couldn't practice because of a stomach virus); and John Weaver limped through the final practice sessions.

"It's the first bowl game," Laughlin moaned to coach Eddie Erdelatz, "and it means so damn much. With the injuries you have, I just don't feel confident."

"Forget it," replied Erdelatz, who was usually pessimistic when discussing upcoming opponents. "We're going to win."

Phil Monahan *(center)*, captain of Navy's "Team Named Desire," and his teammates ride the New Orleans trolley car to the Desire section of the city—and later to victory over Mississippi in the 1955 Sugar Bowl.

Mississippi was dead from the opening whistle. It kicked off to take advantage of a good breeze, and Navy immediately drove seventy yards in seventeen plays for a touchdown. There were two key plays: a gutsy fourth-and-one dive by Joe Gattuso from Navy's thirty-nine yard line that kept the drive alive; and a twenty-four-yard run by Weaver to the Ole Miss three-yard line following a fifteen-yard penalty against Navy. Gattuso, making his first start at fullback since early in the season, then scored the first of his two touchdowns on a three-yard run. One scribe called his work that day "the best all-around, one-man performance of running, blocking, and tackling ever seen on Tulane Field." Gattuso gained 111 yards on sixteen carries and won the game's outstanding player award.

Mississippi assistant coach Junie Hovious called the first drive the turning point of the game. Quarterback George Welsh believed that the key play was the daring fourth-and-one call. "When I got into the huddle the guys said, 'C'mon, George, we can make it. Let's try it.' So we had Gattuso slant off tackle. I knew Joe would make a yard."

John Weaver gains some of his 150 yards against Mississippi during Navy's 21–0 slaughter in the 1955 Sugar Bowl.

Welsh called a perfect game that day in New Orleans. He ran his split-T offense like a magician and carved up Mississippi's secondary with enough passing—eight of fifteen for seventy-eight yards—to befuddle his opponents throughout the game.

Navy's All-America end Ron Beagle, who caught three passes for nineteen yards, noted that "after we went ahead, Mississippi seemed to lose interest, and when we got up by fourteen points, it was just a matter of time how many we scored before the end of the game."

Navy got the 14–0 lead on Welsh's eighteen-yard pass to Weaver, the first of two third-quarter touchdowns. Gattuso and Weaver both tore off huge gains as Navy marched ninety-three yards on its next possession, which Gattuso ended with a short run for the touchdown. While Gattuso never lost a yard in his sixteen carries, Weaver, the team's fastest back, accumulated 150 yards.

Mississippi's offense disappeared under an avalanche of blue jerseys. The defensive hero for Navy was tackle Pat McCool, who handled All-America offensive tackle Rex Reed Bogan and harassed Mississippi quarterbacks Eagle Day and Houston Patton. "McCool was sitting in my lap every time I went back to pass," Day said later. "I didn't get off a good one all afternoon."

"This wasn't our best game," Welsh said afterward. "We played better against Army. Mississippi is a very good and well-coached team, but it was the third-best team we played after Army and Notre Dame and not as good as we expected. They seemed flat, lacked zip. Their initial charge was nothing compared to Army."

Mississippi's players admitted they had not realized Navy was such a tough physical team after watching films of its games against Army and Notre Dame. "It seemed like all eleven men were after you on every play," said Day. "That 'desire' stuff might sound corny, but they had it."

January 1, 1958—Cotton Bowl

Navy 20, Rice 7

Navy had turned down the Cotton Bowl in 1956 because it didn't think its team was good enough after managing only a tie against Army. But in 1957, the fifth-ranked Mids lost only to North Carolina, stomped a very good Army team, and once again was every bowl's choice. The clincher again was money: The Athletic Association still needed more funds to construct the Navy–Marine Corps Memorial Stadium. Navy would receive $175,000 for playing the game; in addition, the program so impressed a group of Texas bankers that they agreed to underwrite the last $500,000 for the stadium project.

The Mids were paired against eighth-ranked Rice, which had won the Southwest Conference title after a rocky start. The Owls had a fine passer in King Hill, who had just been selected as the NFL's "bonus" pick by the Chicago Cardinals.

The scoreboard told the story to a nationwide television audience watching the 1958 Cotton Bowl in which Navy defeated Rice, 20–7.

Stremic: No One Was Tougher

Whither a miracle?

Five days before the 1958 Cotton Bowl game against Rice, Navy's all-America guard Tony Stremic was accidentally kicked by tackle Bob Reifsnider during a scrimmage and suffered a serious shinbone and ankle injury. Stremic was on crutches for two days, and coach Eddie Erdelatz declared, "It will take a miracle for Stremic to play, but if it just took guts, he'd be a cinch to make it."

The day before the game, Stremic was walking gingerly on the injured leg. When the team came out for pregame practice on New Year's Day, he was in full uniform, but his leg was bandaged from knee to ankle, and he had a shot of novocaine to deaden the pain. During the practice, Erdelatz told him to try a full-speed cut-and-run workout for assistant coach Dick Duden. When Erdelatz asked Stremic if he could play, he replied, "Sure coach. It's my last game. Let's go for broke."

Go for broke?

Tony Stremic was chosen the game's outstanding lineman.

Ned Oldham scores Navy's third touchdown in the 1958 Cotton Bowl victory over Rice. Joe Tranchini and Harry Hurst got the other touchdowns.

Two Tickets, Front and Center

When Navy went ahead 20–0 in the third quarter of the 1958 Cotton Bowl game, end Pete Jokanovich decided to have some fun.

He had tucked away some unused game tickets into his uniform when he went out to play, and after Navy's third touchdown, he pulled them out and said to one of the Rice players, "Hey, kid, wanna buy some tickets to the Cotton Bowl game?"

Navy quarterback Tom Forrestal was backed by running backs Ned Oldham, the team captain, and Ray Wellborn. Three years earlier, Wellborn had been a freshman football player at Rice, but he was so enthralled after watching Navy defeat Mississippi in the 1955 Sugar Bowl that he transferred to the Naval Academy. After graduating in 1959, he became a much-decorated combat officer.

With Navy's offensive line, led by Tony Stremic and tackle Bob Reifsnider, helping control Rice's defense, Navy held a 13–0 halftime lead in Dallas. It might have been more had not the Mids fumbled on their first two possessions, missed a pair of field goals, and been stopped once at the Owls' three-yard line.

The first score came after Ron Brandquist recovered Hill's fumble at Rice's thirty-three-yard line. Navy's second unit scored in eight plays; the touchdown came on Joe Tranchini's quarterback keeper. In the second quarter, with Forrestal leading the No. 1 unit, Navy drove sixty-six yards for a 13–0 lead. Forrestal completed all four passes in the drive, and Harry Hurst swept left end for the score, crashing through two tacklers at the goal line. Navy's final touchdown came late in the third quarter after John Ruth recovered a Rice fumble on the Owls' twenty-yard line. Wellborn made a yard, and Oldham swept nineteen yards for the score and kicked the final point.

Navy's famed "jitterbug defense," designed to unnerve opponents, surprised Rice by *not* jitterbugging, which kept the Owls off balance the entire game. Even with the game sewed up, the Mids stopped the Owls' bid for a score on the last play of the game by throwing quarterback Frank Ryan for a loss at their two-yard line.

Navy outgained Rice 375 yards to 274. Oldham and Hurst each gained 50 yards rushing, and Forrestal completed thirteen of twenty-four passes for 153 yards in the 20–7 victory.

Navy's All-America and Heisman Trophy winner Joe Bellino is tackled from behind by a Missouri player during the 1961 Orange Bowl. Joe's only bit of glory was catching a touchdown pass from quarterback Hal Spooner as the Tigers held him to just four rushing yards and won the game, 21–14.

January 1, 1961—Orange Bowl

Missouri 21, Navy 14

Navy had won nine of ten games in 1960, and the Orange Bowl offered it a bid to play against Big Eight Conference champion Missouri.

The plum? A clear profit of a half-million dollars. That, claimed Rear Adm. John Davidson, then the Academy's superintendent, "was the only reason for going to that game."

Navy had stunned Rose Bowl champion Washington and Notre Dame earlier that season, and was itself stunned 19–10 by Duke for its only loss. After beating Army 17–12, Chief of Naval Operations Rear Adm. Arleigh Burke, the secretary of the Navy, and Davidson went to the Navy dressing room in Philadelphia's Municipal Stadium to congratulate everyone.

"By the way," Admiral Davidson said to the team, "would you all like to go to the Orange Bowl?"

Cries of "Yes! Yes! Yes!" filled the room, and the bid was accepted.

In the minds of some, that was the last positive moment in that venture. As Davidson related:

> A month later they were a very unhappy group. [Coach] Wayne Hardin had them practice every day. They lost their Christmas leave, and when they went to Miami a week before the game, Hardin put on a nine o'clock curfew.
>
> Their football officer asked me to intercede with Hardin because he knew the Missouri players were running around Miami Beach having a good time and our kids knew it, too. I refused because that was Hardin's team and he had to take the consequences for his actions just as he was entitled to take the glory for his successes. But I agreed with the football rep that he had made the players give up too much.

However, word got back to Hardin that there was some unhappiness, and he relaxed the curfew to eleven o'clock.

Did it matter? Probably not, because Missouri was thoroughly prepared for Navy. It targeted Bellino, who had won the Heisman Trophy and was the heart of Navy's offense. Bellino gained just four rushing yards in eight carries that day, and Navy lost 21–14 before more than 70,000 persons, including President-elect and No. 1 Navy fan John F. Kennedy.

There were few bright moments. One belonged to Bellino, another to end-kicker Greg Mather. After Missouri marched to Navy's two-yard line, quarterback Ron Taylor gave the ball to Donnie Smith, who was stopped cold. Improvising, Smith tried to lateral the ball back to a very surprised Taylor, but it was Mather who caught the ball. He sprinted ninety-four yards for the touchdown.

On the ensuing kickoff, Hardin, a master of gimmicks, had Mather run forward as if to kick the ball, but Bellino crossed over and executed an onsides kick that was fumbled by a Missouri lineman. Navy recovered the ball at Missouri's forty-three-yard line.

Quarterback Hal Spooner completed two first-down passes to Missouri's fourteen-yard line. The Tigers, reminded of Navy's tendency to pass on first down, were ready when Spooner tried it a third time: Norm Beal intercepted the ball and ran ninety yards for a touchdown.

"That's the play that won the game," said a Missouri coach afterward. "That, and two more interceptions by Andy Russell a bit later. When Navy couldn't run against us, and when their passes started being intercepted, they didn't know which way to turn."

Missouri, which had never won a postseason game, scored two more touchdowns to take a 21–6 lead late in the fourth quarter. Then Bellino unleashed one last bit of magic. Spooner was moving the team primarily by throwing to the sidelines to conserve time. Then he changed up. Bellino cut downfield past a defender toward the far corner of the end zone. Spooner's pass was going over his head, but Bellino sprung forward and made an incredible, diving catch and somersaulted out of the end zone for Navy's final score.

January 1, 1964—Cotton Bowl

Texas 28, Navy 6

Roger Staubach, the 1963 Heisman Trophy winner and College Football's Player of the Year, had captivated an entire nation and fired the buildup for a climactic game in Dallas between second-ranked Navy and national champion Texas.

The matchup was simple: Could Texas harness Staubach, who had had a magical season with his array of scrambling, dodging, dancing, and improvisational football skills? He had already been drafted by both the Dallas Cowboys of the NFL and the Dallas Texans of the new American Football League and, in a delicious bit of irony, Navy practiced for the game at the Cowboys training site where, six years later, Staubach started his Hall of Fame pro career.

Navy's biggest problem was restoring the emotional edge that was lost after the assassination of President John F. Kennedy, who had established a special bond with the team. The team was also drained from the pressure of playing in the national spotlight, and was really an unhappy group that seemed more concerned about its lost Christmas leave than getting ready for Texas.

Practice, and the anticipation of playing the national champion, restored some vitality, but much of that was lost when, before the game, the secretary of the Navy visited Navy's locker room. Although his intentions were good, he cast a pall by reminiscing about Kennedy.

Navy, which had won eight of nine games and had lost only to SMU in the Cotton Bowl Stadium, also suffered a serious setback in practice when Pat Donnelly pulled a hamstring muscle, impairing his mobility as a fullback and linebacker. With the Mids practicing at the Cowboys' facility, it was impossible to keep the Texas coaches completely in the dark about this development. It proved pivotal in getting Texas an early lead: Phil Harris caught two early touchdown passes for the Longhorns when Donnelly simply was unable to get to his coverage area in time to help the defense.

Texas coach Darrell Royal focused on stopping Staubach's ability to run. When Staubach got loose, he spread the defense and created the potential for big plays. Royal feared that more than he did Staubach's straight-away passing game. He drilled his linemen to contain Staubach inside the ends, and he played a three-deep zone pass defense that took away long passes and forced Staubach to settle for small gains.

Texas quarterback Duke Carlisle stunned the Mids with touchdown passes of fifty-eight and sixty-three yards to Harris in the first twenty minutes for a 14–0 lead. Donnelly, a step late because of his injury, just missed intercepting the ball on the second score. Texas added a third touchdown just before halftime on Carlisle's nine-yard run. The game was effectively over.

Navy gained just nineteen net yards in the first half, and the running game lost twenty-eight yards. (For the game, Navy had just one rushing first down and minus fourteen yards on the ground.) Staubach was so harassed by All-America tackle Scott Appleton and ends Knox Nunnally and Pete Lammons that he had one pass intercepted and also lost the ball on a fumble.

National champion Texas flexes its offensive muscle en route to a decisive 28–6 victory over second-ranked Navy in the 1964 Cotton Bowl.

After Texas upped its lead to 28–0 late in the third quarter, Staubach put together his only good drive of the game, moving the team seventy-five yards for Navy's only score, which he made on a two-yard rollout.

The final score was 28–6. Navy could take some consolation in Staubach's statistics: he set a Cotton Bowl passing record by completing twenty-one of thirty-one for 228 yards. But Texas gained 168 rushing yards, and Duke Carlisle, little heralded before the game, did a Roger Staubach number: He completed seven of nineteen passes for 213 yards, and added another fifty-four on eleven runs.

Fullback Kevin Tolbert scores Navy's first touchdown, and the team goes on to win, 23–16, against Brigham Young in the 1978 Holiday Bowl. The Mids won the game on a spectacular sixty-five-yard touchdown pass from quarterback Bob Leszczynski to wide receiver Phil McConkey and three field goals by Bob Tata.

"They outhit us from beginning to end," noted coach Wayne Hardin, "and they did everything a No. 1 team is expected to do—tackled better, blocked better, ran better, and passed better. What more can you ask?"

And what more can you say?

December 22, 1978—Holiday Bowl

Navy 23, BYU 16

In 1978, Navy had its best team since 1963. The Mids compiled an 8–3 record, winning their first seven games and beating Army 28–0. They capped the season in the first Holiday Bowl with a come-from-behind, 23–16 victory over Brigham Young University, champions of the Western Athletic Conference and the host team for the game.

Because of examinations, Navy practiced just one day before leaving for the West Coast, and rain interrupted the practice schedule in San Diego. "Frankly, I was scared to death that we didn't have enough time to prepare," said coach George Welsh. "They did so much offensively, and we were able to put in just one new defensive coverage. All we could do was polish the things we had done all year."

The keys for Navy proved to be clutch play from five-ten, 163-pound wide receiver and co-captain Phil McConkey, and steady, and sometimes superlative quarterbacking from Bob Leszczynski. Leszczynski completed seven of thirteen passes for 123 yards, including a spectacular sixty-five-yard touchdown pass to McConkey, and he added forty more yards with his running.

Defensively, Navy—which was ranked thirteenth nationally—blitzed on virtually every down, hoping to force Brigham Young into keeping some of its receivers back to protect quarterbacks Marc Wilson and Jim McMahon. Late in the game, Navy's defensive pressure indeed forced BYU to scale down its receiving corps in favor of more pass protectors for McMahon, and his multifaceted passing attack had to be run with only two receivers.

Navy players *(from left to right)* Phil McConkey and Nick Mygas (co-captains), and Sandy Jones (89) celebrate with the Holiday Bowl trophy. McConkey is also holding his offensive Most Valuable Player trophy.

Brigham Young went ahead 16–3 early in the second half, and matters looked bleak; all season the Cougars had outscored their opponents during the last two quarters. "I was awfully worried," said Welsh, "because we hadn't come back to win one all year and BYU was playing well."

But Navy was unfazed. In the last twenty-three minutes of the game, the Mids gained 235 yards and scored seventeen points while their defense held the Cougars' noted second-half offense to just twenty-four yards and four first downs.

Navy started its comeback with a twelve-play, seventy-seven-yard drive, punctuated by McConkey's twenty-six-yard reverse and Mike Sherlock's eleven-yard run. Kevin Tolbert scored the touchdown on a plunge. On the next possession, Bob Tata kicked the second of his three field goals, and Navy trailed 16–13.

Navy's defense forced Brigham Young to punt on the next series. On Navy's first offensive play, with less than twelve minutes to play, McConkey ran a streak pattern. Defensive back Bill Schoepflin ran with him step-for-step until McConkey, seeing that the ball was going to be a bit short, stutter-stepped his defender to a momentary stop at the twenty-four-yard line, leaped over him to make the catch, and raced into the end zone. The touchdown gave Navy a 20–16 lead. Tata's third field goal five minutes later made it 23–16 and closed out the scoring.

"Phil gave our offense dimension," Leszczynski said. "Without him, we couldn't really make another team believe we could go forty yards downfield in one play. With him, they had to play us honest."

McConkey said of his seventeenth and last touchdown reception for Navy, "That may not have been the best catch of my life, but it sure was the biggest."

December 14, 1980—Garden State Bowl

Houston 35, Navy 0

Garden State Bowl III is one postseason game Navy would just as soon forget. The Mids did absolutely nothing right. The entire game was one disaster after another as they lost 35–0 to the University of Houston at Giants Stadium in New Jersey's Meadowlands Sports Complex.

The performance was atypical of a team that had been so efficient all season in winning eight of eleven games. But the circumstances simply did not allow coach George Welsh to put together a representative package. For one thing, the players were in the midst of exams during game week; some players even had to take finals at their hotel in New Jersey.

It was a bizarre game—a nightmare, really. This is what happened on Navy's eight possessions in the first half:

1. Lost fumble. Actually, the game was over on this first play—a fumble by running back Eddie Meyers at Navy's twenty-seven-yard line. Eight plays later, Mike Clark's touchdown gave Houston a 7–0 lead. (Clark gained 163 rushing yards on twenty-six carries as Houston's high-powered veer rushing offense shredded Navy's defense for 405 yards. The Mids' defense had allowed just 117 yards per game during the season.)

2. Blocked punt. Houston converted the mistake into a touchdown and a 14–0 lead.
3. Punt, after two first downs.
4. Missed twenty-seven-yard field goal by Steve Fehr, who had made seventeen of twenty-three during the season.
5. Lost Fumble. Houston scored a touchdown for a 20–0 lead.
6. Lost fumble. Houston converted for a 28–0 lead.
7. Interception. Houston missed a thirty-six-yard field goal.
8. Lost on downs at end of first half.

It was not much better in the second half. Navy, with just five possessions, got only as far as Houston's twenty-five-yard line, and that was on its final drive. Meyers, one of Navy's greatest all-time running backs, who had gained 957 yards in 1980, left the game with an injury late in the first quarter and had only thirteen yards in three carries. Kevin Tolbert chipped in fifty-three yards and Mike Sherlock added forty-one, but Navy's most effective weapon was gone. Forced to rely on the passing game, the Mids were stymied by a brisk wind and Houston's defense, which, with a big lead, could tee off on the quarterback. Fred Reitzel completed just five of twelve passes for forty-two yards, and backup Tom Tarquinio was only two-for-twelve for twenty-three. The Mids gained only 200 yards, after averaging 361 a game.

December 30, 1981—Liberty Bowl

Ohio State 31, Navy 28

The 1981 Liberty Bowl in Memphis, Tennessee, was George Welsh's final game as Navy's head coach before he left for the University of Virginia. He left the Naval Academy as its all-time winningest coach.

The invitation was a bit of déjà vu because Navy had been invited by bowl promoter Ambrose "Bud" Dudley to participate in the first Liberty Bowl, in Philadelphia, in 1959. Navy declined the first invitation, but gratefully accepted this one after a 7–3–1 season.

The 1981 team was one of Navy's strongest in the post-Staubach era. For one season it had two of its greatest runners, Eddie Meyers, a senior, and Napoleon McCallum, a sophomore, in the same backfield. Meyers had set both a school season rushing record of 1,318 yards and a career mark of 2,935 yards, and was picked as Navy's outstanding offensive player in this game (defensive end Mike Rouser won defensive honors).

The game started miserably for Navy. The Mids turned the ball over on their first two possessions, and Ohio State turned the mistakes into a 10–0 lead. But the Mids were a resilient team—and a lucky one. They escaped a second straight blocked punt when Ohio State was offside, and then maintained a sixty-four-yard drive, keyed by Steve Fehr's fake punt–pass to Brian Cianella for thirty-nine yards to the Buckeyes' sixteen-yard line. Six plays later, quarterback Marco Pagnanelli completed only his second touchdown pass of the year, a one-yard toss to Greg Papajohn. On its next possession, Navy drove sixty yards, including Meyers's twenty-two-yard run, and tied the score 10–10 on Fehr's forty-one-yard field goal.

Navy kicker Steve Fehr and Ohio State's Cedric Anderson chase a loose ball in the 1981 Liberty Bowl. Ohio State recovered, but Fehr kicked a pair of field goals in the game.

After another Navy turnover, Ohio State's Jim Gayle scored on a two-yard run. Navy came right back with a nine-play, seventy-three-yard drive, including passes of thirty-seven yards to Chris Weiler and eleven to McCallum, and Fehr kicked a twenty-three-yard field goal.

Navy then stunned Ohio State by taking a 20–17 lead four minutes into the second half. Navy's Andy Ponseigo blocked a punt and Ken Olson picked up the ball and rumbled ten yards for the touchdown. But Fehr's poor twenty-four-yard punt set up a nine-play, thirty-seven-yard scoring drive for Ohio State. Later, Art Schlichter passed for his second touchdown, and a seemingly safe 30–20 lead.

Navy was undaunted. After an exchange of punts the Mids put on a magnificent, ninety-seven-yard scoring drive. Meyers punched out twenty-three yards on the ground, and Pagnanelli completed two thirty-four-yard passes, one to McCallum and one to Papajohn. Papajohn scored on a one-yard toss with eight seconds to play, then caught a two-point conversion pass, and Navy trailed by just three points.

Fehr tried an onsides kick, but it was recovered by Ohio State . . . and Navy's gallant effort fell just a bit short. But it made an impact on Ohio State coach Earle Bruce who, by noting that "Meyers might have been a little better than we thought," understated the overall abilities of the Navy team. He was so stunned by the Mids' performance that he stripped his defensive staff and hired a new group of coaches.

It wasn't the coaching that stunned Ohio State. It was Navy football.

December 25, 1996—Aloha Bowl

Navy 42, California 38

It took Navy fifteen years to return to postseason competition. Before their game in 1996, both Army and Navy received bowl bids; the outcome would determine where each team would land. The winner was to go to the Independence Bowl, and the loser got the Aloha Bowl in Honolulu. Army won the game, 28–24, and the next day Navy accepted the offer to play in Hawaii.

In front of a national television audience on Christmas afternoon, Navy engineered one of its most exciting comebacks ever in a 42–38 victory over the University of California, Berkeley. The lead changed hands half a dozen times, and the millions watching on television—as well as a pro-Navy crowd of nearly 40,000 in Aloha Stadium, which is near the huge naval base at Pearl Harbor—were riveted by the up-and-down-the-field action.

Navy also put on one of the greatest offensive shows in its history: 646 total yards, the seventh highest total posted by any school in a bowl game and just seven yards shy of the school record set in 1970 against Colgate. The Mids' average of 9.1 yards per play was the second highest in intercollegiate bowl history. The two teams produced 1,080 yards of total offense and eighty points—sixty-three of them coming in the first half, which ended with Cal holding a 35–28 lead.

Before the game, California coach Steve Mariucci had noted that the contrasting styles of the two teams "would make for an interesting game." The remark was certainly prophetic. His team used conventional backfield and wide receiver sets and had averaged 310.5 yards per game during the season, third best in the nation. Navy coach Charlie Weatherbie's "wingbone" rushing offense, a variation on the old wishbone offenses of the sixties and early seventies, was ranked fifth nationally. But its air attack, which had accounted for more than two hundred yards only twice during the season, stunned everyone with 395 yards from quarterbacks Chris McCoy and Ben Fay. Cory Schemm, a six-foot-one, 205-pound senior wide receiver, gained 194 yards—on just five receptions. He made catches of fifty-two or more yards on three of Navy's six touchdown drives.

In fact, it was a game of big plays by both sides. Cal's Deltha O'Neal returned the opening kickoff for an Aloha Bowl–record one hundred yards and a touchdown, and Cal had a 6–0 lead only thirteen seconds into the game. Navy took a 7–6 lead midway through the first quarter when Tim Cannada's seven-yard touchdown run polished off a three-play, sixty-nine-yard drive that was keyed by McCoy's fifty-seven-yard pass to Schemm. Cal came right back with a seven-play, eighty-one-yard touchdown drive. Quarterback Pat Barnes, who completed twenty-seven of thirty-seven passes for 313 yards and three touchdowns, threw a six-yard pass to Bob Shaw for a 13–7 lead.

The Mids then scored on successive second-quarter possessions. McCoy dove between center and left guard on a one-yard sneak to put Navy ahead again, 14–13; a little more than four minutes later, Ross Scott ended a five-play, ninety-five-yard drive by rushing four yards for a touchdown. Omar Nelson started this lightning-strike

Pat McGrew is off and running after catching a Chris McCoy pass against California in the 1996 Aloha Bowl.

drive with a rollicking forty-four-yard run to the Cal forty-five, and McCoy tossed a thirty-six-yard pass to Pat McGrew to set up Scott's run. At that point Navy held a 21–13 lead.

Cal came back with two scores to take a 28–21 lead with 3:25 left in the first half. But Navy tied the game just thirty-nine seconds later. The McCoy-Schemm combo worked for sixty-two yards on a third-and-four play to Cal's seven-yard line; two plays later, McCoy's two-yard run got Navy a 28–28 tie. That left 2:46 to play in the half, and the Golden Bears used all but thirty-four seconds of it to take a 35–28 halftime lead when Barnes connected for his third touchdown pass, a twenty-yard completion to Shaw.

Navy started to self-destruct in the third quarter when two promising drives were cut short by turnovers. Cal increased its lead to 38–28 on Ryan Longwell's forty-one-yard field goal with just 1:10 left in the quarter.

Navy's defense finally took charge and forced California to punt with 10:45 to play in the game. It was here that Charlie Weatherbie made his most important decision of the day, inserting Fay, one of his co-captains, for a tired McCoy. The coach had done the same thing in the last minutes of the Army-Navy game just three weeks earlier, and Fay had almost pulled out a victory. Now the senior had more time, but a bigger deficit to overcome.

Navy linebacker Jason Coffey goes after California quarterback Pat Barnes on an all-out blitz. Navy's defensive unit was under siege all day—but in the end, they forced a key turnover to set up the winning touchdown drive and sealed the 42–38 victory by sacking Barnes on the game's final play.

"At the time, we needed a spark," Weatherbie said later. "We were bogged down. Ben had been in that situation before, so it wasn't anything new to him. There were many ups and downs, but we picked ourselves up by our bootstraps and found a way."

Fay moved Navy eighty yards in ten plays, spreading the ball around—a ten-yard pass to Howard Bryant first, followed by a sixteen-yard completion to Astor Heaven. Tim Cannada peeled off a fourteen-yard run to the right, and Schemm gained twelve more to the same side. After Cannada caught a

Defensive ends Dennis Kane (14) and Tom Poulter jam up a California running play.

twelve-yard pass, Fay kept the ball and rolled over right tackle for a two-yard touchdown. Tom Vanderhorst's extra point closed the gap to three points, 38–35, with just under eight minutes to play.

Navy's defense and California's offense then settled into a mighty tug of war until, on the thirteenth play of a drive that had consumed more than four precious minutes, Barnes turned a great play into a disaster. On third down from the Mids' thirty-one-yard line, the Cal quarterback scrambled for fifteen yards and a first down. But as he stretched out for an additional yard, he was stripped of the ball; it was recovered at the Mids' sixteen-yard line by Navy tackle Jerome Dixon.

With under three minutes to play, Fay quickly went to work. On a crucial third-and-eight, he passed for fifteen yards to Scott. Then he sent Schemm on a crossing pattern from left to right and hit him in the center of the Aloha Bowl logo at midfield. Schemm finally was driven out of bounds at Cal's sixteen-yard line after a fifty-two-yard gain. Omar Nelson ran to the right side for five yards; on the next play, Fay faked an inside handoff to him, rolled left, and cut upfield through a huge hole and into the end zone for the winning score. Fay celebrated the final big play of his varsity career with a hula-hipped move in the end zone that was every bit as graceful as the one he had used to evade tacklers at the ten-yard line and deliver Navy's first postseason win in eighteen years.

Appendix
Ships Named for Navy Football Lettermen

USS *Antrim* (FFG 20): Commissioned in 1981 and named for Rear Adm. Richard Nott Antrim, a running back from 1928 to 1930, who won the Medal of Honor for saving the life of a fellow prisoner while a POW of the Japanese during World War II.

USS *Bagley* (Torpedo Boat No. 24): Commissioned in 1901; USS *Bagley* (DD 185): Commissioned in 1919; and USS *Bagley* (DD 386): Commissioned in 1937. Named for Ens. Worth Bagley, the first naval officer killed in action during the Spanish-American War. Bagley was a four-year (1891–94) letterman as a running back.

USS *Bauer* (DE 1025): Commissioned in 1957 and named for Lt. Col. Harold Bauer, USMC, a running back (1927–29) who was posthumously awarded the Medal of Honor for his courage as commander of Marine Fighting Squadron 212 in the South Pacific.

USS *Claude Vernon Ricketts* (DDG 5): Commissioned in 1962 and named for Adm. Claude Ricketts, who saved the USS *West Virginia* from capsizing during the Pearl Harbor attack and later was commander of the Second Fleet and vice chief of Naval Operations. Ricketts Hall houses the offices of the USNA Athletic Association.

USS *Douglas L. Howard* (DE 138): Commissioned in 1943 and named for Doug Howard, a three-year letterman, captain of the 1905 football team, and later a Navy head coach. Howard commanded three destroyers and received the Navy Cross for distinguished service during patrol and convoy escort duty in Word War I.

USS *Emory S. Land* (DD 663): Commissioned in 1979 and named for Vice Adm. Emory Land, a halfback on the 1898–1901 teams. Land won the Navy Cross and Distinguished Service Medal for his work with submarines and the construction corps during both world wars.

USS *Halligan* (DD 584): Commissioned in 1943 and named for Rear Adm. John Halligan Jr., who played six years as a guard (1892–97) and graduated No. 1 in the Class of 1898. He was chief of staff to Rear Adm. Hugh Rodman, commander of U.S. naval forces during World War I.

USS *Halsey* (DLG 23): Commissioned in 1963 and named for Fleet Adm. Willam F. Halsey Jr., who was Navy's leading rusher in 1902 and 1903. He was the Navy's most renowned fleet and carrier force commander during World War II.

USS *Heywood L. Edwards* (DD 663): Commissioned in 1944 and named for Lt. Cdr. Heywood L. Edwards, who lettered in 1924 and 1925. Edwards was commander of the USS *Reuben James,* a destroyer that was sunk by a German submarine in 1941 while on convoy duty, and while the United States was still officially a neutral nation.

USS *Hutchins* (DD 476): Commissioned in 1942 and named for Lt. Carlton B. Hutchins, a center on the 1925 team. Hutchins was awarded the Medal of Honor posthumously for his efforts to save the crew of his seaplane after a midair collision during fleet exercises in 1938.

USS *Irwin* (DD 794): Commissioned in 1944 and named for Noble Edward Irwin, center rush on the 1888 team. Irwin won the Navy Cross as director of naval aviation in World War I.

USS *John L. Hall* (FFG 32): Commissioned in 1982 and named for John Leslie Hall Jr., a guard on the 1911 and 1912 teams. Admiral Hall distinguished himself while commanding the Navy's supply forces during Operation Torch in North Africa, the invasion of Sicily, and D-Day in Normandy.

USS *John Rodgers* (Lighthouse Tender); USS *John Rodgers* (DD 574): Commissioned in 1943; and USS *John Rodgers* (DD 983): Commissioned in 1979. Named for Adm. John Rodgers, a four-year letterman who was a tackle (1899–1902) and who was designated Naval Aviator No. 2. Rodgers was a pioneer in naval aviation's first twenty-five years. He won the Distinguished Service Medal for outstanding work on minesweeping operations in the North Sea and later was appointed the assistant chief of the Bureau of Aeronautics.

USS *Jonas Ingram* (DD 938): Commissioned in 1957 and named for Adm. Jonas Ingram, a running back in 1906 and later a head coach and athletic director at the Naval Academy. Ingram won the Medal of Honor for his distinguished service in 1914 while serving on the battleship USS *Arkansas* at Vera Cruz.

USS *Joseph K. Taussig* (DE 1030): Commissioned in 1957 and named for Vice Adm. Joseph Taussig, a back on the 1896–98 teams. During his career, Taussig won the Silver Lifesaving Medal for rescuing a drowning shipmate; the Distinguished Service Medal as commander of the USS *Wadsworth* for convoy escort through German submarines and minefields in World War I; and the Legion of Merit for his staff work during World War II.

USS *Laboon* (DDG 58): Commissioned in 1993 and named for John F. "Jake" Laboon, an end on the 1942 and 1943 teams who, while serving aboard a submarine, won the Silver Star for rescuing a pilot from an atoll in the Sea of Japan. He became a Jesuit priest and senior Catholic chaplain at the Naval Academy, where he also coached the lacrosse and plebe football teams. Laboon later was fleet chaplain for the U.S. Atlantic Fleet.

USS *Martin H. Ray* (DE 338): Commissioned in 1944 and named for Martin Ray, a 1933 letterman. As engineering officer aboard the destroyer USS *Hammann* during the Battle of Midway, Ray was lost while attempting to save the rapidly sinking ship. He received the Navy Cross for his heroism.

USS *Mustin* (DD 413): Commissioned in 1939 and named for Henry Mustin, quarterback on the 1894 and 1895 teams. Mustin was designated Naval Aviator No. 11, piloted the first aircraft catapulted from a ship, and, during the Mexican conflict in 1914, flew the first combat mission.

USS *Raby* (DE 698): Commissioned in 1943 and named after James Raby, who was a halfback on the 1893 and 1894 teams. Raby was awarded the Navy Cross as commanding officer of the USS *Albany* for safely escorting convoys through submarine-infested waters during World War I. Raby was also a longtime commandant of various naval districts.

USS *Reeves* (DLC 24): Commissioned in 1964 and named for Adm. Joseph M. Reeves, who was affectionately known as "Billy Goat" Reeves because of his white goatee. Reeves was the first player to wear a football helmet (as a tackle on the 1892 and 1893 teams). In 1934–36, Reeves was commander-in-chief of the U.S. Fleet.

USS *Richard S. Bull* (DE 402): Commissioned in 1944 and named for Lt. Dick Bull, a tackle and end on the 1933–35 teams. Bull was killed in action as a fighter pilot during the Battle of the Coral Sea; he was posthumously awarded the Distinguished Flying Cross.

USS *Robison* (DDG 12): Commissioned in 1961 and named for Rear Adm. Samuel S. Robison, a member of the 1887 team. Robison was awarded the Navy Cross as commander of the Atlantic Submarine Force. He was later commander in chief, Battle Fleet, and a superintendent of the Naval Academy.

USS *Underwood* (FFG-36): Commissioned in 1983 and named for Gordon W. Underwood, a guard on the 1929–31 teams. Underwood won three Navy Crosses and one Presidential Unit Citation for his work in submarine warfare during World War II. He was one of the leaders in Japanese tonnage sunk.

Bibliography

Books

Bealle, Morris Allison. *Gangway for Navy.* Washington, D.C.: Columbia Publishing, 1951.
Brown, Paul, with Jack Clary. *PB: The Paul Brown Story.* New York: Atheneum, 1979.
Claassen, Harold. *Football's Unforgettable Games.* New York: Ronald Press, 1963.
Clark, Joseph James. *Carrier Admiral.* New York: McKay, 1967.
Clary, Jack. *Army vs. Navy: Seventy Years of Football Rivalry.* New York: Ronald Press, 1965.
Danzig, Allison. *The History of American Football: Its Great Teams, Players, and Coaches.* Englewood Cliffs, N.J.: Prentice-Hall, 1956.
Gunn, John. *The Old Core.* Costa Mesa, Calif.: J & J Publishing, 1992.
Halsey, William Frederick. *Admiral Halsey's Story.* New York: Whittlesey House, 1947.
Hendrickson, Joe. *Tournament of Roses: A Pictorial History.* Los Angeles: Brooke House, 1971.
Koger, Jim. *Upon Other Fields, on Other Days: College Football's Wartime Casualties.* Atlanta: Longstreet Press, 1991.
Morison, Samuel Eliot. *History of United States Naval Operations in World War II.* 15 vols. Boston: Little, Brown, 1947.
Pope, Edwin. *Football's Greatest Coaches.* Atlanta: Tupper and Love, 1955.
Potter, E. B. *Bull Halsey.* Annapolis, Md.: Naval Institute Press, 1985.
Reynolds, Clark G. *Famous American Admirals.* New York: Van Nostrand Reinhold, 1978.
Roscoe, Theodore. *United States Submarine Operations in World War II.* Annapolis, Md.: Naval Institute Press, 1949.
Smith, Stanley E., ed. *The United States Navy in World War II.* New York: Morrow, 1966.
Staubach, Roger. *Staubach: First Down, Lifetime to Go.* Waco, Tex.: Word Books, 1974.
Sweetman, Jack. *The U.S. Naval Academy: An Illustrated History.* 2d ed. Annapolis, Md.: Naval Institute Press, 1995.
Taylor, Theodore. *The Magnificent Mitscher.* 1954. Reprint, with a foreword by Arthur W. Radford and an introduction by Jeffrey G. Barlow, Annapolis, Md.: Naval Institute Press, 1991.
Whipple, Chandler. *William F. Halsey: Fighting Admiral.* New York: Putnam, 1968.

U.S. Naval Institute Oral Histories

Cutter, Capt. Slade
Davidson, Rear Adm. John F.
Dornin, Capt. Robert E.
Edwards, Capt. Frederick A.
Foley, Rear Adm. Francis D.
Hamilton, Rear Adm. Thomas J., Jr.
Jackson, Vice Adm. Andrew M., Jr.
Kauffman, Rear Adm. Draper L.
Kirkpatrick, Rear Adm. C. C.
Laughlin, Capt. C. Elliott
Mack, Vice Adm. William P.
Melson, Rear Adm. Charles L.
Minter, Vice Adm. Charles S., Jr.
Persons, Rear Adm. Harry S., Jr.
Smedberg, Vice Adm. William R., III

Periodicals

Annapolis Evening Capital
Baltimore Sun
Company
New York Times
Shipmate
Sports Illustrated
U.S. Naval Institute *Proceedings*
Washington Post

Index

Note: Page numbers that appear in italic refer to illustrations.

About the Author

Jack Clary's first book was *Army vs. Navy,* published in 1965. For the last two decades he has written the feature article for the Army-Navy game program as well as other pieces for Navy's regular-season programs. He was a sportswriter and columnist for the Associated Press for seventeen years and has also worked at daily newspapers in New York and Boston.

He is the author of more than two hundred magazine articles and fifty-five books, including collaborative efforts with such famous sports figures as Paul Brown, Andy Robustelli, Ken Anderson, Tom Landry, Don Shula, John Madden, Chuck Noll, and Dick Vermeil.

He is a graduate of Fordham University and the Columbia School of Journalism, where he was a Grantland Rice Fellow. He is also a member of Fordham's Athletic Hall of Fame. He now runs Sports Media Enterprises in Stow, Massachusetts, where he resides with his wife, Pat.

The NAVAL INSTITUTE PRESS is the book-publishing arm of the U.S. Naval Institute, a private, nonprofit, membership society for sea service professionals and others who share an interest in naval and maritime affairs. Established in 1873 at the U.S. Naval Academy in Annapolis, Maryland, where its offices remain today, the Naval Institute has members worldwide.

Members of the Naval Institute support the education programs of the society and receive the influential monthly magazine *Proceedings* and discounts on fine nautical prints and on ship and aircraft photos. They also have access to the transcripts of the Institute's Oral History Program and get discounted admission to any of the Institute-sponsored seminars offered around the country.

The Naval Institute also publishes *Naval History* magazine. This colorful bimonthly is filled with entertaining and thought-provoking articles, first-person reminiscences, and dramatic art and photography. Members receive a discount on *Naval History* subscriptions.

The Naval Institute's book-publishing program, begun in 1898 with basic guides to naval practices, has broadened its scope in recent years to include books of more general interest. Now the Naval Institute Press publishes about 100 titles each year, ranging from how-to books on boating and navigation to battle histories, biographies, ship and aircraft guides, and novels. Institute members receive discounts of 20 to 50 percent on the Press's nearly 600 books in print.

Full-time students are eligible for special half-price membership rates. Life memberships are also available.

For a free catalog describing Naval Institute Press books currently available, and for further information about subscribing to *Naval History* magazine or about joining the U.S. Naval Institute, please write to:

Membership Department
U.S. Naval Institute
118 Maryland Avenue
Annapolis, MD 21402-5035
Telephone: (800) 233-8764
Fax: (410) 269-7940
Web address: www.usni.org